Twayne's English Authors Series

EDITOR OF THIS VOLUME

Kinley Roby

Northeastern University

Sean O'Casey

TEAS 245

Sean O'Casey

SEAN O'CASEY

By JAMES R. SCRIMGEOUR

Western Connecticut State College

TWAYNE PUBLISHERS
A Division of G. K. Hall & Co.
Boston, Massachusetts, U.S.A.

Library of Congress Cataloging in Publication Data
Scrimgeour, James.
Sean O'Casey.

(Twayne's English authors series ; TEAS 245)
Bibliography: p. 175–81
Includes index.
1. O'Casey, Sean, 1880–1964—Criticism and interpre-
tation.
PR6029.C33Z84   822'.9'12   78-17352
ISBN 0-8057-6735-5

80 - 3366

for Chris

Contents

About the Author

James R. Scrimgeour received his Ph.D. in English and American Drama from the University of Massachusetts, Amherst, June 1972. He has taught Drama, Composition, and Creative Writing courses at Illinois State University from September 1971 to 1978.   He has published a number of articles including "From Loving to the Misbegotten: Despair in the Drama of Eugene O'Neill" in *Modern Drama*, "O'Casey's Street People: Characterization in O'Casey's Autobiographies" in *The Sean O'Casey Review*, and " 'The Great Example of Horror & Agony': A Comparison of Soren Kierkegaard's Demoniacally Despairing Individual with William Blake's Spectre of Urthona" in *Scandinavian Studies*. He has published over fifty poems in a wide variety of anthologies and little magazines including *Aspect*, *Cave* (New Zealand), *For Neruda/For Chile* (Edited by Walter Lowenfels), *The Louisville Review*, *Lynx*, *Margins*, *Oyez Review*, *Second Coming*, *Uzzano*, and *Wormwood Review*. And finally, he has delivered papers and given poetry readings at various conferences and festivals, published several columns and reviews, and edited *What is that Country Standing Inside You* (an anthology of Contemporary American Poetry).   Professor Scrimgeour now teaches at Western Connecticut State College.

Preface

This book uses close analysis of O'Casey's *Autobiographies*, especially the first four volumes, and selected O'Casey plays to demonstrate that Sean O'Casey was a creative artist of the first rank who in both his *Autobiographies* and his plays succeeds in fusing together an explosive creative imagination with realistic insight into the lives of the exploited peoples of the world in general and into the lives of the slum dwellers in early twentieth-century Dublin in particular. The first two chapters deal with characterization and dramaturgic techniques in the *Autobiographies*, those highly imaginative, if somewhat uneven, books grounded in genuine insight into the harshness of life and the joy of living in spite of this harshness.

The next four chapters deal with the characterization and dramaturgy in representative plays from each of the three distinct periods in O'Casey's dramatic career (early naturalistic, middle expressionistic, late comic-imaginative). Our analysis of these plays not only demonstrates the continuity of O'Casey's dramatic career but shows also that in all three of these periods O'Casey's power is generated by the same fusion of the imaginative and the realistic that illuminates the *Autobiographies*. Although his early plays (*Shadow of a Gunman, Juno and the Paycock*, and *The Plough and the Stars*) emphasize the realistic side of O'Casey and the later plays the imaginative, sparks from O'Casey's imagination light up the early plays and his realistic insight into life darkens both the expressionistic middle plays (like *The Silver Tassie* and *Red Roses for Me*) and the later comic-imaginative ones (like *Purple Dust* and *Cock-a-Doodle-Dandy*).

Sean O'Casey was born John Casey in Dublin, Ireland, on March 30, 1880, the last of thirteen children brought into a lower middle class Protestant household. His father, Michael Casey, worked as a clerk for the Irish Church Mission (a staunchly Protestant organization) until 1883, when he suffered a severe spinal injury, an injury that eventually led to his death three years later in 1886.

After his father's untimely death, six-year-old John Casey and his four surviving siblings (Michael, Tom, Isaac, and Isabella) were raised and cared for by their mother, Susan (Archer) Casey, whose concern for others, cheerful good humor, hard work, and devout faith in life in the face of the continual poverty and hardships of tenement life provided an example of the good life to which O'Casey pays tribute in all of his strongest writing, writing which reverberates with the sound of her gay laugh at the gate of the grave.

Very early in life, the young John Casey contracted a serious eye disease which was to plague him in varying degrees for the remainder of his days. This painful disease, while it made life a continual torment for the young child, John Casey, contributed in many significant ways to the development of the artist, Sean O'Casey. The disease nourished his independence and self-reliance; it insured that Sean O'Casey would be self-educated (and avoid schools like the one described in "Crime and Punishment" in *I Knock at the Door*), that he would fully appreciate the colors and texture of life around him, the concrete details of the lives of human beings struggling to survive in a hostile environment, and that the books he did read (like the plays of his beloved Shakespeare) he would read closely with a true depth of understanding.

John Casey was eleven years old when Parnell, a leader in the fight for Irish rights in general and Home Rule in particular, the "uncrowned king" of Ireland, had his political career (and his life) cut short by his own countrymen who were roused against him by the self-righteous clamor of the Irish clergy after his affair with Kitty O'Shea was revealed. O'Casey's vision of the heroic Parnell attempting to pull the Irish people forward in spite of themselves, and then being betrayed by these same people became etched indelibly in his consciousness at this early age, and thus, in O'Casey's writing, Parnell and his supporters become a larger-than-life symbol of everything that is good in Ireland, and the "piety painted toughs" that down him a symbol of everything that is bad.

John Casey got his first job at fourteen as a stockroom assistant in a hardware store (used as a setting for the Hymdim, Leadem, & Co. chapters of *Pictures in the Hallway*) and went on from there to work at a series of odd laboring jobs for the next thirty-one years, including an eleven-year stint as a laborer on the Irish Railroad. In the middle of this activity, O'Casey met Jim Larkin (like Parnell, a Promethean figure in O'Casey's mythology) and became involved in his Irish Transport and General Workers Union. O'Casey's participation in the climactic confrontation between this union and the

Dublin employers (the lockout, strike, and police riots of 1913) more than any other single event helped shape O'Casey's lifelong social and political philosophy.

Although O'Casey maintained his commitment to the cause of the exploited workers of the world until the day he died, he broke with the Irish labor movement in 1914 when it became clear that this movement was slipping into the hands of flag-waving nationalists. Thus, in 1916, when the ill-fated Easter Rebellion broke out, O'Casey was (as we see clearly in *The Plough and the Stars*) a noncombatant whose sympathies lay more with the tenement dwellers whose lives were disrupted by the war than with either of the warring factions.

In 1925, at forty-five, an age when most of us begin thinking about retirement, O'Casey decided to devote his life to full-time writing, and his life calmed down (as much as O'Casey's life could). He married Eileen Carey Reynolds on September 23, 1927, and they settled in England where he was to live happily with his family in self-imposed exile until his death on September 18, 1964.

Before going on to our discussion of O'Casey's work, we should, perhaps, mention one last incident which significantly affected O'Casey's artistic development. This incident is, of course, the Abbey Theatre's rejection of *The Silver Tassie* in 1928 which culminated in a major confrontation between W. B. Yeats and Sean O'Casey. This confrontation was to O'Casey's aesthetic and artistic philosophy what the confrontation between Larkin's union and the police was to his social philosophy. The artistic principles formulated by O'Casey at this time remained (for better or worse) embedded in his consciousness for his life's duration.

The preceding discussion of some of the most significant events in O'Casey's life should provide enough information so that we may enter the world of O'Casey's *Autobiographies* without being totally lost; that we may enter this world with the understanding that the world which O'Casey creates in his books is not the literal world of late nineteenth-century, early twentieth-century Dublin. We should understand that the world of these books is a world charged with the glory of Sean O'Casey's imagination, a world, however, which grows as naturally out of actual experience in the literal world as a flower grows out of its roots and stem.

Acknowledgments

I should like to acknowledge:

(1) my immense debt to all the O'Casey scholars writing before me—especially David Krause, Ronald Ayling, and Robert Hogan,

(2) the help of the Twayne editorial staff—especially Professor Kinley E. Roby,

(3) my gratitude to Robert Lowery, editor of *The Sean O'Casey Review*, for permission to reprint, in slightly altered form, the article "O'Casey's Street People: Characterization in Sean O'Casey's Autobiographies,"

(4) my thanks to Macmillan Publishing Company for permission to quote from the *Autobiographies* and from *Masterpieces of the Modern Irish Theatre*, ed. by Robert W. Corrigan (Cock-a-Doodle Dandy); to St. Martin's Press for permission to quote from *Three Plays (Juno and the Paycock, Shadow of a Gunman, and The Plough and the Stars)* and from *Three More Plays (The Silver Tassie, Purple Dust, and Red Roses for me)*; and to David Krause for his permission to use the letter from O'Casey to a New York housewife quoted in this book's conclusion,

(5) my appreciation of Chris, without whose patience, understanding, and love this book would never have been written.

Chronology

1880   Born John Casey, 30 March, in Dublin, youngest child of Michael and Susan Casey.

1886   His father, Michael Casey, dies.

1891   First contact with the theater—accompanies older brother (and actor) Isaac to Queen's Theater, Dublin.

1894   First work, stockroom assistant in a hardware store, setting for the Hymdim, Leadem & Co. chapters of *Pictures in the Hallway*.

1901–   Works as laborer on the railroad, longest of many jobs held
1911   before becoming a full-time writer (1925).

1907   First publication, an article in *The Peasant and Irish Ireland*, May 25.

1909   Jim Larkin founds the Irish Transport and General Workers Union, January 4.

1911   Irish railways strike, setting for *Red Roses for Me* (1942).

1913   Climactic confrontation between Larkin's Union and Dublin employers; lockout, strike, and police riots. Probably the single most influential event in the formation of O'Casey's political and social philosophy.

1913   October; Union forms Irish Citizens Army to protect themselves from the police.

1913   November; Nationalists found Irish Volunteers.

1914   O'Casey becomes secretary of the Irish Citizens Army, resigns when his motion to force Countess Markievicz to choose between the Citizens Army and the Volunteers failed by one vote. (O'Casey abstained from voting, the countess voted for herself.)

1916   The Easter Uprising, combined forces of the Citizens Army and the Volunteers last only a couple of weeks in the face of British superiority in numbers of men and quality of weapons, April 9–24. O'Casey not personally involved, but uses strife as setting for *The Plough and the Stars* (1926).

1917–   Time of violence as Irish Republican Army conducts guerrilla
1921   warfare against British forces and the Black and Tans retaliate. Setting for "The Raid" and *Shadow of a Gunman*.

1918   *Songs of the Wren* and *The Story of Thomas Ashe*.

1918   His sister, Isabella, dies, January. His mother dies, November.

1919   *The Story of the Irish Citizen Army*, under the pseudonym of P. O'Cathasaigh.

1921   Peace treaty with England divides Ireland into North and South.

1922–   Civil war in Southern Ireland between the Free Staters (who
1923   favored the peace treaty) and the die-hard Republicans (who did not), setting for *Juno and the Paycock* (1925).

1922   "The Seamless Coat of Kathleen," in *Poblacht Na h-Eireaun* (March), and "The Corncake," in *The Gael* (June).

1926   Visits London to receive Hawthornden Prize for *Juno and the Paycock*. Settles in England for the rest of his life.

1927   Marries Eileen Carey Reynolds, September 23.

1928   Breon O'Casey born. Abbey Theater rejects *The Silver Tassie* (1928), Yeats's letter, O'Casey's reply.

1929   *The Silver Tassie* produced by C. B. Cochran, Apollo Theater, London, October 11.

1932   Refuses (along with Joyce) to become a founder member of Irish Academy of Letters.

1934   Journeys to United States for premiere production of *Within the Gates*, publishes *Windfalls*.

1936   Niall O'Casey born.

1937   *The Flying Wasp*.

1939   *I Knock at the Door* (volume 1 of the six-volume *Autobiographies*).

1939   Shivaun O'Casey born, O'Caseys move to Totnes, Devon.

1945   *Drums Under the Windows*.

1949   *Inishfallen Fare Thee Well*.

1952   *Rose and Crown*.

1954   *Sunset and Evening Star*.

1956   *The Green Crow* and *Mirror in My House* (the collected *Autobiographies*).

1956   Niall O'Casey, twenty-one years old, dies of leukemia.

1957   *The Green Crow*.

1962   *Feathers from a Green Crow*, edited by Robert Hogan.

1963   *Under a Colored Cap*.

1964   Dies of a heart attack in his home in Torquay, Devon, September 18.

1975   Posthumous publication of *The Letters of Sean O'Casey*, V. 1, edited by David Krause.

CHAPTER 1

The Autobiographies:
Characterization

I believe," Lady Gregory told the fledgling playwright Sean O'Casey in the early 1920s, "there is something in you and your strong point is characterization."[1] Now over fifty years and three and one-half million words[2] later we know that there was something in him and that his strongest point (although he has, as we shall see, many other strong points) is still characterization. Sean O'Casey, from the very beginning (the unproduced one-act plays) to the very end *(Behind the Green Curtains)*, has the ability to make us feel that the lives of apparently unimportant little people are important after all. Like the plays of his beloved Shakespeare, O'Casey's *Autobiographies* deal not only with heroic, admittedly great public figures but also with ordinary human beings whose lives would have passed away without comment had not O'Casey's diseased-but-greedy eyes and sharp ears picked up and hoarded precious pieces of their intensely human experiences.

I *The Street People*

We must keep in mind that the following arbitrarily chosen characters are only partially representative, and that many equally important and interesting characters (each with his own distinct contribution to make to the world of the *Autobiographies* as a whole) will not, due to space limitations, receive the attention they deserve. The first of O'Casey's characters with which we will deal is "Mild Millie," whom Sean introduces to us in the "Behold My Family Is Poor" chapter of *Drums Under the Windows*. As the chapter begins, Sean (the character), who hasn't slept for forty-eight hours, is sitting on the curb looking after his sister Ella's meager belongings, protecting them from the street children, "for this sort

19

of thing [someone in trouble] was to them a song, the tapping of a tambourine, or the beating of a drum in their lives."[3] Note that this linking of song and music with the suffering of the poor is, like so much of O'Casey that appears at first glance irrelevant, a perfectly designed introduction to Mild Millie, whose "dance of life"[4] is meant to be a song, a tapping of the tambourine, a beat of the drum to lift up the spirits of the entire family of the poor and exploited people of the world.

The first picture we have of Millie, like the first picture of nearly all O'Casey characters, is a sharply etched one: "A young woman, hatless, a jagged skirt just reaching to her knees, showing a pair of hardy, well-shaped legs, with feet thrust deeply into a man's pair of rusty rough-leather, Blucher boots came unsteadily down the street. A dark-green shawl dangled from her shoulders, and a scaly basket, holding one stale fish, was hooked over her left arm" (*Drums*, p. 96). Sean steals a glance at her and then notes for himself (and us too) that "the line from her chin to her throat was fine, and went curving grandly into a bosom that was rich and firm and white" (*Drums*, p. 96). In this introductory description of Millie we see the strange mixture that we find in so many O'Casey slum characters. We see Millie's fine lines shine through in spite of everything life in the Dublin slums has done to her. Her first words reveal that this unsteady woman with the jagged skirt has both strength of character and a genuine compassion for a fellow fallen being: "—You look dead tired, son, she said to him. Here, sit down on the steps beside me, and she spread out her shawl over them; sit down, an' take it aysey, for, depend on it, God'll look afther th' world when both of us are gone" (*Drums*, p. 97). And then Millie, naturally enough, provides her bosom as a place for the weary Sean to rest his head.

As the chapter develops, O'Casey takes care to insure that we become more and more sympathetic to Millie as he presents instance after instance of her humanity. First, we hear her comments on the politicians, lords, and beer barons as they enter Hutton (the coach building firm across the street, a firm that has a statue of the English lion and unicorn on its front gates); "Aw, Mother o'God," Millie exclaims in one of her typical comments on this unholy procession, "will you look at what's creepin' outa th' sedan-chair, in purple trews an' scarlet cape, but oul' Craddock himself, who, for his vote, was lifted outa Kilmore to be Archbishop of Dublin, with five thousand pounds a year to keep th' poor man from starvin!"

(*Drums*, p. 98). As the procession of Millie's comments, which neatly parallels the procession of creepin' Craddocks, continues, both our admiration for Millie and our disgust for the creepers steadily increases.

Immediately after Millie (and Sean) have finished commenting upon the rich and the super rich of Dublin history, an incident occurs which serves to heighten our admiration of Millie still further. Two policemen come by and order Sean to move his sister's belongings out of the street. Sean (naive character that he is) tries to reason with them, but is getting nowhere when Millie takes over. "Push off, th' pair of yous," Millie warns the officers, as she takes a slug from her bottle. "Push off to where there's genuine throuble, before this red biddy takes effect, or yous'll have something harder than a few scraps of furniture to shift to the station" (*Drums*, p. 101). The two policemen turn tail and walk away rather than take notice of this "fearful female," this "terrible" "powerful woman" whom it takes ten men to carry to the station (*Drums*, p. 101).

Now that this defiance of the police has solidified her hold on our affections, O'Casey can afford to give us a glimpse of things in Millie's past life. "My mother," she tells Sean shortly after the policemen have left, "kicked th' bucket when I was a yearling, an' me father had to drag me up as well as he could til he hurt his spine on the quays tryin' to move a weight it 'ud take a gang to shift" (*Drums*, p. 102). She started drinking while she was nursing her injured father (whose slow, painful death from a spinal injury reminds us of the slow, painful death of Johnny Cassidy's father in "His Da', His Poor Da' " in *I Knock at the Door*). She found out that "a few dhrinks changed a long an' surly night into a short an' gallant hour of thoughts, an' put a merry loveliness into all around us" (*Drums*, p. 103). Note that we are so firmly attached to Millie that her drunkenness and the violence which she uses to get her drink do not repel us but make us sympathize with her still more.

Just in case there might be some reader so insensitive that he still is not captivated by her, O'Casey now gives Millie his ultimate stamp of approval. He has her comment on English and Irish politics in general and on Parnell in particular. Here, as in all of O'Casey, Parnell is a touchstone. By being strongly and unequivocably for him and against the "piety-painted toughs" that downed him, by saying with genuine feeling: "Me uncrowned king, if you were here today it's Millie would go down on her knees an' kiss your

strong, white holy hand, an' daze your enemies with her thrue devotion" (*Drums*, p. 106), Millie passes the final test; and any lingering
doubt we may have had about how we were meant to take Millie's
character should now be resolved.

This removal of all doubt is essential if the climactic dance is to
have its maximum effect. O'Casey has carefully prepared us so that
when Millie finally does wheel into her defiant dance of life, a dance
that makes even the old mournful fife player participate, our spirits
are almost obliged to dance too, whether we will or not. Her leap
into the dance, like everything else in this chapter, is perfectly
timed. She leaps away from Sean and into the dance just as he is
falling into despair, just as he is listening to the mournful tune of the
fife player and thinking: "We all feel it . . . feel it in the deep heart's
core . . . feel the hatred due to that which has turned Ireland's glory
into a half-forgotten fable" (*Drums*, p. 108). We are never sure
whether Millie read Sean's thoughts or whether she saw the tear on
his cheek, but we are sure that the defiant rage she expresses in her
dance in which she sends spit after spit up at the British arms is (in
contrast to the mad Lear's rage on the heath) an affirmative rage for
life, not a destructive rage against it.

Another important ordinary character in whom we see the light is
Ayamonn O'Farrel, the Fenian tram conductor. Ayamonn keeps
"the sword of light" burning in times of trouble even as he grows
old. O'Casey introduces us to the tram conductor (although he
doesn't tell us his name) as early as the second chapter of the first
book of the *Autobiographies*. Here, we do not really get to know
him, but we do hear him make some Millielike comments on "the
castle ball" and sing us a Fenian song. It isn't until "The Red Above
the Green" that we take notice of this man. Here we see Ayamonn
stretch out a helping hand and pull both the half-blind little Johnny
Casside and his mother through the pushing, perspiring crowd to
the top of his tram so that they would have a fine view of a great
orangemen's parade. And we hear him gruffly, but not unkindly,
berate the crowd:

A man 'ud want St. Pathrick's crozier to knock a little decency into
yous, . . . A nice way the whole of yous musta been reared, with your
pushin' an shovin', like a horde of uncivilized savages. . . . I don't know th'
hell why Parnell's wastin' his time thryin' to shape yous into something
recognisable as men an' women. . . . And all of yous riskin' the breakage of
your bodies to see a few twinklin' lights set over our heads to do honour to a

famine queen rollin' about in a vis-a-vis at a time the Irish were gettin' shovelled, ten at a time, into deep an' desperate graves. (*Knock*, pp. 268–69)

These comments serve not only to reveal the tram conductor's rough good humor, his bluntness, his combativeness, his sense of Irish history, and his support of Parnell (that touchstone again) but also to interest us in this tram conductor as a human being. "That conductor's a very sensible man, and shrewd," Johnny's mother tells us after listening to some excellent O'Casey dialogue between the conductor and some of the passengers on his tram. She assures Johnny both that the conductor's Fenian beliefs are "ignorance," and that "he was really kind, though; and we must always remember that kind people are to be met everywhere; for though people often think wrong things, they can often be quite good" (*Knock*, p. 270). Thus, we have it on good authority (John's mother, whose humanity and good judgment have already been clearly demonstrated) that the tram conductor is a "good man" even though he occasionally thinks wrong things.

Our involvement with the tram conductor is increased when we see him standing at the rail watching the parade go by, when we hear him start singing half to himself and half to the passengers gaping at the decorations the ballad "Tone's Grave," by Thomas Davis. Johnny is "moved strangely" by the song and the sight of tears trickling down the conductor's cheeks. Johnny's mother assures Johnny that the Wolfe Tone incident "all happened long ago, an' everyone's forgotten all about it" (*Knock*, p. 275), but the conductor, who obviously hasn't forgotten about it, continues to sing the last verse of his song. This refusal to forget, this keeping of the songs is a necessary, perhaps sacred task that the tram conductor fulfills in spite of innumerable obstacles.

In the "Sword of Light" chapter of *Pictures in the Hallway*, it becomes even more clear that O'Casey is using the conductor as conductor. Here, Ayamonn visits Johnny in his cold, bare apartment for the expressed purpose of passing on the old Fenian songs to Johnny, who in turn learns them and passes them on to us. Johnny (whom the tram conductor vows to call Sean from this point on) listens in hushed silence as the old man sings "soft, low, and simply," one verse from an old Irish ballad, "The Felons of Our Land":

> Let thraitors sneer and tyrants trown, oh, little do we care—
> A Felon's cap's th' noblest crown an Irish head can wear;
> An' what care we, although it be trod by a ruffian band—
> God bless th' clay where rest today, th' felons of our land!
>
> *(Pictures,* p. 294)

And Johnny/Sean feels "the arm round his shoulder quiver, and a strange thrill steals through his own veins, stiffening his body, as he listens to the sad and defiant song" *(Pictures,* p. 294). And, of course, by publishing this verse (along with the other Fenian songs in this chapter) Sean O'Casey hands to all succeeding generations the "sword of Light" that his friend Ayamonn handed to him.

Ayamonn's character is distinguished by an almost uncanny ability to get beneath the blather and deal directly with the issue at hand. In the "Red Above the Green," when the man with the droopy, watery mustache (the spokesman on the tram for law, order, and England) comments favorably on "the glittherin' an' a shinin' show," i.e., the parade, the tram conductor responds incisively: "—It's a shinin' sight to the eye that wants to see it so, said the conductor, with a bite in his voice; but to the Irish eye that sees thrue, it's but a grand gatherin' o' candles, lit to look sthrong, an' make merry over the corpse of our counthry" *(Knock,* pp. 275–76). Note that his response comes directly to the point, which is that these parades, these "shinin' sights," may also be seen as funeral processions. We see this same incisiveness in "The Sword of Light" when Johnny reads Ayamonn a pacifist passage in which Ruskin describes war as the sport of capitalists. "And how," asks Ayamonn of his young friend, as he comes directly to the point that Johnny missed, "are we goin' to get th' English outa Ireland without it?" "Ruskin," Ayamonn assures Johnny, "is only another oul' cod, with th' gift o'gab" *(Pictures,* p. 296).

And finally, in "The Clergy Take a Hand" chapter of *Inishfallen Fare Thee Well,* when "the mane of his hair was very grey now," and his "seamed hands shook slightly while he lighted his pipe" *(Inishfallen,* p. 160), we see that the sharp mind of Ayamonn can still pierce the jugular. "Looka," old Ayamonn says to Sean, laying the blame for the murder of Jack Wogan (and many other republicans) squarely where it belongs, "I'll betcha anything you like, the clergy'll never raise a hand or say a word to stop this quiet, cool killin' of our poor best boys. As men—I say nothin' again' them as priests, mind you, Sean,—as men, it's poor Saint Pathrick himself must be woebegone lookin' down to see th' clergy dumb, while th' counthry's becomin' a murdherin' fiasco" *(Inishfallen*, p. 162). Thus, Ayamonn clearly sums up the point of the entire chapter.

Let us end our discussion of the tram conductor not with an example of his incisiveness but with an example of his kindness. Let us borrow a technique from O'Casey and sum up our comments with a picture. Let us end with Ayamonn's gift to the cold and hungry Sean, the silver shilling that lay glittering on the pages of Ruskin's book.

An equally moving but less famous characterization is that of Mr. Moore, an old man whose republican children (two sons and one daughter) were in Free State prisons and whose wife has just frozen to death in the streets outside their home. We meet Mr. Moore in the "Into Civil War" chapter of *Inishfallen Fare Thee Well*, in which Sean tells us:

. . . the old man walked by himself. . . . He wore no overcoat, not even putting up the collar of the light jacket . . . and with head held up, seemed to be gladly taking any discomfort the rain and the wind could give him. . . . The few white tufts left on his head were saturated, and Sean watched the globules of water gathering at the ends, their stems slowly lengthening till they parted suddenly from the edge of the tufts, now one, then two, two again, then one more, to go swiftly coursing down the nape of the old neck to disappear down inside the collar of the old man's shirt. *(Inishfallen*, p. 130)

Again O'Casey uses the description of minute details to draw us into the man's life; the language drips cold inside our shirts.

When Sean kindly suggests to the old man that he should have brought an overcoat of some kind, Mr. Moore says, "I wouldn't ha' felt easy if I hadda' " *(Inishfallen*, p. 130). "It's the one way," he continues, "I can show her I'm sorry I slep' while she was dying! " *(Inishfallen*, p. 130). "She does know," he assures Sean on the next page, "knows well. An' by standin' up to what I'm standin' up to now, she knows I'd ha' willingly laid down with her on the cold ground in all the sleet fallin' an' all the wind blowin', the time she was dyin' alone, . . . if only I hadda' known"*(Inishfallen*, p. 131). It appears that Mr. Moore, in contrast to both Millie and Ayamonn, has succumbed to the temptation to despair, lay down, and die. His despair is especially appropriate in this chapter, in which Sean tells us: "The whole of Ireland's following a hearse these days . . .

and Ireland herself's driving the horses" (*Inishfallen*, p. 131). The apparently small decision of Mr. Moore not to put on his hat looms large, takes on universal significance. "What's the odds," a neighbor asks Sean; if he does catch his death of cold, "his children are so busy with themselves that they have time only to notice now and again that he's still there." "A tiny vignette" (O'Casey's own words) closes out the Civil War chapter. We see "the big church, with the light on the altar; the chalky statues of glum saints, green, blue, and brown, gawking down at the figure of an old man kneeling beside the coffin that held what remained of one who had been his lifelong comrade" (*Inishfallen*, p. 133). This vignette, like so many of O'Casey's carefully drawn word pictures, speaks eloquently for itself.

A brief discussion of one other minor character will have to suffice to demonstrate O'Casey's sensitivity both to the pain of living in his world and to the glory of living in open defiance of this pain. Although there is a whole gallery with nearly a hundred characters to choose from, we have chosen to conclude our discussion of O'Casey's street people by looking at the "Vandhering Vindy Vendhor," the old Jewish glazier, who has a chapter named after him in *I Knock at the Door*. This particular old man bears not only the burden of the huge, heavy frame filled with sheet glass strapped to his back, but also the additional burdens of being poor and of being a Jew in Christian Ireland. Again a carefully drawn, well-detailed opening description enlists sympathy:

The Jew was short and stocky; bushy-headed, and a tiny black beard, tinged with grey, blossomed meagrely on his chin. A pair of deep black eyes stared out from a fat white face. Long locks of jet-black hair straggled down his forehead. The trousers of a shabby black suit were well frayed at the bottoms; his boots were well down at the heels; a new black bowler tightly clasped his head; his neck was rasped with a high and hard and shining white collar, set off by a gallant red, green, and yellow patterned tie. The Jew's arms were held out in front of his body to strengthen the resistance to the heavy weight on his back. His body was so much bent that the back of his head was sunk into the back of his neck to enable him to look to his front and to see any possible need for his services. The sweat was trickling down his cheeks, and glistening patches showed where it had soaked through his clothes near his armpits and the inner parts of his thighs. He walked with short steps because of the heavy pressure of the burden on his back. As he trudged along, he kept twisting his head as well as he could, now to the right, now to the left, ever on the alert for a possible job, chanting tirelessly as he marched along, Vindys to mend, to mend; vindys to mend! *(Knock*, pp. 206–207)

This description is quoted at length simply because it is so finely sculpted that there is nothing we want to take out. It is solid. Each line, each word in each line, makes a distinctive contribution to our understanding of the old man. It is the kind of "irreducible" passage that Robert Hogan, following Herbert Read, calls a "Gestalt" in his chapter on style in O'Casey's *Autobiographies*.[5]

O'Casey portrays the Vandhering Vindy Vendhor so clearly, with such fine depth of human understanding, that the unthinking cruelty of the children which follows becomes excruciatingly painful. Increasingly disturbed, we squirm as the children laugh at the old man behind his back, call him names, talk him into fixing Mrs. Muldoon's window—even though they know full well he will never be paid, mock him openly with derisive laughter, and finally throw stones at him while he is standing, knocking on Mrs. Muldoon's door, which never opens. Thus, when the old Jew trudges on with the heavy load still on his back, still chanting "Vindys to mend, vindys to mend!" we cheer (as O'Casey intended) not in derision like the boys on the corner but in appreciation of the glow that shines through the grime when one goes on with life in spite of the stupidity of boys (and men).

We dwell on O'Casey's treatment of these street people in some detail because his portrayal of these characters illustrates concretely nearly everything that is good about characterization in O'Casey's *Autobiographies*. It illustrates: (1) his "realistic" (as opposed to "idealistic"—see Shaw's *Quintessence of Ibsenism*)[6] treatment of life as it is and people as they are, (2) his marvelous ear for dialogue (the language the characters use is heightened enough to make it colorful but not so much as to make it ring false), (3) his sympathy with the politically oppressed, the huddled masses of Dublin's poor, (4) his appreciation of "the living glow" that stays in the human heart "like the core of flame in a smoking fire" in spite of the realistic fact that "the lives we have to live are bound to stain the skin with pitch that defileth" *(Drums*, p. 104), and (5) his faith that these gold vermilion embers contain a touch of divinity, that God, as O'Casey (following Joyce) suggests later in the *Autobiographies* *(Rose*, p. 294), may only be a song [or a dance] in the street.

II The Family

O'Casey, in the first four books of his *Autobiographies*, not only creates some marvelous Irish-Elizabethan characters, but also he conducts a realistic in-depth analysis of a human family struggling to survive in the slums of early twentieth-century Dublin. Plays centering on the interrelationships in a human family (O'Neill's *Long Day's Journey into Night*, Williams's *The Glass Menagerie*, Miller's *Death of a Salesman*, Pinter's *The Homecoming*, etc.) are among the most memorable of modern British and American drama, and it is interesting to view the central family in O'Casey's early *Autobiographies* as deserving a place in this dramatic tradition.

One of the more interesting dramaturgic techniques which O'Casey uses in these books is the "absent character" whose spirit hovers over and influences the lives of the family in the drama. O'Casey's father, who dies early in the *Autobiographies*, reminds us of the father in *The Glass Menagerie* in that he remains alive in the minds of the other family members—especially the mother and the poet/son—long after his physical presence is gone. Here, also, the protagonist (young Johnny) is clearly his father's son. Johnny has inherited (among other things) his father's appreciation of Irish history, his love of knowledge for its own sake, and his willingness to defy even God in heaven (*Knock*, p. 14).

The family character upon whom the absent father exerts the least influence is the least important (and least satisfactorily drawn) Casside family member. Brother Archie (Isaac in real life) does not appear to be an integral part of the family unit and is important and interesting primarily for his slight connections with young Johnny. For example, in "Shakespeare Taps at the Window" (*Pictures in the Hallway*), Archie introduces young Johnny to the theater and spends many hours playing Richard III opposite Johnny's King Henry VI. Later, Archie made it possible for Johnny to play the part of the kind priest, Father Dolan, in Boucicault's *The Shaughraun*, and then, after leaving the theater, he helped Johnny get a job at Harmsworth's Agency (a true-blue Protestant firm with which O'Casey deals rather harshly in "All Heaven and Harmsworth Too").

Whether it was because Archie gave up the quick life of the theater for the dead life of a clerk, because he joined the Catholic Church, because he married a snobbish "daughter of a clergyman's son," because he did not attend his mother's funeral, or because of some combination of the above; O'Casey never treats Archie with the compassion and understanding he bestows on the other members of his family: young Johnny "was building a house of his own in which there was no room for his brother [Archie] or his brother's wife" (*Pictures*, p. 326). "Scornful thoughts" were "hardening his heart" (*ibid.*). Johnny knew, O'Casey assures us without irony, "that he was far and away his brother's superior"; for Archie "never ventured to dispute an opinion of his, knowing, if the argument went far, he'd but show an ignorance he was eager to hide" (*ibid.*).

Unfortunately, these scornful thoughts that harden the heart do not help the characterization, and, therefore, there is little room for Archie in the autobiographies. Although O'Casey sometimes portrays Archie sympathetically when, for example, he presents him as a union official giving out too much money to workers on strike or as a frustrated actor keeping the players' receipts for his own train fare back to Dublin from the hick town his company was playing; such scenes in which O'Casey portrays Archie as a realistically drawn human being are scarce. "Poor Archie" is, it appears, "small beer" to Sean O'Casey (*ibid.*).

O'Casey portrays his sister Ella (Isabella) more sympathetically than Archie (Isaac), though less compassionately than the rest of the family unit. O'Casey condemns her, as he condemns Archie, for falling away from the light and for becoming trapped in a disastrous marriage; yet, compassion mingles with the condemnation. The detailed descriptions of her crazy soldier-husband beating her senseless, of her ineffectual struggle to keep her kids alive and well after her husband is put away, and of her deathbed scene all contribute toward making us care about Ella and feel the tragic waste of her life.

The early view of Ella reveals her potential for living a significant life as well as the tragic flaws that make it impossible for her to achieve this potential. In her youth, we learn, she has a talent for drawing and an appreciation of good literature, yet even then she is captivated by the colorful uniforms and fancy dresses of "the Castle Ball," and refuses to read to her dying father (*Knock*, p. 42). Thus, from the beginning Ella is attracted to tinsel and is not strong enough to face the dark side of life. The consummation of her marriage to the colorfully uniformed Benson in spite of her mother's fierce opposition is the kiss of death. After her "smiling morn," her soul seems caught in the coils of ignorance and darkness. Her learning, her artistic talent, her will to live atrophy as Benson takes command until, finally, she goes "about everything like a near-drowned fly in a jar full of water" (*Drums*, p. 70), muttering phrases like "my husband," "my duty," and "God ordained it all" (*ibid.*).

This death-in-life with Benson continues until the final grisly scene when Sean (young Johnny grown up) is called to Ella's to break up yet another fight. Sean goes rather unwillingly, for he knows that "his mother several times had got a shock from a push or a blow meant for Ella when she had thrust her body in between Ella and the flying angry fists of her husband" (*Drums*, p. 71). When Sean arrives, he "quiets" Benson by bringing a chairleg down hard on the madman's thick skull, and then watches over him until the attendants from the insane asylum (the "House of the Dead") take him away.

Unfortunately, however, it is too late for this deliverance from Benson to do Ella any good. The glow that Mild Millie and so many other O'Casey characters keep burning has gone out of Ella entirely. Her defeated, fly-in-water response to life (similar to that of the shattered Laura Wingfield in Tennessee Williams's *The Glass Menagerie*) is clearly demonstrated in the scene in which Sean helps her to move into yet another damp, crowded, cold apartment:

Ella said no word when she came to the room, but just went on, with glazed eyes and thoughtless face, making up the old bed on its rickety iron frame, and the other bed on the floor. (*Drums*, p. 124)

When Sean suggests she make both beds on the frame, off the damp floor for the time being, Ella agrees (again without a word), and the last sight Sean sees before leaving the apartment, the last image we have of Ella alive, is of her sleeping with the two girls and Shawn, the youngest at the head of the bed while the two boys are at the foot—"Six in all in the one room, and six in the same bed" (*Drums*, p. 124).

Although there is no trace of Ella, the schoolteacher and artist, the Ella of long ago in this scene, there is such a trace in the final image, the image of Ella dead on her bed. In this final image, Sean

recognised in the dead face his sister of the long ago, for the swift bloom of a dead youth had come back to mock at the whimpering, squalid things arrayed around it. There were the cleverly chiselled features, tensed by death, the delicate nose and fine brow, the firm oval cheeks, the white throat curving into the breast as gracefully as a swan's neck, and the neatly moulded hands, worn away now, resting confidently by her side. Here lay all that remained of her piano playing, her reading in French of Iphigenia, and of her first-class way in freehand drawing. (*Drums*, p. 134)

This "cleverly chiselled," "neatly moulded" passage helps to illustrate that there is something of classical tragedy in Ella's life and death. Her tragic flaw leads her to sell her soul for "the romance of a crimson coat, a mean strip of gold braid, and corded tassels of blue, yellow, and green" (*Drums*, p. 115), and this sale eventually helps to bring herself, and all those around her (Sean, her mother, and her children) to a "repulsive and confused condition." Like other tragic protagonists, she becomes aware of what has happened to her only after it is too late to do anything except suffer and to invite us, as spectators, to share in her suffering.

O'Casey's treatment of his brother Tom contrasts sharply with both his treatment of Archie and his treatment of Ella. "Tom," Sean affirms, "was a decent fellow. He had done foolish things early and late and often, but who the hell hadn't?" (*Drums*, p. 47). Note how the compassion and understanding we missed in the treatment of Archie shines through Sean's comments on Tom. "Tom was," Sean admits in an important aside, "the one brother whom he liked" (*Drums*, p. 33). Even though Sean paints Tom in softer colors than Archie, or Ella even, he paints Tom's wife, Agatha Cooley (Mary Kelly in real life), in colors as harsh as he paints either Archie's wife or Benson. His treatment of Agatha is especially harsh because Sean intuitively knew "in his heart" that "this marriage would be the end of Tom" (*Drums*, p. 33).

Tom, Johnny tells us at the beginning of the "Death on the Doorstep" chapter of *Pictures in the Hallway*, was a born soldier, but he was also a man. Tom, it seems, could never keep the Lance Stripe long. "Nothing would make Tom put a comrade in the clink, or even report one. What they want, he'd say when the stripe had been ripped from his arm, is not a better soldier but a spying bully" (*Pictures*, p. 220). Tom could never become a "jailer or a judge's lackey." "And so, though he loved a soldier's life, he left it, and came back to his own townland" (*Pictures*, p. 220). This stubborn defiance of the forces that lock up man reveals that in Tom, if not in Ella, the glow of humanity which O'Casey continually celebrates is not completely extinguished.

We see Tom as a simple, honest man whose guiding star ("the pint tumbler in the midst of a pub's glow") guided him truer, O'Casey assures us, than the clergy or policemen guided their flocks. The image of the young, handsome Tom "swanking it" before the hurlers in "The Cat'n Cage" is one that O'Casey would have linger in our minds. Yes, we should see Tom standing "five-foot-eleven in his socks, broad-chested, lithe of limb, ruddy-haired, a handsome ginger mustache sweeping his upper lip, grey eyes that sparkled when he was excited, genial" (*Pictures*, p. 76), gurgling down "more than half of his pint, leaving his fine moustache gleaming with a frothy dew" (*Pictures*, p. 78).

Sean O'Casey gives his handsome, genial brother Tom a special farewell, a farewell that, as Margulies points out in *The Early Life of Sean O'Casey*, he never gave him in real life.[7] The "Poor Tom's Acold" chapter in *Drums Under the Window* is Sean O'Casey's moon for the misbegotten. Here, Sean, beside Tom on his deathbed, lays his hand "gently down on the tawny head, and hears Tom's last words (as Sean O'Casey envisions them) "—Doing me—best—Jack—to—keep—a-live" (*Drums*, p. 57). In contrast to Ella who dies alone in despair, Tom dies with an affirmation of the will to live on his lips. He dies only after the last rites have been administered by the kindly Reverend Fletcher, whom Sean (in this chapter, at least) brought for this purpose just in the nick of time.

Sean O'Casey's treatment of Tom further contrasts with his treatment of Ella in that he puts the blame for Tom's failures in life not on Tom himself (who made mistakes but who the hell doesn't) but on the political and economic powers-that-were (and perhaps still are) in Dublin. A part, a large part, of Sean believes with his mother that Ella made her bed, and, therefore, was responsible for what happened to her while lying in it; but Sean with his whole heart feels that Tom, a born soldier, did not make a bad choice. For Tom was, as Sean tells us in a final moving tribute:

. . . An old tough with a vengeance. Marching to attention, gun on shoulder, to his death. Saluting death, the dark companion, as an officer and a gentleman. (*Drums*, p. 60)

Perhaps God, if he is as much the artist as O'Casey is, will also "conjure up in a distant corner a radiant mirage of a cozy pub" a pub where:

Tom and his Fusilier butties could forever drink without drinking, fight forever without fighting, and die for their Queen and country without dying at all, and gather a harvest of glittering medals on their chests to show themselves off to the wondering saints. (*Drums*, p. 60)

Mick, the oldest brother, is a much darker, much more complex character than Tom, whose geniality and Stoic strength are easy to appreciate and comprehend. O'Casey often used the natural contrast between Tom and Mick to illuminate both of these characters. Tom would stand up for young Johnny when Mick would pester and threaten him. "Tom was," Sean tells us, "a shield that caught the sneering shafts shot by Mick at Sean when he was a kid" (*Drums*, p. 49). Although Tom liked being a soldier (as long as he didn't have to be an informer), Mick "hated the life, and was always eager to get far away from the sound of a bugle." Mick's military life "was a stormy one, and his records were packed with regimental entries" (*Pictures*, p. 220). And finally in "The Cat 'n Cage" it is Mick (not Tom) who instinctively decks the constable (who had just boxed Johnny's ears) with a beautiful one-two combination.

Yes, Mick, the impulsive, active one, had a mean, violent streak in him the gentle Tom never had. It wasn't only constables that were flattened by Mick's fists. In "The Girl He Left behind Him" Sean describes Mick's treatment of "his lovely, sturdily-built Irish Terrier" (*Inishfallen*, p. 310 ff). "Mick," Sean tells us, "when he was drunk, or trying to recover from the effects of drink, used to try to force the animal to crouch before him, after hard beating, so as to show to all who wanted to see how superior man was in thought and deed to the lower animals" (*Inishfallen*, p. 310). Here Sean not only mocks the clergy who in their wisdom deny souls to animals while giving them to men, but also demonstrates in stark, dramatic terms that Mick is often—especially when he has been drinking—in the control of dark, demonic forces that hate life, forces that want to make all other life crouch down and worship them.

Like Jamie Tyrone in O'Neill's *Long Day's Journey into Night* Mick (or at least a large part of him) grows to hate his brother, envies his writing success, and injures the ones he loves for retribution's sake. Significantly enough, the quarrel scene which finally causes Sean to move out of the same house with Mick begins when the drunken Mick staggers into the room,

knocking clumsily and intentionally against the table at which Sean was
sitting, while an envious, dirty hand, sliding along it, sent the little inkbottle flying to the floor . . . –Writin', be God, again! murmurred the
blurred voice of his brother; some fellas are able to give themselves airs!
Scholar, is it? Scholar, me arse! Well, th' ink's gone, so wh'll we do now?
. . . Writin'! If I was someone, I'd thry to be a man first! (*Inishfallen*, p. 47)

By trying to become more of a man, the Mick of the *Autobiographies*, of course, is none. His natural, heroic spirit has been per-
verted into a destructive force that inflicts suffering and violence on
everyone with whom he comes into contact.

However, with Mick, as with Jamie Tyrone, the big part of him
that hates life is not the only part. As in Jamie, the antipathy for life
exists side by side with a love for it. The same hands that beat a dog
haul drowning men to safety. As Sean, giving the "devil" his due,
points out in "Hail and Farewell," he had often seen Mick's
"perished face" "lit up with a courage he could never summon to
himself" (*Inishfallen*, p. 54). To Sean's own knowledge Mick had
pulled more than ten drowning souls to safety "though no mention
of any [of these rescues] appeared on the face of the earth or the
brow of heaven" (*Inishfallen*, p. 55). "Ay. . . . Had he his due," says
Sean, "a streak of red ribbon would be glaring from his faded coat
now" (*Inishfallen*, p. 55).

And so, as the title of the final chapter dealing with Mick
suggests, our view of Mick as a whole is a view of a schizophrenic
character. In this chapter Sean is saying "Hail" (i.e., an appreciation, an introduction) and "Farewell" (a depreciation, a departure)
to Mick. "Paint him as he was twenty golden years ago, and paint
him as he is now," says Sean at the beginning of this chapter,
accurately prefiguring his own achievement, "and one would have a
horrifying picture of a worker Dorian Gray" (*Inishfallen*, p. 45).
Although the closing tableau of Mick lying on the floor in a drunken
stupor (described with the same reminiscent detail that he described Ella on her deathbed), clearly reveals the botched portrait of
his brother, O'Casey's final comment ("Curse of God on the way of
the world today") makes it clear that he blames the botch not so
much on the canvas or the paint as on the forces that splotched the
paint on the canvas in such a haphazard way.

Mick, like so many other tragic characters, is a damned character
viewed by the playwright with compassion. Mick, like Macbeth,
holds our interest and sympathy even as both his external features

and his consciousness become increasingly darkened and as he
spreads more and more destruction around him. Mick is another
once magnificent human being who has been led astray, tormented,
perhaps possessed, by evil powers that instinctively hate life. He
had, as Sean O'Casey puts it, been quietly robbed "by the careless
and criminal indifference of teachers, spiritual pastors, and masters,
who had thoroughly buried [his spiritual talents] for him" (*Inishfallen*, p. 56).[8]

While we feel compassion for Mick in spite of the misery he
inflicts on those around him, we feel even more compassion for the
mother of this family because she continually does all in her power
to relieve suffering. Throughout the first four books of the *Autobiographies* we see concrete example after concrete example of Sue
Casside making little sacrifices which make life a little more bearable
for those around her. We see her give her own blanket for Ella's
children, stay awake all night with the drunken Mick (who would
perversely, deliberately keep her awake), nurse Tom through serious sickness, and last but not least continually watch over her
youngest, half-blind son.

Unlike Mick who—especially when drunk—always found fault
with everything and everyone around him, the mother genuinely
appreciated life. She habitually found beauty in the little things that
nearly all the other characters take for granted. "Everything's grand
to her," Sean thinks, as she lies on her deathbed. "She has accepted
anything given to her without a murmur of complaint. A cup of tea; a
glass of beer; a sip of orange juice; and now a few drops of beef
tea—all grand, and welcome gifts from the giver of all" (*Inishfallen*,
p. 28). If the aging Mick (as presented in the *Autobiographies*) fell
more and more into despair, his mother never wavered in her faith
in life, faith which gave her ample resources to face the worst the
world offered.

The death of this "indomitable" woman tells us much about her
life. She does not whine or cry for attention (like the drunken Mick),
she does not rage against the dying of the light (like Mild Millie), she
does not complain against the way of the world today (as does Sean);
she simply dies "without one murmur for attention; unbreakable,
tireless, and quite confident." This indomitable woman stretches
out "only when all usefulness [has] left her body, possessing nothing
but the sweet peace that gave courage to her fine gay heart" (*Inishfallen*, pp. 32–33). This "sweet peace" (like Cordelia's patience) is

a source of strength not only in her moment of death but in every moment of her life.

Just as her quiet faith contrasts with Mick's raging despair, so too her faith contrasts with Ella's passive despair. Sue spent over forty years of her life bringing up a large family with little money in the Dublin slums, while Ella (as Sean presents her) gives up and dies after a brief, ineffectual struggle. Sue Casey was still living, still caring, still watching over Ella's children even after Ella was gone. She breathed life into her family, into everyone with whom she came into contact, while Ella drained life from them. Life bloomed around her, drooped around Ella.

The mother's plants, "the fuchsia, the geranium, and the musk," bloomed in her house as long as she lived, and so it is fitting that Sean breaks off "a sprig of fuchsia, another of musk, and a crimson disc from the geranium," and carefully arranges them "under a fold of the shroud, near her right hand" (*Inishfallen*, pp. 36–37). These three would be, Sean explains, her passport into heaven. They would be

her gold, her frankincense, and myrrh; her credentials to show to the first guardian saint she'd meet. I cared for these, she'd say, and honoured them, for they were of the gifts that the good God gave me. (*Inishfallen*, p. 37)

After she dies, all the things in her house that had life for her lie dead. "Everything here," Sean laments (including "the clay grimed tins that once held so proudly the geranium, the fuchsia, and the musk"),

was dead and gone; he [Sean] would never set eye on them again, and he never wanted to; without the honour of his mother moving among them, they had fallen from whatever grace they once had, and were damned forever. (*Inishfallen*, p. 53)

Because Sean's mother breathed life into the very things of this world, because she (like Synge's Maurya) spent her life in a heroic yet doomed struggle to keep her family from being destroyed, because she was "in her bravery, her irreducible and quiet endurance, her fearless and cheery battle with a hard, and often brutal, life, the soul of socialism" (*Inishfallen*, p. 36), Sean not only drapes her coffin with "the red cloth that had covered the box on which she had so often sat" (*Inishfallen*, p. 36) but also envisions for her (as he did for his brother Tom) a small spot in heaven, her own spot where she might "sing a few old songs," have "some useful work to do in the daytime," and have "a chance to walk with Michael [her husband] under the evening stars" *(Inishfallen,* p. 37).

The final and in some ways the most interesting family character is of course the character of Johnny/Sean himself. Rather than looking at this character as being schizophrenic (like Mick), we should probably view Johnny/Sean as O'Casey presents him, i.e., as two separate characters. Young Johnny, the first of these two characters, is, like Mark Twain's Huckleberry Finn, torn between the conventional inhuman beliefs being imposed on him by his society on one hand and his not yet buried humanity and common sense on the other. When Johnny is a Protestant kid thinking of the Reformation, or when he goes along with the crowd of boys mocking the vandhering vindy vendhor, he is portrayed as having his mind so cluttered with junk that clear thinking and right conduct become impossible. However, when Johnny questions his uncle about Parnell in "Royal Risidence"[9] or when he conducts his own "dream school" he is portrayed as having insight and a sense of values that the older, more respectable people have lost.

Young Johnny, like Huck, learns his lessons from life outside the schools. He learns that older people's talk on religion is mainly blather and hypocrisy and that God can be found, if he can be found at all, not in dull processions and dreary hymns in dark cathedrals but in the dances and songs of human beings celebrating life in the streets of Dublin. He learns also of cruelty, both of the unthinking cruelty of children (Harry Tait's treatment of Johnny in "A Child of God," the children's treatment of the vindy vendhor, and the children's treatment of each other in the "Battle Royal," for example) and of the thoughtful cruelty of adults (the jailhouse in "Royal Risidence," Slogan's treatment of Johnny in "Crime and Punishment," and Anthony and Hewson's treatment of their employees at Hymdim, Leadem, and Company).

This learning which goes on continually through the first two books is characteristic of Johnny and helps to separate him from Sean, whose character appears fairly well formed when we first meet him "At the Sign of the Pick and Shovel." There, Sean shares with us his rather firmly held opinions of "Arthur Up-Griffith," his fellow workers, the Gaelic Leaguers, W. P. O'Ryan, anticlerical editor of the *Irish Peasant,* and others. Although we find Sean (in contrast to Johnny) much more often in the process of educating rather than in the process of being educated, we find also that his mind is far from being closed.

One of the more interesting characters, introduced only after Johnny has grown into Sean, appears to have been created by O'Casey for the express purpose of pointing out things that the still-naive Sean often misses. Donal MacRory O'Murachadha, the young man from Tourmakeaoy, is first introduced in the "Song of a Shift" episode where he helps educate Sean as to Yeats's greatness and to the mob's (which had been jeering at Synge's *Playboy of the Western World*) ignorance. Similarly, when talking about "Dr. Douglas de Hyde" in the title chapter of *Drums Under the Windows* and in "Gaelstrom" O'Casey again uses Donal to say the harsh words about Hyde and shock the innocent "idealistic" Sean (and us too) into a more realistic appraisal of the man. "Hyde," Donal tells Sean, "has a bend in his back, looking at episcopal rings" (*Drums*, p. 226), and he "has created nothing in Irish literature . . . and he isn't and never was a poet," even though as an editor of "what others greater than he has done . . . he cleans the dust of indifference from many a star; but when he sings himself, he coaxes no music into his song" (*Drums*, p. 166–67).

As Sean grows older, he grows (perhaps unfortunately) less and less in need of Donal's education. By the time O'Casey gets around to dealing with A.E. in "Dublin's Glittering Guy" Sean and Donal are coeducators working as a team to reveal to the young innocent Edwin D. (for droop) Grey that "poor A.E." was little more than a turnip hiding in a mystical light (*Inishfallen*, p. 290). The two of you, Edwin exclaims in righteous anger, are "talking like a couple of barbarians , . . . Good Gawd! Are you two going to set your opinions against these two poets? [Monk Gibbon and Katherine Tynan]" (*Inishfallen*, p. 287–88). "Yes, why not?" replies Sean, confidently providing clear, concrete evidence that the young Johnny Casside has indeed grown up.

The character of Sean in the more hurriedly written last two books of the *Autobiographies* differs from the Sean of *Drums Under the Window* and *Inishfallen, Fare Thee Well* nearly as much as Sean differs from Johnny. Here it appears that the character of Sean has not only become firm, it has rigidified. Sean is almost always educating now. He very rarely looks at himself with the same detachment with which he viewed either Johnny or the Sean of *Drums Under the*

Windows, who resents having to help Ella's children and who would rather play in his piper's band than help the dying Tom home. Sean, as late as "The Raid" chapter of *Inishfallen, Fare Thee Well,* can still laugh at himself, but the Sean of the last two books, like the character of Arthur Up-Griffith, whom he criticizes so severely, cannot. This lack of a sense of humor, this arrogance (there is no softer word for it), is one of the factors responsible for making the last two books of the *Autobiographies* less interesting, less defensible as works of art, than are the first four books.

The Sean of the last two books too often lapses into the self-righteousness he himself so forcefully condemns. Probably the most glaring lapse, certainly one of the most painful chapters to read, is the chapter on "The Dree Dames" in *Sunset and Evening Star,* for as Gabriel Fallon correctly notes, O'Casey, in this chapter, at least, shows he has lost the gift to see himself as others see him.[10] When three women, one of whose husbands has just been taken away by the "ogpu" (the Russian secret Police), come to tell Sean of his disappearance, Sean is harshly unsympathetic. It is hard to imagine the Sean who informed us that ideology is not enough to pay for Johnny Grayburn's "sturdy body, [his] handsome face, [his] promise as a future man" (*Inishfallen,* p. 13), being the same Sean who can tell Creda (who has just lost her husband): "Even the Ogpu don't "arrest people for the pure fun of the thing. And," Sean cruelly adds, if he behaved there as you are behaving here, I don't wonder he was removed as a potential dictator" (*Sunset,* p. 129). It is nearly impossible to imagine the younger Sean saying (as this one does with a straight face) immediately after the women leave: "What an arrogant mind, what a blustering manner, that woman had" (*Sunset,* p. 131) and then go into a three page-disquisition on the arrogance of assuming to know the truth. Here we miss the incisive comments of a character like the tram conductor or Donal O'Murachadha who might deflate such extensive rationalization.

We include the preceding comments on "The Dree Dames" not because we agree with Fallon that this and the "Rebel Orwell" chapter are representative of O'Casey's writing in the *Autobiographies*—or even representative of his writing in *Rose and Crown* and *Sunset and Evening Star*—but because "The Dree Dames" is there and we would do no service to O'Casey, or to ourselves, by ignoring it. We certainly do not subscribe to Gabriel Fallon's (*and* others) theory that O'Casey himself was schizophrenic, that he was a healthy, lovable person while he lived in Ireland and wrote the "blazing masterpieces" *(Juno and the Paycock* and *The Plough and the Stars)* and a sick, bitter, irascible old man while he lived in England and wrote pretentious, narcissistic, propaganda-filled books, the prime examples of which being the *Autobiographies.* [11] Viewing the *Autobiographies* in the light of the preceding discussion, i.e., as works of art, helps us to avoid at least two of Fallon's major errors. It helps us to avoid identifying a character in the *Autobiographies* (whether it be Johnny, the early Sean, or even the later Sean) too closely with a real person (the author, Sean O'Casey, himself), and it helps us to recognize that many of the chapters of the *Autobiographies* blaze as brightly as anything O'Casey ever would write.

III   *The Historical Characters*

Before concluding our discussion of characterization in the *Autobiographies,* let us deflate (slightly) the critical myth concerning O'Casey's treatment of historical characters which is perhaps most clearly stated by Padraic Colum in his article on "Sean O'Casey's Narratives": "I believe," Colum declares, that an "attitude of exclusiveness" is "ingrained in the writer of the *Autobiographies,* though not, needless to say, on the religious or political level. Exclusiveness is in his judgment of persons: Douglas Hyde, Arthur Griffith, A.E., Constance Markievitz—others, too— are put before us in sectarian fashion. One must hope that readers will take certain noted personages in the autobiographies as interesting characters who have somehow got misnamed." [12]

We should like to take this opportunity to suggest that it might be "idealistic" hero-worshiping Irish critics rather than the "realistic" Sean O'Casey who misname Irish historical figures. It appears to us that O'Casey goes out of his way to be excruciatingly accurate when dealing with public, historical figures that he believed would be remembered. We should like to suggest that both his descriptions of literary figures (Yeats, Lady Gregory, Shaw, A.E., etc) and of political figures (Griffith, Hyde, Jim Larkin, Baldwin, etc.) draw so much praise and fire not because they are so imaginative, so removed from reality but because (like his early plays' portrayal of Dublin slumlife) they are so true to it. Although Margulies has demonstrated that O'Casey did make use of the artist's prerogative to invent and change events in his family life, there has been to our knowledge no such objective evidence presented to prove he took such liberties with important historical figures.

Interestingly enough, in the middle of "Black Oxen Passing By," his moving tribute to Yeats, Sean O'Casey goes out of his way to condemn the "odd things" that appear in the English press for their factual inaccuracies, their invention of events that never happened. "A Peter Pan picture," O'Casey says of a particularly imaginative recreation of the English press, containing "all false statements" (*Rose*, p. 139). It is reasonable to assume that this open contempt for these Peter Pan pictures would have an effect on his own writing— not only in this chapter on Yeats but any place in his *Autobiographies* where he is reporting on public personalities.

One reasonably safe way of distinguishing between O'Casey's imaginative and his historical characters is to realize (as O'Casey undoubtedly did) that he could be held accountable (both legally and morally) for his treatment of public figures of whom many other people would write in a sense that he could not be held accountable for the treatment of his "Elizabethan" or his family characters, for O'Casey and O'Casey alone would write of them. Nearly all of his historical portraits in the first four volumes are remarkably true to life, and when occasionally in the last two volumes his treatment of historical characters does tend to fly off into the realm of Peter Pan (as it does in his treatment of Orwell), it is not because he is deliberately creating an imaginative portrait but because the only picture he had in his mind was a picture not of reality but of never-never land.

Even the most imaginative portrait of a historical figure in the first four volumes (that of A.E. in *Inishfallen, Fare Thee Well*), is imaginative only in that his criticism of A.E. is presented as part of a three-way conversation among Donal, Edwin Grey, and himself that probably never actually took place. The criticisms themselves are excruciatingly realistic in that they are grounded in scrupulously accurate quotations from the conversations and the writings of A.E. himself. In fact, the most damning details in the whole chapter can be found in the long quotation in which A.E. talks of the "blind alley" of being "absorbed in character for its own sake" into which Shakespeare had led literature (*Inishfallen*, p. 286).

And so our final overview of the characters (Elizabethan, family, and historical) in O'Casey's *Autobiographies* suggests that in these books Sean O'Casey not only introduces us to a large gallery of always carefully drawn, often imaginatively charged portraits but also introduces us to the equally carefully drawn, often imaginatively charged world in which these characters live and move. By painting the lives of so many different human beings in such fine detail (including, of course, the continually recurring, carefully controlled heightened dialogue) O'Casey succeeds in creating a distinctive world, an imaginatively charged milieu that is uniquely his own. And it is O'Casey's success in creating this milieu (which grows naturally out of his success in creating individual characters) that is the greatest achievement of the first four books of the *Autobiographies*, that in the last analysis makes these books (taken as a whole) a successful, lasting work of art.[13]

CHAPTER 2

The Autobiographies:
Dramaturgy and Content

I *Dramaturgy: Contrast*

ONE of the most frequent, most effective dramaturgic techniques that Sean O'Casey uses to help make so many of the
stories in the *Autobiographies* works of art is that of Shakespearean
juxtaposition for the sake of contrast. Just as Shakespeare uses
the contrast between the comic and the tragic, the low and the high,
the rural and the court as an underlying framework for many of his
plays so too Sean O'Casey uses the contrast between the Dublin
poor and the Dublin rich, the vision of children and the blindness of
adults, the beauty and the ugliness in life, the strength and the
weakness of characters as an underlying framework both for individual chapters and for clusters of chapters throughout the *Autobiographies.*

"This pattern of ironic counterpoint," which, as David Krause
perceptively notes, "is maintained as a tragi-comic rhythm throughout the plays"[1] is also, we should like to suggest, maintained
throughout the first four books of the *Autobiographies.* An early
example of O'Casey's effective use of ironic contrast occurs in "First
the Green Blade," the second chapter of *I Knock at the Door.* Here,
the insensitivity and concern for outward impressions that characterize his sister, Ella, and his brother, Archie, are placed side of the
sensitivity and concern for human suffering that characterize
Johnny's mother. The high life (the pleasures of the lords and ladies
at the castle ball) is placed next to the low life (the pain in little
Johnny Casside's eyes), and the down-to-earth prose of O'Casey's
delightful dialogue is placed alongside of the artificial pseudopoetry
of "The Castle Ball."

As we pick up the chapter's action, the tram that was taking the

Casside family home has just been stopped by a crowd of people.
"It's the ball," the tram conductor tells the passengers in his own
inimitable way, "the Vice-Regal Ball with all the gulls o' Dublin
gawkin' at the notabenebilities flockin' in to a fine feed an' a gay
night in Dublin Castle" (Knock, p. 20). We see Ella and Archie gawk
at the glitter of uniforms and fancy dresses, while the mother is
thinking about the pain in Johnny's eyes. We hear the conversation,
the typical marvelous O'Casey conversation, go on and on as Ella
and Archie comment on the gold braids and the mantles of purple
and velvet while the mother talks about getting Johnny admitted to
the hospital. The last part of this conversation should be sufficient to
demonstrate O'Casey's presentation of this ironic contrast:

The whole thing gives a great amount of employment, said Archie encour-
agingly. Even the photographers benefit, for the whole crowd get their
photos taken after the ball is over . . . to be able to look back at themselves
in their old age in their gala get–up.
  —Sixpence a month, with three visits a week, isn't a lot to charge, if they
can do anything at all for Johnny, murmurred the mother.
  —Some of the dresses of the duchesses cost hundreds an' hundreds of
pounds, said Ella
  —And sweet goodbye to the kingdom, the power, and the glory, if we get
Home Rule, added Archie
  —Well, we'll see what they can do for Johnny on Monday, said his
mother, putting her hand protectingly on his head.
  —Here's a crowd of them coming, said Ella excitedly. . . . (Knock,
pp. 22–23)[2]

We should note in passing that this trick of having one character
bare his or her soul and talk about something that really matters;
while another character (or characters) is not listening is a dramaturgic device that has been used effectively not only by O'Casey but by
O'Neill, Pinter, Beckett, and other modern playwrights.
  In the above conversation not only is Ella and Archie's indifference contrasted with the mother's concern but also the high life (life
that could afford to spend hundreds of pounds on dresses) is contrasted to the low life (the life that can barely afford sixpence a
month for medical treatment). The first few pages of the chapter
which deal with the pain in Johnny's eyes, and all the ineffective
attempts of the superstitious neighbors to cure it (low life), while the
last part of the chapter deals with the pleasures of the castle ball
(high life).

The language which O'Casey chooses to use to describe both the real suffering of Johnny and the artificial pleasures of the lords and ladies at the ball serves to heighten the contrast between the two life-styles. O'Casey tells of the failure of all of the old-wives-tales methods for curing his eye disease in simple down-to-earth prose. One of the most painful experiences occurred when "they" repeatedly pushed his head into a bucket of cold water. And when the stubborn Johnny refused to open his eyes, "they" threatened him, beat him, cursed him, but Johnny (a rebel even then) just:

> stood there obstinately, with his head bent down on his breast, shocked and shaken, the water from his saturated hair trickling, by way of his neck, steadily down his back, and by way of his cheeks, dripping down to his belly; crying over and over again, The bandage, the bandage, put the bandage over me eyes again, they're painin' me terribly. (*Knock*, p. 18)

Of course, this straightforward prose contrasts sharply with "The Castle Ball," a prose poem of sorts inserted into the middle of this chapter of which the following is an arbitrarily chosen sample:

> Having learned fitly sless blessed to give than it is to receive,
> the ambassadors wise and the archdeacons holy,
> with all the great barons and judges most upright,
> followed hard by all the right and left honorables,
> tacked on to the soldier and sailor gewgaws,
> hurried past hurried fast hurried on to the ballroom. . . .
> (*Knock*, p. 27)

"The Castle Ball" could of course be criticized for being the pretentious pseudopoetry that it obviously is, but we would like to suggest that perhaps O'Casey deliberately chose this artificial, stilted, pretentious language to fit its subject matter; namely, the artificial, stilted, pretentious lives of the lords and ladies at the ball. The fact that O'Casey inserts the ribald song beginning: "Oh I could ride a ride a ride a ladie,/ a certain ladie . . ." into the midst of "The Castle Ball" just as he inserts "The Castle Ball" into the midst of "First the Green Blade" supports our contention that in this chapter O'Casey is consciously playing with the various uses of language and that "The Castle Ball" should therefore be taken more as a language game than as serious poetry.

Another interesting example of O'Casey's use of juxtaposition for the sake of contrast occurs in "The Dream School," chapter of *I Knock at the Door*. Here, the main contrast is between the "dream school," the ideal, natural, free school envisioned by Johnny and the real school he was sitting in run by "ol' Slogan," the schoolmaster. This chapter differs from "First the Green Blade," in which an artificial bad world was sandwiched between slices of life in the real world, for here, a good visionary world is sandwiched between chunks of corrupt reality.

In the first part of this chapter Johnny is welcomed to school by old Slogan, whose "thin, pale, bony, bubbly-veined hand" held "a snaky looking cane" in front of Johnny's good eye. Johnny settles into the class which is droning out the multiplication tables, and soon drifts off along a road above which

sailed white clouds so low down that some of them shone with reflected gold from the blossoms of the daffodils. Many beautiful trees lined the road that Johnny walked on, and from some came the smell of thyme and from others the smell of cinnamon. Some of the trees bent down with the weight of blossoms, and numbers were heavy with plums as big as apples, and cherries bigger than the biggest of plums that hung in hundreds on their branches, so that he ate his fill as he walked along that white road. (*Knock*, p. 149)

This road leads Johnny into a far more colorful, more tasty school where he was treated as a "child of God," and as "an inheritor of the kingdom of heaven" (*Knock*, p. 152). Note that in the description of the roadway, as in the description of "The Castle Ball," O'Casey's language mirrors the events described. Here, we see the sentences themselves bent down and laden with fruit shine with reflected gold from the blossoms of the daffodils. This is purple prose, but purple prose with a purpose, purple prose that contrasts vividly with the drab, realistic prose on both sides of young Johnny's vision.

He is snapped back to Slogan's schoolroom as his hand is torn by a bitter pain, and Johnny "with a quick glance at the reddening weals dividing both palms into two parts" put his hands behind his back (as Slogan ordered him to do) and "gazed mournfully at the teacher" (*Knock*, p. 154). "Three-times-one are three, three-times-two are six, three-times-three are nine, three-times-four are twelve, hummed the class" (*Knock*, p. 154) is as unpurple prose as can be found anywhere.

Sometimes in the *Autobiographies* O'Casey carries this dramaturgic technique of juxtaposition for the sake of contrast one step further and contrasts entire chapters with one another instead of merely contrasting elements within a given chapter. "Royal Risidence," one of the best chapters in *Pictures in the Hallway*, becomes even better when contrasted with "The Hawthorne Tree," the chapter which immediately follows it. The "Royal Risidence" of this chapter's title is Kilmainham jail, which Johnny, getting the chance of a lifetime, visits with his kindly, if not quick-witted, uncle Tom.

This chapter, like the jail itself, is just there:

A great, sombre, silent stone building, sitting like a toad watching the place doing its ragged middle-aged minuet. A city of cells . . . [a place] where a haphazard song can never be sung; where the bread of life is always stale; where God is worshipped warily; and where loneliness [is] a frightened hunted thing. (*Pictures*, pp. 40–41)

The first, outermost cells of this city contain the most light. The light-hearted, half-comic dialogue in which the young Johnny ties the kindly old Protestant uncle in knots with questions about the Irish, Parnell, Protestants, Catholics, and English and Irish soldiers helps introduce us to the bleak interior much as the light banter in the first act of Eugene O'Neill's *Long Day's Journey into Night* helps introduce the tragedy that is to follow.

The cells further from the light in "Royal Risidence" are cells like the one in which Johnny can hardly breathe, cells in which he feels "a warm sweat dewing his forehead," cells with "stone and steel surrounding loneliness, pressing loneliness in on itself" cells in which prisioners find only a "black-coated bible" (*Pictures*, p. 43) for company. The dark loneliness, the pressing, surrounding loneliness of the interior is lightened only by one brief spark, a brief moment of human contact, the moment when the old warder confesses to the young Johnny that he is proud of his Fenian son who spent three years in jail.

—I'm proud of me son, he said slowly, proud of him, an' ashamed of me son's father. I'm tellin' that to you, young boy, because you haven't yet been fortified be the world against the things that good men do. . . . I was in the Crimea meself, but I never wear me medal; never since the day me boy was sentenced to three years' penal servitude. Mind you, I'm only saying that there's a lot lyin' soft undher an althar no nearer heaven than a lot of others lyin' hard undher the flagstones of prison yard. (*Pictures*, p. 49)

Note how this small touch of humanity in the midst of all the inhumanity of "Royal Risidence" works to make both the humanity of the old warder more valuable and the inhumanity of the institution more pressing.

In the following chapter the natural beauty of "The Hawthorne Tree" contrasts sharply with the manmade ugliness of "Royal Risidence." The Hawthorne tree, whose first flower would send all the people of Johnny's street "into the center of a new hope," was "a big tree, and its broad branches of rich white bloom" bent so low that young Johnny, "if he sprang into the air," could easily catch one. This "stately" tree "set off the weeds with her ladylike look and her queenly perfume," and "her scented message of summer's arrival came pouring out of her blossoms and went streaming down the little narrow street" (*Pictures*, p. 55). It is under this tree that Johnny dreams of spending an evening "in a circle of peace . . . with curly-headed Jennie Clitheroe, nothing between them save the sweet scent from the blossoms above" (*Pictures*, p. 57). Note that this is the same Jenny Clitheroe he forced his mind to think about in a not wholly successful attempt to relieve the depression caused by visiting the cell of condemned men in "Royal Risidence." Thus, his thoughts of Jenny, love, and spring are linked to "The Hawthorne Tree," but opposed to thoughts of loneliness, darkness, and death that inhabit the cells of "Royal Risidence."

Just as O'Casey used the incident of the old warder to introduce a spark of humanity into the interior of "Royal Risidence" so too he uses the coming of the "dung dodgers" to introduce a little stench into the fragrance of "The Hawthorne Tree." The dung dodgers were "dirt hawks who came at stated times to empty out the petties and ashpits in the backyards of the people, filling the whole place with a stench that didn't disappear for a week" (*Pictures*, p. 58). They trudged filth and stench through all the houses on the street that could only be cleaned out by a full day's work. And so, near the end of the chapter, we see Johnny's mother toil as all in the street toiled "on the day of their purification" until at the end of day (chapter) "the place felt fresh again." And as the chapter ends, Johnny finally becomes free "to eat his chunk of bread in peace beneath the sented shade of the hawthorne tree" (*Pictures*, pp. 64–65). Of course, the stench of the dung dodgers takes up more space in "The Hawthorne Tree" than the humanity of the old warder takes up in "Royal Risidence," but (as O'Casey realized) such proportion is appropriate when dealing with life in the slums of late nineteenth- early twentieth-century Dublin.

II *Dramaturgy: Stories within Stories*

Another dramaturgic device which O'Casey puts to good use in the *Autobiographies* is his own modification of "the play within a play." Here in the *Autobiographies* O'Casey often uses a story within a story or a book within a book. Perhaps the best example of a book within a book is the seven chapters in *Pictures in the Hallway* that deal with Johnny's job at Hymdim, Leadem, and Company. These seven chapters (one for each of the days of creation), beginning with "Coming of Age" and ending with "To Him that Hath Shall be Given," contain (as the title of the seventh chapter might suggest) several examples of pseudobiblical language used for the purposes of satire and parody. And as we shall see, the last line of each of the seven chapters not only parodies Genesis and mocks the self-righteousness of his employers but also reveals that O'Casey viewed these chapters as a single unit.

For example, the last sentence of the introductory chapter in which Johnny gets the job is: "And Johnny felt that it was good; and the morning and the evening were the fair'st day." This mocking use of pseudobiblical language pervades all seven chapters and is especially thick (O'Casey's artistry again) whenever he is making fun of Anthony and Hewson's hypocritical, holier-than-thou attitudes. When Anthony and Hewson, the true-blue owners of the firm, are presenting Enthrews and O'Reilly (two model employees, i.e., informers) with presents, O'Casey describes the scene as follows:

Then, after a fit pause, Mr. Hewson beckoned to Enthrews, and Mr. Anthony beckoned to O'Reilly; and the two came, each from the other end of the earth, trusting, not in their own righteousness, but in the manifold and great goodness of their two masters, who were ready to bestow upon them some of the crumbs that would soon fall from the table covered with the green cloth. (*Pictures*, pp. 111–12)

And this chapter ends, appropriately enough, with the words: "but Johnny felt uneasy, and saw that it was not good; and the morning and the evening were the sicken'd day."

There is simply too much material in these seven chapters for us to deal with this book within a book in the detail it deserves; therefore, we must simply state that the situation gets more and more intolerable for Johnny the longer he works there. He lives through the "tir'd day" ("Work Made Manifest"), "the froward day" ("The Shame of a Thief and a Robber"), "the fivid day" ("Gather Up the Fragments"), "the sexth day" ("Alice, Where Art Thou"), until he is fired by Anthony in the final "seheventh say" ("To Him that Hath Shall be Given").

Before leaving Hymdim, Leadem, and Company, however, let us take time to examine at least one of the many stories within a story within the book within a book within a book. (*Pictures in the Hallway* itself is only a book within *Mirror in My House*.) Although there are many stories in these seven chapters to choose from (including the story of Johnny and Alice, the story of Butolf and his sister being fired for theft, and the story of Suresaint being caught with his hand up the leg of Miss Vaughn's drawers), we have chosen to examine the story of old Biddy within "Gather Up the Fragments." Old Biddy is a sharp-tongued old woman who buys broken and cracked merchandise from Anthony and Hewson and then resells it to the poor. She, like the tram conductor or Mild Millie, has a way with words. And her haggling with Anthony as she brings him down from twelve shillings and sixpence to seven shillings or her muttering to herself as she walks away is akin to genuine poetry. Listen, as she mutters to herself about ol' Anthony:

. . . but praise be to the Almighty God, it's little leisure he'll have to jingle his coins an' count his gains snibbed from an' oul' innocent creature, when his shrinkin', shudderin' body goes woefully down the icy slope o' death, thin an' tottherin', naked as the day he was born on, with the cowld snow fallin' on th' ol' schemer's head, and the nippin' frost askin' him how's he feelin'. (*Pictures*, p. 146)

Ironically, it is the ignorance of this old woman with the touch of the poet in her that causes the climactic quarrel between Johnny and Anthony. As she is leaving, Johnny calls out, "Farewell, sweet Lady o' Shalott!" And she goes after him with a stick yelling as she does: "—Yeh, yeh genteel, gaunty guttershipe! . . . I'll flatten your grinny bake, and knock th' plume outa yer impudence, if you dare again to murmur, let alone to shout afther a decent female th' name of some evil woman of th' long ago" (*Pictures*, p. 148). The ensuing row brings Anthony back on stage. He, naturally enough, takes Biddy's side and tells Johnny, "We don't want any reference to ladies of this or that place here. . . . Business and only business is to be attended to here" (*Pictures*, p. 149). (Note there is no redeeming virtue, no touch of the poet in Anthony's ignorance.) Johnny, who never could attend to "business and only business," talks back, and this insubordination sets the wheels into motion that eventually lead to his being fired.

III   *Dramaturgy: Vignettes*

The vivid pictorial quality of much of the writing in the *Autobiographies*, like the use of contrast and of stories within stories, is deliberate. The use of "tiny vignettes" is, as we saw in O'Casey's treatment of Mr. Moore, often worth more than a thousand words. These miniature portraits, these tableaus, often linger in the consciousness long after the mere words have been forgotten.

One of the most vivid of these vignettes is the final sight that young Johnny saw when he and his mother viewed the parade turned riot from the top of the tram in "The Red Above the Green." "The last sight Johnny saw, as the tram moved slowly away" was the sight of: "a lone huddled figure lying still in the street, midway between the bank and the college, almost hidden in the folds of a gay green banner" (*Knock*, p. 285). This sight, as the title of the chapter suggests, is the point of the whole chapter. In "The Red Above the Green" we see not only the English above the Irish but also the blood from the dead or dying man above the green flag. O'Casey lets this final tableau, painted with the last words of the chapter, do his talking for him. (O'Casey, artist that he is, has the taste, the tact, of knowing when to stop.) This portrait of a huddled figure remains embedded in our consciousness long after the words that painted it have faded away.

In our limited space we can do little more than mention in passing a few of the more memorable vignettes. There is the squealing, bloody pig vainly trying to escape death at the hands of the retreating soldiers in "The Buttle of the Boyne" (a story within the story of the title chapter of *Pictures in the Hallway*). There is his father, his "poor da," just sitting there in the chair dying, telling Johnny: "This is no place for a boy," There is the defiant, bloody Irish worker who is being taken to jail at the end of the chapter on Jim Larkin ("Prometheus Hibernica"):

. . . the wide stitches in his wounded face showing raw against his livid skin, the torn bandages flapping round his neck; shouting, [as] he trudged

on, Up Jim Larkin! No baton, bayonet, nor bishop can ever down us now—
the Irish workers are loose at last. (*Drums*, p. 304)

Also, there is A.E. "at home," Mild Millie dancing, his mother in
the cab with the second Johnny dead in her arms, and Benson
insane and dancing with other dark forms: ". . . round and round a
black stake driven strongly into the darker ground . . . so that it
looked like a maypole dance in a garden of death" (*Drums*, pp.
90–91).

It is not coincidence that so many of the chapters (stories) end with
this kind of picture. From the very first chapter to the very last
O'Casey makes good use of these vignettes. We see the first chapter
end with Johnny's father standing with his arm around Johnny's
mother speaking his defiance of the God who had already taken two
Johnnys away from him:

The circling arm [of the father] tightened round her. She looked up at
him, and saw his face form into a fresh and firmer tightness.
—Sue, he answered, we may yet have another child; that other child may
be a boy; if we should have another child, and that other child should be a
boy, we shall call his name John. (*Knock*, p. 14)

And we see the final chapter end with a picture of the old Sean,
". . . with whitened hair, desires failing, strength ebbing out of
him, with the sun gone down, and with only the serenity and the
calm warning of the evening star left to him" (*Sunset*, p. 339) drinking to "Life, to all it had been, to what it was, to what it would be.
Hurrah!" (*Sunset*, p. 339). Thus both at the beginning and at the end
of his *Autobiographies* O'Casey leaves the closing visual image to
speak for itself, to speak more than words can say.

O'Casey, the artist, does not rest content with using these vivid
pictures at the ends of chapters for dramatic effect. He goes on to
use the repetition of these tableaus (sometimes with slight changes)
both to highlight these changes and to emphasize the lack of change.
For example, this repetition serves to highlight the changes between the two riot scenes (one which he watches from a tram as a
boy and another in which he participates as a man) and between the
two dance scenes (one the dance of Mild Millie which he watches
and the other, the sunset dance on the banks of the Liffey in which
he participates). And on the other hand the repetition of the tableau
of Johnny and his mother together at the end of a chapter usually in

each other's arms³ serves to emphasize the lack of change, the strength of their relationship.

We will close out our discussion of O'Casey's use of dramaturgic techniques by demonstrating as briefly as possible that repetition is a technique that O'Casey uses not only with pictures but also with words and phrases. O'Casey makes effective use of this repetition of words and phrases in many places (including "It was time for Sean to go" in the title chapter of *Inishfallen, Fare Thee Well* and "This was where Chesterton lived among the workers" in "A Drive of Snobs"), but perhaps his most effective use of this technique occurs in "His Da, His Poor Da." Here, we hear the fragment "shrinking from something that everybody thought of, but nobody ever mentioned" repeated three times. The first two strike us in fairly rapid succession at the beginning of the chapter (the first and fourth paragraphs) like two left jabs startling us, lifting up our heads, setting us up for the roundhouse right that closes the chapter. The chapter ends with young Johnny, his da's shouted hoarse whisper: "Go away, go away, you, and shut the door at once—this is no place for little boys," ringing in his ears, running ". . . for his life through the hall out into the street, full of the fear of something strange, leaving his da, his poor da, shrinking from something that everyone thought of, but nobody ever mentioned" (*Knock*, pp. 47–48).

IV   *Dramaturgy: The Imagination*

Just as Blake argued that the sun was not a guinea-sized disc but a choir of angels singing "Holy, Holy!", so too O'Casey—especially the later O'Casey—refuses to worship the "Green goddess of Realism" and worships instead the liberating power of the creative human imagination. For O'Casey, again like Blake, believed that reason and what is should not be worshiped separately from imagination and what might be. O'Casey was aware, as his comments made during his trip to Trinity College clearly reveal, of the difference between the universe "displayed on circling wires, the planets, in due proportion, strung out around a gilded sun perched in the centre—a dead child's dying toy" and "Sean's own imaginative creation of the universe" which "was a far mightier thing than these poor paupered ghosts of planet and sun" (*Inishfallen*, p. 202). As might be expected, Sean O'Casey in his *Autobiographies* as well as in his later plays sets off fireworks, displays these "far mightier things," these creations of the human imagination.

One of the most imaginative (and best) pieces of writing in the *Autobiographies* is O'Casey's treatment of the Adam and Eve story which we find in the midst of "Green Fire on the Hearth" in *Drums Under the Windows* (story within story again). Interestingly enough, Sean O'Casey's correction of the traditional "mistory" of the Garden of Eden is effective not only because it is so imaginative but also because it is so "realistic" (in Shaw's sense of the term). O'Casey's version is certainly more in touch with the discoveries of Darwin and anthropologists than the traditional one.

When Sean (in O'Casey's story) climbs the wall and falls into the Garden of Eden, he finds it "different and disturbed." "It was shaking with the roaaoaring, yelelling, squeealing, and growowling of fierce, huge, and unnatural beasts" (*Drums*, p. 264). Paradise, it appears, was "a vast expanse of slime and swamp" with numerous huge plants "each striving to destroy the other and reign alone."

And everywhere as far as the eye could reach or thought could go, there were sprinkled in and out through it all, funguses. . . . All the colors of the land before him were gloomy browns, sad greens, and fading purples, while overhead a leaden, scowling sky kept the heart low and terrified. (*Drums*, p. 265)

(Picture this on stage.)

Then, lest anyone should think that he had become bogged down in Darwinian naturalism, O'Casey introduces Jeecaysee (an "awethor of the misuses of divorsety"), Daabruin (a priest like figure created to "lead the fiat of heretics to the end of the roaman road"), and a reporter (who is getting the true story of the creation from Adam and Eve themselves) into his swamp-garden. This introduction of twentieth-century characters into a prehistoric swamp is as effective and shocking as Pirandello (whom O'Casey admired) introducing twentieth-century characters into the throne room of his Henry IV.

O'Casey, of course, enjoys playing with these comic characters. Perhaps the best bit occurs when Jeecaysee, trusting tradition, turns to Daabruin for an explanation of "what actually was the deep."

Daabruin stood stiff, held his temples tight like a man in sudden and violent pain. . . . Heaven help me! I used to be fairly good at thinking. Will my head split—or will it see? . . . He buried his face in his hands, and stood in a sort of rigid torture of thought or prayer. Then a convulsion of revaluation swept over the moony face, and the tense lips opened to mutter, The deep was the deep that was where nothing that was not. (*Drums*, p. 268)

This explanation quite satifies the newsman, but for us it remains (like Lucky "thinking" in *Waiting for Godot*) a grotesque caricature of human thought.

The absurdist element in this story is further emphasized when Adam and Eve cannot agree on the story of the creation. Adam gives the traditional chauvinist rib story, while the liberated Eve tells us that that story was "slipped in with [Adam's] connivance to give the excuse for making the woman subject to the man" (*Drums*, p. 269). "But God spoke before you," Eve continues, "and my version, the true version [that there "wasn't a flash of a second of time lost between the making of us"], is there in the book too, for everyone to see" (*Drums*, p. 269). Note that in this confrontation between Eve and Adam we find the conflict which lies at the roots of this chapter, the conflict between the imaginative recreation of the artist (Eve's version) and the romantic, "idealistic" (Shaw again) dreams of fools (Adam's version).

The reporter (fool that he is) ignores Eve, turns his back on the frightening reality of the situation (the death, violence, and slime), listens to Adam's recounting of the Jeecaysee's advice, and puts down only the "glamour" for posterity. Of course, Eve, like so many O'Casey heroines, is not deceived by the "glamour," faces the future squarely and realistically, and leads her man forward up out of the slime to where life may be better. "I've a child coming," Eve declares, "and he won't be born here" (*Drums*, p. 274). And the chapter ends with Eve, showing the strength to face the worst the gods and men can offer, going onward, pulling the unwilling human race forward and upward by the scruff of its mangy neck, as the "dinnaseer" and "dipladoci," "those who are about to die," salute her (*Drums*, p. 275).

Let us note in passing that in the story of Adam and Eve, as in "The Castle Ball" and "The Dream School," O'Casey's language is effectively linked with the content. His imaginatively fused-together words (such as "mistory," "growowlong," "awethor," "Jeecaysee," "dinnaseer," and "dipladoci") work in this fused-together, realistic-imaginative chapter. Each of these words is a microcosmic example of a product of the creative human imagination that more accurately represents reality than tradition has represented it in the past. "Mistory," for example, better represents the traditional story of Adam and Eve than either of the ordinary "mystery" or "story."

In "The House of the Dead" O'Casey again deals imaginatively with the contrast between the creative imagination of the true artist and the foolish "idealistic" blather of insane men. Here, Sean is introduced to a mad patient (bearing a suspicious resemblance to A.E.) who thinks he is a great painter, philosopher, and poet by a logical, reasonable doctor, who turns out to be as mad as his patient. As in Blake's treatment of Urizen and Los, we see that when one state of mind (whether it be reason or imagination) becomes dominant over all others, man becomes mad.

When you have the imagination without reason you have someone like the patient who paints "great mysteries," who brings "infinity to the dotted line." You have this man, who the doctor assures Sean is "far greater" than Constable, Turner, da Vinci, Rembrandt, or Titian. You have this man who paints, as he tells Sean,

the twilight's dream; the star-soul of the earth, and the earth-soul of the star. Yes, I paint great mysteries, revealed to me in sleep. The gods so help me, too, coming down derry down to sit on the rail of my bed to show themselves off, so that I can see to paint them in their thrue colours, pink and light blue and dove grey; with wings sprouting from their foreheads, whence rises the Well of Indra, and plumes of coloured fire, spouting from the spinal cord, by way of the pineal gland. (*Drums*, p. 85)

This is the madness without method that results when the imagination divorces itself completely from reason. This great philosopher-poet-painter is obviously painting things that never were on sea or land, on earth or in heaven.

Naturally, the doctor, the scientific man of reason, also turns out to be mad. He is the walking embodiment of half-digested half-truths that insists he is the whole truth. Socrates, he assures Sean, after living "for ages on locusts and crowds of wild olives" was "roasted to death slowly on a gridiron" for "saying the world moves" (*Drums*, p. 86). When Sean has the temerity to suggest that he might be mistaken, the doctor, "his red face growing redder till it was all a purple glow," responds (like some doctors we all know): "Haven't I made a special study of these questions?" "There's no maybe about it," he shouts at Sean, "I am right!" (*Drums*, p. 86).

After thus demonstrating the insane doctor to be more violent, more dangerous than the relatively harmless, though equally insane, patient, O'Casey goes on to suggest that the madhouse is a perfect symbol for Ireland itself, where the insane lead the insane. Where else but in a madhouse or in Ireland would we find "a scarlet unicorn and a white lion" (remember the statue outside the coachmaker's gates) dancing

a jig like mad to the tune of a Hungarian Rapture, while Eire's King, Lords, and Commons, all in morning-dress, bowler hats upon their heads, tightly rolled umbrellas under their arms, sat around on wool-gathering galleries of clouds, clapping applause, and singing, as they clapped, *A Nation Once Again*, guided in pitch, time, and tone by the dignified little impresario, Art Up Griffith. . . . (*Drums*, pp. 89–90)

And Sean turns and flees from this happy scene in which the magic of Sean O'Casey's creative imagination has turned the "idealistic" into the "realistic," the sane into the insane, and heaven into hell.

No discussion of the imagination in Sean O'Casey's *Autobiographies* would be complete without mentioning his use of dreams. Obviously, the dream school (already dealt with), "The Dream Review," and his sister's wedding-eve soliloquy are all examples of the human mind subconsciously creating visions of life that are better than the reality in which they find themselves mired. Note, however, that the dreams of young Johnny are (like those of Eve and Sean O'Casey himself) creations of a genuine artist, while the dreams of Ella are (like those of Adam and the madhouse caricature of A.E.) the creations of a foolish "idealistic" human being.

In "The Dream Review," as in the madhouse scene, O'Casey's imaginative view of reality (here the parade) helps us to see that the conventional view of this reality is really insane. Here, Johnny livens up the conventional parade in which grown men who "daren't disobey any ordher of the officer commandin'" are "steppin' out with a left-right, left-right . . . never missin' a beat" by imagining (among other things) the Scotch regiment running naked through the streets after the Irish people had torn off their kilts. Note that in "The Dream Review" the genuine entertainment provided by Johnny's imagination is contrasted not only to the ordinary parade the other boys are going to see but also to his drab tenement life with its fleas (which he takes time out to kill) and the spasms of pain in his eyes (which also drag down his imagination).

Although his sister's wedding-eve soliloquy also presents an imaginary world as more beautiful than the world seen by realistic, everyday minds, it differs from Johnny's dream review in that here the realistic mind (represented by the mother) is sane, while Ella's dream's view of Benson as a handsome, educable, reformable man (*Knock*, p. 105) is as insane as the mad poet's view of the Gods. Johnny's dream was good in that it enabled him to triumph over the fleas and the pain for a while, while Ella's dream (as her mother accurately foresees) is the cause of her living with fleas and pain for the rest of her natural life. Johnny's dreams were constructive; Ella's romanticizing is destructive.

The final piece of imaginative writing which we shall discuss is "The Buttle of the Boyne." In this imaginative recreation of time past, as in the imaginative recreation of the Garden of Eden, the protagonist of the *Autobiographies* (this time Johnny) is placed in the midst of it. Here, he is fighting for Sarsfield and the Irish while Glazier, Doosard, and other true-blue bigots, whom Johnny and the Rev. E. M. Griffin had been fighting for control of their church, are fighting for King Billy. As in his treatment of the Garden of Eden and the dream review, Sean O'Casey again succeeds in fusing the imaginative with the realistic.

Perhaps the strongest part of "The Buttle of the Boyne" is the part which deals with the old retreating Irish officer with the bad kidneys. The words and actions of this imaginatively created officer, like the words and actions of Bluntchilli in Shaw's *Arms and the Man*, make it impossible to romanticize, to "idealize" the war. In this "Buttle" six of the twelve cannon the Irish had were taken away by "th' flyin' King [James] for company, and th' other six sent to where they warn't wanted" (*Pictures*, p. 364). We also see the grim reality of starving, retreating soldiers killing civilians and each other for scraps of food or a drink of beer. One of O'Caseys finely drawn pictures says it all.

Farther down the narrow rutty street, a little war waged round a small keg of beer; already wounded men were trying to crawl away from the strife, while two forms lay before the keg, stretched out stiff to show that they were dead, and claimed to be left alone in peace. (*Pictures*, pp. 362–63)

And so we leave them there, these forms which remind us not only that romanticizing war is bad but also that imaginative recreation of it can be good.

V *Content*

After having dealt with O'Casey's use of dramaturgy and with his treatment of the human imagination, let us now turn to the content of these *Autobiographies*. In these books the themes of politics, religion, and celebration of life (joie-de-vivre) rise again and again like pulsing peaks on a blood-pressure graph.

The most difficult task we face when dealing with O'Casey's politics in general and his communism in particular is the task of coming to terms with the obvious split between the pacifist and the partisan. Sometimes, as in "A Terrible Beauty is Borneo," we see O'Casey take a clear partisan stand. And sometimes, as in "Comrades," O'Casey's pacifist tendencies are clearly in control. "Morning star, hope of the people, shine on us!" O'Casey intones at the end of "A Terrible Beauty is Borneo":

> Star of power, may thy rays soon destroy the things that
>   err, things that are foolish, and the power of man to
>   use his brother for profit so as to lay up treasure for
>   himself where moth and rust doth corrupt, and where
>   thieves break through and steal.
> Red Mirror of Wisdom turning the labour in factory,
>   field and workshop into the dignity of a fine song;
> Red Health of the sick, Red Refuge of the afflicted,
>   shine on us all.
> Red Cause of our joy, Red Star extending till thy five
>   rays, covering the world, give a great light to those
>   who sit still in the darkness of poverty's persecution.
> Herald of a new life, of true endeavor, of commonsense,
>   of a world's peace, of man's ascent, of things
>   to do bettering all things done;
> The sign of Labour's shield, the symbol on the people's
>   banner;
> Red Star, shine on us all! (*Inishfallen*, p. 222)

Of course, the Red Star of this passage is as much of an ethical or a religious symbol as a political one. "His Red Star" is, as David Krause notes," a universal symbol of his humanistic creed."[4] Here, the biblical language is not used ironically as it was in the Hymdim, Leadem, and Company chapters and is therefore appropriate and contributes to the total effect of this supplication.

This prayer which is tacked on to "A Terrible Beauty is Borneo" is an excellent, if a bit abstract, presentation of the partisan position which appeals to the intellectual side of our natures, and "Comrades" on the other hand is a tightly controlled work of art every word of which contributes to bringing the pacifist message home to the whole human being. The comrades of the title are: Mick Clonervy, a colonel in the Free State's Army whose "sharp elegant uniform fitted the body" yet "failed to fit the spirit of the man," a man who (O'Casey assures us) "would have felt himself happier in the old clothes spattered with cow dung" (*Inishfallen*, p. 135), and Lanehin, a young man only twenty-two years old, who was Mick's comrade in the struggle against the Tans but who is now a diehard, bomb-throwing republican. "Comrades" centers around the bicycle chase as Mick goes after Lanehin, who had just thrown a bomb through the window of a Free State police station. O'Casey, artist that he is, makes this chase neatly parallel the chase on a nearby lake as a drake moves determinedly after a "modest brown" duck.

The climax of both chases occurs simultaneously, and the chapter ends with two vivid images striking us in rapid succession. First, we see the final confrontation between the two human "comrades," Mick and Lanehin:

—I'm an old comrade of yours, Mick, the young man pleaded.
—Sure I know that well, said the Colonel heartily, and I'll say this much—for the sake of oul' times, we won't let you suffer long.
—Jesus! whimpered the half-dead lad, yous wouldn't shoot an old comrade, Mick!
  The Colonel's arm holding the gun shot forward suddenly, the muzzle of the gun, tilted slightly upwards, splitting the lad's lips and crashing through his chattering teeth.
—Be Jasus! We would, he said, and then he pulled the trigger.

Immediately after this explosion, we see the consummation of the other chase:

—Looka Ma! shrilled a childish voice behind Sean; looka what th' ducks is doin'!
  Sean turned swift to see a fair young mother, her sweet face reddening, grasp a little boy's arm, wheel him right round, saying as she pointed out over the innocent lake: Look at all the other ducks, dear, over there on the water!
  The drake had reached his goal, and he was quivering in the violent effort to fulfil God's commandment to multiply and replenish the earth. (*Inishfallen*, p. 144)

The stark contrast between the natural and the human, between the drake who was fullfilling God's commandment and Mick, who was breaking one of God's commandments, is exceptionally effective.

This existential ending contrasts sharply with the idealistic ending of "A Terrible Beauty is Borneo" and suggests that the emotional side of O'Casey nourished the pacifist in him while the intellectual side of O'Casey nourished the partisan. If these suggested connections are indeed true, then we can understand why it is the younger, more pacifistic O'Casey who strikes a blow for his dear land (although it makes him sick afterwards) and the older, more partisan Sean who refuses to give a piece of rag to the worker whose chin has been just sliced by a policeman's saber, and who, as Krause observes, is always "leaning against the proscenium arch, observing the rapidly changing tableaux of his life and times and offering his commentary, impassioned and defiant, merry and malicious, on the passing parade."[5]

At first glance we are tempted to the conclusion that O'Casey himself did not see this conflict between the pacifist and the partisan either in his characters (Johnny and Sean) or himself, but closer examination of the *Autobiographies* reveals, however, what is perhaps a deliberate progression from the mainly pacifist viewpoint held by the more emotional Johnny to the mainly partisan viewpoint held by the more intellectual, more detached Sean which is so clearly expressed in the panegyric to the Red Star which ends "A Terrible Beauty is Borneo." Although there are some partisan incidents (Johnny hitting oul' Slogan on the head with the stick, e.g.) depicted in the mainly pacifistic section and some pacifistic writing (O'Casey's treatment of the "grim gunner" in "In Cellar Cool") (*Sunset*, pp. 214–17) in the mainly partisan section, the final overall portrait we have of the protagonist of the *Autobiographies* is that of an emotional, pacifistic young man with strong partisan tendencies who develops into an intellectual, partisan old man with strong pacifistic tendencies.

O'Casey's attitude toward religion as expressed in the *Autobiographies* is certainly less complex than his attitude toward war and politics. Here O'Casey easily slips through the horns of the pacifist-partisan dilemma by taking a partisan stand against both their houses. Because he saw that bigotry, prudery, hypocrisy, blind obedience to authority and an intolerable self-righteousness were worshiped in both the Protestant and Catholic churches in

Ireland, he took his partisan stand against all organized religions, although he never questioned the value of religious experience itself. O'Casey had seen these despicable qualities embedded in both Ecret, Massey, Anthony, Doosard, Glazier, McKay, and Mr. Charles Jason on the Protestant side and in Kelly, the "friggin frogs"—Irish (more) Catholic (than) critics—and most of the "clergy" on the Catholic side.

O'Casey also takes pains to point out that human beings often develop into decent, kind (religious, even) people in spite of their religions. "Good people," as Johnny's mother told him on the tram, often "think wrong things." We see these good (though wrong-thinking) people scattered on both sides of the Protestant-Catholic fence throughout all the books of the *Autobiographies*. We see Walter McDonald, D.D., Dr. Michael O'Hickey, Father Flannagan (a priest who lost his job for encouraging his cold, shivering flock to steal the turf they needed for fires), and, of course, our old friend the tram conductor on the Catholic side, and we see the Rev. Fletcher, the Rev. E. M. Griffin, the mother, and young Johnny himself on the Protestant side.

The combination of these two basic beliefs: that a plague should settle on both their houses and that good people often think wrong things help to make the first four volumes of the *Autobiographies* and the early plays better works of art than the last two volumes, the middle plays, and most of the later ones. The later works, in which the Protestants (for the most part) escape whipping and in which people who think wrong things are simply bad, are not as effective as those works written from a less principled, more humane point of view.

Another theme, related of course to the first two, that we find thoroughly imbedded in the *Autobiographies* is the celebration of life, the tribute which O'Casey insists on paying to the beauty inherent in the rebellious human spirit. Nearly all of his stories in the *Autobiographies* and (his wife assures us) all of the plays end on "a note of hope and going on further with life."[6] In the midst of death there is always life. "Comrades," as we have seen, ends with the mating ducks, and "I Strike a Blow for You Dear Land" ends with Johnny making love to a beautiful woman. Violence, death, and the stupidity of men may hold center stage in both of these chapters, yet both chapters end on an affirmative note. And the last word in the *Autobiographies* is "Hurrah."

"The Raid" chapter of *Inishfallen* provides a concrete example of this weird juxtaposition of death and life. Here, Mrs. Ballynoy tries to seduce Johnny between raids by the Auxillaries and the Tans,[7] and the chapter ends with the vignette of "the timid, insignificant Charlie Ballynoy who took no interest in politics" being led away, holding up "his iron locked hands from which clouts of blood still dripped," shouting, "Up the Republic" with "the full force of his voice" (*Inishfallen*, p. 78). This defiance, like Camus's rebellion, is an intense affirmation of life in the face of death, the same kind of affirmation we see in Mild Millie, the bloody worker at the end of "Prometheus Hibernica," the tram conductor, and, last but not least, in Sean O'Casey himself. In fact, this defiant affirmation of life whether it manifests itself stoically (the mother and Tom) or rebelliously (Mild Millie, the tram conductor, Johnny, and Sean), permeates the *Autobiographies* to such an extent that the lack of this affirmation (Ella, the "clergy," Mick Clonervy, Anthony and Hewson, Arthur Up-Griffith, etc.) is a more telling indictment of a character than anything this character could say or do.

O'Casey's genuine appreciation of life can be clearly seen in his imaginative recreations of moments of intensely human experience. O'Casey's moments, like Joyce's "epiphanies," are moments of charged human experience captured in words, charged human experience made accessible to us living fifty years or more later. Examples of O'Casey's eternal moments ("spots of time," Wordsworth called them) would be: Johnny unhorsing the policeman in "I Strike a Blow," Johnny holding Alice's thighs while she is shaking on the ladder in "Alice, Where Art Thou," the mother holding her dead baby in the cab in the midst of Parnell's parade, Johnny watching the tired cow refusing to move in "The Tired Cow," Mild Millie dancing (of course), any one of the aforementioned vignettes, and so many others.

The most famous O'Casean moment is perhaps that colorful spot of time on the banks of the river Liffey in which Johnny and an unknown girl dance until exhausted in the light of the setting sun.[8] This bright moment is found in the midst of a dreary chapter on his job at Harmsworth's Agency (life in the midst of death again). Note how skillfully the artist, O'Casey, builds up to and then fades away from his touch of heaven in the midst of hell. Both his pushing the rackety, continually breaking-down cart filled with Harmsworth magazines which leads into the dance at the bridge and his passing by churches with "the whiff of brimstone" coming through their doors which immediately follows the dance help illuminate the genuine religious experience Johnny and the girl have just shared with us.

In the *Autobiographies* as a whole, as in this epiphanic dance and so many other intense climactic moments, O'Casey's imaginative use of contrast, of stories within stories, of vivid vignettes, and of his own imagination fuse together with his excellent characterization to communicate his distinctive vision of life as forcefully as is humanly possible. In the *Autobiographies* as a whole, as in the best individual scenes, O'Casey shares with us moments of human experience with all the impurities, the dross that we find in life all around us, burned away. Yeats, if he looked at the *Autobiographies* as we do, would have good reason to say at long last, "Perhaps we were not that far apart after all."

CHAPTER 3

Shadow of a Gunman *and*
Juno and the Paycock

I Shadow of a Gunman

FROM the Abbey Theatre's three-day trial run during the last week of the 1923 season to the recent NET production, *Shadow of a Gunman* has always been good "drama" if not good "literature."[1] This melodramatic story of two cronies, the peddler (Seamus Shields) and the poltroon-poet (Donal Davoren, who is mistaken for a gunman on the run by the rest of the tenement dwellers), who find themselves with a sachel full of bombs on their hands in the midst of a Black and Tan raid, but are saved at the climactic moment by a courageous young woman (Minnie Powell, who was then taken prisoner and finally killed by accident when the Black and Tans are ambushed by some genuine gunman) has always held the interest of audiences.

Although the dramaturgy and the characterization of the two major characters reveal real deficiencies, the characterization of the minor characters (Tommy Owens, Mrs. Henderson, Mr. Gallogher, Mr. and Mrs. Grigson, and Minnie Powell) reveals real strength. *Shadow of a Gunman* appeals to us on an emotional (if not an intellectual) level simply because O'Casey's street people, his wonderful Irish-Elizabethan characters, make their debut in this play. It is the minor characters rather than either the peddler Seamus Shields or the poltroon-poet Davoren that give this play its life, its genuine emotional impact. Even though we do get a completely new cast of minor characters in Act II, both sets of characters are interesting in themselves.

One of the more interesting street people in the first-act set of characters is Tommy Owens, a talkative young, would-be patriot who clasps Davoren by the hand and pronounces: "Two firm hands clasped together will all the power outbrave of the heartless English tyrant, the Saxon coward an' knave. That's Tommy Owens' hand, Mr. Davoren, the hand of a man, a man—Mr. Shields knows me well," who then breaks into a gallows tree song, and who finally exclaims "tearfully"; "I'd die for Ireland."[2] The blowin' of this character, who fiercely asks "Why isn't every man in Ireland out with the IRA?" (p. 95) but never himself comes any closer to the IRA than talking loudly about it in the neighborhood pub, anticipates the blowin' of Captain Jack Boyle in *Juno and the Paycock*. The ironic gap between the words and actions of Tommy Owens (and later Jack Boyle) generates real dramatic power.

Like Tommy Owens, Mrs. Henderson and Mr. Gallogher are two other first-act characters who appear to us as distinctive, interesting human beings. It is appropriate that these two characters enter and leave together for the stark contrast between their personalities helps to illuminate both characters. Mrs. Henderson (who lives up to her stage directions) is "a massive woman in every way." She is a "mountain of good nature" who behaves toward Davoren "with deferential self-assurance." "She dominates the room and seems to occupy the whole of it" (p. 96). Contrastingly, Mr. Gallogher "is a spare little man" with "a thin nervous voice." And "he is obviously ill at ease" when talking to Davoren (p. 96).

The scene with the letter in which Mrs. Henderson leads the shy, timid Mr. Gallogher into Davoren's presence and then proceeds to do nearly all the talking for the two of them is vintage O'Casey. "Mr. Gallicker has tried," the good Mrs. Henderson trumpets to Davoren, "to reason with them [unruly neighbors] and make them behave themselves—which in my opinion they never will—however, that's only an opinion, an' not legal—ever since they have made Mr. Gallickers life a HELL! Mr. Gallicker, am I right or am I wrong?" (p. 97). And Mr. Gallogher's comment is limited to the following reassurance: "You're right, Mrs. Henderson, perfectly right—not a word of exaggeration" (p. 97). In fact, it takes three pages of dialogue before Mrs. Henderson stops talking long enough for Mr. Gallogher to read his letter, and even then she interrupts his reading to give her approval or to suggest emendations to the text. (She insists on adding the word "shockin' " to the word abominable to describe more accurately the language used by Mrs. Dwyer.)

Before going on to the second-act characters we should note that the massive Mrs. Henderson is the only resident to offer active resistance when the Black and Tans raid the rooming house and take Minnie away. Although we (unfortunately) never see the battle, we hear Mrs. Grigson tell Seamus and Davoren about "big Mrs. Henderson fightin' with the soldiers" and "nearly knockin' one of them down" (p. 127) before being dragged away in a lorry. This Mild Milly–like resistance to authority is the final frosting on an already delicious character.

Just as Mrs. Henderson and Mr. Gallogher provide most of the entertainment in the first act, so too the minor characters of Mr. and Mrs. Grigson steal the show in Act II. When O'Casey introduces Mrs. Grigson, the long-suffering wife of Adolphus Grigson, early in the second act, we see her worrying about her husband's being out in the streets after curfew. In her first speech she "clares to God" that "me heart is up in me mouth, thinkin' he might be shot be the Black an' Tans" (p. 113). But then an instant later she is asking: "Do the insurance companies pay if a man is shot after curfew?" (p. 114). And she admits to Seamus and Davoren that realistically she'd probably be better off if something did happen to him as she comments "emphatically": "Ah then, if I was a young girl again I'd think twice before gettin' married" (p. 114).

Of course, she stops talking and hurries to offer her arm for "Dolphie dear" to hold onto as he stumbles drunkenly into the room, and another masterful O'Casey mini-portrait is complete. In this short scene O'Casey has presented clearly and unflinchingly the role of the woman in a lower-class Dublin tenement family. We see that Mrs. Grigson is attached to "dear Dolphie" much as his sister Ella was attached to Benson in the *Autobiographies*. Like Ella, she has sacrificed her youth, her creativity, her life for a husband who is not worthy of that terrible price; yet she endures, for there is nothing else for her to do, no place else for her to go.

The unworthy Dolphie is himself an interesting character. Even though he is a Protestant who'll always "abide be the Bible," especially the fear God and honor the King passage quoted by Johnny's Uncle Tom in "Royal Risidence," he insists on shaking Davoren's hand, because Davoren (he believes) "is a man." "Leave it there, mate," Dolphie tells the supposed IRA gunman, "you needn't be afraid av Dolphus Grigson; there never was a drop av informer's blood in the whole family av Grigson. I don't know what you are or what you think, but you're a man, an' not like some of the goughers in this house, that ud hang you" (p. 116). Adolphus Grigson's confused thinking, his shrinking cowardice and his heavy drinking, combine to make him an ancestor of many of O'Casey's finest dramatic characters—especially Jack Boyle of *Juno and the Paycock.*

Dolphus Grigson, for whom every drink was "the first today," is the source of much of the comedy of the second act. This character who protesteth too much that he is a man while firmly—cruelly, even—keeping his wife in her place is the butt of the humor—even when he is offstage. What could have been the funniest scene in the play occurs offstage (unfortunately again) in the kitchen where the Black and Tans force Dolphie (who had carefully opened his Bible to his favorite God and King passage) to "offer up a prayer for the Irish Republic" and sing the hymn "We Shall Meet in the Sweet Bye and Bye" while they loll around drinking his whiskey and laughing at his "terrible sufferins" (p. 125). Now there's torture for Dolphie, but humor for us.

The contrast between this realistic version of the scene (as reported by Mrs. Grigson) and Adolphus Grigson's version which he gives us (after sending his wife to her place in the kitchen) increases the humor even further. "Excitin' few moments," Dolphie assures Shields and Davoren as he "nonchalantly" takes out his pipe, fills it, and settles back, "Mrs. G. lost her head completely—panic stricken. But that's only natural, all women is very nervous. The only thing to do is to show them that they can't put the wind up you; show the least sign of fright an they'd walk on you, simply walk on you . . ." etc. (p. 128). As if the sight of this person, who has just been humiliated, posing and blowing like this weren't funny enough, O'Casey has Dolphie scurry off to the "safer asylum of the kitchen" as the sounds of the shots from the ambush in which Minnie Powell is killed are heard in the distance.

The last minor character, the first of O'Casey's heroic women, is, of course, this same Minnie Powell. She is only twenty-three, "but the fact of being forced to earn her own living, and to take care of herself, on account of her parents' early death, has given her a force and an assurance beyond her years" (p. 88). She, again like later O'Casey heroines, adds to her charm (and to her symbolic significance) by the way she dresses. Her "well shaped figure" is "charmingly dressed in a brown tailor made costume, her stockings and shoes are a darker brown tint than the costume, and all are crowned by a silk Tam-o-shanter of a rich blue tint" (p. 89). She is (as

Donal Davoren appreciatively notes) "a pioneer in action"; she offers to come in and tidy up Davoren's room without being
frightened (as Davoren obviously is) over what the neighbors might
say. "An' do you think Minnie Powell cares," this pioneer asks
Donal, "whether they'll talk or no? She's had to push her way
through life up to this without help from any one, an' she's not goin'
to ask their leave, now, to do what she wants to do" (p. 93).

At the end of the play we see that this self-assured, independent,
charmingly, colorfully dressed young woman has the courage that all
the other characters in this play talk so much about. When the raid
occurs and Seamus and Davoren are in panic, Minnie remains calm.
"Her actions," O'Casey's stage directions tell us, "are performed
with decisive celerity" (p. 122). While Donal is driveling, "Bombs,
bombs, bombs; my God! in the bag on the table there; were done,
we're done" and Seamus is muttering his prayers to St. Anthony,
Minnie picks up the bag and takes it to her room. And finally, when
Minnie is carried away, she's shouting "Up the Republic" as bravely
as Mr. Ballynoy in "The Raid."

If a strength of this play is in O'Casey's handling of the minor
characters in general and Mrs. Henderson and Mr. Grigson in particular, a weakness of this play is inherent in O'Casey's treatment of
the two main characters. In contrast to "The Raid," in which the
main character, Johnny, is a believable flesh-and-blood man caught
up in the absurdity of a Black and Tan raid, both Donal Davoren and
Seamus Shields are cardboard cutouts who are given good lines to
speak now and then. Donal Davoren, half poet and half poltroon,
has, as the extensive stage directions tell us, "in his face an expression that seems to indicate an eternal war between weakness and
strength." "There is in the lines of the brow and chin an indication of
a desire for activity," and "in his eyes there is visible an unquenchable tendency towards rest" (p. 79).

Unfortunately, the conflict so neatly described in the stage directions does not appear in the character in the play. We see little or no
evidence of "desire for activity" in the passive Davoren. He is on
stage (in his own room) doing nothing except talking for the duration
of this two-act play. Davoren himself notes his inability to act as he
compares himself to Minnie. "Minnie," Davoren assures us, "is a
pioneer in action as I am a pioneer in thought" (p. 93). This state-
ment, while perceptive when dealing with Minnie's strengths and

his own limitations, is mostly wishful thinking when dealing with his strengths. He is for the most part as stagnant and inert mentally as he is physically.

Because he is so much the poltroon and so little poet, we find it difficult to become involved with his life. The pioneering, poetic side of his nature (which O'Casey's stage directions tell us about) simply does not appear either in his actions or in his dialogue. Even when he is at his best, as in the following speech: "Right glad I am that she [Minnie] thinks of dress, for she thinks of it in the right way, and makes herself a pleasant picture to the eye. Education has been wasted on many persons, teaching them to talk only, but leaving them with all their primitive instincts. Had poor Minnie received an education she would have been an artist. She is certainly a pretty girl. I'm sure she is a good girl, and I believe she is a brave girl" (p. 109), he is disjointed, illogical, and inconsistent—which is not good for a pioneer of thought. How, we might ask, could an education that teaches people to talk only turn anyone, even Minnie, into an artist?

This disjointedness in Davoren's best speeches is even more apparent when he responds to Seamus Shields's suggestion that "a poet's claim to greatness depends upon his power to put passion in the common people" with the following pseudoserious speech:

Ay, passion to howl for his destruction. The people! Damn the people! They live in the abyss, the poet lives on the mountaintop; to the people there is no mystery of colour: it is simply the scarlet coat of the soldier; the purple vestments of a priest; the green banner of a party; the brown or blue coveralls of industry. To them the might of design is a three-roomed house or a capacious bed. To them beauty is for sale in a butchers shop. To the people the end of life is the life created for them; to the poet the end of life is the life that he creates for himself; life has a stifling grip on the people's throat—it is the poet's musician. The poet ever strives to save the people; the people ever strive to destroy the poet. The people view life through creeds, through customs, and through necessities; the poet views creeds, customs, and necessities through life. The people. . . . (p. 107)

Fortunately for all of us, the speech is interrupted and we never hear all that Donal has to tell us about the people. He does, however, say more than enough to reveal the basic flaw in O'Casey's characterization of Davoren. Although O'Casey apparently designed this speech to reveal a mixture of poltroon and poet, to present some reason in madness, to put some of his own ideas into the mouth of the blathering Davoren; the poet, the reason, and the ideas of O'Casey never shine through the muddle. We never know whether O'Casey lives on the mountaintop, in the abyss, or both. There are no lines drawn to distinguish Davoren from O'Casey, and the result is that key passages in the speech are doubly unsatisfactory. For example, the "life has a stifling grip on the people's throat—it is the poet's musician" part not only appears out of character for Davoren but also it does not represent O'Casey's own opinions on the relationship between the poet and the people.

The character of Donal's roommate, the peddler Seamus Shields, although slightly more human, is also unsatisfactory. Like Davoren, he does nothing but talk for the duration of the play. He is as superstitious and religious as Davoren is rational and philosophic. Seamus, as Hubert Nicholson notes, "the ignorant half phony patriot, is the thing from which O'Casey had striven so hard to emancipate himself"[3] just as, we might add, Donal Davoren is not yet the artist that O'Casey was striving to become. Since O'Casey was only half involved in each of these characters, they both speak only occasionally for O'Casey, and his point of view toward both of these characters appears inconsistent. Why should O'Casey make Davoren so realistic and clear-headed when dealing with religion, and so patroonlike when dealing with poetry and the people? Why make Seamus a farcical, hypocritical coward without a trace of conscience and then give him the following realistic insight into what is actually happening in the Civil War? "I'm a Nationalist meself, right enough, . . . — I'm a Nationalist right enough; I believe in the freedom of Ireland, an that England has no right to be here, but I draw the line when I hear the gunmen blowin' about dyin' for the people, when it's the people that are dyin' for the gunmen! With all due respect to the gunmen, I do not want them to die for me" (p. 111).

Why make the character who has just spoken the best lines in the play say on the same page (almost his next speech): "Thanks be to God I'm a daily communicant. There's a great comfort in religion; it makes a man strong in time of trouble an' brave in time of danger. No man need be afraid with a crowd of angels round him; thanks be to God for His Holy religion." It is a very difficult task to create characters we are involved with and despise at the same time, and O'Casey, in *Shadow of a Gunman*, has not yet sharpened his techniques of characterization to the extent that he is completely successful with this attempted fusion. This fuzzy attitude, this lack of a consistent point of view toward the two main characters, weakens this play considerably and helps make *Shadow of a Gunman* clearly inferior to "The Raid," in which his hand was more firmly in control, his attitudes toward his characters more clearly thought out.

There are other flaws in this play in addition to the fuzzy and inconsistent characterization of Donal Davoren and Seamus Shields. As Robert Hogan convincingly documents, there are serious technical and structural problems with this play. In his discussion of *Shadow of a Gunman* in *The Experiments of Sean O'Casey*, Hogan perceptively notes: that scene iii (with the landlord) is "structurally [and thematically, we might add] a waste," that O'Casey's manipulation of entrances and exits is "too nakedly evident," that the characters of Act I are "virtually discarded," which results in "a lack of unity between acts," that he introduces the important characters Mr. and Mrs. Grigson too late in the play, that the main characters do not hold our interest, that the minor characters "carry the burden of the play in crucial moments offstage," thus making "a diminishing of effect and a blurring of outline seem inevitable," and finally, that O'Casey's attempt at choral fusion in the last scene "is hurt because it [like the speeches of Donal and Seamus] is composed of relevant and irrelevant comments."[4] We agree with all of these criticisms and would like to point out in passing how well "The Raid" chapter of the *Autobiographies* stands up in comparison.

The looseness, the lack of focus, in *Shadow of a Gunman* is apparent not only in the characterization of the major characters, and the structure, but also in the imagery and the literary allusions. Literary allusions like characters are introduced arbitrarily and then forgotten. Prometheus, Paris and Helen, Shakespeare (from Ratcliff to Richard III), Shelley, Morpheus, Baylor of the Evil Eye, and Orpheus are all mentioned by either Davoren or Shields at one time or another, but there is no connection between them, no point to all the allusions except maybe to show that the little learning of these two characters is a silly as well as a dangerous thing. Looking clearly at the play itself, we can not help but wonder whether or not O'Casey was himself fully aware of his characters' limitations, whether or not, at this early stage in his development, O'Casey himself was showing off his own learning to us, much as Davoren and Shields were showing off their learning to the other residents.

This lack of control carries over into O'Casey's use of dramaturgy. For example, the letter, the wonderfully comic letter of Mr. Gallogher, is simply forgotten about in the action at the end of the play. Seamus tells Davoren to burn it, but there are no stage directions to indicate that he actually does so. There are stage directions, however ("Davoren goes over to the bag [with the bombs in it], puts it on the table, opens it, and jumps back, his face pale and limbs trembling"), that indicate both Davoren and Shields suddenly had more important things than the letter to think about. Now, it may be an excellent stroke of characterization to have these two poltroons forget about the letter, but it is a real lapse for O'Casey the dramatist to forget the letter, to leave it in limbo for eternity.

And the final and perhaps most serious problems with fuzziness center around the pictorial quality of this play. In contrast to the *Autobiographies* in general and "The Raid" in particular, in which the images, the tableaus, were vivid, memorable, and often worth a thousand words, the quality of the pictures in *Shadow of a Gunman* (when they appear at all) appears strained. The "seduction scene" (if we can call it that) in *Shadow of a Gunman* between Minnie and Davoren appears pale and thin when contrasted with the more vivid, more robust scene between Mrs. Ballynoy and Johnny in "The Raid." Also we might contrast the perfectly timed, vividly portrayed ending of "The Raid," in which we see Mr. Ballynoy lift up his bloody hands and shout "Up the Republic" as he is being led away by the Black and Tans, with Mrs. Grigson's second-hand account of Minnie's heroism in *Shadow of a Gunman*. And finally, even though we feel that there is real power in the ending of this play as the poltroon-poet and superstitious peddler are left alone to blather and feel sorry for themselves, we realize that this power comes from the words alone and is not reinforced as effectively by concrete visual detail as is the power in the unforgettable final scene of *Juno and the Paycock*.

II   Juno and the Paycock: *Characters*

Almost immediately upon entering the world of *Juno and the Paycock*, we see that O'Casey has learned from his mistakes. In this play the main plot centers around Juno, an unselfish working-class mother who struggles to keep her family together in spite of the "principles" of a daughter on strike (Mary), the whining of a son who lost his right arm in a fight in O'Connell Street (Johnny), and the drinking and shiftlessness of her husband (the "paycock"). When the family disintegrates in spite of her heroic efforts to save it, Juno does not despair; instead, she moves into a new apartment with her abandoned pregnant daughter, and goes on (hopefully) to build a better life. Both this main plot and the still melodramatic subplots (concerning Mary's love affairs, Johnny and the IRA, and the paycock's inheritance) are tighter, more carefully integrated, more under control than were the plots of *Shadow of a Gunman.*

The world of *Juno and the Paycock* not only reveals better structure than the world of *Shadow of a Gunman,* but also the two main characters in this play (in contrast to Seamus Shields and Donal Davoren) are clearly separated from O'Casey and each other. Here O'Casey places two of his most unforgettable Irish-Elizabethan characters in their starring roles. *Juno and the Paycock* is, as the title suggests, a play focused on the ironic contrast between Juno (associated with hard work, concern for others, faith in God, traditional values, marriage, and the family) and the "paycock," Captain Jack Boyle (associated with shiftlessness, selfishness, singing, drinking, and "blowin' "). Strange as it may seem to anyone familiar with his later plays, O'Casey, in this play, clearly sympathizes with the traditional Juno in her conflict with the colorful paycock, whose plumage (his Falstaffian zest for life) engages our sympathy, but not our moral approval.

Juno, like Johnny's mother in the *Autobiographies,* never succumbs to the temptation to despair. She keeps her faith in a Christian God in spite of everything this world can do to her. She is simply a quietly heroic old woman who spends her life in one continual effort to keep her family together and alive in a world that appears to be in a continual state of "chassis." Even though her family does disintegrate and her husband, the paycock, does remain "hopeless until the end of his days," Juno's devotion to life never wavers. She finally gives up on Boyle, but she never gives up on life.

As the play ends, we see her still doing what she can to lighten the burden of life for others, i.e., we see her planning to spend her time and energy helping her daughter Mary and the coming baby. And at the height of their misfortune we hear her strengthen Mary's wavering faith. When Mary suggests that perhaps Jerry Devine (the young socialist union organizer) is right in saying that there is no

God, Juno responds: "Mary, you mustn't say them things. We'll want all the help we can get from God an' His Blessed Mother now! These things have nothin' to do with the Will o' God. Ah, what can God do agen the stupidity o' men!" (p. 70). Thus Juno, good angel of the slums that she is, encourages Mary to bear up under the worst that this world filled with the stupidity of men has to offer, without succumbing to despair and looking forward to nothing but death.

This is not to suggest that Juno did not feel the pain of living in this world so much as it is to suggest that she had the heroic (saintlike?) strength necessary to transcend it. Even though she feels deeply the pain of a mother who has lost her only son, repeats the eternal lament: "What was the pain I suffered, Johnny, bringin' you into the world to carry you to your cradle, to the pains I'll suffer carryin' you out o' the world to bring you to your grave" (p. 71) and goes so far as to ask the Virgin, "Where were you when me darlin' son was riddled with bullets?" (p. 72) she stubbornly refuses to despair, lie down, and die. Instead she prays: "Mother o' God, Mother o' God, have pity on us all! . . . Sacred heart o' Jesus, take away our hearts o' stone, and give us hearts o' flesh! Take way this murdherin' hate, and give us Thine own eternal love! " (pp. 71–72).

If Juno is a saint, she is a saint who has won salvation through good deeds as well as through faith, a saint with dirty hands. For Juno is also very much a flesh-and-blood human being whose face has assumed that "look of listless monotony and harassed anxiety" that "ultimately settles down upon the faces of the women of the working class" (p. 6). Juno is the breadwinner in the family and her own (and her family's) survival depends not only on her faith in God but in her working hard day in and day out. Her faith is a practical working-woman's faith, a faith in hard work rather than in abstract principles. "You lost your best principle, me boy," she tells Johnny, "when you lost your arm; them's the only sort o' principles that's any good to a workin' man" (p. 27). Similarly, when Mary informs us that she is out on strike because a "principle's a principle," Juno realistically responds: "Yis; an' when I go into oul' Murphy's tomorrow, an' he gets to know that, instead o' payin' all, I'm goin' to borry more, what'll he say when I tell him a principle's a principle? " (p. 8)

In addition to her faith in God and her faith in hard work, Juno is characterized by unselfishness. While all of the other characters in this play think only of themselves and act accordingly, Juno's actions (like those of Johnny's mother in the *Autobiographies*) are nearly all grounded in genuine concern for others. Her life is, as we can plainly see, a never-ending series of sacrifices for the other members of her family. Every action, whether a major one like holding down a job to support the entire family or a minor one like getting the whining Johnny a glass of water, reveals this concern. When Mary gets pregnant and the paycock is worrying over what the neighbors will say, over how *he* will be able to "go through this," Juno is thinking about Mary. "What you an' I'll have to go through'll be nothin' to what poor Mary'll have to go through; for you an' me is middlin' old, an' most of our years is spent; but Mary'll have maybe forty years to face an' handle, an' every wan of them'll be tainted with a bitther memory" (p. 61).

As the above exchange indicates, Captain Jack Boyle, in direct contrast to his wife, is characterized by selfishness. Every act, whether it is a major act like borrowing money from all his neighbors on the strength of a will he knows full well will never come in or a minor act like covering Joxer's empty plate with gravy and calling it "sausige," shows him thinking only of himself. Like Davoren, he has an "unquenchable tendency towards rest." "He hates," as his own son observes, "to be assed to stir" (p. 9). He is "at home" in Foley's or Ryan's where he can drink and talk and talk (mostly about himself) to an audience that at least pretends to admire him. The self-aggrandizing quality of Boyle's conversation is best illustrated by the famous speech in which the good captain blows and blows about a life that never was on sea or land: "Them was days," he tells his crony, Joxer Daly,

Them was days. Nothin' was too hot or too heavy for me then. Sailin' from the Gulf o' Mexico to the Antanartic Ocean. I seen things, I seen things Joxer, that no mortal man should speak about that knows his Catechism. Ofen, an' ofen, when I was fixed to the wheel with a marlin-spike, an' the win's blowin' fierce an' the waves lashin' an' lashin', till you'd think every minute was goin' to be your last, an' it blowed an' blowed—blew is the right word Joxer, but blowed is what the sailors use. . . . An' as it blowed an' blowed, I often looked up at the sky an' assed meself the question—what is the stars, what is the stars? " (p. 23).

This speech is quoted in length not only because it shows Jack Boyle at home but also because the gap between this speech and Davoren's poetry and the people speech illustrates the quantum leap O'Casey made in characterization between *Shadow of a Gun-*

man and *Juno and the Paycock*. Here O'Casey succeeds in fusing the poltroon and poet together. Here the blowin' captain who tells us he was "fixed to the wheel with a marlin spike" shows that he has a little spirit left in him still. Captain Jack blows and blows and stimulates the human imagination simultaneously. What are the things that no mortal man who knows his Catechism should speak of? We wonder. What would it feel like to be fixed to the wheel with the fierce wind blowing and the waves lashing? We wonder. What is the stars? We wonder and we wonder. Thus Boyle, blowhard that he undoubtedly is, carries within him the torch of the poet. His bellows send forth sparks capable of kindling the dampest souls.

Because Boyle, like Mild Millie, has not yet lost his zest for music and for life, he remains a character (again like Mild Millie) who is not only vivid and real but a character who invites us to respond to him on different levels simultaneously. Jack Boyle and Mild Millie (and Falstaff)[5] are characters we admire and despise for being precisely themselves. We can, for example, view his moaning about the pains in his back whenever the possibility of work arises as sheer laziness or as a defense mechanism that makes it possible for him to survive in an exploitative economic system. One man's cowardice is, after all, another man's heroism. In the same way the closing scene invites us to rejoice that finally Boyle will get the torment that he so richly deserves and it also invites us to pity this man whose life, like the world around him, has disintegrated into a state of "chassis."

One person who must share at least some of the responsibility for the distintegration of Boyle's life is his drinking "butty," Joxer Daley, who has all of the captain's vices but none of his virtues. There is no trace of spirit in him. He cannot even sing a complete song. He has never had a thought of his own; his knowledge is made up of fragments and first lines; he is a "darlin' " conversationalist. (Anything anyone says is "darlin' " to him.) He is a "twister" who will agree with anyone who has the price of a drink. Like his ancestors, the Elizabethan vice-figures, he torments the protagonist for the sheer fun of it. He seems to take pleasure in hurting Boyle when he is down. When the news about the badly drawn will leaks out, for example, Joxer not only literally pushes Needle Nugent into Boyle's bedroom to make sure that he takes back the trousers the captain has not paid for but also steals his "butty's" last bottle of stout while the repossession is taking place.

In *Juno and the Paycock*, as in *Shadow of a Gunman*, the minor

characters (especially Maisie Madigan and the aforementioned
Needle Nugent) are well-drawn O'Casey street people. These
tenement neighbors, like Mrs. Henderson and Adolphus Grigson,
are interesting in their own right. When Needle complains of the
"bawlin' " of the gramophone while the funeral of Robbie is passing
by on the street below, Maisie responds with a bit of dialogue
worthy of the tram conductor or Mild Millie. "We don't want you,
Mr. Nugent," Maisie says, "to teach us what we learned at our
mother's knee. You don't look yourself as if you were dyin' of grief; if
y'ass Maisie Madigan anything, I'd call you a real thrue Die-hard an'
live-soft Republican, attendin' Republican funerals in the day, an'
stoppin' up half the night makin' suits for the Civic Guards!" (p. 49).
This heightened dialogue not only prefigures the speeches of
characters in the *Autobiographies* but also reveals much about the
characters of Needle Nugent and Maisie Madigan. We see that
Needle is a rare noodle who is more concerned with earning money
and looking after his own welfare than he is concerned with the cause
he so fervently defends, and we see that Maisie has both the insight to
see this side of his character and the courage to tell him of it.

O'Casey's characterization of Maisie Madigan is especially effective. She comes through as more than a birdlike woman with flashes
of insight and a sharp tongue. Although "she is ignorant, vulgar, and
forward," her "heart is generous withal" (p. 40). We see that this
woman with a generous heart has responded to the beauty in life,
but now has to be content with reminiscences about her lost youth.
The mere thought of Mary's proposed marriage sets her off to remembering when she with her own man "was sittin' shy together in
a doty little nook on a counthry road, adjacent to The Stiles" and
"his arm fell, accidental like, roun' me waist, an' as I felt it tightenin', an' tightenin' an' tightenin', I thought me buzzom was every
minute goin' to burst out into a roystherin' song about 'The little
green leaves that were shakin' on the threes, The gallivantin'
buttherflies, an' buzzin' o' the bees! ' " (pp. 42–43). "Ah, me voice is
too husky now," she tells Juno after finishing her latest song (a song
which ends with her building a nest in which she would sleep "on
me Willie's white breast"). "Though I remember the time when
Maisie Madigan could sing like a nightengale at matin' time" (p. 43).
Because Maisie's speeches (in contrast to those of Davoren or Boyle)
deal with actual *lived* experience, we care about her loss and share
her melancholy memories of mating times that never will
return.

Unfortunately, the characterization of the in-between characters, the characters who are neither major nor minor, is the only drawback in a play that is still one of O'Casey's "blazing masterpieces." The characters of Johnny Boyle, Mary Boyle, Jerry Devine, and Charles Bentham—are all nearly as unsatisfactory as Davoren and Shields. They are all too obviously manipulated, too stiff.

Johnny, like Shields and Davoren, is an unsatisfactory character mainly because O'Casey himself appears confused as to what attitude to take toward him. Johnny, the Boyles' only son, is supposedly an ex-IRA man who was shot in the hip in the Easter Rising of 1916 and then later lost an arm in a fight in O'Connell Street. From what we see of him, however, it appears that whatever heroic qualities he may once have had were amputated with his arm. Does O'Casey mean for Johnny's death to take on tragic significance, as the pretentious allusions to Macbeth—i.e., his victim returning to haunt him and his inability to rest—would suggest or does he mean to portray Johnny as a weak, sniveling coward whose continual whining gets on our nerves? O'Casey simply cannot have it both ways. Johnny cannot excite fear and pity at the same time that he makes us sick.

When Robbie comes back, for example, and we hear the terrified Johnny exclaim: "I seen him, . . . I seen Robbie Tancred kneelin' down before the statue . . . an' the red light shinin' on him . . . an' when I went in . . . he turned an' looked at me . . . an' I seen the woun's bleedin' in his breast. . . . Oh, why did he look at me like that? . . . it wasn't my fault that he was done in. . . . Mother o' God, keep him away from me! " (pp. 38–39). We cannot help but feel that Johnny's whining self-pity dilutes the intended tragic effect. Macbeth's sin of aspiring to be more than a man helps make him heroic while Johnny's sin of desiring to be less than a man is pathetic—at best. Even though Johnny's consciousness is continually filled with fear and he has murdered sleep, he lacks both the strength to defy his fate and put gashes on them that come after him and the strength to take his own life.

He also refuses to take the good advice of Juno, who explicitly tells him that "whinin' an' whingin' isn't goin' to do any good" (p. 64) and continues to whine right up to the very end, when Robbie's diehard friends come to get him. As they drag him out, we hear him whining words without thoughts, i.e., his final prayer to the virgin whose light has already gone out: "Mother o' God, pray for me—be with me now in the agonies of death! . . . Hail, Mary, full o' grace . . .

the Lord is . . . with thee" (p. 69). This whining exit, contrasting as it does with the heroic defiance of Macbeth and other genuine tragic characters, further dilutes the tragic effect.

In contrast to Ella, the sister of the *Autobiographies* whom she in so many ways resembles, Mary Boyle is not a fully realized character. She is, instead, more like Davoren in *Shadow of a Gunman*, i.e., she is a character whose dialogue and actions do not measure up to the stage directions. Mary, like Davoren, O'Casey would have us believe, is a character in conflict. "Two forces are working in her mind—one, through the circumstances of her life, pulling her back; the other, through the influence of books she has read, pushing her forward. The opposing forces are apparent in her speech and her manners, both of which are degraded by her environment, and improved by her acquaintance—slight though it be—with literature" (p. 5). With Mary, as with Davoren, the forces pushing her forward are so well hidden that they do not appear to be in her at all. In the play itself it is Juno who pushes her forward while the influence of books pushes her into Bentham's arms. Is, we might ask, the throwing over of Jerry Devine for Bentham an example of enlightenment?

Still, the main problem with Mary Boyle and (we might add) Jerry Devine is not so much in the basic conception of their characters as it is in their dialogue. When dealing with Jerry and Mary, O'Casey seems to falter on what is usually his strongest point. "Mary," we hear Jerry say "appealingly," "what's come over you with me for the last few weeks? You hardly speak to me, an' then only a word with a face o' bittherness on it. Have you forgotten, Mary, all the happy evenin's that were as sweet as the scented hawthorn that sheltered the sides o' the road as we sauntered through the country? " (p. 17). This, O'Casey would have us believe, is the speech of a man standing for the secretaryship of his union, a "good speaker," whom all are saying will get elected (p. 17). At the risk of seeming uncharitable, we must point out that the first sentence (if we can call it that) simply makes no sense. The second asks us to listen to the face of a word. And the third has one "that" too many, and so we are never sure whether it is the evening or the hawthorn which sheltered the sides of the road.

Still it is not clear that the above finely spoken speech is any worse than the melodramatic, hollow-sounding exchange that immediately follows it. Those walks in the country, Mary says, are "all over now. When you get your new job, Jerry, you won't be long findin' a girl far betther than I am for your sweetheart" (p. 17). And Jerry earnestly replies: "Never, never, Mary! No matther what happens, you'll always be the same to me" (p. 17). The ambiguity (perhaps unintentional) of Mary's speech (Is she saying Jerry will find someone "far better than she is" for his sweetheart or is she saying he will find someone far better than she is "for his sweetheart"?) combines with the mawkish sentimentality of the message to ruin the speech for us. And, of course, Jerry's melodramatic answer raises new questions about Jerry's speaking effectiveness. A person cannot be effective if he cannot be believed, and it is rather obvious that Jerry protesteth too, too much, that he is being dishonest both with Mary and himself.

The artificiality of Jerry's speeches becomes even more apparent when they are contrasted to the speeches of the tram conductor of the *Autobiographies* or The Covey, a socialist/communist character in O'Casey's next play, *The Plough and the Stars*. Both Ayamonn and The Covey talk politics continually, but the fine-talking young socialist union organizer Jerry Devine speaks over seventy-seven lines without making one political comment. Perhaps, if O'Casey had shown us Jerry's speaking ability instead of merely telling us about it, the character of Jerry would be more believable. But as it is, he talks mawkishly of love and not of politics at all. This mawkishness is nowhere more apparent than in the last scene in which Jerry and Mary appear together. Here the dialogue is even more painful to read than that of their first encounter. Here is the heart of this overly melodramatic dialogue:

MARY: Oh, Jerry, Jerry, you haven't the bitter word of scorn for me after all.
JERRY: *(passionately)*. Scorn! I love you, love you, Mary!
MARY: *(rising, and looking him in the eyes):* Even though. . .
JERRY: Even though you threw me over for another man; even though you gave me many a bitter word!
MARY: Yes, yes, I know; but you love me, even though. . . even though. . . I'm . . . goin' . . . goin' . . . . *(He looks at her questioningly, and fear gathers in his eyes.)* Ah, I was thinkin' so. . . . You don't know everything!
JERRY *(poignantly):* Surely to God, Mary, you don't mean that . . . that . . . that . . .
MARY: Now you know all, Jerry; now you know all!
JERRY: My God, Mary, have you fallen as low as that? (p. 66)

When the dialogue sinks as low as this, no further comment is necessary.

Last and least, O'Casey's characterization of Bentham, the pseudointellectual Theosophist schoolteacher who seduces then abandons Mary, is the stiffest, the most cardboard character of all. Although more consistently drawn than any of the other in-between characters, he appears out of place in this play. The character of Bentham, which would be appropriate and probably extremely effective in one of O'Casey's later farcical comedies, appears out of place in this Dublin tenement-house play. The characterization of Bentham has more in common with that of Basil Stoke or Cyril Poges in *Purple Dust* or with that of Jeecaysee and Daabruin in the "mistory" of Adam and Eve than with the characterization of any of the other characters in this play.

Bentham's tendency to utter obviously absurd comments can perhaps be best demonstrated by his response to the death of Robbie Tancred and his explanation of Theosophy. The death of Robbie Tancred, this English schoolteacher admits, "is terrible," "but the only way to deal with a mad dog is to destroy him" (p. 46). Cyril Poges himself could not make a more absurd addition. And "Theosophy," Bentham explains, is "founded on The Vedas, the religious books of the East. Its central theme is the existence of an all-pervading Spirit—the Life-Breath. Nothing really exists but this one Universal Life-Breath. And whatever even seems to exist separately from this Life-Breath doesn't really exist at all. It is all vital force in man, in all animals, and in all vegetation. This Life-Breath is called the Prawna" (pp. 36–37). Note how similar this explanation of Theosophy is both to Daabruin's explanation of "the deep" in "Under the Green Hearth" and to Basil Stoke's synthetical consideration of a primrose in *Purple Dust*. And so our analysis of Charles Bentham reveals not only that O'Casey has created a character who is too absurd for the naturalistic play in which he lives and moves but also that O'Casey is, even in the early tenement dramas, experimenting with the kind of farcical character which was to become prominent in his later writing.

III   Juno and the Paycock: *Dramaturgy*

Let us begin our discussion of dramaturgy in *Juno and the Paycock* by examining the stark contrast between our final view of the unsteady, weaving Boyle, and the steadfastness of Juno which immediately precedes it. As in the *Autobiographies*, the juxtaposition of opposites increases the dramatic effect. Directly after we hear Juno repeat a ritualistic eternal lament grounded in unselfishness and a determination to go on with life, we see the final vignette of Captain Boyle adrift, completely lost.

The dramatic strength of this contrast has been almost universally acknowledged. Robert Hogan, for example, asserts that the last two scenes of *Juno and the Paycock* provide one of "the most devastating moments of modern drama."[6] Gabriel Fallon, describing his first view of these scenes together, tells how "Sara Allgood's tragic genius rose to an unforgettable climax and drowned the stage in sorrow," and then he continues, "we in the stalls are suddenly made to freeze in our seats as a note beyond tragedy, a blistering flannel-mouthed irony sears its maudlin way across the stage and slowly drops an exhausted curtain on a world disintegrating in' chassis!"[7] Even James Agate recognized that the "ironic close" was "the work of a master."[8]

Perhaps the most memorable of the many other instances of effective use of contrast in this play occurs in the second act. Here, as so often in the *Autobiographies*, we see the clear contrast between life and death. We see the life (if on borrowed time and money) of these tenement dwellers contrasted with the death passing by beneath their windows. In the foreground of this act we have the comedy of Bentham discussing Theosophy and Joxer trying to sing a song (but never getting past the first line). Here life goes on as Juno and Mary sing "Home to Our Mountains," Masie Madigan sings her "Willie's white breast" song, and the captain recites some of his own poetry. But in the background there are intimations of darker things to come. It is just after Bentham's theosophical discussion that Johnny sees Robbie's ghost. In the midst of the singing Mrs. Tancred enters, says the same words of lament for her dead son that Juno will later say for Johnny, and then leaves. Later, just after the captain has recited his poem, the blaring gramophone is interrupted by Robbie Tancred's funeral procession passing by in the streets below. And finally, this life-filled act ends on a sinister note as "the mobilizer" tells Johnny that he had "better come" to the next meeting for his own sake.

If the second act consists of intimations of death in the midst of life, the third act consists of a flash of life in the midst of death. Just as a touch of the old warder's humanity shines through the gloom of

"Royal Risidence," Juno's heroic affirmation of life shines through the "chassis" of the last act.

Another dramaturgic device that O'Casey borrowed from the Elizabethans along with the use of contrast is that of using the protagonist as a battleground over which the forces of good and evil struggle for control. In fact, we might even go so far as to view *Juno and the Paycock* as a modern morality play in which the "vice figure" (Joxer) leads the "everyman" protagonist (Boyle) away from the magnificent life (Juno). We see Joxer continually tempt his "butty" away from Juno. "I don't like to say anything as between man and wife, but I say as a butty, as a butty, Captain, that you've stuck it too long, an' that it's about time you showed a little spunk" (p. 24). Note the wheedling flattery, combined with the insinuation of lack of "spunk" that this "butty" uses to lead the paycock away from Juno and the good life she represents. "Be firm, be firm, Captain," Joxer counsels, "the first few minutes'll be the worst: if you gently touch a nettle it'll sting you for your pains: grasp it like a lad of mettle an' as soft as silk remains!" (p. 24). Of course, Joxer, typical vice figure that he is, does not stand firm. At the mere sound of Juno's voice outside, we see Joxer go "flyin' out the window" with the same instinctive antipathy that evil angels felt for good ones in earlier drama.[9]

It is interesting to note that Boyle, like so many protagonists,[10] vacillates between the two forces vying for control of his soul. We see Boyle choose Juno's counsel when he first hears about the inheritance, and life looks good to him. As the first act ends, he renounces his old "butty" and reaffirms his faith in Juno. "Juno," Boyle declares, "I'm done with Joxer. I'm a new man from this out. . . . (*Clasping Juno's hand and singing emotionally*) O, me darlin' Juno, I will be thrue to thee; / Me own, me darlin' Juno, you're all the world to me" (p. 30). To the surprise of no one, Jack Boyle does not remain true to his darling Juno for long. As soon as the second act opens, we see him with Joxer again, assuring Joxer not to worry about Juno; for, the captain's "masther now, an' . . . goin' to remain masther" (p. 31).

As the second act develops we see these "butties" together more and more often; we see these two fallen beings eating, drinking, singing, and being merry on borrowed time. In contrast to the forward-looking Juno or the backward-looking Mrs. Madigan, Boyle appears totally immersed in the present, and lives with total disregard for the consequences of his actions. Appropriately enough, his view of the world (faithless twice-fallen figure that he is) is of a world in which nothing is fixed, in which all is flux and motion. The world, as Captain Jack Boyle tells us with more and more conviction as the play draws to a close, "is in a terrible state o' chassis!"

This previously mentioned final scene in which the drunken Boyle is left alone on a bare stage with only Joxer to comfort him (the same Joxer who has just stolen the captain's last bottle of stout) is a scene in which his mind mirrors his view of the world. The mind of this man who has just been deserted by Juno is shown to be in a terrible state of "chassis." "The Counthry'll have to steady itself . . . it's goin' . . . to hell. Where'r all . . . the chairs . . . gone to . . . steady itself, Joxer. . . . Chairs'll . . . have to . . . steady themselves. . . . No matther . . . what any one may . . . say . . . Irelan' sober . . . is Irelan' . . . free" (p.72). The whole material world, chairs and all, has become unsteady, and Captain Boyle appears to have drunk himself into a state of mind similar to Elizabethan "distraction" in order to avoid responsibility for the havoc his unthinking devotion to Joxer (and everything he represents) has brought upon himself and his family.

As the critical acclaim for this final scene clearly demonstrates, O'Casey has in this play finally learned to use tableaus effectively. In contrast to *Shadow of a Gunman*, in which there was too much talk, too few tableaus, *Juno and the Paycock* contains numerous scenes in which vivid visual images reinforce the thematic content. We see Juno bring Johnny a glass of water (after Mary has just refused to do so). We see Joxer go flying out of the window. We see the inhabitants of the tenement participating in the dance of life. We see the recurring ritual of a mother lamenting the death of her son reenacted before our very eyes. We see the votive light on the virgin's statue go out (just before Johnny is taken out to be executed). And finally, we see concrete image after concrete image as thing after thing is removed from the Boyle apartment in the last act. Needle takes his pants; Maisie, the gramophone; Joxer, the bottle of stout; the furniture movers, the furniture; and the irregulars, Johnny, until finally nothing at all is left and the stage is cleared for the searing final scene.

And in conclusion let us note that *Juno and the Paycock*, like the best chapters in the *Autobiographies*, is carefully put together. There are no loose ends, no forgotten letters, no irrelevant landlord scenes. Here every scene and every character in every scene contributes to the overall effect of the play. The minor character—Maisie Madigan, with her reminiscences of her youthful sexual encounters, for example,—fits nicely into a play in which Mary becomes pregnant and young Johnny's light is senselessly snuffed out. Mrs. Tancred, the mother of the dead republican, is integrated carefully into the story as her similarity to Juno (they are both poor working-class mothers who have lost their sons) becomes more important than their political differences. Even the will, which like the bombs in *Shadow of a Gunman* is a bit melodramatic, is woven carefully into the fabric of the plot. But O'Casey's increased control over all his material is perhaps best demonstrated by his treatment of the light before the virgin's statue. He brings this light to our attention early, casually mentions it a few times to keep it glowing in our minds, thus preparing us well for the climactic snuffout.

CHAPTER 4

The Plough and the Stars

I *The Collective Protagonist*

IN *The Plough and the Stars*, as in *Shadow of a Gunman* and *Juno and the Paycock*, O'Casey's finely chiseled characters immediately engage our attention. In *The Plough and the Stars*, however, O'Casey seems more sure of himself and his characterization breaks away from that of his two earlier plays in a few important respects. There is, for example, no main character or pair of characters that dominate the action. Whereas O'Casey used Davoren and Shields (unsuccessfully) in *Shadow of a Gunman* and Juno and the "paycock" (successfully) in *Juno and the Paycock* as central figures around whom the other characters revolved, in *The Plough and the Stars* he uses no such figure or figures. In this play all of the tenement dwellers whom we see struggle to survive in spite of the stupidity of men (especially flag-waving nationalists) are, taken together, the collective protagonist of this play. Nora Clitheroe, Bessie Burgess, Mrs. Gogan, Peter Flynn, The Covey, and Fluther Good are all linked together in an elemental struggle against the forces of death and destruction. Although this collective loses a battle or three (Mollser, Nora, and Bessie) they do not lose the war. For by continuing to support each other (they even protect the nationalist Captain Brennan from the British soldiers) they manage to survive in a world that really is in a state of "chassis." By sticking together, these characters, like O'Casey's strongest individual characters, affirm life in the face of death. It is fitting and proper that O'Casey dedicates this play, this tribute to the resilience of the human spirit, "to the gay laugh of my mother at the gate of the grave."

Whenever any of these interrelated characters speaks, he or she reveals not only something significant about him or herself but also something significant about at least one other character. This doubly revealing conversation is especially effective in the opening act, in which O'Casey introduces his characters. Mrs. Gogan's opening conversation with Fluther Good, for example, is a perfect introduction to this world in which all characters are defined according to their relationships with each other. "God," Mrs. Gogan says, "She's [Nora] goin' to th' divil lately for style! That hat, now, cost more than a penny. Such notions of upperosity she's gettin'. (*Putting the hat* [of Nora's] *on her head*) Oh, Swank, what! " (p. 137). This speech reveals not only that Nora Clitheroe has been "goin' to the divil lately for style" and that she has "notions of upperosity," but also that Ginnie Gogan knows the price of the hat, would like to own it herself, and doesn't mind opening another person's package. And Fluther Good's reply, "She's a pretty little Judy, all the same" (p. 137), tells us both that Nora is attractive to men and that Fluther is a man to appreciate this attraction. And then Ginnie Gogan's next speech, beginning, "Ah, she is, an' she isn't. There's prettiness an' prettiness in it. I'm always sayin' that her skirts are a little too short for a married woman. . ." (p. 137), reveals both Nora's "immodesty" and Mrs. Gogan's tendency to be easily scandalized, and hints again at Mrs. Gogan's envy of Nora.

The conversation between Mrs. Gogan and Fluther continues with only a short interruption from Peter Flynn until in the short space of four pages (about six minutes' playing time) we have learned the basic traits of five major characters and incidental information about a number of others. Especially important is the knowledge we gain concerning Peter Flynn and Nora's husband, Jack Clitheroe. We learn, for example, that Peter Flynn, who is fond of dressing up in the "full dress of the Foresters," is a "funny-lookin' little man. . . . Like somethin' you'd pick off a Christmas tree" (p. 139), that Peter appears dumb but becomes very talkative when "you get his goat, or he has a few jars up" (p. 140), and that Peter and The Covey cannot abide one another. We also learn, in these opening pages, that Captain Jack Clitheroe is nearly as vain as Uncle Peter. "He was so cocksure," Mrs. Gogan tells us, "o' being made [a captain] that he bought a Sam Browne belt, an' was always puttin' it on an' standin' at th' door showing it off, till th' man came an' put out th' street lamps on him. God, I think he used to bring it to bed with him!" (p. 140). This Commandant-to-be sulked and refused to attend meetings because he wasn't made a captain. He was a man; he "wasn't goin' to be in anything where he couldn't be conspishuous" (p. 140). And we even learn the bonus information that his belonging to the Irish Citizen's Army was a sore spot in his relationship with Nora. "But I'm tellin' you," Mrs. Gogan tells Fluther (and us), "herself was delighted that that cock didn't crow, for she's like a clockin' hen if he leaves her sight for a minute" (p. 140).

By now it should be clear that the opening conversation between Mrs. Gogan and Fluther does indeed introduce the basic traits of Mrs. Gogan, Fluther, Nora, Peter Flynn, and Captain Jack Clitheroe and emphasize the interrelatedness of their lives. For better or worse Ginny Gogan's life is connected with Nora's and Fluther's, Fluther's life is connected with Nora's and Peter Flynn's, and Nora's life is connected with Peter Flynn's and her husband's. In short we see that we cannot deal with the life of one of these tenement dwellers (Nora, for example) without dealing with the lives of all the characters with whom he or she is connected. Thus, the conversation between Fluther and Mrs. Gogan which may appear rambling is actually to a point. Every word of this tightly controlled opening dialogue is designed to shed light on one or another part of this play's collective protagonist.

One character who tempts us to see her as she sees herself, i.e., as a person who has a taste for the finer things in life (the paintings of *The Gleaners* and *The Sleeping Venus* hang on her walls) that the other more common tenement dwellers cannot appreciate or understand, is Nora. At first glance she does appear to stand out from the others. She does dominate the action in the first act of the play. As the first act develops, we cannot help but notice that it is her hat, her house, her husband, her manipulation of Peter and The Covey, and her defiance of the traditional woman's role that are the main topics of conversation, the main subjects of interest. She certainly starts off as a strong character who is used to getting her own way—one way or another. "When her firmness fails her," O'Casey's stage directions explain, "she persuades with her feminine charm" (p. 147).

Similarly, in the struggle between husband and wife, Nora, at first, appears to be the stronger of the two. Until Brennan arrives, we see her manipulate Jack almost at will. When her liberated complaints about being used ("Oh, yes, your little, little red-lipped Nora's a sweet little girl when th' fit seizes you; but your little, little red-lipped Nora has to clean your boots every mornin', all the same" (p. 154) or about her having to limit her thoughts and words to his,

understanding offends him, she deftly shifts gears, becomes coaxing, and "sits down beside him and puts her arm around his neck"
(p. 154). And before long Jack is singing "their song" with genuine
emotion to her as she nestles her head on his breast and listens
delightedly.

This tableau of the Clitheroes at home is shattered when Captain
Brennan enters with the news of Jack's promotion to Commandant
(news which up to this time Nora had succeeded in hiding from
him). When the Commandant confronts her with her obvious decep-
tion, shakes her by the shoulders, and demands, "What did you do
with th' letter?" Nora flares up, "I burned it, I burned it! That's
what I did with it! Is General Connolly an' th' Citizen Army goin' to
be your only care? Is your home goin' to be only a place to rest in?
Am I goin' to be only somethin' to provide merrymakin' at night for
you?" (p.158) This flash of spirit does not keep Clitheroe at home but
it helps illuminate his choice. When he renounces Nora for the life
of a soldier, he not only chooses to have a Sam Browne belt rather
than Nora's arms wrapped around him but also he destroys any
chance he and Nora might have had to build and maintain a whole
relationship grounded in shared moments of human experience (like
the moment Brennan interrupted) rather than in sexual experience
alone. And when Jack finally leaves with Brennan (who had been
humming "the soldiers song" throughout the Clitheroes' conversation) we first suspect that perhaps Nora is not quite as strong as she
had appeared to be.

Nora's inability to hold her man becomes even more apparent in
the climax of Act III. In this scene, which mirrors the climactic
scene of Act I just discussed, we see Jack Clitheroe fall for the
second and final time as he reaffirms his faith in death instead of life.
In this scene Nora uses every ounce of strength (both mental and
physical) that she has, but she is simply not strong enough. The
warm, red-lipped Nora is no match for the cold Brennan. Nora
perceptively notes "th' anger in [Brennan's] face," and "th' fear
glintin' in his eyes" (p. 197) and points out Brennan's coldness to her
husband. "Turn around an' look at him," Nora implores Jack, "look
at him, look at him! . . . His very soul is cold . . . shiverin' with th'
thought of what may happen to him. . . . It is his fear that is thryin' to
frighten you from recognizin' th' same fear in your own heart! "
(p. 197). But Brennan appeals to Jack's manhood: "Why are you
beggin' her to let you go? Are you afraid of her, or what? Break her

hold on you, man, or go up, an' sit on her lap" (p. 197), and Jack Clitheroe again chooses the shiverin' cold life of a soldier over the lovin' warm life Nora represents. With Lieutenant Langon dying in the background, Jack again turns violent and hurts Nora as he "roughly loosens her grip and pushes her away from him" (p. 197). Nora sinks to the ground and the soldiers go back to the wars.

After Fluther comes in drunk and provides us with a few minutes of comic relief, O'Casey redirects our attention to Nora. Her offstage cries of anguish as her baby is being born stillborn emphasizes that all life, literally and figuratively, has been killed in Nora as a result of Jack's final rejection of her which we have just witnessed. As the "mad" scenes in the last act clearly demonstrate, all the fire, the spirit that once moved Nora, is gone. Nora from this point on is not driven so much as she is drained.

The first "mad" scene reveals that Nora, like Mary Tyrone in the last scene of *Long Day's Journey into Night*, has been almost completely wiped out. "Her eyes," O'Casey's stage directions point out, "are glimmering with the light of incipient insanity; her hands are nervously fiddling with her nightgown. She . . . looks vacantly around the room, and then comes slowly in" (p. 204). Her mind, again like Mary Tyrone's, simply cannot, will not grasp painful reality. "I can feel comfortable," the vacant Nora informs the characters assembled in Bessie Burgess's apartment, "only in our own familiar place beneath th' bramble tree" (p. 204). The once-warm, red-lipped Nora is now cold, "feelin' very cold; it's chilly out here in th' counthry" (p. 205). She talks distractedly about her baby and her husband, and refuses to respond to Bessie's helping hand. "I won't go away for you," she tells Bessie, "I won't. Not till you give me back my husband. *(Screaming)* Murderers, that's what yous are; murderers, murderers! " (p. 205). Note that this mad scene is timed so that Brennan returns just in time to view the effects of the war on Nora and to listen to her "murderer" speech. Brennan, as might be expected, ignores Nora's distress; for his only concern, as Nora had previously recognized, is with saving his own skin.

Nora's reversal from concern over other human beings (especially her husband) to withdrawal from them is demonstrated with stark dramatic effectiveness in the play's final scene. In this second "mad" scene she is completely wiped out; she has lost all touch with the present entirely. At least before she could recognize Bessie and Fluther and respond to the soothing influence of Bessie's hymns.

Here, however, she simply has no idea where she is. She puts the kettle on for her husband's tea, sings a few verses of "their song," "When You Said You Loved Me," and then goes to the window and screams: "Jack, Jack, for God's sake, come to me! " (p. 215). And finally, when the good samaritan Bessie is shot after pushing the glazed Nora away from the window, Nora refuses to recognize that Bessie is slowly bleeding to death. While Bessie's life is draining away, Nora, "her hands trembling," "her lips quivering," and "her breast heaving," stands staring "wildly" at Bessie, saying to herself in a whisper: "Jack, I'm frightened. . . . I'm frightened, Jack. . . . Oh, Jack, where are you?" (p. 216).

The preceding threadbare discussion of Nora Clitheroe deals not only with Nora but also with her husband, Brennan, and Bessie. Of these, Bessie Burgess certainly deserves fuller treatment. Bessie appears to gain the spirit that drains out of Nora during the progress of this play. Bessie Burgess grows in stature from a character apparently tossed in because O'Casey needed a spokesperson for the loyal Protestant Irish to a character who earns our genuine admiration. In the first act Bessie appears to be uninvolved in the lives of the other tenement dwellers. Her support of England, her Protestantism, and her hymn-singing combine to set her apart and to cause her to quarrel with her neighbors. The extent of her first-act querulousness is clearly demonstrated when we see the "well oiled" Bessie shake Nora by the shoulders and exclaim, "You little over-dressed throllop, you, for one pin I'd paste th' white face o' you" (p. 149).

Bessie's estrangement from the other characters is most extreme in the second act. In this act all the characters are shown to be in a continual state of excitement because of the impending war in the background; and as a direct result of this excitement their ideology takes precedence over their humanity. When Bessie and The Covey (another character isolated by politics from the rest) enter the pub where all the action of Act II takes place, they sit at the opposite end of the counter from Peter, Fluther, and Mrs. Gogan. And it appears that Bessie sets out deliberately to anger the group and thus force them to acknowledge her existence. Bessie, speaking ostensibly to The Covey but really to the other group, declares, "I can't for th' life o' me undherstand how they can call themselves Catholics, when they won't lift a finger to help poor little Catholic Belgium" (p. 168). "Take no notice of her," Peter Flynn (who takes notice of the faintest whisper people make about him) advises Mrs. Gogan, "pay no attention to her. She's just tormentin' herself towards havin' a row with somebody" (p. 168).

But Ginny Gogan, of course, does take notice. "Isn't it a nice thing," Mrs. Gogan says, speaking loudly to Peter Flynn and Fluther but really to Bessie, "to have to be listenin' to a lassie an' hangin' our heads in dead silence, knowin' that some persons think more of a ball of malt than they do of th' blessed saints" (p. 168). Fluther tries to calm Mrs. Gogan down a bit by reminding her that Bessie is "a female person that has moved out of th' sight of ordinary sensible people" (p. 169), but this reminder only serves to emphasize for Mrs. Gogan and for us the wide chasm between Bessie and the other characters at this point in the play.

This gap reaches its widest point just after the background figure makes his speech about the exhilaration of war and Bessie and Mrs. Gogan begin to insult each other in earnest. "Thanks be to Christ," Bessie says passionately, Bessie Burgess "knows when she was got, where she was got, an' how she was got; while there's some she knows, decoratin' their finger with a well polished weddin' ring, would be hard put to it if they were assed to show their weddin' lines" (p. 170). And Ginnie, "plunging out into the center of the floor in a wild tempest of hysterical rage" (p. 170), replies in kind: "Y' oul' rip of a blasted liar, me weddin' ring's been well earned be twenty years be th' side o' me husband . . . an' any kid, livin' or dead, that Jinnie Gogan's had since, was got between th' bordhers of th' Ten Commandments! . . . An' that's more than some o' you can say that . . . use th' innocent light o' th' shinin' stars to dip into th' sins of a night's diversion" (pp. 170–71).

At this point Bessie jumps out to face Mrs. Gogan, and breaks out into a typical O'Casey rhetorical frenzy: "Liar to you, too, ma'am," Bessie replies with as much zest as Mild Millie cursed the English, "y' oul' hardened threspasser on other people's good nature, wizenin' up your soul in th' arts o' dodgeries, till every dhrop of respectability in a female is dhried up in her, lookin' at your ready-made manoeuverin' with th' menkind! " (p. 171). And finally, just before the barman pushes the cooing doves out the door, Bessie calls Peter (who is trying to quiet her down) a "little sermonizin', little yella–faced, little consequential, little pudgy, little bum" (p. 171) and sends him away "with a push of her hand that sends Peter tottering to the end of the shop." This pushing away of the little consequential Peter is a high point of the second act and leaves us with a vivid image that further emphasizes Bessie's isolation from the other characters in this tenement unit.

As the third act opens, the characters are back in their native tenement surroundings, away from the excitement of the speeches and the pub, and Bessie, although still singing "Rule Britannia," is presented as being an essential part of the tenement unit. She gives a mug of milk to the tubercular young Mollser "silently" just before she loudly denounces the "sham battle soldiers" that have landed them all "in a nice way." "A lot of vipers," Bessie concludes, "is what th' Irish people is" (p. 186). But the little gesture of kindness toward Mollser takes a lot of the sting out of her anti-Irish statements.

When the looting starts, the battle lines are completely redrawn; the other tenement dwellers join Bessie in looting while the soldiers of the Irish Citizen's Army fire on the looters. When Bessie enters with her "new hat on her head, a fox fur round her neck over her shawl, three umbrellas under her right arm, and a box of biscuits under her left" (p. 187) and announces that they are "smashin' th' windows, battherin' in th' doors, an' whippin' away everything! " (p. 187), the people begin to treat her as one of their own. After Bessie takes time in the midst of all the excitement to help the "curious" feeling Mollser into the house, the following exchange occurs between Fluther and her. *FLUTHER (running over to the door of the house and shouting in to Bessie).* Ay, Bessie, did you hear of e'er a pub gettin' a shake up. *BESSIE (inside).* I didn't hear o' none. *FLUTHER (in a burst of enthusiasm.* Well, you're goin' to hear of one soon" (p.188). Fluther now feels close enough to Bessie to joke with her as he would with any other member of the group. Bessie's newfound closeness to the other characters is further emphasized when the old sparring partners of Act II (Bessie and Mrs. Gogan) leave together, sharing a pram which they plan to fill with general plunder. When they return, Bessie and Ginnie are still together, still sharing the pram, and there is "the pride of a great joy illuminating their faces" (p. 192) as they chat pleasantly about how grand they will look in their plundered clothes.

In order to illustrate clearly how completely Bessie's relation to the group has changed, O'Casey ends the third act with Bessie going bravely out into the streets to get a doctor for Nora. Mrs. Gogan is by her own admission too afraid to go; Fluther is too drunk. And so Bessie risks it. Just as the best chapters of the *Autobiographies* end with a sharply etched picture worth a thousand words, the third act of *The Plough and the Stars* ends with the vivid image of the previously unwanted Bessie Burgess tightening her shawl around her "as if it were a shield" and then firmly and swiftly going out into the sound of rifle shots and the tok, tok, tok of machine guns protected only by her Protestant prayer: "Oh God, be Thou my help in time o' throuble. An' shelter me safely in th' shadow of Thy wings" (p. 199).

Thus we are not surprised when, "a few days later," the curtain rises on Act IV, and we see the characters huddled together in Bessie Burgess's attic apartment. These small, cramped quarters have an expressionistic "look of compressed confinement." And "there is an unmistakable air of poverty bordering on destitution" (p. 200). Apparently the Protestant, Loyalist Bessie Burgess is, if anything, slightly worse off than her Catholic, nationalistic neighbors. Our first view of Bessie in this last act clearly reveals how completely Bessie's humanity has triumphed over her ideology. "Do ye want to waken her [the drained Nora] again," a weary Bessie asks the card players in a hoarse whisper, "when she's just gone asleep? If she wakes, will yous come an' mind her? " (p. 202). Note that Bessie is here trying to nurse back to health the "over-dhressed little throllop" whom she tried to strangle with her bare hands in the first act. Bessie, we find out, has stayed up with Nora for three nights running even though she realizes that Nora will "never be much betther than she is," and sees that Nora's eyes "have a hauntin' way of lookin' in instead of lookin' out, as if her mind had been lost alive in madly minglin' memories of th' past" (p. 203). Here, in this last act, Bessie's realistic, clear vision of the present contrasts sharply with Nora's "madly minglin' memories of th' past."

Even Bessie's response to her own unnecessary, absurd death is realistic. When the heroic Bessie is shot by mistake by the British soldiers, she does not die as Brennan tells us that Commandant Clitheroe did (i.e., in "a gleam o' glory"), saying that she's glad to die for Ireland— or even that she's glad to die for the other members of the tenement unit. Rather, she curses the insane Nora, who was the direct cause of her being shot: "Merciful God, I'm shot, I'm shot, I'm shot! . . . Th' life's pourin' out o' me! *(to Nora)* I've got this through . . . through you . . . through you, you bitch, you . . . . You wouldn't stop quiet, no, you wouldn't, you wouldn't, blast you! Look at what I'm afther gettin', look at what I'm afther gettin' . . . " (p. 215). Nora, as we have already seen, remains blankly unaware of these insults while Bessie slowly bleeds to death. This final image of Bessie dying while the mad Nora calls out for her Jack brings vividly home to us the fact that war can destroy human life both physically (Bessie) and spiritually (Nora). War, O'Casey realistically tells us, not only wastes the human lives of its participants but also the lives of the street people, the innocent bystanders, whose lives are certainly tough enough without it.

Bessie Burgess's death helps to clarify the crucial role that Bessie plays in this tenement drama. When Bessie dies, we see Mrs. Gogan genuinely grieving over her and vowing "to gather some neighbors to come an' give th' last friendly touches to Bessie in th' lonely layin' of her out." (p. 217). As this final gathering shows, Bessie's life, like Nora's, is inextricably bound up with the lives of all the other characters in this play. Bessie, O'Casey finally makes clear, is not a character (like Bentham) thrown into a setting in which he does not really belong, but she is a finely chiseled character who plays a carefully thought-out part in the drama of this tenement house collective.

Fluther Good is another character who at first glance may appear to be the central figure in this play, but who in reality is like Nora and Bessie merely another essential part of the tenement unit. Fluther, like Bessie and unlike Nora, grows in stature as the play progresses. He becomes less clownish and more heroic. Although the life force can always be seen in Fluther, the first act presents Fluther's love of life in what he might call a "derogatory" way. Here, O'Casey dwells not so much on Fluther's love of life as on the other side of the coin, i.e., his fear of death. When Fluther's cough is noticed by Mrs. Gogan, he assures her "a little nervously" that "it's only a little cold I have" (p. 141). And Mrs. Gogan, who by her own admission loves funerals, increases his nervousness considerably by telling him: "There's many a man this minute lowerin' a pint, thinkin' of a woman, or pickin' out a winner, or doin' work as you're doin', while th' hearse dhrawn be th' horses with the black plumes is dhrivin' up to his own hall door, an' a voice that he doesn't hear is muttherin' in his ear, 'Earth to earth, an' ashes t' ashes, an' dust to dust'" (p. 141). This muttering works on Fluther so that by the time that he "faintly" says, "A man in th' pink o' health should have a holy horror of allowin' thoughts o' death to be festerin' in his mind, for (with a frightened cough) be God, I think I'm afther gettin' a little catch in me chest that time—it's a creepy thing to be thinkin' about"

(p. 141), we laugh outright; for, the comic side of his character is laid out for us all to see.

We continue to laugh at Fluther as his fear of death works on him for the next two pages. During this time we see Fluther in turn feel "a curious kind o' gaspin' for breath," feel himself "suddenly gettin' hot an' then cold," feel himself getting "dizzy as bedamned" before finally wondering whether all the above symptoms could have been caused by giving up beer too suddenly. These symptoms magically vanish and the comedy is further increased as the communist Covey's comments on "mollycewels an' atoms" rouse Fluther to defend his religion. The voice which had become faint gets louder and louder as Fluther responds to The Covey while Uncle Peter struggles with his collar in the background:

FLUTHER: Mollycewels an' atoms! D'ye think I'm goin' to listen to you thryin' to juggle Fluther's mind with complicated cunundhrums of mollycewels an' atoms?

THE COVEY (*rather loudly*): There's nothin' complicated in it. There's no fear o' the Church tellin' you that mollycewels is a stickin' together of millions of atoms o' sodium, carbon, potassium o' iodide, etcetera, that, accordin' to th' way they're mixed, make a flower, a fish, a star that you see shinin' in th' sky, or a man with a big brain like me, or a man with a little brain like you!

FLUTHER (*more loudly still*): There's no necessity to be raisin' your voice; shoutin's no manifestin' forth of a growin' mind. (p. 143)

This comic dialogue continues for a while, interrupted only by comments from Peter Flynn and Mrs. Gogan that serve ironically to undercut and thus further emphasize the comic quality of these characters' speeches. Just as the coal vendor appears, shouting, "Coal blocks, coal blocks" immediately after Jack Boyle's "what is the stars" speech in *Juno and the Paycock*, so here Mrs. Gogan says the Irish soldiers are "formin' fours, an' now they're goin' to march away" (p. 144) immediately after The Covey's speech on evolution ending with " . . . for it's not long since th' fathers o' some o' them crawled out o' th' sheltherin' slime o' the sea" (p. 144). And Peter Flynn, talking of his collar, says, "Blast it, blast it, blast it! " immediately after The Covey tells Fluther about the "skeleton of th' man o' Java" (p. 144).

The second act not only shows Bessie at the height of her alienation from the other characters, but also it shows Fluther at the

height of his clownishness. The pub scene in which Fluther is emotionally flustered, in which "the blood is boilin' in [his] veins," in
which he gets into yet another quarrel with The Covey (Fluther,
comic figure that he here is, does not heed the good advice he had
just given to Ginnie Gogan to ignore her tormenters), shows Fluther
as a mock hero rather than as a real one. In fact, the high point of
Fluther's comic career occurs near the end of this quarrel scene
when Fluther, in mock-heroic fashion, "suddenly springs into the
middle of the shop, flings his hat into a corner, whips off his coat and
begins to paw the air." "Come on, come on, you lowser," Fluther
roars at The Covey at the top of his voice, "put your mits up now, if
there's a man's blood in you! Be God, in a few minutes you'll see
some snots flyin' around, I'm tellin' you" (p. 176).

As is the case in most mock battles, the sparring is all in good fun.
No one gets hurt. The Covey is ejected from the bar and Fluther
remains behind with Rosie Redmond, a prostitute who increases the
comedy by playing up Fluther's pugilistic prowess. "Be God," the
wide-eyed Rosie squeals, "you put th' fear o' God in his heart that
time! I thought you'd have to be dug out of him" (p. 177). "Sure,"
she continues, exaggerating as much as she dares, "you'd ha' broken
him in two if you'd ha' hitten him one clatther" (p. 177). "Oh,
Fluther," Rosie exclaims, perhaps a bit too innocently, "I'm afraid
you're a terrible man for th' women" (p. 177). And finally, when at
the end of the act Fluther and Rosie exit with their arms around
each other as Clitheroe's battalion marches by in the background,
the portrait of Fluther, the mock hero, is completed.

As is the case with Bessie Burgess, we begin to take Fluther
seriously in the third act. The first reference to Fluther in Act III,
for example, is not a reference to his blustering, his drinking, or his
eye for the Judies, but to his genuine heroism. Mrs. Gogan, who
comically intensified Fluther's fear of death in the opening act, here
tells us that she stayed up all night worrying about Fluther, who was
out in the streets looking for Nora Clitheroe. (Again note the in-
teraction of these tenement characters.) "I was kep' awake," Mrs.
Gogan tells us, "all night with th' shootin'. An' thinkin' o' that madman, Fluther, runnin' about through th' night lookin' for Nora
Clitheroe to bring her back when he heard she'd gone to folly her
husband" (p. 181).

Thus, we are not surprised when, a short time later, Fluther
enters with Nora half leading, half carrying her in and speaks his

first words of this act: "Ah, she's all right, Mrs. Gogan; only worn out from thravellin' an' want o' sleep. A night's rest, now, an' she'll be as fit as a fiddle. Bring her in, an' make her lie down" (p. 183). This speech (which is neither comic nor mock heroic) both reassures Mrs. Gogan and illustrates Fluther's genuine concern for Nora. Shortly thereafter, Nora herself acknowledges that she would still be lying out in the streets if it were not for Fluther, thus removing any lingering doubt of Fluther's heroism. From this point on, Fluther is a different man; his speeches are markedly different in tone from his mock-heroic speeches in Acts I and II.

Even though Fluther still gambles and drinks in Acts III and IV, his gambling and drinking are no longer laughing matters so much as they provide momentary escape from the reality of war that affects all of the tenement dwellers' lives. Just as the patriotic speeches in the background of Act II helped separate the tenement collective from one another and make them comic and querulous figures, so the actual war in the background of Acts III and IV helps unite them and make them more serious, more tragic characters than they were before. When the big guns begin to sound in the distance, it becomes clear that O'Casey is using the games of the tenement dwellers both as an escape from and a contrast to the war raging outside. Fluther, who is tossing coins with Peter Flynn and The Covey, exclaims upon hearing the big guns: "Aw, holy Christ, that's not playin' th' game" (p. 187). When the cowardly Peter Flynn is worried about a shell from one of the big guns landing on top of them, Fluther becomes intensely involved in the game. "Go on, toss them again, toss them again. . . . Harps, a tanner. . . . Let them roll, let them roll. Heads, be God! " (p. 187). Note that both here and later in the card-playing scene of Act IV the characters in the games are not really playing against each other. In both gambling scenes the game is a device that unites the characters and focuses their attention on something a bit more pleasant than their common enemy, the war.[1]

And even in the final scene of the third act, in which Fluther enters "frenzied, wild-eyed, mad, roaring drunk," singing "Fluther's a jolly good fella! . . . Fluther's a jolly good fella! . . . That nobody can deny" (p. 198), the sheer intensity of Fluther's frenzied, wild-eyed appearance reveals clearly the difference between Fluther's drinking here and his drinking in the previous act. His drinking, like Jack Boyle's drinking in the final act of *Juno and the*

Paycock, has suddenly shifted from pleasant social drinking to something darker, more sinister. Fluther's world has also collapsed around him; for the war brings "chassis" to the tenements. Nora's screams and moans provide ironic background music for Fluther's third-act song. Of course, getting "roaring drunk" does not really allow Fluther to escape from his relationship to the other characters; for by getting drunk he, like Bessie singing "Rule Britannia" or Nora going insane, is merely playing his essential assigned role.

Finally, in Act IV we see that Fluther's progress from the comic mock hero of the first two acts to the tragicomic antihero of the last two is completed. Although Fluther, in the second act especially, may be viewed as "the knight errant of the tenements,"[2] the last act reveals that Fluther and the other card players are distracted not so much by windmills as by the moans of Nora. Both Fluther and The Covey, listening to Nora moaning in the back room, have to be reminded by Peter Flynn that the "thray o' hearts" was led.[3] "It's damned hard lines," Fluther (very un-Quixotelike) tells his old sparring partner, "to think of [Nora's] deadborn kiddie lyin' there in th' arms o' poor little Mollser. Mollser snuffed it sudden too, afther all" (p. 201). And when The Covey replies, "Sure she never got any care. How could she get it, an' th' mother out day an' night lookin' for work, an' her consumptive husband leavin' her with a baby to be born before he died! " (p. 201), we see that even The Covey is beginning to respond in a human way to the injustice inherent in a capitalistic system, injustice that up to this point had been little more than an abstract message out of Jerensky's *Thesis on the Origin, Development, and Consolidation of the Evolutionary Ideas of the Proletariat.* Here O'Casey shows us that Fluther and The Covey, who had been brandishing fists at each other in the first two acts, are now united in sympathy for the suffering of Mollser, Nora, Mrs. Gogan, and the rest of the street characters in this play.

In the fourth act we see that it becomes even more difficult for the characters to continue playing their games. Even the comic play-fights (games, if you will) in which the characters engage during Acts I and II are no longer possible while living in the war zone. When Peter Flynn's mind wanders from the game so that he does not see Fluther's ace, the developing argument is immediately stifled by Bessie's reminding them that Nora is in the next room.

Even though Fluther is still drinking in this final act, he does not become "frenzied" and "wild-eyed"; instead he maintains control and deliberately sets out to enjoy each drop that may be his last. When The Covey asks Fluther, "Why don't you spread that [bottle of whiskey] out man, an' thry to keep a sup for to-morrow?" Fluther responds, "Spread it out? Keep a sup for tomorrow? How th' hell does a fella know there'll be any tomorrow? If I'm goin' to be whipped away, let me be whipped away when it's empty, an' not when it's half full" (pp. 202–203). Here his drinking is not comic. It is an existential act, a gesture of defiance of the forces that whip us.

Just as Fluther's refusal to be whipped away while his bottle is half full is a serious treatment of Fluther's love of life which was treated comically in the first two acts, so too his defiance of the British soldiers is a serious treatment of his combativeness, which had been previously used as a source of humor. Instead of pawing the air foolishly as he does when he threatens The Covey, he "aggressively" asks Corporal Stoddart (who is dressed in his full war kit), "You're not fightin' for your counthry here, are you?" (p. 209). When the English Sergeant Tinley complains that the Irish snipers are not playing the game fair, Fluther, "unable to stand the slight," bursts out, "Fight fair! A few hundhred scrawls o' chaps with a couple o' guns an' Rosary beads, again' a hundhred thousand thrained men with horse, fut, an' artillery . . . an' he wants us to fight fair! D'ye want us to come out in our skins an' throw stones" (p. 213). And finally, just before the four tenement males are taken out of the house at gunpoint we hear Fluther exclaim, "Jasus, you an' your guns! Leave them down, an' I'd beat th' two o' yous without sweatin'" (p. 213). The comic side of Fluther's character, although still present, is clearly in the background. We fear for Fluther much more than we laugh at him as he exists for the final time.

Although we have managed to touch briefly on the important traits of all the tenement dwellers in the preceding discussion of Nora, Bessie, and Fluther, at least three other characters deserve at least a concluding paragraph or two. The first of these three, Ginny Gogan, is as talkative as anyone in the play (with the possible exception of Fluther). She has more lines than either Bessie or Nora and only a few less than Fluther. She, like Bessie, grows in stature as the play progresses until finally, when Bessie is killed, she takes on the burden of going on with life in general and with caring for Nora in particular. Note that this woman who picks up the burden of life and goes on is no longer the comic figure who abandoned her baby in the pub in Act II. Her preoccupation with death changes in the last two acts to an appreciation of life. Even though Fluther still views her as being "in her element, now [that Mollser is dead] mixin' earth to earth, an' ashes t' ashes an' dust to dust, an' revellin' in plumes an' hearses, last days an' judgements" (p. 208), her genuine tribute to Fluther which begins: "I'll never forget what you done for me Fluther, goin' around at th' risk of your life settlin' everything with the undhertaker an' th' cemetery people . . ." (p. 209) and her equally genuine tribute to Bessie: "Indeed, it's meself that has well chronicled, Mrs. Burgess, all your gentle hurryin's to me little Mollser, when she was alive, bringin' her somethin' to dhrink, or somethin' t' eat, an' never passin' her without liftin' up her heart with a delicate word o' kindness" (p. 210) should make it clear that Fluther is mistaken, that in these last two acts, life, not death, is Ginny Gogan's element.

The cowardly uniform lover, Peter Flynn, like Mrs. Gogan, plays a larger part and is more an integral part of the tenement unit than he is generally given credit for. He comes closer to remaining a comic figure right up to the very end than does any other tenement dweller. This is appropriate, for a tenement unit without someone to laugh at would be a unit incomplete. It is the comic character who appears separate from the others as things begin to darken in the third act. Peter refuses to join the others in looting because he is afraid of the sound of the big guns. And then when Bessie and Mrs. Gogan return with their plunder, Peter "in a panic" shuts the door in their faces. Here in the third act, where all the other characters are changing, Peter remains a cowardly, mock-heroic old fool.

And in the final act, when the war outside makes everyone else's life a serious concern, Peter Flynn remains the only character we can wholeheartedly laugh at. When Fluther and The Covey make derogatory comments about his looking like a "fancy hearse man," Peter responds as only he could. "As long as I'm a livin' man, responsible for me thoughts, words, an' deeds, to th' Man above, I'll feel meself instituted to fight again th' sliddherin' ways of a pair o' picaroons, whisperin', concurrin', concoctin', an' conspirin' together to rendher me unconscious of th' life I'm thryin' to live! " (p. 211). This outburst gives us one moment of pure laughter as we, like poor Corporal Stoddart, are "dumbfounded" by this torrent of empty rhetoric. And so Peter Flynn plays his assigned role, represents his assigned state of mind in the consciousness of the collective protagonist, and remains a buffoon in spite of everything.

Last but not least, we must deal with The Covey (slang for smart aleck). The Covey is a convincing, realistically drawn character who makes a fool of himself occasionally but who also often appears to speak for O'Casey himself. He is an essential part of the tenement unit, the need for which grows clearer as the play develops. His avowed communism and his avid commitment to Jerensky's *Thesis on the Origin, Development, and Consolidation of the Evolutionary Ideas of the Proletariat* appear to set him as far outside the bounds as Bessie's loyalty to the King and her hymn-singing set her. However, the human bonds that connect him to the other tenement dwellers are stronger than his ideological differences with them. And at the end of the play The Covey not only shows genuine sympathy for Mollser but also sides with the others in their looting and in their defiance of the British soldiers. We see a concrete example of the new togetherness when The Covey joins forces with Fluther in a verbal attack on Corporal Stoddart (who was a socialist himself and rationalized his behavior by claiming to be doing his duty for his country). "Dooty," The Covey ironically tells the corporal, "th' only dooty of a socialist is the emanicpation of th' workers" (p. 208).

Our final view of O'Casey's collective protagonist in *The Plough and the Stars* reveals that each character represents a state of mind that grows naturally out of the depressing environment of early twentieth-century Dublin. (See Krause for the statistics.[4]) As we have seen, each character has developed his or her distinctive way of surviving. The Covey has his communism and Jerensky's *Thesis*, Peter Flynn his uniforms and his cowardice, Mrs. Gogan her curiosity and her fascination with death, Jack Clitheroe his position of Commandant and his idealistic nationalism, Rosie Redmond her professional duties, Nora her aspirations, her love, and later her madness, Bessie her religion and her loyalty to the King, and Fluther his drink, his gambling, and his pretty Judies. As the play develops, each character's consciousness (with the exception of Peter Flynn) becomes raised; he or she becomes aware of his or her existential predicament, and the differences (real as they are) between these characters become less important than their similarities. It becomes important that these characters are human beings united together in an absurd, frightening battle against forces that won't play the game fair. Fortunately, their common suffering in this struggle is an integrating force which brings them together, a force stronger than the disintegrating force of ideologies, nationalities, and religions which is tearing them apart.

II *Dramaturgy*

O'Casey's introduction of a collective protagonist is only perhaps the most startling of many effective dramaturgic techniques (both conventional and experimental) that we see in *The Plough and the Stars*. In this play, as in *Juno and the Paycock*, we see that O'Casey is in firm control of his material. We see, as in almost all of O'Casey, that one of his most effective dramaturgic techniques is a masterful use of contrast. First, and perhaps most important, he uses the contrast between characters to help sharpen his characterization. Fluther's blather, which doesn't mask his real courage, is contrasted with Peter Flynn's blather, which doesn't mask his real cowardice. Nora's movement from practicality to insanity is contrasted to Bessie's movement in the opposite direction. And The Covey's distant attitude toward women in general and prostitutes in particular is contrasted with Fluther's close appreciation of same.

The scenes in Act II in which Rosie accosts The Covey and Fluther in turn serve as well as any scenes to illustrate how O'Casey uses contrast to heighten characterization. When Rosie ("all business") moves in on The Covey, we see him stir uneasily and then "move a little further away." Rosie, of course, moves after him, but he is more interested in leaving Rosie a copy of Jerensky's *Thesis on the Origin, Development, and Consolidation of the Evolutionary Idea of the Proletariat* than he is in responding to her "thransparent stockin's showin' off the shape of a little lassie's legs! " (p. 165). In fact, the mere mention of these legs frightens The Covey into moving even farther away. Undaunted, Rosie pursues her game a little further. She moves on from shapely legs to "kissin' an' cuddlin' " and actually tries to put her arms around him. This is the last straw for the so-serious Covey, who has "something else to do besides shinannickin' afther Judies! " (p. 166). But even when he turns away, the game continues. We see Rosie clip her "little ducky," her "shy little ducky," under the chin until The Covey, who can no longer stand it, breaks away, and runs out.

Note that The Covey's aversion to "kissin' an' cuddlin' " (which fits so well into the comedy of the second act) concretely illustrates his lack of involvement in the lives of the people whose lot he wants to improve. His frightened response to Rosie's advances contrasts nicely with Fluther's already well-documented, more appreciative response and helps us to see more clearly one of the essential differences between these two characters; namely, that the churchgoing Fluther appreciates, feels at home with, and is actually a part of the huddled masses of Dublin's poor, while The Covey supports these masses theoretically, but shrinks (in the first two acts, at least) from actual contact with them.

In *The Plough and the Stars*, as in both *Juno and the Paycock* and the *Autobiographies*, O'Casey uses contrast not only to illuminate character but also to heighten the main dramatic conflict. Here he uses contrast to emphasize the stark differences between the life of those in the tenement unit and the lives of those who have renounced this life for the sake of "Ireland." By the end of this play, this conflict, which started out as a conflict between Nora and her husband, has escalated into a conflict between the tenement dwellers and the soldiers (both Irish and English), i.e., into a grim struggle between the forces of life and death. The words of the nationalistic speaker, who appears in the window from time to time during the second act, contrast sharply with the words of the tenement dwellers in the pub.

The speaker's first speech, for example, celebrates the shedding of blood and declares: "It is a glorious thing to see arms in the hands of Irishmen. We must accustom ourselves to the thought of arms, we must accustom ourselves to the sight of arms, we must accustom ourselves to the use of arms. . . . Bloodshed is a cleansing and sanctifying thing, and the nation that regards it as the final horror has lost it's manhood. . . . There are many things more horrible than bloodshed, and slavery is one of them" (p. 162). This speech contrasts not only with Rosie's complaints to the barman about a lack of customers but also tempts the ordinary people to give up on life and jump into the middle of death and destruction. "If I was only a little younger," the barman assures Rosie, "I'd be plungin' mad into th' middle of it" (p. 162). Even Peter and Fluther (whose mock-heroic acts in this act contrast with the apparently heroic acts of the soldiers) are "hot and full and hasty with the things they have seen and heard" (p. 162) as they enter the pub for a drink.

The contrast in this act between life in the pub and the speeches of nationalistic patriots in the streets outside is unmistakable. P. S. O'Hegarty notes that the speech of Padraic Pearse "cuts like a trumpet call, like the sword of the Lord, like a gleam of beauty, right across the squalidity, the maudlinism, the spinelessness, which was Ireland at that time; just as the Rising itself came, suddenly and like a sign from Heaven."[5] Whether the speech of Pearse is the "sword of the Lord" or whether it is "dope, dope" as The Covey calls it is, of course, debatable, but the fact that it cuts across the life in the pub "suddenly and like a sign from Heaven" is not. This sudden light reveals not only differences in subject matter, but differences in the language itself. The language of Pearse's speech is the language of propaganda. It uses rhetorical repetition of phrases, appeals to authority, associates the cause of the speaker with all that is Holy, and is, therefore, a kind of pseudopoetry as artificial in its own way as the poetry of "The Castle Ball." The speeches of the pub customers, on the other hand, especially the speeches of Fluther, Bessie, and Mrs. Gogan, often explode into the authentic proletarian poetry we saw in the *Autobiographies*, poetry which derives its power from the human experience of living day to day in the streets of Dublin. We might note in passing that the speech of the figure is linked with wars, death, tragedy, and heroic sacrifices while the speech of the people in the pub is linked with love, life, comedy, and mock-heroic actions. The figure is "idealistic," the people "realistic" (Shaw's terms again).

Just as the *Autobiographies* used stories within stories as a device to give depth to the work as a whole *The Plough and the Stars* uses a play within a play for this same purpose. The second act of *The Plough and the Stars* contains a world of its own, a world that people live in when they are high on religion and/or patriotism. This pub world is distinctive and separate from the tenement world in which the rest of this play takes place. All the action in the second act world is fast-paced—frenzied, even. Everyone is talking fast, talking loud, and running in and out of the pub. The blood is clearly boiling in the veins of the tenement dwellers, who are shown in their worst light. The "pub" in the second act may be viewed as a microcosm of all of Ireland just before the uprising. The common people are excited. Pearse's speeches are in the background. The hostility that had been held in check is just beginning to bubble to the surface in just about everybody. Everything and everybody is ready to explode. Here, as in "The House of the Dead" chapter of the *Autobiographies*, O'Casey makes life in a small, vividly described room a microcosm of life in Ireland and perhaps of life in the whole world.

As suggested before, one of the main conflicts in this play, a conflict concretely illustrated in the "pub" world, is the conflict between Shaw's "idealist" and "realist." The Irish Nationalist soldiers, Clitheroe, Brennan, Langon, and the voice, are all devoted to the idealistic abstraction of Ireland, and as a direct result of this devotion have torn themselves away from life in the real world and become lost in a never-never land of their own minds' creation. Because they have lost contact with real human beings, they are willing to sacrifice human lives—even their own—for mere words, for abstractions that never were on sea or land. Although O'Casey's attitudes toward these idealists and the realists (represented by the tenement dwellers) should be clear, the apparent willful blindness of certain critics (the aforequoted O'Hegarty, for example) makes it necessary to emphasize as Krause does that O'Casey "was more concerned with human beings than national politics,"[6] that O'Casey fervently believed that the lives of the tenement dwellers were worth more than the forces that threatened to destroy them. O'Casey's sympathy for the realistic characters is perhaps most clearly illustrated by the sharp contrast between the deaths of Jack Clitheroe and Bessie Burgess. There is more glory, more genuine heroism in the death of the realistic Bessie (who dies cursing Nora) than in the death of Commandant Clitheroe (whose last words, as reported by Brennan, were, "I'm proud to die for Ireland").

The Plough and the Stars, even though primarily realistic, contains many experimental, expressionistic elements that will be emphasized more strongly in the later work of O'Casey. Even the Irish playwright Denis Johnston, writing in 1926 of *The Plough and the Stars,* recognized that "as a realist he [O'Casey] is an imposter. . . . His dialogue is becoming a series of word-poems in dialect; his plots are disappearing and giving place to a form of undisguised expressionism under the stress of a genius that is much too insistent and far too pregnant with meaning to be bound by the four dismal walls of orthodox realism."[7]

One very minor but significant scene which reveals O'Casey moving away from naturalism and toward more expressionistic drama occurs when an unnamed character identified only as "The Woman" appears in the middle of the third act to ask the way to Wrathmines. This "fashionably dressed, middle aged, stout woman" who is "almost fainting with fear" is ignored by the members of the tenement collective, whose refusal to give aid and comfort to this woman illuminates by way of contrast the comfort they give each other during this time of crisis. This unnamed figure, who is more caricature than character and is not worthy of our sympathy, gives us a preview of many other such characters who will wander around in later O'Casey plays.

Close examination of *The Plough and the Stars* also reveals that O'Casey often compresses time in a very nonnaturalistic way for dramatic effect. In both the third and the fourth acts, for example, O'Casey (like Marlowe at the end of *Dr. Faustus* or Synge in *Riders to the Sea*) compresses action that should take an hour or so into a few minutes. The first and most obvious of these time compressions occurs in the third act just after Bessie Burgess and Ginny Gogan have left to loot the shops. The two advocates of law and order return from their looting in the length of time it takes The Covey (staggering "with a ten stone sack of flour on his back") to get the door open (about one page of dialogue). Here this compression works for O'Casey in at least two important ways. First, it helps to make the time that Peter Flynn (and O'Casey) causes The Covey to stand outside on the doorstep with the sack of flour on his back seem longer than it really is. And second, it emphasizes the speed with which the tenement dwellers can get things done when they work together.

The scene in the last act which shows O'Casey using this same technique of compression is Bessie's climactic death scene. She listens to Nora sing a song, gets shot pushing Nora away from the window, and then slowly dies while Corporal Stoddart and Sergeant Tinley are taking the males down to the church. The corporal and the sergeant return immediately after Bessie dies, and the effect again is to make a short scene seem longer. But this time it is not our laughter at The Covey but the excruciating pain of Bessie's absurd death that is drawn out. Although the quick return of the English soldiers could be accounted for within the text of the play (the sergeant and the corporal could have carried out their threat to send all the men west in retaliation for the sniper's next score), the primary effect of this quick return is to intensify Bessie's death scene.

And the most obvious, most important nonnaturalistic device is the use of the "figure" whose speeches produce in his listeners, especially the soldiers, a religious, ritualistic effect. The speeches of this figure, like the chants in *The Silver Tassie*, help to involve the soldiers in a mock-religious experience. The final scene of the feverish second act, in which Commandant Clitheroe, Captain Brennan, and Lieutenant Langon are high on the dope of the figure's speeches, prefigures the battlefield scene in *The Silver Tassie* in which the soldiers chant their devotion to the Gun. Here all three soldiers are "in a state of emotional excitement. Their faces are flushed and their eyes sparkle; they speak rapidly, as if unaware of the meaning of what they said" (p. 177). These zombielike, hypnotized characters respond to the last speech of the figure in a stylized, ritualistic way. The voice speaks from the platform outside the window for the last time, and then we see Captain Brennan (who is later to be imprisoned) catch up the Plough and the Stars and shout, "Imprisonment for th' Independence of Ireland"; we see Lieutenant Langon (who was later to be wounded) catch up the tricolor and shout, "Wounds for th' Independence of Ireland!"; and finally we see Clitheroe (who was to be killed) stand up and shout, "Death for th' Independence of Ireland" before they chant together in unison, "So help us God" (p. 178). These men drink mechanically to their own respective destinies, then leave when the bugle calls.

The death-in-life of these soldiers' chants contrasts sharply with Rosie's life-affirming song in the very next scene. There Rosie sings her song about the tailor who could do nothing for her and of the sailor who could. Although this song was exorcised in the original production, the dramatic necessity for having this zestful song side by side with the zombielike chants of the soldiers is obvious. As O'Casey himself said when informed by Yeats of the censorship, "Yes, it's a pity. It would offend thousands. But it ought to be there."[8]

The figure in the window is not the only nonnaturalistic background that O'Casey uses in this play. There are the already-mentioned grotesquely cramped quarters of Bessie's attic flat. And there are the flames of the burning buildings in the distant sky, the sounds of the big gun, the tok-tok of machine guns, and the chants of "Red Cross . . . Ambulance" that continuously remind us of the death and destruction that hovered over the Dublin tenements during Easter Week 1916. These background sights and sounds help to emphasize that the world of this play is a distinctive world, an absurd world in a state of chassis, a world that helps shape the lives of all the characters (the tenement unit) struggling to stay alive within it.

In summary, *The Plough and the Stars*, in terms of dramaturgy and characterization, is both a culmination and a beginning. It is a culmination of his earlier, more realistic writing—if you do not count chapters of the *Autobiographies;* it is a work in which he expresses clearly and forcefully his commitment to and love for the poor, exploited, yet undaunted tenement dwellers whose gay laughter we hear at the gate of the grave. The characterization in this play (taken as a whole) is stronger than the characterization in *Juno and the Paycock*. This is not to say that Fluther Good and Bessie Burgess are stronger or more finely sculpted characters than Jack Boyle and Juno, for they are not, but it is to say that all the characters in this play are strong, are believable, and belong in the world of the play in which they live. Here, there is no Johnny Boyle, no Mary Boyle, no Jerry Devine, whose unconvincing, overly melodramatic dialogue distracts the reader and detracts from the total effect of the play. There are no cardboard Benthams in the *The Plough and the Star*'s flesh-and-blood world. Even the British soldiers are finely drawn portraits, rather than Benthamlike caricatures.

The Plough and the Stars is also the culmination of his earlier plays in terms of dramaturgy and construction. The concentration on the tenement-dwelling collective, the compression of events, the carefully controlled use of language combine to make this play the tightest, the best-constructed of all his earlier, more naturalistic dramas—perhaps of all his dramas, period. As the preceding discussion suggests, each line of dialogue, each offstage noise, every action of every character has a purpose and contributes toward the main goal of illuminating the life of this tenement collective in all its complexity. The end result of this improved tightness is, as Robert Hogan says, a play "of much greater complexity and tension"[9] than *Juno and the Paycock*.

But, as we have seen, *The Plough and the Stars* is not only a culmination of O'Casey's naturalistic period but also it is the beginning of what, for want of a better word, we will call his "expressionistic" period. In addition to being the best play ever written about life in the Dublin tenements and one of the best about life in any housing whatsoever, it is also a play that gives us previews of coming expressionistic attractions. We have seen ironic use of religious ritual, characters without specific names, compressed time, symbolic background material, and heightened poetic dialogue—all techniques which we will see O'Casey use extensively in his later plays.

CHAPTER 5

The Silver Tassie *and* Red Roses for Me

I   The Silver Tassie: *Act I*

MUCH of the critical confusion surrounding *The Silver Tassie* disappears if we view this transition play as a microcosm of O'Casey's entire dramatic work. This play is also divided into three distinct styles, the naturalistic (with expressionistic undertones)—the first act; the expressionistic—the second act; and the absurd-comic—the third and fourth acts. The first act portrays a basically naturalistic world populated by the tragicomic street people we find in the early plays and in the *Autobiographies*. The second act portrays life in "the war zone," a world filled with ruins, ruined land, ruined civilization, and ruined men. And the third and fourth acts portray life in an absurd-comic world strangely resembling Ireland peopled by caricatures strangely resembling Irishmen.

This shift from characters to caricatures which we first see in this play can perhaps be best understood if we view this shift as O'Casey's response to criticism of himself as a "slum dramatist." At this point in his life, O'Casey was becoming impatient with "the Green Goddess of Realism" and was eager to set free his imagination to explore the world beyond Dublin's streets. He had already shown that he could create interesting Irish-Elizabethan street characters, and the caricatures we see in the last two acts of this play represent the beginning of O'Casey's lifelong search for something else.

At the outset, the difference between the tragicomic characters of *The Plough and the Stars* and the first act of *The Silver Tassie* and the caricatures of the later O'Casey and the last two acts of *The Silver Tassie* must be made clear. We care about the Irish-Elizabethan tenement dwellers of the first act, who appear as real human beings struggling to survive, and whatever comedy there

111

is in their characters grows naturally out of these human roots, whereas when these characters get transplanted into the absurd-comic world of the third and fourth acts we laugh at their puppet-like machinations much more than we become involved with their lives.

As might be expected, O'Casey develops the characters of the tenement dwellers in the first act of *The Silver Tassie* much as he developed the characters of the tenement dwellers in *The Plough and the Stars*. While *The Plough and the Stars* opens with Mrs. Gogan and Fluther talking about Nora, this play opens with Sylvester Heegan and Simon Norton bragging about the exploits of Sylvester's son, Harry. Harry, we learn, has snapped a chain with his biceps, won the Cross-country Championship, and "punched the fear of God into the heart of Police Constable 63C."[1] As in *The Plough and the Stars*, we learn about the talkers as well as about the talked about. We learn that both Simon and Sylvester admire Harry's exploits (especially the decking of the constable which "caps the chronicle") even though they cannot agree whether it was a left hook or a right hook to the jaw that finally put the constable to sleep.

In the opening scene Simon and Sylvester's appreciation of Harry's zest for life is neatly contrasted with the "tambourine theology" of the frustrated Susie Monican, who, appropriately enough, is polishing some kind of war gear (rifle, bayonet, and helmet) each time that we see her in this act. "When the two of yous stand quiverin' together on the dhread day of the Last Judgement," the evangelistic Susie pointedly asks the two cronies, "how will the two of yous feel if yous have nothin' to say but 'he broke a chain across his bisseps'? Then the two of you'll know," she equally pointedly adds, "that the wicked go down into hell, an' all the people who forget God" (p. 23). Similarly when Sylvester is waxing eloquent over Harry's encounter with Constable 63C, Susie interrupts with: "We don't go down on our knees often enough; that's why we're not able to stand up to the Evil One: we don't go down on our knees enough. . . . I can hear some persons fallin' with a splash of sparks into the lake of everlastin' fire. . . . An account of every idle word shall be given at the last day" (p. 24). Although O'Casey has Susie speak more than her share of "idle words," he still takes care to strengthen her position at Simon and Sylvester's expense. Her question concerning what these old idlers will have to say for themselves on judgment day strikes as squarely as Harry's fist on the constable's jaw.

A short time later, Susie begins to preach at them in earnest, and we learn more about both preacher and preachees. "God shows his love by worrying, and worrying, and worrying the sinner" (p. 26), the self-righteous Susie explains as she takes it upon herself to worry Simon and Sylvester. "God," she assures them, "is never tired of waiting and waiting and waiting; and watching and watching and watching; and knocking and knocking and knocking for the sinner—you, Sylvester, and you, Simon—to turn from his wickedness and live" (p. 27). All this waiting and watching and knocking effectively increases the uneasiness and self-consciousness of the two old "butties" and is, we might add, an excellent example of O'Casey using exaggerated language to increase the dramatic effect. "Oh, if the two of you only knew," Susie continues, laying it on thicker and thicker, "what it was to live! Not to live legstaggering an' belly-creeping among the pain-spotted and sin-splashed desires of the flesh; but to live, oh, to live swift-flying from a holy peace to a holy strength, and from holy strength to a holy joy, like the flashing flights of a swallow in the deep beauty of a summer sky" (p. 27). Again Susie's genuine insight into the characters of Simon and Sylvester (she realizes that they do not know what it is to live) helps flesh out her otherwise thin character.

Just as Susie has this insight into the limitations of the lives of these two elegant swallows, so too Simon and Sylvester have insight into the limitations of Susie's evangelical religion. Simon and Sylvester unite when Susie shakes them (both mentally and physically). "Desist, Susie, desist," Simon pleads. "Violence won't gather people to God. It only ingenders hostility to what you're trying to do." "You can't," Sylvester adds, "batter religion into a man like that." "Religion," Simon continues, "is love, but that sort of thing is simply a nullification of religion." And then after Susie briefly breaks in to defend her bitterness and wrath, Sylvester continues with the cronies' counteroffensive. "Don't try to claw me into the kingdom of heaven. An' you only succeed in distempering piety when you try to mangle it into a man's emotions." "Heaven," Simon concludes, "is all the better, Susie, for being a long way off" (p. 29). Thus, it appears that Sylvester and Simon's reactions to Susie's theology (like Susie's reactions to these two "cockatrices") help to give some depth to O'Casey's characterization, i.e., these reactions help to make Simon and Sylvester more complex characters than they would be otherwise. Simon and Sylvester, it appears, see that Susie's clawing religion is a nullification of true religion, yet they, by their own admission, are quite a way from heaven—and glad to be there.

Another pair of well-drawn minor characters that vitalize the first act of *The Silver Tassie* much as Mr. and Mrs. Adolphus Grigson enliven the second act of *Shadow of a Gunman* are Mr. and Mrs. Teddy Foran. Both husband and wife (as they appear in the first act, anyway) are among O'Casey's finest minor characterizations. Teddy Foran is especially effective as a soldier who realizes that his wife is anxiously waiting for him to board ship so that she can be single again. When we see Teddy for the first time, he is, like the main protagonist, Harry Heegan, an impressive figure. "He is big and powerful, rough and hardy. A man who would be dominant in a public house, and whose opinions would be listened to with great respect" (p. 35). He is carrying his wedding bowl in one hand and a hatchet in the other. Needless to say, he is in the center of attention. His first words, directed to his wife, who is cowering under the bed with Sylvester: "Under the bed, eh? Right place for a guilty conscience. I should have thrown you out of the window with the dinner you put before me. Out with you from under there, an' come up with your husband" (pp. 35–36), reenforce his dominance, his ability to control a situation.

He continues to dominate the action until he breaks the bowl with the hatchet (an interesting preview of the fourth-act scene in which Harry mangles the cup) and exits dramatically, leaving the following angry words echoing behind him. "Damn it [the bowl] and damn you [Mrs. Foran]. I'm off now to smash anything I missed, so that you'll have a gay time fittin' up the little home again by the time your loving husband comes back. You can come an' have a look, an' bring your mon amee if you like" (p. 37). And even when he is offstage Teddy Foran's presence is felt. We are at least as interested in Teddy, whom we hear breaking things in the room above, as we are either in Sylvester, who is on stage puffing himself up in fine Joxerian fashion, or in Mrs. Foran, who is lamenting the demise of her poor little wedding bowl which, she tells us, she "might have had for generations."

Mrs. Foran, who was personally going to hold a wedding bowl for generations, is an interesting character in her own right. She is in her own way a good match for Teddy. She is "one of the gay, careworn women of the working class" who is liberated enough to be mindful of her own needs as well as the needs of her husband. She puts a steak on the fire to show she is mindful of his needs and sings the following song to show us that she's mindful of her own.

> For I'll be single again, yes, I'll be single again;
> An' I eats what I likes, . . . an' I drinks what I likes,
> An' I likes what I likes, when I'm—(p. 25)

Although this song is interrupted by Simon and Sylvester's quarrel over the hand of the hook, the undaunted Mrs. Foran finishes the song later immediately after informing us that she'll be "in a doxological mood tonight, not because the kingdom of heaven'll be near me, but because my husband'll be far away" (p. 27).

When Susie, Sylvester, and Simon let the steak burn, Mrs. Foran, Irish-Elizabethan that she is, sizzles, shrieks:

The steak, the steak; I forgot the blasted steak an' onions fryin' on the fire! God Almighty, there's not as much as a bead of juice left in either of them. The scent of the burnin' would penetrate to the street, an' not one of you'd stir a hand to lift them out of danger. Oh, look at the condition they're in. Even the gospel-gunner couldn't do a little target practice by helpin' the necessity of a neighbor. [As she goes out] I can hear the love for your neighbors almost fizzlin' in your hearts. (p. 31)

This speech is flavored with the genuine poetic dialogue that spices O'Casey's characterization in the *Autobiographies* and his early plays, and leaves us savoring the exuberant use of language we have come to expect from O'Casey's Irish-Elizabethan street people.

The four characters who round out the cast of characters in this first act are: Harry Heegan, himself; Barney Bagnal, his friend and teammate; Mrs. Heegan, his mother; and Jessie Taite, his girl friend. It is interesting to note that his girl friend and his mother pull our hero in opposite directions. The mother is anxious to send him off to the world of death in the trenches while Jessie is anxious to hold him in the world of life in her arms. Like an old watch, Mrs. Heegan has just about wound down. She is an old woman who is "unknowingly lumbering toward a rest" (p. 22), and who does everything she has to do "with a mechanical persistence" (p. 22). Jessie Taite, on the other hand, is young and "responsive to all the animal impulses of life" (p. 38). This contrast between the mechanical and the vital shows up clearly in the scene in which Harry returns from the game victorious. Here the mother repeats over and over again empty phrases filled with nothing but her desire to get Harry on the boat so she can collect her government checks while Jessie is brimming full of life. For Jessie, on the other hand, this time of triumph, is (as O'Casey tells us) "a time of spiritual and animal exultation" (p. 39).

Harry and Barney are two more O'Casey characters whom it is interesting to contrast with each other. Harry is a "typical young worker" who goes "to the trenches as unthinkingly as he would to the polling booth" (p. 38). In this first act he is, like Jessie, filled with life. He is excited "with the sweet and innocent insanity of a fine achievement." He is a big man who, like Teddy Foran, dominates the action while he is on stage, while Barney, his teammate in the games of soccer and war, stands shyly in the background. We see Harry get away with lifting Jessie's skirt, while we see Barney get pushed away for trying the same thing with Susie. It appears that in Act I Barney is clearly subordinate to Harry, which is fitting since even though Barney is just about the same age and just as strong, he is "not so quick, less finely formed, not so sensitive" (p. 39) as Harry Heegan.

Note that the characters of the first act (with the possible exceptions of the mechanical mother and the all-star Harry Heegan, who even in this act appear at times too stereotyped, too symbolic to be true) are tragicomic human beings. Like the characters of O'Casey's earlier, more naturalistic dramas, these characters are characters we care about—even though they often think wrong things. In the first act of *The Silver Tassie*, as in the whole of *The Plough and the Stars*, each of the tenement dwellers engages our interest and fits precisely into his or her own distinctive niche in a distinctive world.

In the first act of *The Silver Tassie*, as in the whole of *The Plough and the Stars*, O'Casey takes care to fuse expressionistic elements to an otherwise naturalistic play. Here, as in *The Plough and the Stars*, we see various characters participate in ritualistic scenes. Here we see O'Casey the craftsman carefully weave comic ritual (Simon and Sylvester knocking out their pipes while Susie expounds her tambourine theology), celebration of life ritual (Harry drinking from the graillike tassie and then kissing Jessie with wine-wet lips), and premonition of doom ritual (the voice of the crowd repeatedly chanting,

"You must go back" to the embarking soldiers) into the very fabric of this first act.

Expressionistic elements help to make the final parting scene especially effective. As in the second act of *The Plough and the Stars*, the soldiers act as if possessed. Harry, Teddy, and Barney, like Clitheroe, Brennan, and Langon, appear as puppets manipulated by external environmental forces. These soldiers succumb to the siren's call which lures them back to the ship much as Clitheroe et. al. succumb to the voice of the figure in the window. By having Barney continually echo the last line of each stanza of the title song just after Harry finishes singing it, O'Casey creates an hypnotic effect similar to the effect achieved when Clitheroe, Brennan, and Langon vow imprisonment, wounds, and death for the independence of Ireland. O'Casey concludes this scene with a nice symbolic flourish as the light on the top of the center mast which had been visible in the window during the entire act slowly disappears.

Because this final scene is so well done, because the irony of Mrs. Heegan's last words ("Thanks be to Christ that we're after managin' to get the three of them away safely" [p. 46]), makes for as blistering an ending as anything in O'Casey—except, perhaps, the ending of *Juno and the Paycock*—because the structure of this act is so tight, with every little detail connected with and leading up to the departure of the troops; because the characters in this act all fit together in a distinctive world of their own; because of all these things, the first act of *The Silver Tassie* may be profitably viewed as a successful one-act play. In fact, we might suggest that if O'Casey had played down Harry Heegan a bit, built up the roles of Mr. And Mrs. Foran, and retitled it "The Wedding Bowl" the first act of *The Silver Tassie* would be a near-perfect-one-act play.

II   The Silver Tassie: *Act II*

The second act of *The Silver Tassie*, if taken by itself, is perhaps O'Casey's finest achievement in his "expressionistic" style. This act, like the first, has an internal consistency of its own. It is an act in which the mood evoked in the audience is the thing, an act in which the setting becomes more important than either the characters or the language. The setting in this act is crucially important because it is the only link between this act and the concrete reality of war. The characters are abstract, the language (as Hogan notes) is mostly chants in "verse of rather poor quality,"[2] and even the enemy is

unseen "out there" somewhere. It appears that it is precisely this
movement away from the concrete to the abstract in both characterization and dialogue that leads some critics (like Hogan, again) to
say that this act "depends for effectiveness less upon the dramatist
than the set designer."[3]

Of course, such critics should realize that even the most gifted set
designer does not create a set out of thin air. We might go so far as to
suggest that Augustus John created his strikingly effective set for the
second act of *The Silver Tassie* out of O'Casey's stage directions as
much as Sara Allgood created her strikingly effective Juno out of
O'Casey's dialogue. The set is an integral part of the second act, but
this does not necessarily mean either that the second act is ineffective theater or that O'Casey should not be given credit for conceiv-
ing the set in exactly this way. In fact, we believe that O'Casey
should be complimented for doing what so many playwrights ne-
glect to do, i.e., for thinking about how important an ingredient the
setting is in the total flavor of a play.

As we have seeen in the *Autobiographies,* one of O'Casey's
strengths is his ability to communicate sharply etched vignettes.
Perhaps his stage directions describing the setting for *The Silver
Tassie* are the first step in his development of this talent. Here,
O'Casey's picture (and it is his picture) is worth more than a
thousand words. In the second act of *The Silver Tassie* O'Casey
deliberately transforms the set from background into foreground.
Here the setting, which traditionally has been used for reenforcing
characterization or plot, becomes its own reason for being. Here
O'Casey, with a startlingly original stroke of genius, uses characters,
plot, and dialogue to reenforce the mood created by the set. Thus,
saying that the effectiveness of this act depends on the set designer
is like saying that the effectiveness of a traditional act depends upon
the actors and is really no criticism at all.

Yes, the setting, "the war zone," should be kept firmly in mind
throughout our discussion of the second act. The scene, as O'Casey
describes it, is:

a scene of jagged and lacerated ruin of what was once a monastery. At back a
lost wall and window are indicated by an arched piece of broken coping
pointing from the left to the right, and a similar piece of masonry pointing
from the right to the left. Between these two lacerated fingers of stone can
be seen the country stretching to the horizon where the front trenches are.
Here and there heaps of rubbish mark where houses once stood. From

some of these, lean, dead hands are protruding. Further on, spiky stumps of trees which were once a small wood. The ground is dotted with rayed and shattered shell-holes. Across the horizon in the red glare can be seen the criss-cross pattern of the barbed wire bordering the trenches. In the sky sometimes a green star, sometimes a white star, burns. . . . In the wall, right, near the front is a stained-glass window, background green, figure of the Virgin, white-faced, wearing a black robe, lights inside making the figure vividly apparent. Farther up from this window is a life-size crucifix. A shell has released an arm from the cross, which has caused the upper part of the figure to lean forward with the released arm outstretched towards the figure of the Virgin. Underneath the crucifix on a pedestal, in red letters, are the words: PRINCEPS PACIS. Almost opposite the crucifix is a gun-wheel to which Barney is tied. At the back, in the center, where the span of the arch should be, is the shape of a big howitzer gun, squat, heavy under-part, with a long, sinister barrel now pointing to the front at an angle of about forty-five degrees. At the base of the gun a piece of wood is placed on which is chalked, HYDE PARK CORNER. On another piece of wood near the entrance to the Red Cross Station is chalked, NO HAWKERS OR STREET CRIES PERMITTED HERE. In the near center is a brazier in which a fire is burning. Crouching above, on a ramp, is a soldier whose clothes are covered with mud and splashed with blood. Every feature of the scene seems a little distorted from its original appearance. Rain is falling steadily; its fall worried now and again by fitful gusts of a cold wind. A small organ is heard playing slow and stately notes as the curtain rises. (pp. 47–48)

Note that this description, like the description of the "Vandhering Vindy Vendhor", is so finely sculpted there is nothing we want to take out. Each of the details in this setting, whether it is the lacer-ated fingers of stone, the dead hands protruding from rubbish heaps, the criss-cross pattern of barbed wire, the "vividly apparent" figure of the Virgin, the arm released from the cross, the menacing shape of the howitzer, the fire, the rain, or even the organ music, is symbolically significant. Thus, unless we have a strong pictoral imagination, an ability to visualize this set and keep all its rich detail in our mind's foreground while reading, this whole act will appear as a flat "undramatic" act in which "nothing happens."[4] But if we can keep this vivid, concretely detailed set continually in mind and view the characters and language as background reenforcement for this pictorial masterpiece, then we readers may leave this act as audi-ences leave the theater—strangely moved by the total experience.

It should be obvious that to keep the characters and language in their proper reenforcing positions, to create the war-zone mood, is

no small artistic achievement. If we examine closely the opening
scene with the Croucher and the four soldiers, we see that O'Casey
deliberately forces us to view the language and the characters not as
ends in themselves, as objects of primary interest, but as the secondary background material that in this act they ought to be. From the
very beginning O'Casey makes it clear that the pictorial effect of
his figures is more important than their characters. The nonin-
dividualized croucher is merely a soldier "whose clothes are covered
with mud and splashed with blood" crouching above on a ramp. The
"Act" begins as this figure, "without moving," utters dreamily:

And the hand of the Lord was upon me, and carried me out in the spirit of
the Lord, and set me down in the midst of a valley.
And I looked and saw a great multitude that stood upon their feet, an
exceeding great army.
And he said unto me, Son of man, can this exceeding great army become a
valley of dry bones? (p. 48)

This grotesque distortion of biblical language helps to call attention to the grotesque, lacerated monastery and to the slow and
stately organ music. When the croucher stops speaking, the music
stops also, and a "*voice in the part of the monastery left standing
intones:* Kyr . . . ie . . . e . . . eleison. Kyr . . . ie . . . e . . .
eleison, *followed by the answer:* Christe . . . eleison" (p. 48). The
effect is as if the set itself were speaking, as if the soul of the
lacerated ruins were commenting on the croucher's desolate and
despairing description of the valley of dry bones. "Christ is risen,"
this unseen voice assures us. This voice from inside the monastery
continues to dominate the scene, providing counterpoint to the
croucher's chants and always getting the last word. The croucher,
for example, asks that the four winds of Ezekiel "breathe upon the
living that they may die," and the voice answers in Latin, saying,
"Glory to God and peace to men of good will" (p. 48). And finally the
croucher tells of the fires of war turning "the exceeding great army"
into "a valley of dry bones" while the voice tells of the eternal flames
of God's love. "Ah," the set seems to be saying (echoing Juno),
"what can the will o' God do agin the stupidity of men? "
   Like the voice of the croucher, the voices of the four soldiers
serve mainly to throw into relief significant details in the set. "Cold
and wet and tir'd" are the first words of the first soldier. "Wet and
tir'd and cold," says the second, and "Tir'd and cold and wet," says
the third. Then the fourth soldier sums up the soldiers' feeling of

fatigue in one longer phrase: "Twelve blasted hours of ammunition transport fatigue" (p. 49). This exchange not only indicates that these human beings are as interchangeable as the order of their words and that it is the wetness, the coldness, the tiredness of life in the war zone that is important but also this exchange reveals that the conversation of the soldiers occurs in a highly structured, artificial pattern (three short lines followed by one longer one) which O'Casey repeats three times while introducing the soldiers.

By the third time this pattern is repeated ("*2nd Soldier.* Lifting shells. *3rd Soldier.* Carrying shells. *4th Soldier.* Piling shells. *1st Soldier.* In the falling, pissing rine and whistling wind" [p. 49]) we respond more to the monotonous effort involved in lifting, carrying, and piling the shells than we do to the soldiers lifting them. The environment (as O'Casey intended) has obviously become more important than the people in it. O'Casey further emphasizes the importance of the environment by breaking his pattern for the first time in order to let two more soldiers comment on the drenching rain and the whistling wind. This scene appears designed to focus our attention on the hard rain falling rather than on the soldiers on whom it falls.

In *The Plough and the Stars* O'Casey showed us the horrors of war by having wounded characters (both participants and innocent bystanders) bleeding to death on stage, but here in the second act of *The Silver Tassie* O'Casey shows us the horrors of war by creating a mood of sadness, waste, and desolation. After watching *The Plough and the Stars,* we feel sorry for Lieutenant Langon and Bessie Burgess, but after watching the second act of *The Silver Tassie* we feel a world-sorrow, a sorrow for all the waste of life in this world. For the most part, this act maintains its focus on this waste of life that is so graphically displayed by the set and concentrates on capturing the essence of life in the war zone, thus making it possible for us to feel sorrow not for an individual character or two but for the whole misbegotten lot of humanity caught up in the senseless activity of war.

In a few scenes, however, O'Casey shifts into a more naturalistic presentation of character and gives us a preview of the absurd comic characters that dominate the third and fourth acts and so much of the later O'Casey. The scenes with the Visitor and the Staff-Wallah are fused as carefully into this expressionistic second act as the expressionistic elements were fused into the basically naturalistic first act. And even though the dialogue in these scenes (which according to Hogan provides the only vital bits in the act)[5] is more naturalistic than the dialogue of the scene with the Croucher and the four soldiers, the dialogue of the Visitor and the Staff-Wallah is not the Elizabethan dialogue that is so prevalent in the earlier plays and in the *Autobiographies*.

The Visitor for example, hardly ever speaks a complete sentence. When rebuking Barney (tied on the wheel, remember) for stealing the cock, he says: "Sacred, sacred: property of the citizen of a friendly state, sacred. On active service, serious to steal a fowl, a cock. The uniform, the cause, boy, the corps. Infra dignitatem, boy, infra dignitatem" (pp. 52–53). The Visitor's language is as choppy as his thoughts and not only reveals that his mind is incapable of thinking out a complete sentence but also contributes to the overall surrealistic effect and seems especially appropriate in this act in which every feature of the set is slightly distorted. Like the speeches of the Visitor, the orders of the Staff-Wallah consist of mere phrases, idle words from which all human associations have been carefully removed and contrast sharply with the variety of distinctively human voices we heard in the first act. And so it appears that the language of even the most naturalistically drawn characters in this act is still deliberately artificial and designed especially to reenforce the war-zone mood much as the language of Vladimir and Estragon in Beckett's *Waiting for Godot* reenforces the absurdity of their situation.

This haunting theatrical experience ends appropriately enough not with dialogue but with a picture. The setting at the end of this act, as in the beginning, requires our undivided attention. The soldiers all shout, "To the guns" and then "hurry to their places led by the Staff-Wallah to the gun. The gun swings around and points to the horizon; a shell is swung into the breech and a flash indicates the firing of the gun, searchlights move over the red glare of the sky; the scene darkens, stabbed with distant flashes and by the more vivid flash of the gun which the soldiers load and fire with rhythmical movements while the scene is closing. Only flashes are seen; no noise is heard" (p. 67). Note how the lack of sound helps emphasize the pictorial quality of this close. Our attention remains focused on the tableau of the gun dominating all around it—especially dominating those dark, huddled forms that were once human beings that are now servicing the gun with rhythmical movements as the act ends.

Like the first act, the second act taken by itself is not far from being an excellent one-act play. The main drawback to this act is, of course, the language, which is not always as felicitously chosen as it is in the scenes with which we have previously dealt. Often the language degenerates into the pseudopoetry of "The Castle Ball" episode in the *Autobiographies*, and we are never sure whether or not this decline into pseudopoetry is intentional. We hope it is, but fear it is not. O'Casey could certainly add something to this act by cutting (or at least revising) most of the chants in stanza form which appear particularly weak and unpoetic and serve mainly to detract from the intended tragic effect. Stanzas that grate especially hard on our sensibilities are:

> Jazzing back to his hotel he now goes gaily,
> Shelter'd and safe where the clock ticks tamely.
> His backside warming a cushion, down fill'd,
> Green clad, well splash'd with gold birds red-beak'd. (p. 62)

> Each sparrow, hopping, irresponsible,
> Is indentur'd in God's mighty memory;
> And we, more than they all, shall not be lost
> In the forgetfulness of the Lord of Hosts. (p. 56)

> God, unchanging, heart-sicken'd, shuddering,
> Gathereth the darkness of the night sky
> to mask his paling countenance from
> The blood dance of His self-slaying children. (p. 63)

and

> Remember our women, sad-hearted, proud-fac'd.
> Who've given the substance of their womb for shadows;
> Their shrivel'd, empty breasts war tinselled
> For patient gifts of graves to thee. (p. 65)

In this act, as in the Catholic Mass, it is the *sound* of the chants more than the mere words out of which the chants are made that makes the most essential contribution to the total experience of the religious ceremony which O'Casey deliberately designed this second act to be. Thus, as long as the actors playing the parts of the soldiers have good voices (as they apparently did in the first production of this play in London, 1929), they can make the chants effective as an

integral part of this religious ceremony (the second act) in spite of
the chants' ineffective "poetry."

Since our main criticism of this act is merely a criticism of
background material, i.e., the language of the chants, this criticism,
even if valid, should not significantly detract from the act's effectiveness when performed on stage. Certainly O'Casey's occasional
lapses in his choice of words ("empty breasts war tinselled/For
patient gifts of graves to thee") often make this act difficult to read in
the study, but even these lapses can be endured if (as advised in our
opening paragraph) we keep in mind that grotesque yet hauntingly
beautiful set and skim lightly over the chants.

III   The Silver Tassie: *Acts III and IV*

The third and fourth acts could probably be condensed into yet
another one-act play that could work on its own terms, but jar our
sensibilities when read in conjunction with Acts I and II. The problem lies not so much in the disparity between the expressionistic
second act and the farcical third and fourth acts as in the discrepan-
cies between the characters in the last two acts and the characters in
Act I. Characters that were Elizabethan human beings in Act I are
now slapstick caricatures.

It is especially significant that Surgeon Forby Maxwell is not
present in the first act but is one of the most important characters in
Acts III and IV. Like Bentham in *Juno and the Paycock,* he is out of
place in the tenements. He is primarily a comic creation, an absurd
caricature who may make us laugh occasionally but who is by no
stretch of the imagination a flesh-and-blood human being we can
care about. He enters singing a song (similar in many respects to
Rosie Redmund's song at the end of Act II of *The Plough and the
Stars*). His conversation centers mainly around sex and often sounds
as silly as that of the Visitor in the war zone. He takes particular
relish in telling Susie Monican the story about Nurse Jennings, who
was "caught doing the tango in the Resident's arms in the Resident's room. Naughty girl, naughty girl" (p. 77). Note how the
broken sentences and the repetition of "naughty girl" help produce
the same comic effect produced by the "sacred property" speech of
the Visitor in the second act. The absurdity of this character is
plainly visible when he leaves Sylvester and Simon's hospital room
tickling Susie and singing: "Kiss in a corner; ta-ra-ra-ra, kiss in a
corner" (p. 79). "Think of sinkin' your body," Sylvester tells Simon

immediately after the surgeon's exit, "to the level of a hand that, ta-ra-ra-ra would plunge a knife into your middle, haphazard, hur-ryin' up to run away after a thrill from a kiss in a corner (p. 79).

Although Simon and Sylvester never sink as low as Surgeon Forby Maxwell, they do sink enough so that they are barely recognizable. The clownish and farcical Simon and Sylvester of the third and fourth acts appear to be fundamentally different from the tragicomic Irish-Elizabethan Simon and Sylvester of Act I. Their Falstaffian gusto has been replaced by slapstick. We could easily identify with Simon and Sylvester when they were being persecuted by Susie's tambourine theology, but we do not so easily identify with characters who avoid soap and water as if they were the plague and who cannot use a telephone.

This shift in characterization is especially striking in the cases of Mr. and Mrs. Foran. These characters, who were the life of the party in the first act, have in the last two acts been reduced to wallpaper. Although the change in Teddy can be at least partially explained by the fact that he lost his eyes in the war, that "[his] best is all behind [him]" (p. 105), the change in his wife is unjustifiable and totally inexplicable. She changes from a person who dances and sings at the thought of being single again into a prudish old woman who is shocked at the way girls nowadays "are advertisin' their immodesty." She degenerates from a worthy antagonist of Teddy into a person who cannot even help Sylvester and Simon handle a telephone. And even the change in Teddy is not completely satisfactory. Why, we wonder, should the loss of physical sight destroy a man spiritually? Why must Teddy (and Harry, for that matter), who was such an impressive human being in Act I now feel so sorry for himself, be so lacking in tragic dignity?

As we try to answer these questions, we become involved in what is perhaps an even more serious problem than the irritating phenomenon of characters with the same names not being the same people. This more serious problem is that we are never sure what is the point of it all, i.e., what O'Casey in the last analysis intends for this play as a whole to accomplish. What, we wonder, is the world-view of this play? Does O'Casey intend to satirize the ball with its gaily colored ribbons and streamers or does he expect us to feel tragic empathy with Harry and Teddy, who have lost the ability to participate in this dance? If in the third and fourth acts the only purpose of eyes is to watch slapstick routines and the only purpose of legs is to join with Surgeon Maxwell in the tinseled dance, then the world of these acts (in contrast to the world of the first act) appears to be a world well worth losing. In this play the part of O'Casey who severely chastized his sister Ella for selling her soul for the sake of gaily colored ribbons and handsome appearances and views the climactic dance of the fourth act like "the castle ball" is in conflict with the part of O'Casey who loves color and spectacle and views this dance as a dance of life. Clearly part of O'Casey feels that Harry and Teddy are fortunate in being excluded from a society in which characters such as Mrs. Foran, who were once human beings, now love nothing more than "the ukelele's tinkle tinkle in the night-time" (p. 106) while another part approves of their bitterness (e.g., Harry's mangling the cup, and Teddy's repeated blasphemy, "Blessed be the name of the Lord") at this exclusion. And so this play ultimately fails not only because O'Casey never resolves this conflict between the two sides of himself, but more importantly because O'Casey never gives us the slightest indication that he is aware that this conflict exists.

The foregoing comments are not meant to suggest that the third and fourth acts are nothing or that they are more poorly written than the first two acts so much as they are meant to suggest that the last two acts are as fundamentally different from Act I as they are from Act II. The world of the last two acts is an absurd, comic world in which cardboard caricatures trip all over themselves rather than a naturalistic tenement world peopled by tragicomic human beings. There is nothing inherently wrong with creating such a world and such characters; for O'Casey often uses such creations effectively in his later farcical comedies (especially *Purple Dust*). We believe, however, that this comic world and these absurd caricatures simply do not belong in a play that pretends to tragedy, in a play that asks us to share the protagonist's rage against the injustice and evil in the world.

IV   *Yeats vs. O'Casey*

Perhaps the best way to conclude our discussion of *The Silver Tassie* is to share our responses both to Yeats's famous letter of rejection of *The Silver Tassie* and to O'Casey's equally famous reply.[6] In general terms Yeats believed that the first act was the best first act that O'Casey had written, that the second act was an interesting technical experiment which was "too long for the material," and that after that there was nothing. His more specific criticisms included: (1) that the play was written "out of opinions," (2) that these opinions were illustrated "by a series of almost unrelated scenes," that there was "no dominating character, no dominating action, neither psychological unity nor unity of action," (3) that the subject matter (the Great War) was so much dead wood that would not burn with dramatic fire, and (4) that O'Casey did not get into his characters, but instead used them as mouthpieces for aforesaid opinions.

O'Casey's reply adequately refutes some of these criticisms, but sidesteps at least two major issues. He appears justified when he argues for the necessity of "opinions" and for the Great War as being proper subject matter for his drama, but he appears evasive when responding to Yeats's comments on the play's lack of unity and its cardboard characterization. Instead of dealing directly with the unity issue, he chides Yeats for reading leading articles; instead of dealing with the play's characterization, he merely snaps: "Whether Hamlet or Lear educated Shakespeare, or Shakespeare educated Hamlet and Lear, I don't know the hell, and I don't think you know either."[7]

As the preceding comments suggest, our response to *The Silver Tassie* controversy is to side sometimes with O'Casey and to side sometimes with Yeats. We believe (with Yeats) that the first act is one of the best first acts O'Casey has written and that the second is a striking (if perhaps too long) technical experiment, but we do not believe that after these first two acts there is nothing. The third and fourth acts are for O'Casey the beginning of a new kind of drama, a drama in which lantern-slide characters flit about in an absurd comic world. Although O'Casey (as we have mentioned before) will make excellent use of such characters in his later plays, the cardboard characters that bumble around in the last two acts of *The Silver Tassie* weaken the tragic effect of the play considerably.[8]

O'Casey's opinions do not bother us, for we agree with O'Casey that the only way to burn up a playwright's opinions is to burn up the playwright himself. But, as should be obvious by now, we are disturbed by the lack of unity in this play. This play, interesting as all the diverse parts may be, is simply not well put together. The construction of this play reminds us of *Shadow of a Gunman* in that O'Casey again seems to have forgotten what he did in the first half of the play while writing the second half. We are not very concerned about the lack of a dominating character, for *The Plough and the Stars* (perhaps O'Casey's best play) has none, but we are concerned about O'Casey's inability to interrelate all the characters and the action harmoniously together.

Undoubtedly, the rejection of *The Silver Tassie*, for better or worse, marks a crucial turning point in the career of Sean O'Casey. From this point on he is a playwright without a theater, and the overall quality of his drama declines a bit as a direct result of this loss. Also, from this point on, O'Casey, perhaps overreacting to the adverse criticism of *The Silver Tassie*, deliberately, defiantly refuses (for the most part) to create any more of those marvelous Irish-Elizabethan characters that infuse life into both the earlier plays and the *Autobiographies*. And so, even though O'Casey, thanks to the increase in his imaginative powers and his new style of characterization, would write some very fine comic plays, he would never again write drama in which a fully realized Irish-Elizabethan character would play a leading role; he would never again write a fully successful tragic (or tragicomic) play.

V   Red Roses for Me

Red Roses for Me provides perhaps the best example of O'Casey's attempts to write serious, tragic drama in his new style after *The Silver Tassie* controversy had separated him from the Abbey Theatre once and for all. The plot in this most autobiographical of the plays is fairly simple. Ayamonn Breydon, the protagonist (modeled on O'Casey hero Jim Larkin), ignores the warning of his mother (modeled on Sue Casey), the pleading of his girl friend (modeled on "the girl he left behind"), the company's offer of a job as foreman, and the threats of the police and leads the workers in a climactic strike (modeled on the 1913 lockout and strike) in which Ayamonn is killed. The first two acts deal with the preparations for the strike; the third act presents O'Casey's vision of the better life toward which the workers are striving; and the fourth act provides some comic relief by Dowzard and Foster (modeled on Doosard and Glazier of the autobiographies) neatly juxtaposed to the final laying out of the martyred Ayamonn.

As serious drama, however, *Red Roses for Me* is even less successful than *The Silver Tassie* because this play lacks the intensity of *The Silver Tassie* and because O'Casey has still not accomplished a fusion of his older Elizabethan characterization and his newer, more expressionistic characterization into an organic whole. Ayamonn Breydon, for example, is a dutiful son, a lover, a union organizer, a Protestant church member in good standing, a poet, an art collector, and a student of Shakespeare (among other things). Although Hogan's comment that Ayamonn "is a combination of Red Jim [Larkin] and Christ and the president of the local Browning society"[9] is perhaps a bit unfair, Ayamonn is definitely a character that does too many things too well. Perhaps O'Casey himself, like Ayamonn, is overdoing it. "Ayamonn," his kind mother advises him, "you're overdoing it. Less than two hours' sleep today, and a long night's work before you. Sketchin', readin', makin' songs, an' learnin' Shakespeare: if you had a piano, you'd be thryin' to learn music. Why don't you stick at one thing, an' leave the others alone?" (p. 229).

When Sheila Moorneen, his Catholic girl friend, reproaches him for all this varied activity: "You lead your life through too many paths instead of treading the one way of making it possible for us to live together" (p. 239), Ayamonn, attempting to justify not only himself, but perhaps O'Casey also, replies:

We live together now; live in the light of the burning bush. I tell you life is not one thing, but many things, a wide branching flame, grand and good to see and feel, dazzling to the eye of no-one living it. I am not one to carry fear about with me as a priest carries the Host. Let the timid tiptoe through the way where the paler blossoms grow; my feet shall be where the redder roses grow, though they bear long thorns, sharp and piercing, thick among them! (p. 239)

Ignoring the ineffective "poetry" of this passage and focusing on the content of the first half, we see that for Ayamonn (and probably for O'Casey as well) life is fire, a wide branching flame each tongue of which savors different human experience. This vision of Ayamonn's life as fire is perhaps more basic, more effective dramatically than the vision of his life as walking through a bed of red roses (thorns and all) which appears to be artificially grafted both onto this speech and his character.

Ayamonn's strength lies in the fact that his fire is contagious. He continually sends off sparks that help light up the darkness of the external world of early twentieth-century Ireland, light up the darkness within other characters, and light up the darkness in the lives of all men for all time. Ayamonn's flame burns on at least three levels;

it sets afire the minds of individual human beings, the minds of all human beings living in his time, and minds of all mankind—past, present, and future. Ayamonn turns on Finnoola, Eeada, and Dympna, he turns on the strikers, and in the magical sunset dance scene on the banks of the river Liffey, he may still turn on people today. If O'Casey through Ayamonn succeeds in passing the torch of enlightenment from generation to generation, if this scene can still set our minds aglow, then the play is a success in at least one important respect no matter how many other flaws it may have.

Before we can determine whether Ayamonn succeeds in setting aglow the minds of the other characters in the play, we should know a little more about these characters. This play's cast of characters includes Ayamonn's Mother, Sheila Moorneen, Brennan O' the Moor ("owner of a few oul' houses"), Mullcanny ("a mocker of sacred things"), Roory O'Balacaun (a staunch Fenian), the Reverend E. Clinton ("Rector of St. Burnupus"), and Dowzard and Foster (two Protestant bigots and members of St. Burnupus's Select Vestry).

Ayamonn's mother, like Susan Casey of the *Autobiographies*, is a strong, sensitive, unselfish woman who is always thinking of other people before she thinks of herself. When Ayamonn "irritably" suggests that perhaps she shouldn't go out in a heavy rainstorm to spend the night with a dying neighbor, that she shouldn't spend so much time "goin' out on one silly mission or another like an imitation sisther of charity" (p. 235). Mrs. Breydon responds: "I couldn't sit quiet knowin' the poor woman needed me. I'd hear her voice all through the night complainin' I never came to give her a hot dhrink, settle her bed soft, an' make her safe for th' lonely hours of th' slow-movin' night" (p. 235). There is, this indomitable woman goes on to assure Ayamonn, "no harm to use an idle hour to help another in need" (p. 235). Ayamonn, still not convinced, points out that his mother is wearing herself out in the process, but she answers "with a sigh," "I'll wear out, anyway, sometime, an' a tired ould body can, at least, go to its long rest without any excuse" (p. 235).

This exchange between mother and son reveals that in this early scene Ayamonn, our flaming hero, is something of a wet blanket. Here it is the mother's genuine concern for others, her determination to go on helping life in spite of the storms of heaven and the stupidity of men, that lights up the surrounding darkness.

The selfishness of Ayamonn's "sweetheart" (Sheila Moorneen) in the first two acts, at least, contrasts sharply with the unselfishness of his mother. His mother has the strength to let Ayamonn go his own way (even when she does not approve) but the Sheila of the first two acts, like the girl he left behind in the *Autobiographies*, is too Catholic, too bourgeois to let him do anything but settle into "the one way" to live. Both Sheila and Mrs. Breydon disapprove of many of the branches of flame in Ayamonn, but we see Mrs. Breydon don the robes in order to help Ayamonn rehearse *Henry VI* while we see Sheila angrily walk out on Ayamonn and his disruptive friends.

Just as Mrs. Foran of *The Silver Tassie* and The Old Woman of *Within the Gates* appear to be wholly different characters at the beginning and at the end of their respective plays, so too the Sheila Moorneen of the first two acts is not the Sheila we see in Act IV. It is almost impossible to believe that the Sheila who pleads with Ayamonn to sell out his comrades for the sake of a foremanship miraculously gains the vision to see in the extra shilling for which the workers were fighting "the shape of a new world" (p. 310).

This same inconsistency in characterization can be seen in O'Casey's portrayal of Brennan of the Moor, who, like Sheila, is simply not the same character at the end of the play that he was at the beginning. In Act I Brennan is a capitalist caricature, a comic figure we laugh at (despise, even) for worrying so much about his stocks and bonds in the Bank of Ireland, but then in Act III this Stoke-Poges figure suddenly becomes a wandering minstrel with whom we are supposed to sympathize and identify. What kind of songs, one might legitimately ask, could a mind so worried with stocks and bonds sing? And when the play ends with this miserly character of whom O'Casey made such a fool in the first act playing the final requiem for Ayamonn, the effect is not quite so moving as O'Casey intended.

It is interesting to contrast O'Casey's disapproving attitude toward Sheila's attempts to keep Ayamonn to herself with his more approving attitude toward Nora's attempts to hold on to Jack Clitheroe in *The Plough and the Stars*. Here the act of trying to keep one's love from being killed in war is presented as an act of cowardly weakness instead of an act of heroic defiance. Both Sheila and Nora lose their struggle to keep their men; yet in Nora's case we are meant to feel the injustice, the absurdity of Commandant Clitheroe's decision to leave while we are meant to feel the essential rightness of Ayamonn's devotion to his cause.

Just as we saw two different, ultimately unreconciled views of war (that of the pacifist and the partisan) in the *Autobiographies* so too we see these two views reflected in his plays. We see the "realistic" (Shaw's term again) pacifist view in *Juno and the Paycock*, *The Plough and the Stars*, and *The Silver Tassie*, and we see the "idealistic" partisan view in *Red Roses for Me* and nearly all the plays which follow. In *Red Roses for Me* O'Casey asks us to take seriously the sacrificial vision of bloodshed that he treated ironically in the second act of *The Plough and the Stars*. In this play Ayamonn (and O'Casey, apparently) sides with the figure in the window of *The Plough and the Stars* who insists that though the foes of the righteous are strong "they cannot undo the miracles of God, who ripens in the hearts of young men the seeds sown by the young men of a former generation."[10] The death of Ayamonn is presented as a ritualistic heroic sacrifice on which young men will feed and gain the strength necessary to create a better world. This straight "idealistic" treatment of Ayamonn's sacrifice makes ironic counterpoint impossible, and takes away an important dimension from this drama.

Since *Red Roses for Me* is the most autobiographical of the plays, it is not surprising that there are many scenes which, with minor variations, occur in both this play and the *Autobiographies*. What is surprising is that in each of these overlapping scenes, the scene in the *Autobiographies* is more effective. The most obvious comparison (and the one in which the play fares best) is the comparison of the epiphanic dance scenes which occur near the bridge over the river Liffey. The third act of this play which echoes the dance scene in "All Heaven and Harmsworth Too" is, like the second acts of both *The Plough and the Stars* and *The Silver Tassie*, a play within a play. Here, as in "All Heaven and Harmsworth Too," O'Casey takes time out from his portrayal of the drab, bleak, economically depressed and politically oppressed Dublin of the early twentieth century to portray the shining, poetic world that this city might become.

The stage directions in the third act of *Red Roses for Me*, like those of the second act of *The Silver Tassie*, are an essential ingredient in the total play. But here it is the bridge, rather than the howitzer, which "fills most of the scene before the onlooker" (p. 275). "The distant end of the bridge," O'Casey tells us, "leads to a street flowing on to a point in the far distance; and to the right and left of this street are tall gaunt houses, mottled with dubious activities, with crowds of all sorts of men and women burrowing in them in a pathetic search for a home" (p. 275). Note that these dark burrowing characters have, like the Down-and-Outs of *Within the Gates*, given up on life. "Their expressionless faces" are "hidden by being bent downwards towards their breasts" (p. 275). One character (appropriately enough) has an "unlit pipe [no fire here] dropping from his mouth apparently forgotten." "A gloomy grey sky is over all, so that the colors of the scene are made up of the dark houses, the brown parapets of the bridge, the grey sky, the silver spire, the red pillar, and Nelson's black figure" (p. 275). Although the sun shines on the red of the pillar and the silver of the spire, there is no sign of the sun where the people are.

As the act begins, the three superstitious old women, Finnoola, Eeada, and Dympna, are, like the Down-and-Outs, drowsy despairing shapes whose conversation serves to reenforce the gloomy mood spawned by the setting. "This spongy leaden sky's Dublin," Eeada drowsily intones, in the opening lines of the play within a play, "those tomby houses is Dublin too—Dublin's scurvy body; an' we're Dublin's silver soul. *(She spits vigorously into the street.)* And that's what Eeada thinks of th' city's soul an' body" (p. 276). "You're more than right, Eeada," Dympna echoes, "The sun is always at a distance, an' th' chill grey is always here" (p. 276). And Finnoola, third member of this despairing chorus, comments on the "half-mournin' skies for ever over us, frownin' out any chance of merriment that came staggerin' to us for a little support" (p. 276). This eerie, gray mood, created by means of this fusion of set and dialogue, is marked by a lack of spirit. The characters are mechanical and lifeless. The only prophets that these Dubliners care about are the ones who can pick horse races. "Things here" (beside the darkened bridge), the perceptive Rector tells the not-so-perceptive Inspector, "are of a substance I dare not think about, much less see and handle. Here, I can hardly bear to look upon the same thing twice" (p. 280).

The strength of this third act, like the strength of the "Heaven and Harmsworth" chapter of the *Autobiographies*, is grounded in the conflict between the dullness, darkness, and spiritlessness of human life depressed by institutional religion and economic exploitation and the fire of the rebellious human spirit that may for a brief moment or two light up this darkness. Here in *Red Roses for Me*, Ayamonn is able to arouse the walking dead from their lethargy in spite of themselves. The chorus of old men and women can see only bleakness, bitterness, and blackness when Ayamonn first tries to rouse them, but Ayamonn does not succumb to their despairing vision. Ayamonn persists because he, like O'Casey himself, understands that the city is only black to the eyes that see it so. Even though "meanness, spite, and common pattherns are woven thick through all her glory," "her glory's there for open eyes to see" (p. 285).

At this point the darkness becomes even darker, but Ayamonn still keeps the faith. He tells Roory and all the other "impatient people" to "be still, man; it was dark when th' spirit of God first moved on the face of the waters" (p. 286). And so it is appropriate that just before the mood changes the scene becomes "so dark that things are but dimly seen," with only Ayamonn's head "set in a streak of sunlight, looking like the severed head of Dunn-Bo speaking out of the darkness" (p. 287).[11] We see the spirit moving on the boards of the stage as the words from this illuminated head rouse Eeada, Dympna, Finnoola, and the other dark shapes from their death-in-life. "We who have known, and know the emptiness of life shall know its fullness," the prophetic head proclaims. "Take heart of grace from your city's hidden splendour. *(He points with an outstretched hand)* Oh look! Look there! " (p. 287).

And sure enough, "the scene has brightened, and bright and lovely colors are being brought to them by the caress of the setting sun. The houses on the far side of the river now bow to the visible world, decked in mauve and burnished bronze; and the men who have been lounging against them now stand stalwart, looking like fine bronze statues, slashed with scarlet" (p. 288). The whole of the drowsy chorus has wakened. Eeada, rising into the light, "now shows a fresh and virile face"; Dympna's face is aglow; the men, also glowing, look like bronze statues; and Finnoola, who rises last, is "dressed in a skirt of a brighter green than the other two women" and is especially beautiful. The once-drowsy onlookers realize, for a moment at least, that their "tired heads have always haunted far too low a level" (p. 289). We hear the First Man exclaim, "Oh, hell, it's grand! " (p. 289). And finally we hear everyone join in a song the last stanza of which goes like this:

> We swear to release thee from hunger an' hardship,
> From things that are ugly an' common an' mean;
> Thy people together shall build a brave city,
> Th' fairest an' finest that ever was seen! (p. 290)

The climax of this scene which bridges the chasm between life as it is and life as it ought to be is, as in the *Autobiographies*, a spontaneous dance of life. Here, as in the *Autobiographies*, we see the dancers move from golden to purple pools of light. Ayamonn and the now strikingly beautiful Finnoola (who had in her youth chosen the "patched coat, shaky shoes, an' white hungry face of th' Irish rebel" [p. 281]) dance opposite each other, "move around in this spontaneous dance, she in a golden pool of light, he in a violet-colored shadow, now and again changing their movements so that she is in the violet-colored shadow, and he in the golden pool" (p. 290). As the dance reaches its climax these colors, which in the *Autobiographies* were "the finest colors God has in His keeping,"[12] and here are "the finest colors God has to give" (p. 290), are shining their brightest. In both scenes we see the "sword of light" stab through the darkness for a brief illuminating moment.

After the dance ends and Ayamonn bids farewell to Finnoola, using almost exactly the same words and actions with which Johnny bid farewell to the strange girl in the *Autobiographies*, the figures begin to shrink, the colors begin to fade, and the characters become "bewildered." Still, the characters have all been strangely moved by their "dream." It is significant that the act closes with the voice of the strikers singing, albeit quietly, the last stanza of the song that inspired the dance.

This act, if produced as O'Casey envisioned it (i.e., if the director pays attention to O'Casey's stage directions), certainly should move an audience. The problem with this act, as we see it, is that it is not successfully integrated into the rest of the play. Perhaps the most serious incongruity concerns Ayamonn's participation in the dance. While it appears natural for a young man like Johnny, who had been pushing a cart filled with Harmsworth magazines all day, to welcome the respite and join in a dance with a strange girl, it is not so natural for a young labor leader (even one with as many interests as Ayamonn) to take time out of the day of a crucial confrontation with the police to dance, sing, and enjoy beautiful sunsets. As the play stands, part of us may feel that Ayamonn is poetic and sensitive, but another part of us feels that he ought to be out in the streets with the men rather than dancing with the women.

Also we should note that the three old women whom O'Casey had deliberately deindividualized and dehumanized in the first two acts, suddenly, even in the beginning of this act, appear as distinct human beings. Finnoola especially has to be singled out from the others so that she will be worthy to dance with Ayamonn. Although this change may have been made deliberately in order to contrast the bleakness of the lives of the characters in the first act with the color in the lives of these same characters in the third act, the total effect of this change is at best mixed. When these characters who have been used as a chorus suddenly become individualized and a part of the action, we are not quite sure whether O'Casey is deliberately using these characters in an imaginative, unconventional way or if he is making the same kind of mistake he makes in the characterization of Brennan and Sheila.

As the preceding comments indicate, the third act of this play, like the second act of *The Silver Tassie* stands well by itself, has an internal logic of its own, and could be an excellent one act play. Unfortunately, here, as in the second act of *The Silver Tassie*, O'Casey's attempt to fit a play within a play is simply not as successful as it was in both *The Plough and the Stars* and the "All Heaven and Harmsworth Too" chapter of the *Autobiographies*, and the overall effect of *Red Roses for Me* suffers as a result.

Another scene with correspondences in the *Autobiographies* is the scene at the end of Act I in which Roory O'Balacaun passes on the "sword of light" to Ayamonn much as the old tram conductor passed on this same sword to Johnny in the *Autobiographies*. Again the key difference in these two treatments of the same event is in the characterization. Roory, like Brennan and Finnoola, is too comic to take seriously.

Because Roory is such a fool (he has nothing but contempt for books and thinks the singer's song is "indecent"), Ayamonn, when he joins him in his Fenian song and stands silent, clasping his hand, appears a bit of a fool himself. In contrast to the Elizabethan tram conductor whose devotion to the Fenian cause made that cause important to us, Roory's devotion to this same cause discredits it in our eyes.

O'Casey's treatments of these two old Fenian characters reveal a fundamental difference in kinds of satire. His treatment of the old tram conductor, while still satirical, is grounded in love and compassion for the man, while his treatment of Roory is grounded in an intention to make fun of him. This latter type of satire may be effective in the later comic plays but it makes it extremely difficult, if not impossible, to achieve any kind of tragic empathy with the characters in this one.

One final comparison between corresponding characters in *Red Roses for Me* and the *Autobiographies* reveals that even when the satire in both cases is of the uncompromising variety, the satire in the *Autobiographies* still works better. O'Casey's treatment of Dowzard and Foster (the true-blue Orange bigots in *Red Roses for Me*), for example, is less effective than his treatment of Doosard and Glazier in the title chapter of *Pictures in the Hallway*. Although it is true that Sean O'Casey shows as little compassion for Doosard and Glazier as he does for Dowzard and Foster, Doosard and Glazier are much more formidable antagonists, much less straw men, than are the uniformed scarecrows, Dowzard and Foster. In *Pictures in the Hallway* the mock-heroic "buttle of the Boyne" ends with Glazier and King Billy the victors over Johnny and Sarsfield. It is impossible to imagine the cowardly Dowzard and Foster grappling with Ayamonn the way Glazier grapples with Johnny not only because the character of Ayamonn is not ironically undercut, i.e., made human (the way Johnny is), but also because the characters of Dowzard and Foster are not ironically understrengthened as are Doosard and Glazier.

Note also that the Dowzard and Foster episode in *Red Roses for Me* is not an integral part of the whole, as is the Doosard/Glazier episode in *Pictures in the Hallway*. Here, as in *Shadow of a Gunman*, O'Casey's introduction of characters in the last act whom we have never seen before disturbs us a bit. The Dowzard and Foster episode, interesting and funny as it may be, is simply not integrated into the overall structure of the play. Perhaps the play would be more structurally coherent if O'Casey had let the chorus of old women perform the function for which it was originally designed and tell us about the events occurring offstage rather than introducing these two extraneous characters for this purpose.

At this point it occurs to us to question whether or not we have been pushing the virtues of structural unity and consistency of characterization a bit too strongly. O'Casey, or someone speaking for him, might suggest that the absence of structural unity and consistency of characterization in O'Casey's middle plays is a deliberate stroke of O'Casey's original, unconventional genius. One might argue, as John Gassner does, that when O'Casey "abandons the realistic technique, he makes one unalterable demand, namely, the right to let the play alternate between fact and fancy, verisimilitude and exaggeration or intensification, without regard to *literary consistency.* The only consistency he accepts is *theatrical consistency.*"[13] It is our position, John Gassner notwithstanding, that *The Silver Tassie, Red Roses for Me,* and most of the middle plays have neither literary nor "theatrical consistency" (whatever that is) and that these plays are seriously flawed as a result.

And so our final evaluation of *Red Roses for Me* is mixed. The magical third act, if produced properly, should be a moving theatrical experience, but the play as a whole suffers from a lack of consistency in both characterization and structure. The play, like some of its important characters, (Brennan, Finnoola, and Sheila, e.g.) is simply not integrated together. The various episodes within the play do not work together and strengthen each other so much as they weaken and distract us from each other. This lack of literary and theatrical unity is in direct contrast with both the tragicomic early plays (*Juno and the Paycock* and *The Plough and the Stars*) and the comitragic later ones (*Purple Dust* and *Cock a Doodle Dandy*), all plays which O'Casey puts carefully together.

CHAPTER 6

Purple Dust *and* Cock-a-Doodle Dandy

B OTH *Purple Dust* and *Cock-a-Doodle Dandy* are much tighter both in terms of structure and characterization and are therefore more effective drama than either of the last two plays we have discussed. Because his dramaturgy and his characterization are more tightly focused, because his targets are more clearly defined, these two plays succeed where *The Silver Tassie* and *Red Roses for Me* do not.

I   Purple Dust: *Characterization*

In *Purple Dust*, the lesser of these two plays, for example, all of the events of the subplots reenforce the thrust of the main plot rather than distract us from it. Here, everything contributes to a more complete understanding of the interrelationships between two Englishmen who come to rural Ireland to restore an old Tudor mansion for themselves to live in for the duration of the Second World War, their Irish mistresses, and the Irish workmen hired to remodel the mansion. As the play develops, we see concrete example after concrete example of the Irish workmen making fools of the Englishmen and of the Englishmen making fools of themselves in scene after scene of broad slapstick comedy until finally the mistresses leave the Englishmen for two leaders of the workmen just before the mansion (with the bumbling Englishmen still in it) is swept away by the waters of an apocalyptic flood.

Purple Dust zeroes in on the contrast between the English, as represented by Stoke and Poges, and the Irish, as represented by O'Killigan and O'Dempsey. In *Purple Dust* nearly every line of dialogue, every farcical episode, helps throw light on the contrast between the two life-styles. The English on one hand have their

139

quattrocento furniture, their stock exchange, their Tudor mansion, and their mistresses, while the Irishmen on the other have their singing and dancing, their life in "the Hills" filled with "laughter round a red fire when the mists are risin', when th' roads an' fields are frosty, an' when th' nights is still" (p. 205).

One of the most important differences between the English and the Irish in this play is their approach to nature. Stoke and Poges, idealists that they are, attempt to go back to a nature that never existed except in their minds, but O'Killigan and O'Dempsey, realists that they are, go forward to a nature that does exist. Stoke and Poges, much like the hero of A.E.'s novel who goes back to nature in an air-conditioned automobile, have not thought very clearly about the natural life to which they are going back. Their thinking about the natural life in Ireland, like their thinking about everything else, is hopelessly divorced from reality and is continually contrasted to the thinking of the Irish workmen (especially O'Killigan and O'Dempsey) which is grounded in the sensual and the real. For the Englishmen reality is "what every right minded man the world over knows—or ought to know" that wherever the English have gone

progress, civilization, truth, justice, honour, humanity, righteousness, and peace have followed at our heels. In the Press, in the Parliment, in the pulpit, or on the battlefield, no lie has ever been uttered by us, no false claim made, no right of man infringed, no law of God ignored, no human law, national or international, broken. (p. 179)

And O'Killigan, on the other hand, finds reality "with the bittherness an' joy blendin' in a pretty woman's hand; with the pity in her breast; in th' battlin' beauty of her claspin' arms; an' rest beside her when th' heart is tired" (p. 132).

This basic contrast between the "English" and the "Irish" is established in the opening scene of the play. As the play begins, the first Irish workman comments on the "wondhers" of people being crazy enough to "come to live in a house that's half down and it's wanin' over," of people crazy enough to trick "th' rotten beams into a look o' sturdiness with a coat o' white and black paint." And in this same scene the second workman, Philib O'Dempsey, prophetically quotes the old Irish poets' view of the relation between the English and the Irish: "Time'll see th' Irish again with wine an' ale on th' table before them; an' th' English, barefoot, beggin' a crust in a lonely sthreet, an' th' weather frosty" (p. 120). This contrast remains in the foreground of this play right up to the last scene in which we hear the splash of the oars as the Irish O'Killigan rows away with Avril and we see the English Stoke and Poges run from the green waters tumbling into the room.

The characterization in *Purple Dust* is more consistent than in any play since *The Plough and the Stars* and contributes a great deal to the overall tightness of the play. Basil Stoke and Cyril Poges are caricature capitalists who are not in tune with nature. Their song-and-dance routine (in contrast to Brennan's mandolin-playing) does not help to turn on a beautiful sunset over the bridge of the river Liffey. Even though O'Casey takes care to distinguish Basil and Cyril from each other, they both (like Shaw's Brittanicus in *Caesar and Cleopatra* or Tom Broadbent in *John Bull's Other Island*) remain English for the duration of their play. As Englishmen, they are both concerned with appearances and the surfaces of things. The comedy of the play is heightened as Stoke and Poges make comments about others that we can apply to them. The mean, tightfisted Poges notes that men of the present day are: "Paltry, mean, tight, and tedious" (p. 170), while the irresponsible, wordy Basil Stoke moans about Irish people (and horses) being "irresponsible, irresponsible" (p. 153) and accuses his fellow Englishman, Poges, of "merely using words" (p. 139).

Cyril Poges, the first of the Englishmen that we meet, is sixty-five years of age with "perceptible bags of flesh under the eyes." "He has a fussy manner, all business over little things; wants his own way at all times; and persuades himself that whatever he thinks of doing must be for the best" (p. 121). Cyril's characteristically idle, insignificant comments are scattered throughout this play. Cyril Poges is a man who sees "swarms" of rabbits, thinks Genghis Khan was "the bounder driven from Jerusalem by the Lion-hearted Richard" (p. 134), assures his mistress, Souhaun, that "Shakespeare knew what he was talking about when he said 'the glory that was Rome and the grandeur that was Greece' " (p. 136), and insists that "Gog and Magog were giants killed by David" (p. 151).

The idleness and ignorance of the self-made capitalist, Cyril Poges, are surpassed only by the idleness and ignorance of the

younger, more aristocratic Basil Stoke who, thanks to his remark-
able connections, passed through Oxford. Basil's pseudophilosophi-
cal speech in which he takes a primrose into his "synthetical consideration" is a classic example of idleness, for it consists of nothing but
one idle word after another:

> . . . If we take the primrose, however, into our synthetical consideration, as
> a whole, or, *a priori*, as a part, with the rest of the whole of natural objects
> or phenomena, then there is, or may be, or can be a possibility of thinking
> of the flower as of above the status, or substance, or quality of a fragment;
> and, consequently, correlating it with the whole, so that, to a rational
> thinker, or logical mind, the simple primrose is, or may become, what we
> may venture to call a universal. See? (p. 138)

Here, as is often the case in this play, we see more than the Englishman intends; we see that Basil Stoke will have a bit of difficulty
accounting for these words on judgment day. "Every idle word, not
in bunches, but one by one. A terrible thought," O'Casey tells us in
the *Autobiographies*, and we echo here—a terrible thought indeed.

Both Basil and Cyril live in the past because they fear and are not
prepared to cope with life in the present or the future. The old
decaying Tudor mansion, which symbolizes the collapsing British
empire (among other things), is an appropriate environment for
them. The beams of the house are rotten and worm-eaten, the
colors are dull brown or gray (like Dublin before the Liffey sunset),
and the rooms are drafty cold and without fire. (The English cannot
even start a fire to warm their own old house.) Here, as in *Red Roses
for Me*, fire is linked with the imaginative, creative life and the lack
of fire with sterility, inanity, and the old order to be cleared away.

Just as O'Casey carefully distinguishes between his two English
characters, so too he carefully distinguishes each of the three Irish
workmen and their foreman from one another. The third workman,
for example, is distinguished from the other workmen by his puritanical attitude toward sex. In the first scene he suggests that good
Irish girls like Avril and Souhaun should be ashamed of themselves
for becoming mistresses. And his puritanism is even more clearly
revealed, later in the play, when he takes Basil's "naked and un-
ashamed the vixen went away" quotation literally. At this point, he
self-righteously exclaims: "This'll denude the disthrict of all its self-
denyin' decency" (p. 154), and bemoans the fact that "th' poor men

workin' in th' fields had to flee to th' ditches to save th' sight of their
eyes from th' shock o' seein' her!" (p. 155)

The personality of the first workman is even more clearly de-
lineated than is that of the third workman. The first workman is a
cunning hypocrite who manipulates the English for his own advantage by telling them what they want to hear. When Poges has just
been scared silly by the sight of a cow he thought was a bull, the first
workman helps Poges maintain his idealistic illusions. "Just a harmless innocent cow, sir," he "cunningly" tells Poges. "Frightened the
poor girl, now, did it? But I see it didn't frighten you, sir" (p. 166).
Later on the first workman goes so far as to tell Poges what an
"honor" it is to be working in this "wondherful house" (the same
house which he has just told us is half down and wanin' over). And
finally, the first workman assures Poges (with a straight face) that
although they came late they were still in time "to see the finery
fade to purple dust, an' th' glow o' th' quality turn to murmurin'
ashes" (p. 171).

But, of course, it is the second workman, Philib O'Dempsey,
who, like the tram conductor in the *Autobiographies*, keeps the
sword o' light burning in times of trouble, shining through heaps of
purple dust. Yes, Philib is a visionary who hears strange things by
day and sees strange things by night. He often feels the "touch of
the long-handed Lugh," he tells the incredulous Poges, "when the
Dagda makes a gong o' the moon, an' th' Sword o' Light shows the
way to all who see it" (p. 175). Philib hears the hallo of Finn Mac-
Coole on the hills outside and sees his spear in the stars; he is a man
who sees further than the edge of a coin. Whereas Stoke and Poges
see history in abstract, "idealistic" terms, O'Dempsey sees history
in vivid, concrete images. He awes Poges into interest with his
vision of Wolfe Tone, "a stern-fac'd man in the blue-gold coat of the
French Armee, standin' alone on th' bridge of the big dim ship, his
eyes fixed fast on the shore that was fallin' undher the high-headed,
rough-tumblin' waves o' th' sea!" (p. 176). Thus, Philib takes the
long view of mankind, is not limited by ordinary calendars (as Blake
was not limited by clock time), and has the genuine understanding
of and respect for tradition about which Stoke and Poges continually
talk.

The visionary Philib is also gifted with an exceptionally musical
tongue. Whether he is describing his vision of the glorious past in
which he sees "Ireland crinkle into a camp," and "every rib o' grass

grows into a burnished fighter that throws a spear, or waves a sword, an' flings a shield before him" (p. 175), or he is realistically appraising the contemporary situation:

. . . what is it all now but a bitther noise of cadgin' mercy from heaven, an' a sour handlin' o' life for a cushion'd seat in a corner? There is no shout in it; no sound of a slap of a spear in a body; no song; no sturdy winecup in a sturdy hand; no liftin' of a mighty arm to push back the tumblin' waters from a ship just sthrikin' a storm. Them that fight now fight in a daze o' thradin'; for buyin' an' sellin', for whores an' holiness, for th' image o' God on a golden coin; while th' men o' peace are little men now, writin' dead words with their tiny pens, seekin' a tidy an' tendher way to the end. Respectable lodgers with life they are, behind solid doors with knockers on them, an' curtained glass to keep the stars from starin'! (p. 177)

Philib himself becomes a burnished fighter wielding words that live not behind closed doors but out in the open with nothing but clean air between them an' us an' th' starin' stars.

As the preceding comments on Philib O'Dempsey reveal, the contrast between the vivid language the Irish characters use and the abstract, idle words of Stoke and Poges often illuminates the contrast between the characters themselves. The language of the Irish characters says something, is vivid and concrete, appeals to the senses, and even when used artificially, as in the Avril-O'Killigan exchange, is always under control. The speech of the first workman which opens the play is a case in point. His language, like Philib's, is both vivid and imaginative. The old house is *"wanin'* over." The English are *"thrickin'* th' rotten beams into a look o' sturdiness" (italics mine). Neither Stoke nor Poges, whose minds are trapped in half-understood phrases, are free enough to use language in this creative way. We should note in passing that the Irish speeches (in contrast to the English speeches) have something to say. The first workman, for example, makes a perceptive point about the essential nature of the old house, and Philib makes a similar score on the respectable lodgers.

And finally we come to the foreman, O'Killigan (the Ayamonn Breydon of this play), who is the acknowledged leader of the Irish workmen in their fight against the English and their Irish allies (represented here by Canon Chreehewel, who is as hostile to the life force as Basil and Cyril are oblivious of it). What Stoke and Poges (and their Irish flatterers) idealistically view as "loveliness,"

O'Killigan realistically views as rottenness and ruin. "Give a house a history," O'Killigan tells his fellow workmen at the beginning of the play; "weave a legend round it, let some titled tomfool live or die in it—and some fool mind will see loveliness in rottenness and ruin" (p. 126).

By comparing O'Killigan to Basil Stoke we see both characters more clearly. Basil Stoke is (the stage directions tell us) "a long thin man of thirty, with a rather gloomy face which he thinks betokens dignity, made gloomier still by believing that he is something of a philosopher. His cheeks are thin and their upper bones are as sharp as a hatchet" (p. 122). "He is clean shaven, and the thin hair on his half bald head is trimly brushed back from his forehead" (p. 122). And he goes out riding in a "dark green kind of hunting coat, buckskin breeches, and big gleaming top-boots with spurs; he carries a whip in his hand, and a high, handsome, shining tall hat on his head" (p. 149). Contrastingly, O'Killigan, although also tall and young, is "handsome when he is in a good humour, which is often enough. . . . His hair, though cut short, is thick and striking. When he speaks of something interesting him, his hands make graceful gestures.... He is dressed in blue dungarees and wears a deep yellow muffler, marked with blue decoration, round his neck" (p. 125). Note that the Irish O'Killigan has thick hair (while Basil is prematurely bald), is often in good humor (while the hatchet-faced Basil is always gloomy), is graceful (while Basil is awkward), and dresses plainly with a true appreciation of color (while Basil wears gaudy colors topped off by the infamous top hat).[1] And last but not least, while Basil Stoke was passing through Oxford reading "every word written by Hume, Spinoza, Aristotle, Locke, Bacon, Plato, Socrates [*sic*] and Kant among others" and learning the art of riding at a London riding school, exercising regularly in Richmond Park, O'Killigan was fighting the fascists in Spain.

A comparison of the songs that Basil and O'Killigan sing in their respective opening scenes reenforces the differences revealed in their external appearances. Basil sings:

Our music, now, is the cow's sweet moo [this from a man who later in the play will shoot a harmless cow, thinking it is a wild bull]
The pigeon's coo
The lark's song too,
And the cock's shrill
cock-a-doodle-doo, (p. 123).

O'Killigan lilts:

> They may rail at this life, from the hour I began it,
> I found it a life full of kindness and bliss;
> And until they can show me some happier planet
> More social and bright, I'll content me with this. (p. 125)

Now, Basil's song is as inane and pretentious as his clothing. His "oo"'s ooze out of strained rhythm and forced rhyme. O'Killigan's song, on the other hand, at least expresses his characteristic acceptance of life in lines that nearly reach the level of greeting-card verse.

At this point, let us pause to ask ourselves whether or not we have been perhaps too kind to O'Casey's Irishmen. These natural, "realistic" Irish characters may at first appear as artificial stock characters whose language is self-conscious, strained, sentimental—even fatuous. Closer observation, however, reveals (to us, at least) that O'Casey is usually in control of the situation. He *uses* (we believe) these stock characters for his own original, artistic purposes. The dialogue is adjusted by O'Casey's usually firm, controlling hand to fit each character, thus gracing the Irish characters in this play with the same heightened poetic dialogue spoken by the colorful street people of O'Casey's *Autobiographies*. Only in the case of O'Killigan (an admittedly large exception) does the language sometimes ring false.

Although O'Killigan (like his immediate predecessors, Ayamonn and The Dreamer in *Within the Gates*) is not a particularly realistic or believable character, he is reasonably effective in this play in which none of the characters is realistically portrayed. In contrast to *The Silver Tassie* and *Red Roses for Me*, *Purple Dust* presents to us a distinctive, consistent world peopled by characters who are cut from the same cloth. The character of O'Killigan is a foil, but he is a foil with a purpose. O'Casey uses this foil to score point after glittering point on the hapless, half-dead Stoke and Poges. Part of the enjoyment we get from this play is the enjoyment that comes from watching an expert swordsman (O'Casey) toying with his adversaries, i.e., using his Irish characters continually to make flashing, slashing scores on the English characters (both sets of characters being especially designed for this purpose). Such swashbuckling heroes and such straw villains would, of course, be inappropriate for more naturalistic, more tragic drama, but here, we believe, as in a Marx Brothers movie, the cardboard characterization—especially the artificial villains—contributes to the intended slapstick effect.

The two women of this play, the Irish mistresses of Basil and Cyril, whom O'Killigan and O'Dempsey lure away from the choking dust, are perhaps the most realistic characters in the play. Avril (the younger and the prettier of the two) and Souhaun are the only characters who grow during the course of this play—a growth that is more carefully prepared for and more convincing than the change that took place in Sheila Moorneen in *Red Roses for Me*. As the play begins, Avril and Souhaun appear as part of the English entourage—mere possessions of Stoke and Poges respectively, but we learn very early that these Irish possessions have more learning and more depth than their English masters. The lyrics to Avril's opening song, for example, make some sense and contain an appropriate allusion to Marvell's poem "The Garden."

In the first act, also, we see Avril take part in two dances—one with the rich Englishmen and one with the poor Irish workers. And we see that Avril, although she may not want to admit it, is more at home with the workers. When the Irish reel Avril dances with O'Killigan is done, O'Killigan gives her a playful "skelp on the behind," and she reacts first like the mistress of Basil Stoke: "You low fellow, what did you dare do that for! How dare you lay your dirty hands on a real lady! That's the danger of being friendly with a guttersnipe! Wait till you hear what Mr. Basil Stoke'll say when he hears what you've done" (p. 128). But a little later after the other workmen leave she responds more as an Irish girl, more in the spirit of the game: "Never again, mind you—especially when others are here to stand and gape. [*She goes over and feels the muscle of his arm.*] There's too much power in that arm to give a safe and gentle blow to a poor young girl" (p. 129). These responses reveal not only that Avril is a divided character but also that the playful, Irish Avril rather than the haughty, English Avril is the deeper, the more real person.

And so we are not surprised that by the time the play ends O'Killigan has succeeded in exorcising the English from Avril's soul, thus making it possible for her to row away with him to a new life in the Irish hills. Unlike Synge's Pegeen Mike, she responds to the "dint o' wondher" in O'Killigan's playboylike proposal and leaves the dying to graft herself on to the living. She spits out the purple dust to go to

"where love is fierce an' fond an' fruitful," where "there's things to
say an' things to do an' love at the endings!" (p. 206). Because from
the very beginning we have seen not only her underlying love of the
Irish but also her underlying contempt for the English (even in the
opening scene she sees Basil as "That thing [with bitter contempt]!
A toddler thrickin' with a woman's legs; . . . a perjurer in passion; a
gutted soldier bee whose job is done, and still hangs on to life" [p.
130]), her acceptance of O'Killigan's romantic proposal is dramatically convincing and surprises no one except the hopelessly dense
Basil Stoke.

Souhaun's position between the English Poges and the Irish Philib
O'Dempsey parallels Avril's position between Stoke and O'Killigan.
Like Avril, she is divided with the deeper, more basic side of her
character attracted to the Irish while the surface, superficial side
is attached to the English. In the first act Souhaun (like Avril
and the Irish servant girl, Cloyne) is instinctively attracted to
O'Killigan and feels, despite Poges's assurance to the contrary, that
the old Tudor house "is a little cold and damp." Her contempt for
the English surfaces immediately following the primrose argument
between Stoke and Poges. Here, the older, more experienced Souhaun counsels the younger Avril to "go on up, and flatter and comfort your old fool by ridiculing my old fool; and, when he's half
himself again, wanting still more comfort and flattery, wheedle a
cheque out of the old prattler" (p. 144). But the Irish side of her
character soon becomes submerged again and just two pages later
she is "raptuous" over Basil's riding outfit and haughtily assures
O'Killigan that frequent exercise in London riding schools has made
good riders of both Basil and Avril.

The Irish in Souhaun (like the Irish in Avril) rises to the surface
more and more often as the play develops. In the second act she
begins to show interest in Philib, who with his own distinctive vision
sees her as only "a week or two oldher than [her] younger friend" and
looking "like an earlier summer kissin' a tardier spring good-bye" (p.
180). Here, she admits that it "is ridiculous for [her] to be with
Poges," for she feels like a young bird "that has just got command of
its wings" (p. 180). And in the last act this young bird takes flight.
She responds to the second workman's visionary call, much as Avril
responds to O'Killigan's, and gallops away into the hills with Philib
O'Dempsey, the man with "thrancin' talk" who has the habit of
"makin' gold embroidery out o' dancin' words" (p. 206).

II   Purple Dust: *Dramaturgy*

"Indeed," Robert Hogan tells us, "*Purple Dust* is O'Casey's finest structural achievement since *The Plough and the Stars*. . . . [It] has a unity and coherence that O'Casey's other experiments, even the often supurb *Silver Tassie*, did not have."[2] We basically agree with this judgment (although we believe that sections of the *Autobiographies* are also fine structural achievements). The dramaturgy of *Purple Dust* is well controlled indeed. O'Casey's use of contrast, his use of song and dance, his use of sensory appeal, his use of slapstick comedy, and his judicious use of nonnaturalistic techniques all reinforce each other, all contribute to making this play a harmonious whole.

Since our study of characterization included a discussion of O'Casey's use of contrast and song and dance, we shall begin our analysis of dramaturgy in *Purple Dust* by examining in some detail O'Casey's enormously effective appeal to our immediate sensory experience in general and to our senses of sight and hearing in particular. The sound of all the Irish animals' noises which wake up the English at the break of dawn, the lowing of the cow, the sound of the shot while Basil is wandering around outside with a loaded gun, the crash of breaking chinaware (which we know is Poges's Annamese vase and Cambodian bowl), the sound of the galloping horses as Souhaun rides away with Philib, and the increasingly louder peals of thunder all are especially effective not only in themselves but also in that they serve to remind us that life is going on in the world beyond the crumbling walls of the old Tudor mansion. Throughout the course of this play the sound of things collapsing reverberates in our consciousness.

O'Casey, naturally enough, uses color as effectively as he uses sound. The colors of the clothing of all the characters (not just the aforementioned Basil and O'Killigan) are designed not only to sharpen the symbolic contrast between the Irish and English but also to help make this play the colorful spectacular that it should be when performed on stage. Even the heavy iron discs of the roller, which so appropriately knock a wall out of the dark gray brown mansion, are "vividly painted in panels of red, white, green, and yellow" (p. 181). Every visual detail in this play (and there are many of them), whether it is minor like the black and blue striped vase and the brightly colored, geometrical-patterned rug; more impor-

tant like the head of the yellow bearded man poking through the
ceiling, and the stylized cow head poking over the barricade; or
crucial like the apocalyptic green waters that tumble into the room
at the end of the play, helps to illuminate the key contrast between
the English and the Irish on which this play is focused. Yes, the
visual details in *Purple Dust* are coordinated in a way that the visual
details in some of the earlier experiments (most noticeably *The
Silver Tassie* and *Red Roses for Me*) are not.

This coordination of visual detail helps tremendously in the creation of the roisterous, circus atmosphere that permeates the entire
play, that provides the background as Stoke and Poges engage in
incident after incident of slapstick comedy. This play, as Krause
perceptively notes, "represents a new and original development of
O'Casey's stagecraft—and of modern drama. He uses the stage as if
it were a combination music hall and circus ring, whirling through a
profusion of burlesque turns and clowning acts, and bringing the
whole performance to a spectacular conclusion with a supernatural
extravaganza."[3]

Although at first glance the slapstick scenes which propel this play
appear arbitrarily selected and interchangeable, closer examination
reveals that these scenes are carefully fitted together, that each act
rises to an increasingly serious climax of its own and each scene in
each act helps to make these climaxes the memorable dramatic
moments that they are. Avril riding away with O'Killigan, Basil
shooting the cow, and the tumbling green waters are all appropriate, effective endings for their respective acts.

We have already seen how the games O'Killigan and Avril play,
and Basil's inept horsemanship, help set up O'Killigan's riding away
with Avril at the end of Act I. Now let us examine how the scenes in
Act II build up to Basil's offstage shooting of the cow. As the act opens,
Stoke, Poges, and their servants are wakened by a cacophony of
animal sounds (including of course the lowing of cattle). They shiver
in the cold a bit until Cloyne arrives with the news that a "wild bull"
(the harmless cow that Basil is destined to destroy) is out in the
entrance hall. Stoke and Poges play Alphonse and Gaston with the
gun (thus focusing our attention on the weapon) until "the cow puts
a stylised head, with long curving horns, over the barricade and lets
out a loud bellow" (p. 165). The ensuring panic of the English is
neatly contrasted with the calm voice of the first workman easily
shooing the cow outside. Next follows the flattery scene in which

this same first workman helps Poges to convince himself that he stood his ground while the cowardly Basil ran for his life.

Basil's cowardice remains in the background as the second workman tells Poges about the Irish warriors of time past and the respectable lodgers (see Basil with his gun) of today. A short time later Poges accidentally knocks down a wall of the house with an oversized roller, and just as we are thinking that this is the most absurd thing anyone (even an Englishman) could do O'Killigan enters to inform Poges (and us) that Basil is going about the grounds carrying a fully cocked gun. Poges sends someone else (Souhaun) to take the gun (about which we are beginning to worry a bit ourselves) away from Basil, and stays behind to lecture O'Killigan for being seen in public with Avril. This lecture is especially well timed, for it helps make Poges's mistake (he thinks Basil has shot Avril) understandable and ridiculous at the same time. Note that the few incidents in this act which are only tangentially related to Basil and the "bull," such as the introduction of the vase and bowl and the Souhaun-O'Dempsey conversation are still necessary ingredients in the overall concoction which is *Purple Dust.*

Because of the tighter structure, O'Casey's nonnaturalistic experiments are more carefully integrated into this play than they have been in any play since *The Plough and the Stars.* Here, the stylized head of the cow, the exaggerated characters, the heightened language, and The Figure representing the spirit of the river are all carefully fitted into place. Even the entrance of The Figure does not surprise us that much, coming as it does immediately after the entrance of the postmaster, who is a little weird in his own right. This Figure, who "is dressed from head to foot in gleaming black oilskins, hooded over his head, just giving a glimpse of a blue mask, all illuminated by the rays of flickering lightning" (p. 213), makes only one speech, but this speech, like the speech of the figure in *The Plough and the Stars,* is the most important speech in the play. "The river has broken her banks," this Figure says in a deep voice,

Cattle, sheep, and swine are moaning in the whirling flood. Trees of an ancient heritage, that looked down on all below them, are torn from the power of the place they were born in, and are tossing about in the foaming energy of the waters. Those who have lifted their eyes unto the hills are firm of foot, for in the hills is safety; but a trembling perch in the highest place on the highest house shall be the portion of those who dwell in the valleys below! (p. 214)

This message from the spirit sums up the whole play. "Trees of an ancient heritage" (Stoke and Poges) are "torn from the power of the place they were born in," tossed about in the foaming energy of the Irish people, and left trembling on the roof of the house, while O'Killigan, O'Dempsey, Avril, and Souhaun have lifted their eyes unto the hills and are saved.

And so the fault of this play (if there is one) is not so much in either the characterization or the dramaturgy, as it is in the underlying thought. There appears (to us, at least) something about the message of the play and the final action of O'Killigan that just does not ring true. There is something incongruous about a rebel who fought the fascists in Spain retreating with his love to the "little house on the hill." Is O'Casey advocating involvement in or escape from the struggles of life? And if he is advocating both simultaneously (which may be the answer after all), he should make it clear that that is what he is doing.

Yet, our final assessment of *Purple Dust* is a positive one. O'Casey, in this play, may not set out to do as much as he sets out to do in some of his earlier experiments, but he does do everything he sets out to do, and he does it well. We believe that consistent characterization, tight structure, and imaginative use of language and dramaturgy all contribute to the creation of an internally consistent Calliope world driven round and round by the joyous celebrating human spirit, which more than makes up for whatever philosophical shortcomings may be embedded in this play.

III   Cock-a-Doodle Dandy

Like *Purple Dust*, *Cock-a-Doodle Dandy* is tightly focused on one central conflict. Here, however, the conflict is not between the English and the Irish but between the forces of life (represented by The Cock, Loreleen, and The Messenger) and the forces of death (represented by Father Domineer, Shanaar, and One-Eyed Larry). During the three "scenes" of this play these conflicting forces vie for the control of the minds of the inhabitants of the little Irish village of Nyadnanave in general and for the control of the members of Michael Marthraun's household in particular. In contrast to the similar struggle in *Within the Gates*, which the forces of good won too easily, the results of this psyche-warfare are mixed. The life force wins control over the women of the house (Lorna, Michael's young wife, and Marion, the maid) while the death force wins control over Michael and the rest of the inhabitants of the town. Just as O'Casey's imaginative recreation of the Garden of Eden ended with Eve leaving the garden so that her children would not be born there so this play ends with the women leaving this nest of knaves going forward to a place "where life resembles life more than it does here."[4]

Like so many of O'Casey's earlier plays, this play opens with two members of a community discussing another member who is not there. As this play opens, Michael Marthraun, the owner of a lucrative turf bog (the dowry he received when he married Lorna), and Sailor Mahan, the owner of a fleet of lorries that carries the turf from bog to town, are discussing young Loreleen, who is, Mahan informs us, Michael's daughter by his first wife. Michael, himself, is not so sure: "So it was said at th' time, an' so it's believed still; but I had me doubts then, and I've more doubts now. I dhread meetin' her, dhread it, dhread it. [*With a frightened laugh.*] Michael Marthraun's daughter! [*Gripping Mahan's arm.*] Is she anyone's daughter, man?" (p. 247). This last question, linking Loreleen with the supernatural, helps prepare us for Michael's description of the invisible wind that follows Loreleen around, turning holy pictures to the wall and helps introduce us to the absurd, comitragic world of this play. Michael has seen, he assures Sailor Mahan, "th' image of our own St. Pathrick makin' a skelp at her with his crozier; fallin' flat on his face, stunned, when he missed!" (p. 247). Since we have already seen The Cock enter, dance around the "cynical looking" evergreen, and then exit before the start of the play, we are not quite as sure as Sailor Mahan that Michael is deluding himself.

As in so many other O'Casey plays, the opening dialogue reveals as much about the talkers as about the talked about. The opening dialogue of *Cock-a-Doodle Dandy* not only reveals that Loreleen is a beautiful, independent young woman associated with supernatural forces that are in polar opposition to the forces represented by traditional religion but also that Michael is a superstitious, foolish man who sees evil in that woman while Sailor Mahan has much more common sense and can see (here in the beginning at least) "nothin' evil in a pretty face, or in a pair of lurin' legs" (p. 248).

Michael Marthraun's clothing (as might be expected) reveals

some significant information about his character. It reveals, for example, that this clean shaven, lean, grim-looking, sixty-year-old man does not take much to gay colors. He is "dressed in a blackish tweed suit, and his legs are encased in black leggings. A heavy gold chain stretches across his waistcoat, and he wears a wide–leafed collar, under which a prim black bow tie is tied" (p. 246). Note that the only trace of color is his gold chain which serves mainly to show how rich he is.

The black-robed, gold-laden Michael Marthraun represents the life that The Cock (and O'Casey) so justifiably detest, a life grounded in hypocrisy and self-deceit. Michael, for example, seconds Shanaar's comments on woman's ungodliness, laments the "evil" in women, and then playfully pinches Marion's bottom the first chance he gets. Similarly, he inveighs loudly against the "materialism" that is edging his workers into "a revolt against Christian conduct" (p. 254) and then refuses to give the workers the shilling a week they so dearly need and he can so well afford. When Lorna (who keeps his books for him) has the temerity to remind him that he is making more than enough to meet the workers' meager request he angrily responds: "Listen, you: even though you keep th' accounts for me, it's a law of nature an' a law of God that a wife must be silent about her husband's secrets!" (p. 303). Michael's "Cristian" conduct, it appears, includes making up laws of God and nature to keep his woman in her place.

As this play develops, Michael Marthraun remains the center of attention, the butt of most of The Cock's pranks. Because he, like Peter Flynn in *The Plough and the Stars,* is consistently a fool and a coward, we laugh at him right up to the very end. We laugh at his fear when the "crek, crek" of a corn crake punctuates Shanaar's story, his shock at seeing the pretty maid, Marion, sprout horns just as he is about to kiss her, his being amazed by the bottle of whiskey that glows red hot but won't pour, his surprise as his chair (like his language) collapses under him, and his clumsy attempts to hold up his pants in the stiff wind (which The Messenger, Robin Adair, and the women never even notice). In fact, we laugh at nearly everything he does, every word he says, until the final scene.

It is difficult to laugh at anyone, even Michael Marthraun, in the final scene, for in this scene the fantasy is over, The Cock has been exorcised from Nyadnanave, and grim reality has set in. *Purple Dust* moves from a realistic beginnning to a fantastic surreal conclusion, but in *Cock-a-Doodle Dandy* that process is reversed. Here, the ending is as realistic, as ironic as the endings of his earlier, more naturalistic plays. Just as the final image of Captain Jack Boyle in the bare room with only Joxer for company lays out the waste of his life clearly for us all to see, so too the final image of Michael Marthraun alone with his rosary beads reveals a similar waste. This stark image of a lost soul in the complete control of the forces of darkness, a lost soul who has nothing to do but die, again enlists our sympathy as well as our contempt, for we see that though he has inflicted pain upon others, he has inflicted worse pain upon himself.

The common sense of Sailor Mahan (who as his name suggests may be viewed as an everyman figure, a battleground over which the forces of good and evil struggle for control) contrasts sharply with Michael's superstitious foolishness. In contrast to Michael, Sailor Mahan "is of a more serene countenance," "his face is of a ruddier hue," and is "in no way unpleasant" (p. 246). His double-breasted royal blue suit is noticeably brighter than Michael's black. Again, as in so much Elizabethan Drama (and so much O'Casey), external characteristics mirror internal ones. Thus, we are not surprised that this man with the "more serene countenance" has both a healthy skepticism and a Flutherian appreciation of woman that Michael (for the most part) lacks. When they both succumb to Shanaar's way of looking at women and see horns growing out of the beautiful Marion's head, Sailor Mahan (in contrast to the hysterical Michael) tries to remain cool, wants to "think it out," and asks for a drink to steady him down. And when Julia (Lorna's younger, dying sister) goes off to Lourdes, the idealistic Michael is sure the prayers of the Nyadnanavians are "bound to get th' higher Saints goin' " while the realistic Mahan "impatiently" exclaims: "Arra, man alive, d'ye think th' skipper aloft an' his glitterin' crew is goin' to bother their heads about a call from a tiny town an' disthrict thryin' hard to thrive on turf?" (p. 270). Also, Sailor Mahan stands up to Father Domineer (as the overly submissive Michael could never do) when the good father asks him to fire his best lorry driver, who is living "in sin." And finally, he responds to Michael's definition of a virtuous man (one who must "always be thinkin' of th' four last things— hell, heaven, death, an' th' judgement" with the realistic reply: "But that would sthrain a man's nerves, an' make life hardly worth livin' " (p. 275).

Unfortunately, Sailor Mahan's more realistic view of the world (including, of course, the genuine appreciation of women which he maintains from the opening of the play to the very end when he is caught in a car with Loreleen and stoned back to his wife and children) is not sufficient for his salvation. At the end he is stoned back to the one right way to live and sentenced, presumably, to spend the rest of his days in this land "where a whisper of love bites away some of the soul" (p. 313). This sturdy man whose "mind is fitted together in a ship shape way," who even though "forced out of his thrue course be a nautical cathastrope, . . . an act of God," still "ploughed a way through th' Sargasso Sea, reachin' open wathers, long afther hope had troubled him no longer" (p. 271) cannot plow through the Nyadnanavians to reach freedom. Instead, he remains landlocked like the lifeless lumps that impede his progress.

One of the more noticeable of these impediments is One-Eyed Larry, a foolish, fawning follower of Father Domineer. The face of this half-person "is one alternately showing stupidity or cunning. . . Where his left eye was is a black cavity, giving him a somewhat sinister look." "He is wearing a black cassock or soutane, piped with red braid." "He is carrying a small bell, a book, and an unlighted candle" (p. 294). He, appropriately enough, "shuffles along" behind Father Domineer, his spiritual pastor and master. Note that One-Eyed Larry is a comic, cowardly character who would not be that dangerous by himself. When Father Domineer, Michael Marthraun, and he are exorcising The Cock from Michael's house, Larry breaks ranks, comes running out of the house, "his face beset with fear." By his own admission he left just as the struggle was starting in earnest. When Father Domineer and Michael emerge from the battle victorious, One-Eyed Larry "at once runs out, and takes his place reverently behind them, standing with his hands folded piously in front of his breast" (p. 299). Larry's actions in this scene reveal that he, like Stoke or Poges, is an ineffectual buffoon who, by himself, would have as little chance against The Cock as Basil Stoke has against O'Killigan.

Shanaar, the "very wise old crawthumper," is, like Larry, a buffoon in league with the forces of darkness, but he is also, unlike Larry, "a dangerous old cod" (O'Casey's own comment). He is certainly more dangerous than One-Eyed Larry, even though he too, by himself, is no match for The Cock. When this "very, very old man" "wrinkled like a walnut, . . . with longish white hair, and a white beard—a bit dirty—reaching to his belly" (p. 254) sets his Latin against the crowing of The Cock, the lusty crow of The Cock wins a decisive victory. In response to Shanaar's "fervent," if spurious, Latin ("Oh, rowelum rande, horrida aidus, sed spero spiro specialii spam!" [p. 259] The Cock "lets out a violent and triumphant crow" which not only causes Shanaar to disappear behind a wall but also causes Michael to "fall flat in the garden, as if in a dead faint" (p. 259).

This old cod who is driven into hiding behind the wall by The Cock's crow is still dangerous, however, because his view of women (as creatures having horns on their heads) is contagious. Shanaar is, as Sailor Mahan realizes in the beginning and as Michael admits in a moment of strength, a bit "too down on the women." "Watch that one, Marion," Shanaar tells Michael in one of his typical antiwoman speeches, "Women is more flexible towards th' ungodly than us men, an' well th' old saints knew it. I'd recommend you to compel her, for a start, to lift her bodice higher up, an' pull her skirt lower down; for th' circumnambulatory nature of a woman's form often has a detonatin' effect on a man's idle thoughts" (pp. 262–63). Unfortunately, both Michael and Sailor Mahan catch this spiritual sickness and see the women as Shanaar would have viewed them.

Note that Shanaar, who fears "the circumnambulatory nature of a woman's form" does not have the control over language that he thinks he does. When he warns Michael to be on guard "against any unfamiliar motion or peculiar conspicuosity or quasimodical addendum, perceivable in any familiar thing or creature common to your general recognisances" (p. 263), he joins the gallery of comic O'Casey characters (including Bentham, Peter Flynn, Daabruin, and Basil Stoke) whose explanations need to be explained. His English, it appears, is even more incomprehensible than his Latin.

Clearly, the most formidable power set in opposition to The Cock is Father Domineer, a symbolic representation of the repressive power of institutions in general and of the Catholic Church in Ireland in particular, whose language we understand only too well. Father Domineer, archvillain that he is, is much more formidable, more dangerous than the wishy-washy liberal bishop in *Within the Gates*. Although David Krause believes that Father Domineer "is too much a straight villain to be an entirely satisfactory symbol," that making the enemy a monster weakens the drama, and that O'Casey should perhaps "have made Father Domineer more of a comic villain,"[5] we believe that O'Casey's characterization of Father

Domineer is apt. Father Domineer's inhumanity is his strength. The comic human Larry and Shanaar are no match for the Dionysian Cock with the spirit of God in him. If The Cock is to be driven out of Nyadnanave, the force driving it must be a devil of some kind.

Loreleen, closely associated with The Cock as she is, naturally notices that Father Domineer has actually set himself up against God. "When you condemn a fair face," Loreleen tells Father Domineer, "you sneer at God's good handiwork. You are layin' your curse, sir, not upon a sin but on a joy. Take care a divil doesn't climb up your own cassock into your own belfry" (p. 311). "You fool," Loreleen angrily exclaims when Father Domineer is about to engage in the devil's favorite pastime of burning books, "d'ye know what you're thryin' to do? You're thryin' to keep God from talkin' " (p. 300). Father Domineer, it appears, is like Blake's Urizen jealous of all other Gods before him and deliberately attempts to destroy the creative human imagination.

Father Domineer's opposition to God is an essential component of his character, a component clearly illustrated when he kills the lorry driver with the "blessing" of the force to which he is aligned. This act of murder which climaxes the second scene is, of course, dramaturgically necessary for it starkly reveals the full extent of Father Domineer's demoniac power and prepares us for the third scene in which the crucial battle between the Father and The Cock takes place. This act of murder reveals that the "God" of Father Domineer is not the God who commanded, "Thou shall not kill!" In fact, Father Domineer should, as the messenger of the true God suggests, whisper the act of contrition into his own ears. By having Father Domineer commit this murder on stage O'Casey demonstrates as vividly as possible that Father Domineer is possessed by dark supernatural powers that hate life and want it dead.

Because some critics feel this murder scene is in bad taste or extraneous,[6] we must emphasize as strongly as possible the dramatic necessity for Father Domineer having a very real devil in his belfry. Without this devil The Cock's exorcism from Nyadnanave would be unbelievable. It is one of the strengths of this play that in it O'Casey has finally created a demoniac force worthy of doing battle with his life-affirming characters. In both *Within the Gates* and *Purple Dust*, for example, the life-denying forces were represented by such ineffective, bumbling characters that no one could possibly take them seriously. Just as *The Plough and the Stars* and "The Buttle of the

Boyne" are effective precisely because the death forces are formidable so too *Cock-a-Doodle Dandy* is effective precisely because Father Domineer has the power to strike dead those who oppose him.

Whereas One-Eyed Larry, Shanaar, and Father Domineer are all possessed by evil, Lorna, Marion, Loreleen, The Messenger, and, of course, The Cock are all, by the time the play ends, at least, possessed by the life force. Lorna and Marion, being more human, have more doubts than Loreleen and the messenger and so it takes them longer to decide which side they are on. As the play progresses, Lorna and Marion gradually come to realize that turning holy pictures to the wall and pecking at a tall hat are not necessarily evil acts. Both Marion and Lorna continue to submit to the forces led by Father Domineer until the climax of the last scene, but they do it less and less willingly. In the opening scene both Lorna and Marion are uncomfortable in The Cock's presence. When The Cock sends the altar light flying, claws the holy pictures, and pecks at the tall hat, Marion is "in great distress," and Lorna barricades herself under a bannister. And when the messenger, who understands "there's no danger an' there never was," calmly leads The Cock out of the house, Lorna orders him to "take that bird away at once. Hand him over to th' Civic Guard, or someone fit to take charge of him" (p. 260).

Later, just after the "dance of life" in scene two ends with the appearance of Father Domineer, both Lorna and Marion fall on their knees with the men and face the priest with "their heads bent in shame and some dismay" (p. 289). And we see that in spite of this "some dismay" these women are submissive and know their place. Still later, just after the exorcism of The Cock from the house in scene three, Michael Marthraun at the behest of Father Domineer asserts his authority as head of the household and orders his wife back "to th' place, th' proper place, th' only place for th' women" (p. 299). Although both Marion and Lorna go back into the house, Marion goes "with a sour looking face" and Lorna looks "anything but charmed," and we see that the seed of "some dismay" has grown considerably since we saw it in scene one.

Finally, when Loreleen (who throughout the play has steadfastly refused to submit to the authority of Father Domineer) is dragged before him by the Nyadnanavians, over whose hearts and minds the forces of evil now have complete control, Lorna and Marion begin to realize that there is no place for them in this town. When the priest drives the bloodied, barefoot Loreleen into exile, they are sure of it. Lorna packs her bags and leaves with Loreleen in order "to be free from th' priest an' his rabble." "Lift up your heart lass," the finally saved Lorna exclaims, "we go not towards an evil, but leave an evil behind us" (p. 312). Shortly later Marion leaves without letting her boyfriend, the messenger, kiss her good-bye; for, as she tells him, "a whisper of love in this place bites away some of th' soul" (p. 313). These two women have come a long way from the beginning of this play when their minds were cluttered with impressions to this ending where their minds see clearly where they are going and what they are leaving behind.

The messenger joins the tram conductor as being one of O'Casey's most successful attempts to create a character who sanctifies the things that matter with song. Whereas The Dreamer of *Within the Gates* is adolescent, Brennan o' th' Moor inconsistent, Ayamonn and O'Killigan too busy with other things, the messenger, Robin Adair, is an insightful, consistently drawn character who appreciates life and communicates this appreciation to others. Robin Adair, like so many of O'Casey's finer creations, is a fusion of the archetypal and the individual; he is a messenger of the gods and he is a man. An Irish Mercury, he has "a flash of a pair of scarlet wings" on the right side of his silver gray coat, and "a bright green beret is set jauntily on his head and he is wearing green-colored sandals" (p. 258). Yet he also works for the post office and has spent time in jail for kissing Marion in a public place. He illustrates his affinity with The Cock with the symbolic gesture of marching offstage in goose step with the magical bird. Yet he illustrates his support for Loreleen with the very human gesture of forcing the rough fellows to let Loreleen's arms go. (Note even Father Domineer does not interfere with the messenger when he frees Loreleen from these bullies which suggests that the messenger comes from a power that Father Domineer, himself, cannot control.)

The music of the messenger, like the messenger himself, has symbolic depth. His music is not merely accordion music; it is also the spirit of God moving in Nyadnanave. It is his music that the characters all dance to in that magical dance of life near the end of scene two. When Father Domineer stops the dance, the messenger continues to play the tune "very softly, very faintly" (p. 289). And later when the wind is literally pulling the pants off the followers of

Father Domineer, "the messenger is coaxing a soft tune from his accordion" (p. 306). In fact, the messenger's music is always in the background of this play; i.e., the spirit of God is still faintly alive,· until the very end. But after the women leave, and Julia comes back from Lourdes without a cure, the messenger realizes that Nyadnanave is now a town fit only to die in and leaves, singing the last song, gracing the inhabitants of this doomed town with the last touch from the spirit of God they will have in their lifetime.

The Cock, the most imaginative creation in all of O'Casey, also is infused with the spirit of God. The Cock is the source of all singing and dancing in Nyadnanave (and by extension the world), and "broadly signifies," in Hogan's words, "vitality, the life force, fertility."[7] The "enchanted cock," David Krause adds, is an "inspired magician," a merry champion of "Original Joy."[8] We learn early that this inspired creature is the polar opposite of priests and politicians in general and Father Domineer and Michael Marthraun in particular. There appears to be a mutual instinctive antipathy between The Cock on one side and holy pictures, altar lights, and top hats on the other.

O'Casey's stage directions (always a good place to begin) emphasize the stark black and color contrast between Father Domineer's forces and The Cock. The Cock "is of a deep black plumage, fitted to his agile and slender body like a glove on a lady's hand; yellow feet and ankles, bright green flaps like wings, and a stiff cloak falling like a tail behind him. A big crimson crest flowers over his head, and crimson flaps hang from his jaws. His face has the look of a cynical jester" (pp. 245–46). The Cock has an "agile slender body" while the bodies of all his antagonists are older, more awkward, more crooked, and crinkled. The Cock is associated with crimson flowers and is glowing with life; Shanaar is wrinkled like a walnut. The Cock moves supply and gracefully; Michael's lips twitch. And The Cock has the look of a "cynical jester"; the tight surly lines in Father Domineer's face will not let him smile.

The Cock, the cynical jester who is driven from Ireland, not only represents a Dionysian life force but also represents O'Casey himself. This figure, as his green wings indicate, is indeed a transformation of the green crow. O'Casey himself, in his *Autobiographies,* in *Red Roses for Me,* and in this play is an inspired magician whose imaginative vision brightens up barren landscape. Both The Cock and O'Casey run afoul of the coalition of black-garbed priests and top-hatted polititians. The Cock, like O'Casey, may be banished in this play, but he gives the black-garbed, top-hatted, craw-thumping, would-be religious, would-be patriots the slapstick beating they deserve and then sets out for more fertile climes.

Thus, the incident in which the coalition of church and state (Father Domineer and Michael Marthraun) succeeds in exorcising the inspired cock from the house is perhaps a microcosm of the play as a whole. Here, in the opening of scene three the demoniac power of Father Domineer (who has just killed the lorry driver, remember) begins to assert itself. The play gets darker as we realize that there is truth in the good father's boast: "Th' bell is powerful, so is th' book, an' th' blessed candle, too" (p. 294). When the struggle begins in earnest, "the house shakes; a sound of things moving and crockery breaking comes from it; several flashes of lightning spear out through the window over the porch; and the flagpole wags drunkenly from side to side" (p. 297). The frightened One-Eyed Larry's account of the opening shots of the battle shows that the spirits aligned with The Cock are at least holding their own. "One o' Father Domineer's feet is all burned be a touch from one o' them, an' one o' Micky's is frozen stiff be a touch from another" (p. 297).

The battle continues to rage and soon we see the house shake even worse than before and seem "to lurch over to one side. The flagpole wags from side to side merrily; there is a rumble of thunder, and blue lightning flashes from the window" (p. 298). The thunder which we had not heard before and the change in color of the lightning indicate that the battle is getting more intense. It is either, One-Eyed Larry declares, "them or us." Finally, the battle reaches its climax. "The house shakes again; the flagpole totters and falls flat; blue and red lightning flashes from the window and a great peal of thunder drums through the garden. Then all becomes suddenly silent" (p. 298). After the orgasm of red and blue lightning flashes, the flagpole can no longer remain erect. The evil spirits (Kissalass, Velvethighs, etc.) are dispersed, and Father Domineer and Michael emerge disheveled and tired, but elated over their conquest. "Be assured, good people," Father Domineer sums up the results of the battle for his parisheners, "all's well now. . . . The Civic Guard and the soldiers of Feehanna Fawl will see to the few who escaped. We can think quietly again of our Irish Sweep" (p. 299).

This house that shakes, lurches, and is lit up with flashes of white, blue, and finally red lightning is not only a strikingly effective dramaturgic device but also it is, like the Tudor mansion in *Purple Dust* and Dame Hatherleigh's house in *Oak Leaves and Lavender*, a symbol of a decaying culture, a symbol of Ireland under the control of puritanical priests and bourgeois politicians. The Cock, like O'Casey, can infuse the life force into this dying structure for only so long. In this play, as in the historical situation, the red lightning and the drums of thunder under the window only serve to strengthen the control of the unholy alliance and make the possessed priest and polititian even more dangerous to those living under them.

The battle of Marthraun's house is only one of many flowers that O'Casey's fertile imagination drives through the stem in *Cock-a-Doodle Dandy*. There is the scene in which horns sprout from Marion and Lorna's heads, the scene in which the liquor glows red hot, but will not pour, the scene in which O'Casey portrays yet another magical dance of life, and the scene in which Father Domineer leads his troops in an assault on the wind—just to name a few of the blossoms. In *Cock-a-Doodle Dandy*, in contrast to some other plays we have discussed, the blooming is well timed, consciously designed for the most dramatic effect.

Whereas the confrontation scenes between the young woman and the bishop in *Within the Gates* are repetitive and not coordinated well with one another, the confrontation scenes in *Cock-a-Doodle Dandy* are coordinated especially well. The first of the confrontations in which Father Domineer frustrates the spirit of God by stopping the dance of life marks the turning point in the play. In this dance scene the women succeed in enchanting Sailor Mahan, the Sergeant, and even Michael Marthraun so that these dry old men can live for a brief moment, at least, and it appears that The Cock has the situation well under control. Unfortunately, as soon as Father Domineer makes his entrance ("in a green light") the dance immediately ceases, everyone (except Loreleen and the messenger) falls on his or her knees, and the play darkens. When Father Domineer in the beginning of the next scene drives the spirits from Michael's house, the atmosphere becomes even darker, more oppressive. And finally, when the spirit of God (in the form of the wind) is driven from even the land outdoors, the victory of the forces of darkness is complete.

In this final exorcism scene, we see Father Domineer lead a successful assault on the spirit of God which has become angry after being driven from the house. We see the swifter, stronger wind move nothing in the garden with its "whistling violence" except the followers of Father Domineer. The women and the messenger remain unmoved while Michael, the bellman, One-Eyed Larry, and later the sergeant all struggle to stand still and hold up their pants. This zestful, jestful spirit which the wind represents "declines in a sad wail" when Father Domineer enters "with a wild look in his eyes" and organizes his forces for the counterattack. We watch this ragtag army make feeble progress (but progress nevertheless) until the sound of Loreleen's capture in the distance ends the fray. "Listen to th' band," Father Domineer says "jubilantly," "we're closin' in; we're winnin'!" (p. 308). Note that with the capture of Loreleen, The Cock is captured also, and the wind disappears for the duration.

We see the same care in the construction of individual scenes within scenes that we see in the play as a whole. The scene, for example, in which the impatient Michael and Sailor Mahan try to get the sergeant to tell them what The Cock turned into works especially well. Here, O'Casey builds up the frustrations of his characters by making them stay in an uncomfortable situation for an extended period of time. Just as Peter Flynn in *The Plough and the Stars* refuses to open the door and leaves The Covey standing outside with the heavy sack of flour on his shoulders, the sergeant refuses to tell Michael and Mahan what they are so anxious to hear. Although the anguish of these two cronies is more mental than physical, it is still very real. Between them Michael and Sailor Mahan have to ask the sergeant at least nine different times (in the space of a page and one third) before the sergeant gets around to telling them what happened the third time he shot at The Cock. "As I was tellin' you," the sergeant finally concludes, "there was th' crimson crest of th' Cock, enhancin' th' head lifted up to give a crow, an' when I riz th' gun to me shouldher, an' let bang, th' whole place went dead-dark; a flash of red lightning near blinded me; an' when it got light again, a second afther, there was th' demonised Cock changin' himself into a silken glossified tall-hat! " (p. 279). Note that this speech is a miniature of this scene as a whole, i.e., it contains a lot of unnecessary verbiage which takes time to say thus building the suspense in Michael and Sailor Mahan (and in us) and leading up to the final absurdity of The Cock changing itself into a silken glossified tall hat.

At this point we must interject a word or two about the language of *Cock-a-Doodle Dandy*. Not since *The Plough and the Stars* has the language of each character been so distinctly his or her own. Sailor Mahan's speech, for example, as revealed in his opening conversation in which he accuses Michael of "haulin' in a rope that isn't there" is spiked with vivid sea imagery. Close examination of each character's speech reveals similar distinctive traits. The sergeant's speech reveals his military orientation, Michael's reveals his business orientation, Marion's her servant station, Lorna's her youth, Shanaar's his senility, Father Domineer's his harshness, the messenger's his music, etc.. A scene which illustrates this diversity in language as well as any is the ritualistic send-off scene in which Julia leaves for Lourdes. A ritualistic effect, similar to the effect of Harry Heegan's send-off in *The Silver Tassie*, is created as Lorna, Michael, Sailor Mahan and Father Domineer bid Julia farewell each in his or her distinctive style. Father Domineer appropriately concludes the send-off by urging her off to Lourdes with the same hardness that Mrs. Heegan urged Harry aboard ship. "Now, now, no halts on th' road, little daughter! The train won't wait . . . . Bring her along, Brancardiers! Forward, in th' name o' God and of Mary, ever virgin, ever blessed, always bending to help poor, banished children of Eve!" (pp. 268–69). Note that Father Domineer's language won't wait, bounds impatiently forward, and is as mechanical and automatic as the train.

The Lourdes episode has (along with the murder of the lorry driver) often been criticized, even by otherwise sympathetic critics, for having little, if any, relation to the central conflict of the play,[9] and we would like, therefore, to take a paragraph or two to show that the Lourdes episode, like the previously discussed murder of the lorry driver, is carefully designed to heighten the total effect of the play. It is our position that there are no loose ends in this play, that this play is as tightly controlled as anything O'Casey ever wrote (including the best sections of the *Autobiographies* and *The Plough and the Stars*). Far from being gratuitous, the Lourdes episode, which culminates in Julia's return in despair "without even a gloamin' thought of hope" (p. 314), provides a vivid example of the end that lies in wait for those who believe in Father Domineer's miracles. Julia's return without a miracle from "the Coney Island of misery, agony, and woe,"[10] from Lourdes, with "all its crowds and all its candles," illustrates as starkly, as concretely as possible, that Father Domineer is indeed a devil whose advice conducts one down the path to despair and death. And Julia's return also makes it possible for us to see that the "questionable blessing" of the messenger, whose whole soul is wishing he could cure her, but who can only say, "Be brave . . . . Evermore be brave" (p. 314), is much more valuable than either the "somersaultin' prayers" of Shanaar or the traditional blessing spouted by Father Domineer.

And last but not least Julia's return from Lourdes contributes to the shock of the dark, realistic ending of this colorful, imaginative play. It is refreshing to see O'Casey return after years of oversimplification to a reasonably realistic appraisal of the human condition. Here O'Casey keeps his faith in life, but it is the faith of Mild Millie, the old Jewish glazier, Juno, and the tenement collective of *The Plough and the Stars*, not the faith of the adolescent dreamer or the boy scout Ayamonn. It is to O'Casey's eternal credit that the faith that shines through the darkness in this play is a hard-won faith, a faith that will endure in spite of the demonically possessed political and religious fellas.

CHAPTER 7

Conclusion

I   Autobiographies

SEAN O'Casey's position as one of the major creative artists of the twentieth century is becoming more secure with every passing day. As more and more people are beginning to recognize, Sean O'Casey is both a seminal force in modern British and American drama and a prose artist of the first rank. The first four volumes of the *Autobiographies* are a mother lode especially rich in ore, much of which has yet to be mined. Even though space limitations made it impossible for us to deal with the *Autobiographies* in the detail they deserve, we have hopefully dealt with them in detail sufficient to demonstrate their finely sculpted quality, their colorful, imaginative explosions, and their human strength. Others following us will (we are sure) pick up where we have left off and demonstrate clearly that the first four volumes of the *Autobiographies* (at least) are the creations of an artist of the first rank working at the height of his powers.

II   *Plays*

We have seen O'Casey's plays shift from the more naturalistic Irish-Elizabethan early plays to the experimental, expressionistic plays of his middle period (represented here by *The Silver Tassie* and *Red Roses for Me*) and then to the later comic-imaginative plays (represented here by *Purple Dust* and *Cock-a-Doodle Dandy*). This shift (Irish critics notwithstanding) was not caused by O'Casey's leaving Ireland to live in England. The primary reasons for this shift, we believe, are: (1) the essential nature of Sean O'Casey's unique, restless, creative imagination and (2) the Abbey Theatre's rejection of *The Silver Tassie*. The rejection of *The Silver Tassie* appears especially important since O'Casey deliberately (perversely, perhaps) restrained himself from writing any play to which

167

Yeats could point and say, "I told you so." And it is this restraint (as evidenced by his refusal to create consistently drawn Irish-Elizabethan characters and his refusal to give his plays unity of action) rather than his departure from Ireland which perhaps accounts for much of the weakness inherent in the expressionistic middle plays. Although his colorful, creative imagination and his sympathy for the exploited peoples of the world are clearly present in these middle plays, they cannot save them; for neither his imagination nor his sympathy appears (to us, at least) to be under artistic control.

Finally, in the comic-imaginative phase of O'Casey's playwriting career, he achieves this control over his imagination and his politics. In the last plays, as in *The Plough and the Stars* and in the best stories of the *Autobiographies*, there is unity of action. Here, as we have seen, O'Casey's comic, imaginative genius is directed to specific ends. If we, for example, compare *Cock-a-Doodle Dandy* (the best of the comic-imaginative plays) to *The Plough and the Stars* (the best of the early plays) these two dramas appear approximately equal in terms of overall effectiveness. Both plays reveal tight artistic control and consistent characterization, and the sheer imaginative vitality of the later play balances off with the greater depth of characterization of the earlier one.

III *Poetry*

O'Casey, as might be expected, puts his best poetry into his best works and his worst pseudopoetry into his lesser achievements. The speeches of Fluther Good, Captain Jack Boyle, Mild Millie, the tram conductor, etc., are spiced with genuine poetry while the speeches of the dreamer in *Within the Gates* and Ayamonn Breydon in *Red Roses for Me* are not. *Purple Dust* is an interesting play in that we can see poetry and pseudopoetry side by side. O'Killigan sounds sometimes like Ayamonn while Philib O'Dempsey sometimes has the "dint o' wondher" of a genuine poet in his talking. When we hear the imaginatively charged dialogue of colorful street people, we are hearing the best poetry O'Casey will ever write. When we hear self-conscious attempts to write poetry (as in the chants of *The Silver Tassie* and the speeches of Ayamonn and the dreamer), we are hearing his worst.

IV *"for the light is there always"*

Of course, there are many reasons for O'Casey's continually increasing popularity. One reason emphasized by David Krause in his final ringing knock on O'Casey's door is O'Casey's "comic genius." O'Casey, as Krause illustrates in this moving tribute, is a "master of knockabout" who achieves "catharsis through profanation."[1] We also appreciate the Dickensian side of O'Casey, but we would, in the final analysis, like to shift the emphasis slightly. For us, the catharsis is more important than the profanation. We believe that O'Casey's slapstick comedy, his unique comic imagination (valuable as it is) is ultimately less important than his ability to capture in words the strength of the human spirit that can keep the sword of light shining through the grime. It is, we should like to suggest, his Shakespearean empathy with all kinds of characters (especially the outcast and the exploited) which insures his literary immortality.

As we said in the beginning, we believe (O'Casey himself to the contrary) that O'Casey's greatest gift (though he has many gifts) is still the gift that makes possible his characterization. The man who draws us into the lives of the old Jewish glazier, Old Biddy, Mild Millie, the tram conductor, the brother Mick, the mother of the *Autobiographies,* Juno Boyle, Jack Boyle, Joxer Daly, the entire tenement collective in *The Plough and the Stars,* Mr. and Mrs. Grigson (from *Shadow of a Gunman*), Mr. and Mrs. Foran (from the first act of *The Silver Tassie*), Philib O'Dempsey, Sailor Mahan, and Michael Marthraun (at the very end); the man who could write the following letter to a despondent New York housewife:

My dear Mary, It is not for me to say nay to your sad letter; but surely it is the lot of all of us to know the feverish brow, and the body hot with illness, or cold with the many hopes vanished, a voice lost, & no light, apparently, before us. Only apparently, for the light is there always, tho' we often keep our eyes shut so that we cannot see. I am aware of all you say about underpaid workers, of many a funeral; thro' many strikes, I have eaten dry bread & bitter waters, with my half-famished comrades; but never lost the will to keep fighting. Ireland misses Larkin just as the USA misses Debs, for such flames are rarely kindled; but they, in the work of others, will flame again, if not in America or Ireland, then somewhere else to lighten & warm the whole family of man.

I know what a housewife has to face & has to do. I've scrubbed bare floors—no oil cloth for the poorer slums—kindled poor fires, washed my own & my mother's poor shirt & shift; but it was no treadmill task to do what we could to keep ourselves alive, & go about; at least, dishonestly clean; for no tenement dweller could keep honestly clean under the conditions, around, about & above them. I did chores before I became ill, to help my wife; & am beginning again—washing up, peeling spuds, carrying down the garbage, etc. It is partly good for us, for it is routine, & this checks the excitement of the mind, & gives us a rest. We cannot always suffer ecstasy. There must always be a lot of "petty service," if not for others, then for ourselves. Each has to go thro' the routine of petty life day by day, year in & year out; there is no escape, nor should there be, for we are civilized animals that must accept civilization's laws.

I wish I could write you a long letter, but I'm still away from normal activity, & soon grow tired.

You have my sympathy, and a faraway touch of a hand that wishes you well, and (your son) Michael, too. I still have the same view of life; I love it, even in the midst of pain, when the candle of activity gutters. Shake Michael's hand for me, and give me your own.[2]

(a letter which even now we cannot read without tears squeezing between the frames of our glasses and the bridge of our nose); the man who sees that "the light is there always" is the man we salute, the man to whom we extend our hand in gratitude and friendship.

Hurrah yourself, Sean.

Notes and References

Chapter One

1. Lady Gregory's Journals, 1916–30, edited by Lennox Robinson (New York, 1947), p. 72.

2. David Krause, "A Self-Portrait of the Artist as a Man," *Sean O'Casey: Modern Judgements*, ed. by Ronald Ayling (London, 1969), p. 235.

3. Sean O'Casey, *Mirror in My House* (New York, 1956), *Drums under the Windows*, p. 96. All subsequent quotations from the *Autobiographies* are referred to by abbreviated book name and page number in the text.

4. William A. Armstrong, "Sean O'Casey, W. B. Yeats and the Dance of Life," *Modern Judgements*, p. 131 ff., convincingly demonstrates that Millie's dance is indeed a "dance of life."

5. Robert Hogan, *The Experiments of Sean O'Casey* (New York, 1960), p. 163.

6. George Bernard Shaw, *The Quintessence of Ibsenism* (New York, 1961), pp. 37–45. This discussion of an imagined community's views on marriage clarifies what we (following Shaw) mean by these terms.

7. Martin Margulies, *The Early Life of Sean O'Casey* (Dublin, 1970), p. 61.

8. For more detailed information on the contrast between Mick, the character presented here, and Mick, who became "something of a legend" in the "streets and pubs of the North Wall area" of Dublin, see Margulies, pp. 86–7.

9. See David Krause, *Sean O'Casey: The Man and His Work* (New York, 1975), pp. 265 ff. for a more detailed treatment of this conversation.

10. Gabriel Fallon, *Sean O'Casey, the Man I Knew* (Boston, 1965), p. 163.

11. *Ibid.*, p. 160. Here we see Fallon's three main objections to the *Autobiographies:* (1) "the narcissism of the style," (2) the "unreliability of the content," and (3) the "unaccountable bitterness." The irrelevance, inaccuracy, and sheer silliness of these comments should speak for themselves.

12. Padraic Colum, "Sean O'Casey's Narratives," *Modern Judgements*, p. 225.

13. By creating this distinctive imaginatively charged milieu O'Casey becomes part of an impressive literary tradition including as diverse figures as the Beowulf Poet, Shakespeare (in the History Plays), Marcel Proust, and William Faulkner.

Chapter Two

1. Krause, *Sean O'Casey*, p. 71.

2. Carmella Moya in her article "The Mirror and the Plough," *Sean O'Casey Review*, V.2, N.2, p. 147, also notes the effective use of contrast in this dialogue. This useful article also views O'Casey as using similar techniques of dramaturgy and characterization in the autobiographies and the plays—especially *The Plough and the Stars*.

3. E.g., tableaus of Johnny and his mother together against the world can be seen at the end of "First the Green Blade," "His Father's Funeral," "We All Go the Same Way Home," "Crime and Punishment," and "The Lord Loveth Judgement."

4. Krause, *Sean O'Casey*, p. 274. (Krause's discussion of O'Casey's communism, pp. 272 ff., is the best discussion of this subject which we have come across.)

5. *Ibid.*, p. 269.

6. Eileen O'Casey, letter quoted by Saros Cowasjee in his forward to *Sean O'Casey: The Man behind the Plays* (New York, 1964), p. vii.

7. The Black and Tans were much more ruthless and feared than the Auxiliaries, and this ruthlessness can be seen whenever O'Casey deals with them, whether it is in the beginning of his career *(Shadow of a Gunman)* the middle *(The Star Turns Red)* or the end (the prerumble to *The Drums of Father Ned).*

8. See Armstrong, pp. 131 ff., for a more detailed description and fuller treatment of this "dance of life."

Chapter Three

1. See Hogan, p. 36.

2. Sean O'Casey, *Three Plays* (London, 1961), pp. 94–95. All subsequent quotations from *Shadow of a Gunman, Juno and the Paycock,* and *The Plough and the Stars* are referred to by page number in the text.

3. Hubert Nicholson, "O'Casey's Horn of Plenty," *Modern Judgements*, p. 216.

4. Hogan, pp. 30–35.

5. Krause, *Sean O'Casey*, pp. 76 ff., presents a perceptive detailed discussion of the similarities between Jack Boyle and Falstaff.

6. Hogan, p. 41.

7. Fallon, p. 22.

8. James Agate, "Juno and the Paycock," *Modern Judgements*, p. 77.

9. See my "The 'Ougly Shape': Despair in Early English Drama," *Mas-*

sachusetts Studies in English, pp. 78 ff., for a more exhaustive examination of the treatment of this antipathy in early English Drama.

10. Faustus, Macbeth, Lear, and the "typical" morality protagonist, for example. See also *ibid.*

Chapter Four

1. Krause, *Sean O'Casey,* p. 74, also views "the war" as the tenement dwellers' "common enemy."

2. *Ibid.,* p. 80.

3. Note the parallels between this card game and the card game between Edmund Tyrone and his father in the last act of O'Neill's *Long Day's Journey into Night* (New Haven, 1973), pp. 137 ff.

4. Krause, *Sean O'Casey,* pp. 2–8, presents a detailed account of these depressing conditions, including some interesting statistics. (E.g., early in 1880 the death rate in Dublin was 44.8 per 1,000 people, the highest of any city in the world at that time.)

5. P. S. O'Hegarty, "A Dramatist of New Born Ireland," *Modern Judgements,* p. 65.

6. Krause, *Sean O'Casey,* p. 86.

7. Denis Johnston, "Sean O'Casey, An Appreciation," *Modern Judgements,* p. 85.

8. Sean O'Casey, quoted by Hogan, p. 43.

9. Hogan, p. 50.

Chapter Five

1. Sean O'Casey, *Three More Plays* (London, 1965), pp. 23–24. All subsequent quotations from *The Silver Tassie, Purple Dust,* and *Red Roses for Me* are referred to by page number in the text.

2. Hogan, p. 64.

3. *Ibid.,* p. 65.

4. *Ibid.*

5. *Ibid.,* p. 64.

6. See Hogan's Appendix, pp. 184–206, for extensive coverage of *The Silver Tassie* controversy including the full text of both Yeats's letter of rejection and O'Casey's reply. Krause's coverage of the controversy in his *Sean O'Casey, the Man and His Work,* pp. 94–109, is also useful, although slightly biased against Yeats.

7. O'Casey's letter to Yeats, quoted by Hogan, pp. 195–96.

8. For an opposing view which sees the last two acts as a "ruthless return" to "the fiercest ironic realism" see Shaw's letter to Lady Gregory, quoted by Hogan, pp. 198–99.

9. Hogan, p. 91.

10. Sean O'Casey, *Three Plays,* p. 178.

11. Armstrong, p. 140, summarizes relevant details of Eleanor Hull's

treatment of the Dunn-Bo legend in *Pagan Ireland* (Dubliin, 1923), pp. 1–3.

12. Sean O'Casey, *Pictures*, p. 339.

13. John Gassner, "The Prodigality of Sean O'Casey," *Modern Judgements*, p. 117.

Chapter Six

1. To fully understand the extent of O'Casey's contempt for the tall hat, see *Inishfallen*, pp. 207 ff, in which Sean comments with "some bitterness" on the seventy-seven men executed by the Free State Government so Irishmen could afford the privilege of donning a top hat.

2. Hogan, p. 103.

3. Krause, *Sean O'Casey*, p. 187.

4. Sean O'Casey, *Cock-a-Doodle Dandy*, *Masterpieces of the Irish Theatre*, edited by Robert Corrigan, p. 315. All subsequent quotations from *Cock-a-Doodle Dandy* are referred to by page number in the text.

5. Krause, *Sean O'Casey*, p. 201.

6. Hogan, p. 121, e.g., feels that this scene does not add to the "story's essential development," and the Irish critics, as might be expected, feel the bad taste.

7. Hogan, p. 118.

8. Krause, *Sean O'Casey*, p. 188.

9. See Hogan, p. 121.

10. O'Casey, *Inishfallen*, p. 383 (also quoted by Krause, *Sean O'Casey*, p. 199).

Chapter Seven

1. Krause, *Sean O'Casey*, pp. 305 ff.

2. O'Casey, quoted by Krause, *Self-portrait of the Artist as a Man*, pp. 250–51.

Selected Bibliography

PRIMARY SOURCES

Behind the Green Curtains. London & New York: Macmillan, 1961.
The Bishop's Bonfire. London & New York: Macmillan, 1955.
Blasts and Benedictions, ed. Ronald Ayling. London: Macmillan; New York: St. Martin's Press, 1967.
Cock-a-Doodle Dandy. London & New York: Macmillan, 1949.
Collected Plays, 4 vols. London & New York: Macmillan, 1949–51.
The Drums of Father Ned. London & New York: Macmillan, 1960.
Drums Under the Windows. London & New York: Macmillan, 1945.
Feathers from the Green Crow, ed. Robert Hogan. Columbia: Univ. of Missouri Press, 1962.
The Flying Wasp. London & New York: Macmillan, 1937.
The Green Crow. New York: George Braziller, 1956.
I Knock at the Door. London & New York: Macmillan, 1939.
Inishfallen Fare Thee Well. London & New York: Macmillan, 1949.
The Letters of Sean O'Casey, Volume 1: 1910–1941, David Krause, ed. New York: Macmillan, 1975.
Mirror in My House; the Autobiographies of Sean O'Casey, 2 vols. New York: Macmillan, 1956.
More Wren Songs. Dublin & London: Maunsel, 1918.
Oak Leaves and Lavender. London & New York: Macmillan, 1946.
Pictures in the Hallway. London & New York: Macmillan, 1942.
The Plough and the Stars. London & New York: Macmillan, 1926.
Purple Dust. London & New York: Macmillan, 1940.
Red Roses for Me. London & New York: Macmillan, 1942.
Rose and Crown. London & New York: Macmillan, 1952.
The Silver Tassie. London & New York: Macmillan, 1928.
Songs of the Wren. Dublin & London: Maunsel, 1918.
The Star Turns Red. London & New York: Macmillan, 1940.
The Story of the Irish Citizen Army. Dublin & London: Maunsel, 1919.
The Story of Thomas Ashe. Dublin & London: Maunsel, 1918.

Sunset and Evening Star. London & New York: Macmillan, 1954.
Two Plays (Juno and the Paycock and Shadow of a Gunman). London & New York: Macmillan, 1925.
Under a Colored Cap. London: Macmillan; New York: St. Martin's Press, 1963.
Windfalls. London & New York: Macmillan, 1934.
Within the Gates. London: Macmillan, 1933.

SECONDARY SOURCES

ARMSTRONG, WILLIAM A. "History, Autobiography, and *The Shadow of a Gunman*," *Modern Drama*, II, 4 (February 1960), 417–24. *Shadow* does much more than merely provide cross section of life in a Dublin slum in 1920.
———. *Sean O'Casey*. London: Longmans, Green, & Co., 1967. Balanced biography, relates the man to the period in which he lived.
———. "Sean O'Casey, W. B. Yeats, and the Dance of Life," *Sean O'Casey*, ed. by Ronald Ayling. London: Macmillan, 1969, 131–42. Perceptive, intelligent analysis of the "Dance of life" in O'Casey— especially good on Mild Millie and *Nannie's Night Out*.
———. "Sources and Themes in *The Plough and the Stars*," *Modern Drama*, IV, 3 (December 1961), 234–42. Perceptive article containing useful material on O'Casey's editing of Pearse's speeches before putting them into the mouth of the orator in the window.
AYLING, RONALD. "Character Control and 'Alienation' in *The Plough and the Stars*," *James Joyce Quarterly* (Tulsa, Oklahoma), VIII, 1 (Fall 1970), 29–47. Insightful analysis of the means whereby characters and their actions are "distanced" from each other and the audience.
———. "The Poetic Drama of T. S. Eliot," *English Studies in Africa*, II, 2 (September 1959), 247–50. Comparison of the "poetic drama" of Eliot and O'Casey to O'Casey's advantage. Discusses O'Casey's possible influence on Eliot's technique.
———. *Sean O'Casey: Modern Judgements*. London: Macmillan, 1969. Excellent collection of the most influential and best O'Casey criticism. The introduction contains the most perceptive summary of O'Casey criticism yet done.
———. "Sean O'Casey: Fact and Fancy," *Dublin Magazine*, IV, 3–4 (Autumn-Winter 1965), 69–82. Convincing demonstration of the "fancy" which permeates Fallon's book on O'Casey.
BARZUN, JACQUES. "O'Casey at Your Bedside," *Griffin Magazine* (London), III (October 1954), 4–9. "At the Last Judgement O'Casey can submit that he has written two first rate plays and set adrift forty characters—more than enough good works for literary salvation."

BENSTOCK, BERNARD. *Paycocks and Others: Sean O'Casey's World.* New York: Barnes and Noble, 1976. An expanded, more thorough treatment of the O'Casey character types presented in his earlier book; a perceptive, useful study.

———. *Sean O'Casey.* Lewisburg: Bucknell Univ. Press, 1970. Part of Irish Writers Series. Competent, if not imaginative, treatment of O'Casey's "cast of characters."

COLUM, PADRAIC. "Sean O'Casey's Narratives," *Sean O'Casey*, ed. Ronald Ayling. London: Macmillan, 1969, pp. 220–27. Reasonably perceptive Irish criticism of O'Casey's *Autobiographies.*

CORRIGAN, ROBERT W., ed. "The Irish Dramatic Flair," *Masterpieces of the Irish Dramatic Theatre.* New York: Collier, 1967, pp. 6–8. Finds "Irish flair" in Yeats, Synge, and O'Casey.

COSTON, HERBERT. "Prelude to Playwriting," *Tulane Drama Review*, VI (September 1960), 102–12. Useful material on first forty years of O'Casey's life.

COWASJEE, SAROS. *O'Casey.* Edinburgh & London: Oliver & Boyd, 1966. Better than his first, but not by much.

———. *Sean O'Casey: The Man behind the Plays.* New York: St. Martin's Press, 1964. Devoted but often insensitive criticism—*The Plough and the Stars* is, for example, a play in which "O'Casey has little to say after the third act."

DA RIN, DORIS. *Sean O'Casey.* New York: Ungar Publishing Company, 1976. Part of World Dramatists Series; an "armchair guide," competent description of plays, little originality, no significant evaluation of the plays.

DE BAUN, VINCENT C. "Sean O'Casey and the Road to Expressionism," *Modern Drama*, IV, 3 (December 1961), 254–59. Documents the "expressionism" in *The Plough and the Stars.*

DUMAY, EMILE JEAN. "Merriment and Celebration in Sean O'Casey's Plays," *The Sean O'Casey Review*, II, 1 (Fall 1975), 12–21. Adequate, if somewhat superficial, treatment of "Merriment etc."

EDWARDS, A. C. "The Lady Gregory Letters to Sean O'Casey," *Modern Drama*, VIII, 1 (May 1965), 95–111.

ELLIS-FERMOR, UNA. "Poetry in Revolt," *Sean O'Casey*, ed. by Ronald Ayling. London: Macmillan, 1969, pp. 106–109. Praises O'Casey for being "the embodiment of poetry in revolt" and turning bitter social criticism into "new channels."

FALLON, GABRIEL. *Sean O'Casey: The Man I Knew.* Boston: Little, Brown, 1965. Interesting reminiscences of O'Casey's relationship to the Abbey Theatre, not reliable as criticism, especially perverse on the late plays and the *Autobiographies.*

FRAYNE, JOHN P. *Sean O'Casey.* New York: Columbia University Press,

1976. Damns O'Casey with faint praise; O'Casey, for example, growing old, *"forgets* that the real experience of life in a country is the sum total of small details which resist abstraction" *(my italics).*

GASSNER, JOHN. "The Prodigality of Sean O'Casey," *Theatre Arts* (N.Y.), XXXV (June 1951), 52–53; (July 1951), 54–55; (August 1951), 48–49. O'Casey's "prodigal creativity" sets him apart from the "largely trivial and constricted" contemporary theater.

GOLDSTONE, HERBERT. *In Search of Community, the Achievement of Sean O'Casey.* Dublin: The Mercier Press, 1972. Valuable, enthusiastic treatment of O'Casey, grounded perhaps in too arbitrarily defined categories ("commitment," "community," etc.).

HOGAN, ROBERT. *The Experiments of Sean O'Casey.* New York: St. Martin's Press, 1960. A valuable, often perceptive discussion of O'Casey's dramaturgy—especially good on the late plays and the *Autobiographies,* weakest on *The Silver Tassie.*

————. "The Haunted Inkbottle: A Preliminary Study of Rhetorical Devices in the Late Plays of Sean O'Casey," *James Joyce Quarterly,* VIII, 1 (Fall, 1970), pp. 76–95. Interesting, perceptive article; focuses on the language of the later plays (especially *Purple Dust, Cock-a-Doodle Dandy, The Drums of Father Ned,* and *Behind the Green Curtains*).

————. "In Sean O'Casey's Golden Days," *Dublin Magazine,* V, 3–4 (Autumn-Winter 1966), 80–93. Useful, perceptive examination of O'Casey's place in the pastoral tradition.

JOHNSTON, DENNIS. "Sean O'Casey: An Appreciation," *Daily Telegraph* (London) March 11, 1926), p. 15. Silly asides on sex and O'Neill offset by insight into the expressionistic elements in O'Casey's early plays.

JORDON, JOHN. "Illusion and Actuality in the Later O'Casey," *Sean O'Casey,* ed. by Ronald Ayling. London: Macmillan, 1969, pp. 143–61. Contains provocative, if not convincing, defense of *The Star Turns Red.*

KAUFMAN, MICHAEL W. "The Position of *The Plough and the Stars* in O'Casey's Dublin Trilogy," *James Joyce Quarterly,* VIII, 1 (Fall 1970), 48–63. Insightful, if somewhat unfocused, comments on *The Plough and the Stars*—especially good on the second act.

KILROY, THOMAS, ed. *Sean O'Casey, a Collection of Critical Essays.* Englewood Cliffs, N.J.: Prentice-Hall, 1975. Part of Twentieth Century Views Series; useful, balanced (perhaps too balanced) anthology of contemporary O'Casey criticism.

KNIGHT, G. WILSON. "Ever a Fighter: On Sean O'Casey's *The Drums of Father Ned,*" *Stand,* IV, 3 (Summer 1960), 15–18. Sympathetic, Christian analysis of *The Drums of Father Ned.*

KOSLOW, JULES. *Sean O'Casey, the Man and his Plays.* New York: Citadel Press, 1966. Oversimplified "political" approach to O'Casey, superseded by more balanced studies.

KRAUSE, DAVID. "O'Casey and Yeats and the Druid," *Modern Drama*, XI (December 1968), 252–62. Reflections provoked by the publication of *Blasts and Benedictions*—contains good summary of the O'Casey-Yeats relationship.

―――. "'The Rageous Ossean': Patron-Hero of Synge and O'Casey," *Modern Drama*, IV, 3 (December 1961), 268–91. Oisin (Ossean)/ St. Patrick = Synge and O'Casey / early twentieth-century Ireland.

―――. *Sean O'Casey: The Man and his Work*. New York & London: Macmillan, 1975. The best book out on Sean O'Casey—excellent background material in first chapter—moving tribute in the last—perceptive criticism in between—perhaps a bit too sympathetic to O'Casey's middle plays.

―――. *Self-portrait of the Artist as a Man*. Dublin: Dolmen, 1968. Uses quotation from O'Casey's letters to illuminate O'Casey, the man.

LINDSAY, JACK. "Sean O'Casey as a Socialist Artist," *Sean O'Casey*, ed. by Ronald Ayling. London: Macmillan, 1969, pp. 192–203. Stresses "central socialist focus" which finds consistent expression even though "O'Casey's artistic vision" grows "deeper and richer as he goes on."

LOWERY, ROBERT G. "O'Casey, Critics, and Communism," *The Sean O'Casey Review*, I, 1 (Fall 1974), 14–18. A perceptive, realistic analysis of O'Casey's communism, a necessary corrective to much criticism on this subject.

MAGALANER, MARVIN. "O'Casey's Autobiography," *Sewanee Review*, LXV, 1 (Winter 1957), pp. 170–74. Comparison of Stephen Dedalus and Johnny Casside opens "interesting avenues of approach to *Mirror in My House*."

MALONE, MAUREEN. *The Plays of Sean O'Casey*. Carbondale: Southern Illinois University Press, 1969. Everything related to O'Casey's "socialist convictions" and adherence to "the tribe of labor." Some convincing documentation of O'Casey's charges against the Catholic Church in modern Ireland.

MARGULIES, MARTIN B. *The Early Life of Sean O'Casey*. Dublin: Dolmen Press, 1970. Provides valuable information about O'Casey's early life—especially interesting comments on O'Casey's older brother Mick.

MCCANN, SEAN., ed. *The World of Sean O'Casey*. London: The New English Library, 1966. Predominantly unreliable Irish gossip—noteworthy exceptions being the articles by Kevin Casey, T. P. Coogan, John O'Donovan, and David Krause.

MIKHAIL, E. H. *Sean O'Casey: A Bibliography of Criticism*. Seattle: University of Washington Press, 1972. The complete bibliography of O'Casey criticism.

————, and JOHN O'RIORDAN, eds. *The Sting and the Twinkle*. London: Macmillan, 1974. Anthology of biographical and autobiographical writing about O'Casey, little new.

MOYA, CARMELA. "The Mirror and the Plough," *The Sean O'Casey Review* II, 2 (Spring 1976), 141–53. Excellent discussion of O'Casey's use of similar dramaturgic techniques in the *Autobiographies* and in *The Plough and the Stars*.

MURPHY, ROBERT P. "Sean O'Casey and 'The Bald Primaqueera,' " *James Joyce Quarterly*, VIII, 1 (Fall 1970), pp. 96–110. "It is clear from the many parallels in structure, use of language, and dramaturgical techniques that O'Casey, despite his protestations to the contrary, is firmly in the tradition of Artaud's theater of cruelty as translated into practicable drama by Ionesco."

NICHOLSON, HUBERT. "The O'Casey Horn of Plenty," in *A Voyage to Wonderland and other Essays*. London: Heinemann, 1947. Sympathetic treatment of *Autobiographies*—especially good on the prison scene in "Royal Risidence."

O'CASEY, EILEEN. *Sean*, Ed. and with Introduction by J. C. Trewin. New York: Coward, McCann & Geoghegan, 1972. Contains much valuable information on and many valuable documents from O'Casey's later life.

ROLLINS, RONALD G. "Clerical Blackness in the Green Garden: Heroine as Scapegoat in *Cock-a-Doodle Dandy*," *James Joyce Quarterly*, VIII, 1 (Fall 1970), pp. 64–75. "O'Casey utilizes ancient scapegoat ceremonials as the formula for arranging and accenting his material, thereby charging his play with a symbolism that is encyclopedic and multi-dimensional."

ROLLINS, RONALD. "Desire vs. Damnation in O'Casey's *Within the Gates* and Donleavy's *The Ginger Man*," *The Sean O'Casey Review*, I, 2 (Spring 1975), 41–47. "O'Casey's mythical drama and Donleavy's picaresque novel emerge as trenchant criticisms of clerical authoritarianism."

RUDIN, SEYMOUR. "Playwright to Critic: Sean O'Casey's Letters to George Jean Nathan," *Massachusetts Review*, V, 2 (Winter 1964), pp. 326–34.

SCRIMGEOUR, JAMES R. "O'Casey's Street People: Characterization in the Autobiographies," *The Sean O'Casey Review*, IV, 1 (Fall 1977), 57–64. Part of chapter one of this book.

SMITH, BOBBY L. "O'Casey's Satiric Vision," *James Joyce Quarterly*, VIII, 1 (Fall 1970), 13–28. Unlike most satirists, "O'Casey's satiric vision includes ample room for joy and laughter, for having a good time, and loving life in the process."

TEMPLETON, JOAN. "O'Casey and Expressionism," *Modern Drama*, XIV (May 1971), 47–62. "Techniques of Expressionistic Drama . . . are found throughout O'Casey's plays [and] his early attempts at Expressionism became a kind of proving ground for his last plays."

TODD, R. MARY. "The Two Published Versions of *Within the Gates*," *Modern Drama*, X, 4 (February 1968), 346–55. Details differences in the two versions focusing on changes in the characters of The Bishop, The Dreamer, and The Young Woman.

WORTH, KATHERINE J. "O'Casey's Dramatic Symbolism," *Modern Drama*, IV, 3 (Kansas, 1961), pp. 183–91. Useful study—especially good on "clothes" and "house" symbolism in O'Casey.

Index

DARE
TO BE
SCARED
4

THIRTEEN MORE
TALES OF TERROR

Dare to Be Scared:
Thirteen Stories to Chill and Thrill

Double-Dare to Be Scared:
Another Thirteen Chilling Tales

Triple-Dare to Be Scared:
Thirteen Further Freaky Tales

DARE
TO BE
SCARED
4

THIRTEEN MORE
TALES OF TERROR

Robert D. San Souci
Illustrations by David Ouimet

Cricket Books
Chicago

Library of Congress Cataloging-in-Publication Data

San Souci, Robert D.
  Dare to be scared 4 : thirteen more tales of terror / Robert D. San Souci ; illustrations by David Ouimet. — 1st ed.
      v. cm.
  Contents: Heading home — Lich gate — Principal's office — Woody — Snow day — Fairy godmother — Violet — A really scary story — Witch — Red rain — Cabin 13 — Smoke hands — Moonrise.
  ISBN-13: 978-0-8126-2754-1
  ISBN-10: 0-8126-2754-7
  1. Horror tales, American. 2. Children's stories, American. [1. Horror stories. 2. Short stories.] I. Ouimet, David, ill. II. Title. III. Title: Dare to be scared four.

PZ7.S1947Dau 2009
[Fic]—dc22
                              2009018490

To all the fans of the
DARE series:

This book is for you!

Contents

Heading Home

Gabriel Carter was supposed to get a ride home from evening basketball practice with Mrs. Jenkins, his friend Kirk's mom. But the two fifth-grade boys, shooting hoops in the gym while waiting for Mr. Atkins, the coach, to arrive, had gotten into an argument over who was likeliest to win the NBA play-offs. This led to on-court showing off, gibes, and name-calling (all encouraged by the other players).

Finally Kirk shouted, "Heads up!" at Gabe's back. As the other boy turned, Kirk launched a "baseball pass" toward his friend's shoulder, but the basketball impacted Gabe in the chest, momentarily knocking the wind out of him and dropping him to his knees. Kirk seemed startled, but offered no apologies. Two of the other players helped Gabe to his feet. When he'd caught his breath, Gabe suddenly launched himself at Kirk, swinging his fists. Kirk began windmilling his own arms defensively.

"Freeze!" bellowed Mr. Atkins. The coach had entered the gym just in time to catch the boys battering at each other. Striding angrily over, he grabbed each by the shoulder and yanked them apart. Ignoring their protests that "*He* started it," the man dragged the boys, now reduced to glaring at each other, to the bleachers and sat them down several feet apart. After a short lecture about sportsmanship, he announced they were sidelined for the rest of the practice — and wouldn't be in the starting lineup against Freeman Elementary on Friday night. Then the coach shooed the other boys, who had been mightily enjoying the bawling out, onto the court to begin the drills.

After watching a few minutes, Gabe stood up, muttering, "I'm going home."

"I don't think Atkins is going to like that," Kirk warned. "Besides, we're giving you a ride. My mom promised to pick us up at 8:30."

But Gabriel ignored this and, with an airy wave, walked away from his former friend. "I'm going home with Maggie Mae," he said. "She's better company than you any day of the week." He headed toward the door at the back of the school auditorium.

"You can't do that," Kirk protested, starting to follow. "If you're not here, I'll get in trouble."

"Good," Gabe replied. Then he thought of Mrs. Jenkins nervously calling his house to be sure he'd arrived safely. That could be a problem. So he added, "Just tell your mom I was feeling sick, and someone drove me home awhile ago. Then neither one of us will get in trouble." That said, he retrieved his backpack from the assortment lining the bleachers farther down, pulled open the gym door, and walked out.

Maggie Mae, the family pet, who had accompanied Gabe to practice, was waiting patiently on the slab of concrete just outside the entrance. She was big — a mix of German shepherd and who-knew-what. Gabe had left her a pie tin of water and a paper plate of kibbles, both of which she had finished. "Good dog! Good girl!" the boy said as she stood up and excitedly licked his face. He wiped the pie tin with Kleenex and put it in his pack while Maggie barked enthusiastically — clearly as eager to be off and away as he was.

He quickly untied the end of her leash from around the guardrail and deposited the Kleenex and the paper plate in one of the trash cans at the foot of the steps. He stood for a minute listening to the muffled shouts and whistle-blowing from inside the gym. He'd half expected Kirk to follow him and try to get him to wait. But the gym door remained tightly closed.

Standing alone, Gabe was suddenly aware of just

how dark it was growing, and how isolated the school was. Bartlett Elementary was only two years old. It had been built as an overflow school to accommodate the large numbers of new families moving into the housing tracts springing up around the town of Parkdale. At the moment, it sat apart on a broad expanse of grassland, though people said it was only a matter of time before Bartlett Elementary found itself in the middle of new housing complexes. In the morning or afternoon, a few kids like Gabe walked or rode bikes to and from school, but most relied on buses or parents to transport them each day.

No youngsters walked or rode bikes after dark. There had been several burglaries and car thefts in the recent past. Though no one had been hurt, parents tended to keep a nervous watch on their children once the sun had set.

Gabe knew his parents would have a cow if they discovered he was walking home this late — even with Maggie Mae as a guard dog. But he didn't intend for them to find out. He planned to take the shortcut along the railroad tracks, which would bring him home much sooner than following the road back. If he was a few minutes late, he'd just tell his big sister, Marlena, who was babysitting while his parents had dinner with friends, that practice had run extra long. She'd probably be so busy talking on her cell phone or texting or watching scary DVDs, she'd never even notice the time.

4

He unhooked the leash from Maggie Mae's collar, and the dog, savoring her freedom, bounded happily away. Maggie returned once to check on him, then raced off again into the tall grass that grew on either side of the dirt path that led to the railroad tracks and the creek running beside it. Kids were supposed to stay away from these twin attractions; they never did.

Children were warned, in particular, *never* to use the railway as a shortcut. Of course, during the day, when no adults were around to stop them, plenty of kids trudged along, jumping from tie to tie or balancing themselves on the rails, often making it a contest to see who could get farthest without a misstep. There were dire warnings about careless walkers run over by a train, but the children shrugged them off. Trains only came through twice a day — once at noon, when kids were in school or under the watchful eyes of their parents; once around midnight, when they were safely tucked in bed. Besides, it was argued, everything was so flat you could see a train coming a mile away — and hear its whistle *two* miles, at least.

But no kid would go near the railroad tracks after sunset. It wasn't parental warnings that stopped them: it was the ghost stories — especially ones the older children told about Dead Man's Curve. But since it wasn't *that* late, and he didn't have *that* far to go, Gabe thought he was safe enough.

The evening was pleasantly mild. The half-moon

gave a soothing soft sheen to the grasses and occasional tree. Ever since the family had moved from Columbus to this quieter stretch of Ohio, Gabe had been fascinated by the sheer numbers of stars he could see without the city glow filtering them out. As he walked along the path, he had to keep reminding himself to watch where he was going and not be so distracted by the show the stars were putting on. He didn't want to step in a gopher hole or trip over a rock.

Now Maggie Mae was barking at something deeper in the grasses. She might have scented a rabbit or a meadow vole. He'd let her run around a little more and then call her back. She was a good dog and always came when she heard her name.

He had reached the railroad tracks and begun following them off to his right, heading north. At the moment he was balancing himself, arms extended, on a rail, trying to set a new personal record for distance. He hoped he could make it all the way to Dead Man's Curve.

It was called that because a long time ago, way back during World War II, there had been a horrible train wreck at that spot. No one ever quite figured out the cause, but the engine had jumped the tracks, jackknifed, and most of the cars, which at the time were filled with troops and civilian passengers, had piled up on top of one another. Lots of people had been hurt or killed — some of them really torn up. Gabe had peeked, with gruesome fascination, at a newspaper photo one of his classmates had gotten from an older brother, who'd found the paper in an antique shop. It was the sort of picture they usually didn't print in papers — except the weird kind at grocery store checkout lines or at newsstands that sold candy, cigars, cigarettes, and magazines or newspapers from all over the world. But, if you knew what you were looking for, you could find all kinds of nasty or creepy images — including dead bodies.

The picture his friend had secretly passed around ranked with the awfulest of the awful. It showed a woman whose head had been cut off. The photo was blurry and yellowed, but you could clearly see that one outflung hand still clutched the strap of a fancy purse while her head was facing up at a totally impossible angle away from her body. Her open eyes gazed sightlessly at the camera, her long black hair spread around her like a fan, and she wore a pretty, if old-fashioned, hat. Gabe had felt sorry, even across the years, for the lady, who was probably on her way into Parkdale for an afternoon of shopping and fun and had died so horribly. Afterward, he wished he hadn't looked at the photograph, because the image came back to haunt him from time to time.

Even without the chilling photo, plenty of ghost stories had grown up around the site of the wreck. An older kid would tell spellbound younger children that, on certain nights, you could see "Awful Annie's" ghost. Lowering his or her voice, the storyteller would force the audience to come closer while describing the ghost as the spirit of a woman sliced in two in the train wreck. If you were lucky, you'd only see her lower half, walking along the tracks. The unfortunate, however, would run into her upper torso, clawing its way from crosstie to crosstie. "Have you seen the rest of me?" she'd ask, sounding very sad. "I've lost my legs." The storyteller would drop his or her voice to a whisper, and the little ones would lean in. Then the storyteller would suddenly shout, "MAYBE I'LL TAKE YOURS!" and grab the knee of the nearest child, bringing shouts and screams from all the listeners, not just the victim.

Gabe had been caught by this "Gotcha!" story the first week he transferred to Bartlett.

Thinking about the old picture and the story, he lost his concentration and dropped with a *crunch!* onto the gravel ballast between two ties. He was close, but he hadn't actually reached Dead Man's Curve.

A breeze rippled the grass and rattled the leaves of a nearby oak. Suddenly, he was no longer interested in setting a record for rail-walking. He just wanted to get home. It registered how empty and extremely quiet the landscape around him was. Even the normally loud buzzing of crickets seemed subdued. He began to walk faster, taking two ties at a time. "Maggie Mae!" he called, then whistled. "Here, girl!"

To his relief, the dog ran up to him, barking a greeting. Gratefully, he patted her head and scratched behind her ears. "Stay!" he commanded, when she looked ready to charge off again. "Heel!"

She gave a disappointed soft whine, but she obeyed. Together they trotted toward the point where the train tracks veered in an easterly direction. In the distance, Gabe could see pinpoints of light that marked the outermost houses of Meadowview, the tract where his family had their home. This, added to Maggie Mae's cheerful presence, made him feel better yet.

Suddenly, to his surprise, the boy saw a shadowy figure following the tracks, walking slowly away from him. He stopped, peering ahead into the gloom. For a terrifying moment he recalled the story of "Awful Annie" haunting the nighttime tracks. Then he realized the figure was a tall, thin female — a *complete* woman — making her unhurried way toward the scattered lights. He guessed it was someone else taking the same shortcut. The fact that it was a woman made her unexpected appearance much less frightening. It might even be someone he knew. He was too far away to see much, except that the breeze was lightly billowing her skirt, and her head was covered with a scarf of some pale, shiny fabric.

Still, the sight made him pause. Beside him, Maggie Mae whined and suddenly balked, refusing to go farther. Impatient to get home, Gabe reached down and

hooked the leash to the dog's collar. He began moving ahead, slowing his pace to match the woman's more easygoing stride. For no particular reason, he hung back, not wanting to overtake the retreating figure. Maggie Mae was even more reluctant to follow. She tried to dig her paws into the gravel of the track bed, but her master tugged more firmly on the leash and ordered her to "Heel!" and she obeyed, though she continued to make the unnerving whine.

To his growing unease, Gabe realized the woman was slowing down. Then she stopped and glanced back at him; he could make out a black oval of a face framed by the pale scarf. She made no effort to move; clearly she was waiting for him to catch up.

Uncertain what to do, Gabe stopped walking. Obviously happy to stay put, Maggie Mae lay down to wait along with him. The chirrups of the crickets seemed pretty well hushed. The moon was sliding down the sky, and shadows were growing darker. Ahead, just around the curve where the woman stood waiting, the lights of Meadowview teased him with their nearness.

I've got my dog, Gabe assured himself. *If she's a crazy person, I'll just take off running.* He was confident he could leave any troublemaker eating his dust since he was always the fastest at laps during P.E. "Get up," he urged Maggie Mae. At first she refused, but a rough yank on her leash roused the dog. Yet Gabe found he had to keep tugging at her; the whine in her throat had thickened into a persistent growl.

The woman waved them forward. Her voice was faint and slightly muffled. "Come along, boy; I won't bite." He heard soft laughter. "I'd enjoy a little company the rest of the way home."

As he approached, he saw that she was carrying a bright red paper shopping bag. On the side, in fancy white script, was the name *Gaynor's Department Store*. The words rang a bell, though there was no Gaynor's in downtown Parkdale or in any of the newer strip malls springing up as the town expanded ever outward.

It was getting more difficult to haul Maggie Mae forward. If he pulled any harder on the leash, he was afraid he might hurt her. "What's the matter with your puppy?" the woman asked. "She's a stubborn one. I haven't got all night." Her voice was pleasant enough, but he sensed a hint of mockery in it. Even stranger was that her voice seemed to come from somewhere *outside* her. It must be a trick of the uncertain light, he decided.

He still couldn't make out her face. Now she was gazing down at the shopping bag clutched in her right hand. It seemed to hold something good-sized and fairly heavy. Reading the store name a second time suddenly brought back memories to Gabe.

Years ago, during World War II and right after, his grandaunt Gretchen had been a saleslady at Gaynor's Department Store — then the biggest store for miles around. She used to talk about it when he and his family went to visit her in an assisted-living facility on the south side of town. The old woman had died of pneumonia six months ago; but though bedridden for the last part of her life, she remained clearheaded right to the end. Mostly she'd reminisce about "the old days" — fondly recalling her long employment at Gaynor's.

"I had lots of good friends there," she'd say. "Of course, it was the war. Most of the men were in uniform in Europe or Asia, so the place was pretty much run by us gals. My two best friends were Maxine Parr and Laura Trask. We were called 'Parkdale's Own Andrews Sisters' back then." (She always said this with a laugh.) "We would sing together at the big in-store Christmas party, at weddings, whenever people would ask us. Mostly we'd sing swing numbers — we actually *did* sound like the Andrews Sisters — well, a *little*." (Another laugh.) "But Laura had the best voice. Sometimes she'd sing a solo or two, and Maxine and I would just hum along and back her up. People always said she should have had a career singing with a big band — one of those famous ones like Glenn Miller's."

Here the old woman would close her eyes, and Gabe guessed she was remembering.

"Well, it doesn't matter now. But she could have been a real star like Dinah Shore or Rosemary Clooney —"

Abruptly, she'd give a laugh, much softer this time, and say to the boy, "I'm boring you, aren't I?"

"Oh no," he would protest, not very convincingly.

"You're not much of a liar," she'd say. Then her smile would fade. "Poor Laura," Grandaunt Gretchen would always add, with a sad little shake of her head. "Poor thing." Then she'd change the topic.

It was about two years ago when Gabe had asked, "Why do you call her 'poor thing'?"

With a sigh, the old woman explained. "She died in that horrible train crash in 1945. She had taken the morning off, but was coming into Parkdale for the afternoon shift. The three of us were going out to dinner afterward. She had something 'wonderful' to tell us. I think she had finally become engaged to that airman — I can't even remember his name now — who was sweet on her, and who had been visiting her a lot while he was on leave. She had spent the morning with him. I saw him at her funeral, and then none of us ever saw him again. Whatever happened to her that day must have been terrible. They kept her casket closed at the wake and during her funeral. It was too awful to see," she added with a shudder.

Suddenly Maggie Mae gave a ferocious yank on the leash, jerking Gabe out of his memories. Her unexpected, frantic movement pulled the leather loop out of his hand, nearly taking a couple of fingers with it. Then the dog was loping away into the grass with the leash trailing behind her. Gabe shouted after her, but she was clearly bent on getting out of Dodge. In a moment the shadowed grass had swallowed her up.

"It looks like someone doesn't want to be sociable," commented the woman. Again, Gabe thought he heard the tiniest bit of amusement in her voice.

But he wasn't really paying attention. "She's never done anything like that before," he said, puzzled. "If she doesn't head home pretty quickly, I'm going to be in deep doo-doo." He waved his hand in the cool air to relieve the sting of the leather burn.

"Well, it sounds as if we both need to get on our way," said the woman.

More concerned about his dog and what his parents would say if she managed to get lost, Gabe hardly realized that he was now walking beside the woman, on her right. He peered at her more closely, but she was looking away, apparently examining something far off on her side of the track.

Curious, he snuck a peek into her shopping bag. Inside, a large roundish something was wrapped in layers of white tissue paper. It was impossible for him to guess what it might be.

She had started walking again. This time her long, thin legs were making rapid strides, so he had to speed up to keep pace with her.

From time to time, he'd cup his hands around his mouth and call, "Maggie Mae!" But there was no answering bark, no sudden reappearance from the emptiness on all sides.

Gabe regretted passing up the chance to ride with Kirk — even if they weren't speaking. *I'd be safe by now,* he thought miserably, *and so would Maggie Mae.* He tried to tell himself there was a good chance the dog had headed for home and was already waiting for him.

With so many thoughts crowding his mind, it took him a minute to realize he was hearing soft music. Someone — a woman — was singing faintly, sweetly. It sounded like radio or TV music heard from afar, maybe through a closed door or window.

The voice couldn't be his shadowy companion's, but it was coming from the shopping bag she carried. *Is the tissue-wrapped item a radio or a portable CD player that's accidentally turned itself on?* he wondered.

Suddenly he stopped, chilled to the bone. He recognized the tune as one that his grandaunt Gretchen had often sung, a famous song the old woman had said always reminded her of her doomed friend.

His grandaunt's stories flooded back into his mind.

"I know that song," he said, his voice little more than a whisper.

"Do you?" The voice seemed to float into his ears from nowhere, from everywhere.

"It's an old song. It's called 'Laura.'"

"Oh yes. It's my favorite." Now she began to laugh, light and bubbly, clearly mocking him. But the laughter, he realized to his horror, wasn't coming from the woman. *It was coming from inside the shopping bag!*

With a groan of pure fright, he took a big step backward, then another.

The woman whirled about to confront him; the wind, toying with the edge of her scarf, blew it across her face, still hidden in shadow. The laughter pouring from the bag came loudly and shrilly now. Gabe backed away, afraid to take his eyes off the woman.

"Don't you think we should meet face to face?" she asked. Abruptly, she grabbed the sides of the shopping bag and dumped the contents onto the ground. Something heavy bounced and rolled toward him, the tissue paper shredding as it snagged on the gravel ballast and the splintery wood of the crossties, leaving a trail of white ribbons behind.

"Don't be standoffish, boy!" the unwrapped head cried. The woman raised her hands and pulled back her scarf. The shiny cloth draped itself across her shoulders, revealing only empty air. As Gabe watched, the figure's shoulders shook, but the sound of the laughter poured from the head that had rolled to a stop inches from his feet.

After a moment or two in which he was too paralyzed with fear to do anything, the boy took off running down the tracks, back the way he had come — faster than he had ever run before. When he dared to look over his shoulder, he saw that the woman was holding the head, dangling it at the end of its long black tresses. Then she began shifting it from hand to hand as if making ready to hurl it. For a crazy moment, he thought of Coach Atkins casually tossing a basketball from palm to palm while lecturing his young players on the finer points of the game.

Swiveling his head back and forth to keep safe footing on the track, yet see what was happening behind him, Gabe watched her launch the dreadful thing. It was an amazing toss, a perfect one-handed "baseball pass." The horror flew past him into the wild grasses and weeds a little distance ahead. Then, impossibly, it rolled out of the weeds, over the metal rail, and righted itself, facing him midpoint on a crosstie. The eyes were glittering in a cruel way, and it was snapping its teeth dangerously, for all the world like an angry dog. He turned instinctively and saw the body, its arms outstretched, loping toward him from the other direction.

He tried to decide which way to flee. To the side of the tracks that was closer to the housing developments and the road? To the side that led to the fields and distant edge of a wood beyond the stream?

He knew the potholes and barbed wire fencing on the town side might trip him up. Maybe he could avoid the nightmare figure by running his fastest and zigzagging across the level meadow. He leaped off the tracks, splashed across the creek, and ran a good ways into the field before he looked back.

He was surprised to see the animated torso now

carrying the head in its arms, like a mother cradling an infant, as it paced up and down the bank of the stream. But something seemed to prevent it from coming after him. Puzzled, poised to break into a run at a second's notice, Gabe stood panting, catching his breath, as he watched the figure in its wind-whipped skirts and billowing scarf tramp up and down the edge of the creek. At times it would stand stock-still, holding the head at chest height. Though it was only a shadowy shape, the boy was sure he could feel the glittery eyes in the head watching him, just as he was sure, even from so far away, he could hear the teeth snapping in frustration.

Then came a scream of anger so loud that the boy had to clap his hands to his ears. But as the sound died away, the figure melted into the shadows and vanished.

Still shaken, he stumbled in the direction of home, keeping resolutely to the safe side of the creek, always on the alert for the return of the dark figure. As his fears gradually ebbed, he remembered another thing his grandaunt Gretchen had told him. She had come to America from England just before the war. She was very serious about things like ghosts and other supernatural creatures, and he would often get a thrill from listening to her old stories. Now he remembered her telling him once, long before, "If you are ever troubled by a ghost, cross the nearest stream. A ghost cannot pass over moving water."

The lights of Meadowview were comfortably close.

In a little while, he'd dare to wade the creek and reach home. He knew he was going to be very late, and he'd probably walk into a buzz saw of questions and accusations from his parents. He wasn't sure what to tell them, but he was certain they wouldn't buy the truth.

He had just recrossed the creek, anxiously watching for a return of the ghostly figure, when Maggie Mae came bounding up, barking and running in circles around him, as though they'd just shared a wonderful adventure together. With a laugh, he called to her, and the two set off running for home. It had been a terrifying encounter. But when he saw his classmates tomorrow, he would have a great story to tell. Better even than "Awful Annie."

He knew one other thing for sure: he'd never use the railroad tracks again as a shortcut.

Never, ever!

Lich Gate

Amanda Henderson had never been to England; she had never met her grandparents, her mother's father and mother. Her mother rarely spoke of them. To Amanda, it seemed she was more than content to be in San Jose, California, half a world away from the place she had grown up. Amanda's mother and her grandmother exchanged occasional letters, and once a year Mrs. Henderson called to wish her own mother happy holidays. When she was old enough, Amanda was put on the line to say "hello" and "Merry Christmas" to the old lady with the funny accent.

She was never invited to speak to her grandfather. When the girl asked her mother about him, the woman's eyes and mouth grew hard. "He had a cruel streak and a ready fist," she'd say. "Once he nearly dislocated my jaw when he said I'd sassed him. I hadn't — only had the nerve to suggest he was wrong about something. I don't remember the reason, only the hurt."

To Amanda, now nine, it seemed sad that she had never met her grandmother, at least. But Amanda's grandmother was only a thin, worn voice on the phone. Apparently "Nana-there," as she called her to distinguish from her father's widowed mother, "Nana-here," had never had a computer, so there was no way to exchange e-mails or photos. Her mother had a couple of cheap photographs tucked in a drawer, but the colors were fading, and everyone's skin looked orangey. Most were just of "Nana-there," sitting in a chair or standing in a garden. She never smiled — just stared into the camera as if she wished whoever was taking the picture would go away and leave her alone.

Only one photograph had both grandparents in it. The picture looked like it had been snapped in a kitchen. Her grandmother was sitting on a straight-backed chair; on the table in front of her was a blue glass mixing bowl, a dented flour tin, and a wooden spoon. Amanda's grandfather was standing right behind his wife, his two hands resting on her shoulders. He was brawny, broad-featured, with hands the size of shovels. Amanda shivered at the picture, imagining that hand slamming into her mother's tender jaw. In contrast, his wife was petite, tight-featured, with doll-like hands clasped on the table before her. But they had the same grin — like two people who shared a secret no one else could ever guess. It was the only picture of Nana-there in which she looked contented.

When Amanda said, "They look happy," her mother replied, "Maybe they were. It was hard to know what they were thinking most of the time. They had little use for the world outside the farm. And the world returned the favor. As a child I was shunned because of them. I never felt wanted anywhere when I was little. Leaving that place, that town, the whole country was the easiest thing I ever did."

The girl took a final look at the picture. The old man wore round metal-rimmed glasses with lenses thick as bottle bottoms. They made his eyes seem huge. And there was something about the way he was staring directly into the camera that led Amanda to think, when she was smaller, that somehow he was gazing hungrily across the years and miles right into her own eyes. She still found it uncomfortable to look at the photograph.

But now, her grandfather was dying. There had been a flurry of phone calls from her grandmother. From things half heard, Amanda gathered that her mother did not want to go back for a last visit, even though, apparently, her father was asking for her and her mother was begging. It was Amanda's father, Jerry, who decided the issue. "If you don't go," she heard him tell her mother while they were sitting in the kitchen, sure that Amanda was absorbed in cartoons in the adjoining room, "you'll always feel a twinge of guilt." It struck the girl as funny that adults didn't think she could be doing two things quite comfortably at once. Yes, she was watching the *Powerpuff Girls*, and, yes, she was also tuned in to what her parents were discussing.

"I don't think I can face him," her mother said. "He was an awful parent."

"He's *dying*, Mona," her father said. He was such a gentle, kind man; he always tried to see everyone's point of view. *Even when they don't deserve it*, thought Amanda, remembering what her mother had been through.

"The world will be better off when he's gone," her mother said bitterly. The girl was shocked to hear such a thing said about a parent, any parent.

"Then let this be closure," her father said doggedly. "Support your mother, and let the past go. Show him what a good, strong person you've become. He may be regretting what happened; that may be why he's called you back."

"I know him," her mother said. "He'll regret nothing. I can't imagine why, after so many years, he even wants to see me."

"*Us*," her father said. "He asked for the family. I don't think he gives a hoot for me, but Amanda — she's blood kin. Don't deny him this one chance to see his only grandchild. Anything else would seem cruel," he said. Then he added, "And, Mona, I know you're not a cruel person. I realize he hurt you, but this is the end. For all our sakes, I think we'd better go."

Amanda heard her mother make a small, choking sound in her throat. Then, glancing away from the TV to the kitchen table, she saw her mother clasp her father's hand in her own. "You're right," she said. "I only wish I had a heart and soul half as big as yours. I hope Amanda takes after you, not me."

"She's a part of both of us," her husband said. He leaned over and kissed Mona. Amanda returned her attention to the TV, but now she was trying to imagine what England would be like.

They left shortly after a final call to her English grandmother, outlining their plans. It was December, two weeks before St. John's Episcopal School was out for the holidays, but her parents had cleared everything with Sister Imelda, calling the visit a "family emergency." But all the time they were planning and packing, Amanda could see her mother was struggling, as her father kept putting it, "to go with the program." Every minute that brought them closer to departure seemed to make her mother more uneasy. When they were finally boarding the plane at San Francisco International Airport, Amanda felt excited, but her mother was so jittery, she seemed almost ready to run away. Her father kept patting her shoulder, like somebody comforting a frightened child.

Whatever expectations Amanda had about England were sadly disappointed. She had been expecting an exciting world of trendy music and musicians; amazing, glittery shopping districts; glorious castles filled with antiques and armor and history; and royalty and rock stars *everywhere*.

What she found was distressingly otherwise. She only had a glimpse of London the one night between their arrival at Heathrow Airport and their departure the next morning in a rented car for the town where her grandparents lived. She was so tired from seemingly endless hours on the plane that she fell asleep in the taxi to their hotel. She only woke up when her mother roused her for a late breakfast before getting ready for the last part of their trip.

Amanda was surprised to find the steering wheel on the wrong side of the dashboard and to realize that cars were all traveling on the wrong side of the road. She had been so sleepy the evening before, she'd never even noticed. She asked her father, who was driving, if it wasn't a problem, but he reminded her he'd been in London several times on business (though he had never attempted a visit to his in-laws). *"No problemo,"* he announced, and they were soon heading north to the little town called Weeming Downs that, Amanda understood, wasn't very far from the coast. Maybe there'd be sunny beaches to visit and even a boardwalk with rides like the one she'd visited in Santa Cruz on a recent family outing. Maybe there'd be a chance to get away from the sad business of her grandfather's dying.

But the closer they got to their destination, the worse things looked. The sky, which had already been gloomy in London, had turned into a solid sheet of wintry gray. Looking out the car window, Amanda saw unpleasant, unbroken, slightly misty marshlands with nothing but clumps of ugly brown reeds and the black outlines of scraggly trees to break the monotony. The only signs of life were occasional black crows or white gulls screeching above the waste.

Amanda's mother grew more quiet and worried-looking with every mile that passed. From time to time her father would reach over and squeeze her mother's hand, as though reassuring her that everything would work out fine.

The town of Weeming Downs turned out to be little more than a sad collection of dingy stone houses and a few shops whose windows looked dark and uninviting. The people Amanda saw on the twisty streets appeared withered and bleached — as lifeless and colorless as the landscape.

Her grandparents' house on the far side of town, down a stretch of country lane that branched off from the main road. It was already getting dark when they saw the house. It stood on a slight rise, ringed by dying trees. A waist-high brick wall, covered with damp, mossy gunk of blue, green, and white, separated the house and garden from the lane. Jerry Henderson brought the car to a halt near the rusty garden gate.

Amanda's mother said simply, "Oh," then gave a shuddering sigh and stared at the house — a good-sized, two-story place with a tiled roof. Like everything else, it looked dank and mildewed to Amanda. Her father tried his best to sound cheery as he announced, "Here's the welcoming committee — your mother."

Now Amanda could see her grandmother, who looked even thinner and more worn than her photographs, walking down the brick path to greet them. Jerry quickly opened the passenger-side doors so Amanda and her mother could climb out. Mona Henderson just stared at the figure; Amanda, feeling her tension, half hid behind her mother, watching the pale, white-haired, ghostly-looking woman approach.

Jerry tried to break the ice. "Hello, Mother Bowen — Flora — at last we meet." He gave the old woman a gentle hug to which her only response was to look vaguely uncomfortable.

Mona went next, taking her mother's hands in her own, leaning down and kissing the slightly sunken cheek. "Hello, Mother," she said. "How is *he* today?"

"It's a better day," the older woman said. "*Himself's*

asleep now. We can look in on him later." Amanda could hear the coolness in her voice.

Then the old woman's faintly blue and watery eyes locked on Amanda's. The dullness there gave way to an unexpected brightness. The ghost of a smile played around the thin, dry lips. "And this would be Amanda," she said, reaching out her hand to the girl. After a moment's hesitation, Amanda gave it a tentative shake. "Surely you can do better than *that*," said the woman teasingly. "Give your nana a kiss." Helplessly, Amanda glanced at her father and mother, who both nodded. Dutifully, she kissed the dry, powdery cheek that smelled both flowery and sour at the same time.

"Now, come inside," said Flora, more animated. "Let's get you unpacked and settled in, and then we'll have tea. Your grandfather rarely wakes from his afternoon nap before five," she told Amanda.

As they carried suitcases into the house, the girl saw that the garden was badly neglected — nothing but patches of weeds, rangy shrubs, and the occasional skeleton of a dead rosebush propped up by a rotting trellis. But the windows of the house were sparkling clean, with crisp white curtains, and the brass doorknob and knocker looked freshly polished. The interior, though filled with shadows that Amanda found unsettling, was pleasantly warm and fragrant with scents of baking and cleaning.

Her mother and father were given the larger guest

bedroom at the back of the first floor. Amanda was given a small room at the end of the upstairs hallway. To reach it, she had to pass the closed door behind which her grandfather lay asleep. "Always be very careful not to disturb him," Nana Flora said in a whisper. Her grandmother slept in a small room at the opposite end of the hall. But she could climb the stairs and go to her room without passing the sickroom door. Amanda wished their rooms were reversed, but there was nothing she could do about it. She was very careful to tiptoe past her grandfather's door, scarcely daring to breathe, for fear of disturbing the unseen sleeper.

It turned out her room had been her mother's years before. While mother and daughter unpacked Amanda's things, Mona looked around, occasionally murmuring, "I remember the vanity. How do you like that? The bottom drawer still sticks, though Pa was always promising to fix it. I saved up my allowance to buy this comforter with the flowery ruffles." To Amanda, her voice had the flatness of a tour guide at a museum, as if she felt nothing about her past.

"The picture of the wintry meadow and river there was a gift from an old aunt of mine. I hated it. I thought it was too dark and depressing," Mona continued. "I wanted something with flowers and bright colors, but your grandfather said it was the gift of a very important family member: his aunt Elspeth. I only saw her a few times. She was ancient when I knew her." Amanda's mother gave a bitter little laugh. "I always thought she was a witch and tried to hide when she came to visit. My father didn't like that one bit." She quickly changed the subject. "Let's hurry and put the last of your things away so we can have tea. I'm starved."

They "took tea" in the parlor (Amanda would have called it the "living room"), with a couch and heavy matching chairs upholstered in thick, slightly shiny green material. Everything was covered, arms and backrests, with lacy cloths Amanda called "doilies," until her grandmother said, "They're anti-macassars — to keep everything clean."

It was a nice tea with delicious almond-flavored cookies (Nana Flora called them "biscuits"), berry shortcake, and lemon scones. Amanda hungrily sampled them all. She would have preferred a Coke, but she politely accepted the cup of tea her grandmother served, though she did add a lot of extra sugar. The food and drink and talk seemed to make even Amanda's mother feel more comfortable. Suddenly, Flora Bowen glanced at the clock on the mantel and stood up. "I'd better check on *himself*."

After Nana Flora left the room, Amanda helped her mother gather up the tea things. Her father picked up a magazine from the rack beside the couch and began thumbing through it without much interest.

There was no dishwasher in the kitchen. Mona

washed things up in a plastic dishpan and set them in a drainer to dry, while Amanda sat at the little table, doodling on paper napkins from the holder. Out of the corner of her eye, she watched her mother, who seemed nervous again. One teacup slipped out of her soapy hands and broke in the sink. As she cleaned it up, she said, more to herself than Amanda, "Thank goodness it's only the everyday china — not the service Aunt Elspeth left them. I'd *never* hear the end of that!" She wrinkled her nose at the mention of the dreadful relative.

By the time they had rejoined her father in the parlor, Amanda's grandmother was coming downstairs. She paused in the hall doorway to announce, "*Himself* is awake and asking for all of you." She turned and started back up the steps.

"The moment of truth," Jerry said softly. He gave his wife a squeeze. Mona looked tense and brittle as a bundle of sticks — as if she would snap in half if he squeezed too hard. Together, holding hands, Amanda's parents followed Nana Flora upstairs. Amanda, without being told, came after them — curious and fearful of finally meeting her grandfather.

The bedroom door was open. Nana Flora stood just inside, her eyes fixed on her bedridden husband, her arms folded across her chest. *She looks like a nurse,* Amanda thought.

The room was big — maybe the biggest room in the

house. The huge double bed was of polished dark wood with a waxy look to it. Fancy scrollwork decorated the footboard, while the elaborately carved headboard had what looked like a rising sun — the upper half of a circle with rays surrounding it, coming up over a low mountain range.

Her grandfather lay like a long, skinny shape under a heavy gray comforter. He was propped up on mounded pillows piled against the headboard. His head had only a few strands of wispy hair. He wasn't wearing his glasses, and his eyes looked tiny and red and rabbity to Amanda. The flesh of his neck and his arms, which lay outside the blanket, hung loose, as though the man inside had shrunk far smaller than his skin.

Her mother, still holding tight to her father's hand, walked to the side of the bed. Amanda trailed after them.

"Hello, Father," said Mona, her voice shaky.

"*Glasses!*" the old man snapped, the sound like a frog's croak. He hitched himself higher on his pillows. Mona glanced down, located the familiar round spectacles on the nightstand, and held them out to her father.

When these were securely perched on the bridge of his nose, his eyes looked as big and round as in the photograph back in California. *Why, Grandpa, what big eyes you have,* Amanda thought and felt herself dangerously near a fit of the giggles. *Don't you dare,* she

told herself sternly. She knew she would embarrass all of them.

"So, the prodigal daughter returns," James Bowen said in his dust-dry voice. "Sorry there's no fatted calf, but I'm sure your mother will be able to rustle up a veal loaf." Amanda didn't understand what he was referring to, but she was sure his words were a put-down of some kind.

"It's nice to see you, too," his daughter responded. To Amanda, it sounded as if she didn't see *anything* nice about their reunion.

"And this is — sorry, sir, forgive an old man's fading memory" — he waved a bony hand vaguely at Amanda's father — "your name escapes me." He made it sound as if Amanda's father were someone not worth knowing.

"Gerald," the younger man said, adding hastily, "Please call me Jerry."

"Of course, *Jerry*. We're all family here. Together again for the very first time." He chuckled as though he'd made a joke, but no one else was smiling. Abruptly, his rasping laugh turned into a bout of coughing that shook his body. Mona took a half-step toward him, but he waved her away. "It will pass," he managed to gasp out, "it and everything." He pressed a wad of tissues to his mouth, and the spasms gradually subsided.

Once he had the coughing fully under control, he looked past his daughter and son-in-law at Amanda.

"And this must be Amanda," he said, crooking his finger, beckoning her to come closer. Her parents backed away to let her approach the bedside. "I won't bite," he said. "But these old eyes don't see as well as they once did."

He studied her closely a moment or two. Again, she had the crazy feeling that she was Little Red Riding Hood facing the wolf-as-grandma (or grandpa). She choked back another nervous giggle. At last he said, "Oh yes, you've got Mona's red hair and her nose. And your grandaunt Elspeth's chin — lots of strength and determination there. Yes, yes, you're a Bowen through and through." At this, a look passed between him and his wife that only Amanda seemed to notice.

She wanted to say, *I'm Amanda HENDERSON,* but she knew it would be wrong to argue with such a sick person. Somehow she managed to rearrange her face into what she hoped was a sweet expression. More than anything she wanted to be away from the sickroom smell, the tension that crackled in the air all around her, and the old man whose words sounded mean even when they didn't seem to be saying anything cruel, and whose eyes gazed at her wolf-hungry.

"I'm so very glad you've come to see me," her grandfather said. His words could have been addressed to her mother and father, as well as herself, but Amanda had the feeling they were meant only for her — and she sensed something deeper hidden inside them.

Unexpectedly, the old man seemed to weaken. Behind the circles of his glasses, his eyelids drooped. With a small grunt, he fell back onto the pillows.

Nana Flora, who had remained silent during the brief exchanges, said, *"Himself's* tired. You go now; I'll make sure he's comfortable." Amanda was glad to leave the room, but she was sure her mother was even more relieved. As they slowly made their way downstairs, Amanda wondered, *How are we going to stand two weeks here?* It hadn't even been a full day yet, and she already hated and feared the place for reasons that made no sense to her.

That night she had a nightmare. She was standing in what was sometimes the hallway, facing her grandfather's sealed bedroom door, and other times she seemed to be outdoors, where she stood before a curious closed wooden gate beneath a small peaked roof supported by two high walls. On either side of the gate, a rusty iron fence ran left and right as far as her eyes could see. In her dream, blood-red mist seeped from under the closed bedroom door, and blood-red mist filled the meadow beyond the gate. Dream-Amanda sensed something waiting on the other side of the door, while a shadowy shape made its way through the mist toward the gate. *Run!* she warned her dream-self, but she couldn't move. What would soon yank open the door, and somehow at the same time wrench open the gate, was coming for her, but she remained frozen in place.

The doorknob began to turn; a dark shape loomed out of the crimson mist. In her dream, she heard the click and creak of the door as it opened; she heard the squeal of rusty hinges on the gate. Through door and gate, large arms, the skin pale and sagging like loose rags, reached for her. Terrified, she found her voice and screamed. . . .

She awoke suddenly in her mother's old room. She wondered if she really *had* screamed, but since no one rushed in to find out what was happening and to warn her not to disturb the sick old man down the hall, she figured her cry had only been a dream-scream. Fortunately, the details of the nightmare were already fading like morning mist under a warming sun.

By now she was wide awake. Though she was thirsty, too, she didn't want to drink the bathroom water. When she had brushed her teeth earlier, the water from the tap had tasted rusty and gritty. But she knew there were plastic bottles of Evian water in the refrigerator, left over from the family drive to Weeming Downs. Climbing out of bed, she opened the door a crack.

The night-light was on in the hall. Her grandfather's and grandmother's doors were closed. Opening and shutting her door as quietly as she could, she started down the hallway. Again, she took special care past the old man's door, dreading his calling out and demanding who was making a disturbance.

She reached the head of the stairs without a problem. The second step down gave a loud *creak* underfoot; she froze, afraid she might have woken up the household. But all she heard was the ticking of the parlor clock.

A lamp on the narrow table in the hall below had been left on at its lowest setting; it gave more than enough light for her to reach the kitchen. There she eased the refrigerator door open and took out a water bottle. On an impulse, she lifted the lid on Nana Flora's pig-in-a-wig cookie jar and helped herself to two of the almond-flavored "biscuits" she'd liked at tea. She slipped these into the pocket of her robe and went back upstairs, being especially careful of the second step from the top.

She was just passing her grandfather's door, when she heard someone whisper, *"Amanda."* She paused in midstep. Deciding it was only her imagination, she continued down the hall toward her room.

"Amanda." There was no mistake. Someone *was* calling her. To her horror, she realized the sound was coming from her grandfather's room.

"Amanda, come in, girl. Come in." There was no mistaking James Bowen's raspy voice.

Could she run to her room and pretend she hadn't heard his call? But something warned her he knew she *had* heard and would be very angry if she disobeyed.

"*Now*, girl. Time is precious." She dared not ignore him. With a shaking hand, she turned the glass knob on the bedroom door and entered.

Someone — Nana Flora, of course — had draped a red cloth or scarf over the lamp on the nightstand. Her grandfather lay propped up in bed as Amanda had seen him earlier. In the half-light, his spectacles glowed like two circles of pure red. To Amanda, it was like looking into a robot's eyes on a *Star Wars* DVD. But, in a way, it was a relief not to have to look into his real eyes.

"So you couldn't sleep, either," said the old man. He patted his side of the bed, indicating she should sit with him. Not wanting to hurt his feelings or make him angry, Amanda perched at the foot of the bed, leaning her back against the footboard. She was aware of her grandfather's legs shifting under the comforter beside her. He continued, "I can sleep during the day, but not very much at night. Night is important to the Bowens. We do our best . . . thinking . . . at night. It doesn't surprise me you're a night owl, too; it's in our blood." He gave her a smile that, under the twin red circles of his glasses, looked not at all pleasant.

"I was thirsty," Amanda said. "I went to the kitchen for some water." She held up the bottle she was clutching in her hand.

"Yes. I heard you going *and* coming."

"I tried to be quiet. I didn't want to bother you."

"Oh, you couldn't be a bother. I was waiting for you.

I wanted to have a private little talk." There seemed to be so much meaning lurking just below the words.

"What did you want to talk about?" she asked.

"About when I pass on." He said this so matter-of-factly that Amanda was startled. She asked herself, *How can he talk about his own death and sound as if it were no more important to him than running an errand or planning a vacation?* Unable to think of anything to say, she said nothing.

Her silence didn't seem to bother him. He explained, "You're going to play a very important part in my crossing over. *Very important.*" He tented his fingers under his chin and stared at her for a long time before continuing, "When you attend my funeral — "

"But," she interrupted, "we're only staying two weeks. We'll be back in California before . . . before . . ." She stopped, unsure how to express herself. It seemed the very height of cruelty to agree with him that he might be dying — might soon be dead.

"Hush, girl! Just listen! We Bowens always know — well, sometimes more than we might want to know. But it can be an advantage. It gives us time to prepare." He nodded eagerly; the legs under the comforter shifted as though a momentary burst of energy had filled his body. "I couldn't go until you were here. Now things are falling into place just as they should." He paused and gasped for breath. Amanda was afraid he was going to have a coughing fit, but he seemed to cut it short by sheer will power.

"It won't be long now," he said, suddenly sounding very tired. "But you and I must make a pact."

"What's a pact?"

"A special agreement. A bargain."

"'Kay," she said, hesitantly.

"On the third night after my funeral, I want you to come to the lich gate of the churchyard where all the Bowens — even the disgraced — are buried." He gave her a knowing smile. "No one would dare deny us passage through that gate."

"But what *is* a lich gate?"

"Oh," he said with a chuckle, "it sounds scary, but it's not. *Lich* is an old word meaning 'body.' Every coffin is carried into the cemetery through the lich gate. The one at the village church is simple — not much more than a shed with two open ends, and the special gate in the middle. I want you to promise that on the third night after I'm buried, you'll come to the gate."

"What else do I have to do?"

His voice was now so soft, Amanda had to lean toward him to hear. "It's very simple. At exactly midnight, just unlatch the gate and call my name three times."

"What happens then?"

"Then my soul will find its true resting place."

"I don't understand. Won't you be in heaven already?" She was remembering what Sister Imelda had taught her at school. Nothing that her grandfather was talking about seemed to match what the nun had said about dying and what the Bible said happens next.

Without warning, he leaned forward and grabbed her two hands in his. They were bony, with skin like old tissue paper, but his grip was strong.

"Ouch, Grandpa, you're hurting me," she protested, trying to pull her hands free.

He ignored her, saying fiercely, "You've promised me. If you don't do what you promised, something bad — *very bad* — will happen to you." He wasn't smiling now. With the grim line of his mouth, his painful hold, and his threatening words, Amanda glimpsed what her mother must have seen when she was a girl. She understood why her mother had left this place as soon as she could.

"I promise," she said, making her voice sound as sincere as possible.

He let her go, sinking wearily back onto the pillows. "Go on, girl. I have a lot of thinking to do, and a short time left. Don't you dare forget our pact."

Her legs felt shaky underneath her, but she made it to the door. She whispered, "Good night," before closing it. Either he didn't hear or couldn't be bothered to respond, because he just lay staring up at the ceiling.

In her room, Amanda took a sip of water. She pulled out an almond cookie and bit into it, but now it tasted crumbly and bitter. She spat it out into a tissue, wrapped the two cookies up, and dropped them in the waste-basket. Everything in the house seemed bad in some way. She took a second sip of water — her throat was the driest she could ever remember. Then she climbed into bed and pulled up the covers.

If she had any dreams, she didn't remember them the next morning.

Amanda woke to the sound of voices in the hall. Feet were hurrying upstairs and down. When she peeked out her door, trying to make sense of what was going on, she saw two men — one holding an old–fash-ioned doctor's medicine bag — talking to her parents and grandmother. They were all standing outside her grandfather's room. The door stood open, and she won-dered how they dared to disturb the old man so.

Then she guessed, even before her mother peeled herself away from the others and came toward her, saying, "Your grandfather's gone. He passed away last night. At least he didn't suffer." At some level Amanda realized her mother was saying all the things she should properly say, but was really and truly feeling nothing except relief.

For reasons she didn't fully understand herself, Amanda decided to keep quiet about her midnight visit to the old man's bedside. She had made a worrisome promise she was sure she couldn't keep. She knew it wasn't right, but she was glad he was gone so they could go home and she could forget about the past twenty-four hours.

"He's at rest, poor soul," her father said kindly. Amanda just nodded, trying to make herself look sad, but she could still feel a faint soreness where her grandfather had crushed her hands in his just hours before. In her heart, she really felt angry and afraid — not a bit sad.

He must have known he was dying while he was talking to me, she thought. Well, maybe her empty promise made him feel a bit better at the end. *And now he's in heaven, and that's the end of it,* Amanda told herself — but somehow, she couldn't believe the awful visit was nearly over.

The funeral took place two days later. The night before, Nana Flora held the wake in the tiny funeral parlor that served Weeming Downs. When they arrived, Amanda followed her mother and father to gaze for a moment into the casket. James Bowen was laid out in his coffin in a blue suit that looked hastily repaired and cleaned. There was the faintest of smiles on his too-red lips. Though his eyes were closed, Amanda had the uncomfortable feeling that they might pop open at any moment and she'd hear him remind her of her promise to him. Then they all knelt to say a silent prayer. Amanda couldn't think of any words, so she just remained with her hands folded until the adults got up to sit beside

Nana Flora in one of the front chairs.

A few townspeople came. Except for patting Nana Flora's hand or shoulder, and doing the same with her mother, Amanda noticed that the strangers kept to themselves, as if they were almost afraid of the Bowens, but felt obliged to give James Bowen this final sign of respect.

At the funeral, she recognized the same group of villagers clustered in pews near the back of the church — again keeping away from the family, and as far from the coffin, as possible. Amanda sat between her mother and grandmother in a front pew. The little stone church was between the Bowen place and the town — so close that the family decided to walk there. The pastor, a young man with a nervous squint, hurried through the service. He gave a little sermon that seemed like something he'd memorized and repeated dozens of times. Except for the occasional mention of "James Bowen" or, simply, "James," the words he spoke would have fit anybody's funeral, Amanda thought.

Then they followed the coffin, carried by several men of the parish, out the back door of the church and along the path to what looked like a little house, with two side walls, but no front or back. Halfway through was a heavy wooden gate. From either wall extended iron fencing that surrounded the cemetery. *The lich gate,* Amanda realized. It was just the way her grandfather had described it — and, she was sure, it was the same gateway she had seen in her nightmare two days before. The pastor unlatched the gate and pushed aside the two halves to let the coffin and mourners pass through. Amanda felt a chill as she stepped into the shaded space with red-and-black tiles underfoot. The last man through carefully closed and latched the gate behind him.

The graveside rites were even shorter and more rushed. When the necessary things had been said, and last gestures made, the pastor murmured a few words to the family and hurried off. That was a signal to the rest. The townspeople hastily let themselves out through the main gate and vanished, seeming to have said everything they had to say at the wake or in the few minutes before the funeral began.

Nana Flora lingered by the coffin that would soon be lowered into the earth by the workmen Amanda could see hovering at a respectful distance, anxious to get the job done. Nana seemed to be whispering to the man inside the casket; Amanda was surprised to see her smiling. It was almost as if she were sharing a secret with her dead husband. Abruptly, she turned and looked directly at Amanda and smiled even more broadly. "You're the only one who could help him in the last days," she said. "I'm not family by blood — just marriage. You're the *real* Bowen here." At this, the old woman shot a look of such anger and bitterness and even, Amanda was sure, *hatred* at the girl's mother.

Fortunately, Mona had her back turned and didn't see it.

For the thousandth time, Amanda felt that everything around her was wrong, that nothing was what it seemed to be. She couldn't wait to get away from the whole nasty place. She was glad she didn't have to go back through the lich gate. Everyone left by the big main gate with its iron scrollwork.

As they strolled back to Nana Flora's house, her mother said, "Your father and I have decided to stay on two more weeks, to help your grandmother through the holidays."

"But we'll miss Christmas at home," Amanda said, her heart sinking.

"It's more important to be here," her father said. "The worst is over; now it's a matter of helping your grandmother start to heal. Maybe, next summer, we can persuade her to visit us in California."

Amanda thought of the look Nana Flora had shot her mom. She hoped her grandmother wouldn't agree to a visit. Amanda wanted nothing more than to put distance between herself and Weeming Downs. The thought of her grandmother coming to California, bringing memories and worse, upset her. But she didn't dare say anything. Her mother, holding her hand, took Amanda's silence only for disappointment over a Christmas away from her friends. "We'll have a late Christmas when we get back," Mona said, trying to sound cheerful. "You'll see; we'll do just fine. Like your father says, the worst is over."

But the worst wasn't over for Amanda. The first night after the funeral, terrifying nightmares haunted her sleep, and twice she woke up screaming. Her parents dismissed the night terrors as the result of stress from her grandfather's death and all the strain of the wake and burial. Her grandmother had little to say, except to murmur, "Poor child." But she watched Amanda continually, as if she sensed that something beyond the stressful situation was at work.

The second night, Amanda was brought awake by someone shaking her. She sat up, rubbing her eyes, wondering who had disturbed her sleep. When she turned on her bedside lamp and looked around, the room was empty, and her door was shut. The clock showed a few minutes after midnight.

Then, quite clearly, she heard her grandfather's voice warning her, "If you don't come to the lich gate as you promised, you're going to be very sorry." She looked wildly around the room, but saw nothing — though, for just a moment, she thought she glimpsed a tall, thin, misty shape with red eyes watching her from the corner. But it was gone in the blink of an eye — so quickly, she wasn't sure she had seen anything.

She stayed awake the rest of the night, with the lamp on, but she saw and heard nothing more. She knew it was pointless to tell her parents; they'd think she'd just had another nightmare. She was keeping as far away from her grandmother as she could, without looking too obvious. Ever since the funeral, Amanda had felt afraid of the old woman, though on the surface nothing seemed out of the ordinary. But she constantly felt the woman's eyes on her, watching her for some unguessable reason.

She was so tired, she felt like a zombie moving through the next day. Her mother insisted she go to bed early. For a long time, Amanda lay tossing and turning, exhausted but unable to sleep, wrestling with her conscience and her fear of what might happen if she failed to keep her promise to her grandfather. She was sure that two nights before he had really been there in her dreams and then, last night, in her room. And he had promised to make her very sorry if she failed to keep her word.

Finally she made up her mind. She would have to do it. After all, she told herself, it was only a short distance to the church. It would only take a minute to open the lich gate, say her grandfather's name three times, then relatch the gate and return home. After that she wouldn't have to worry about breaking her promise anymore. And, just maybe, whatever part of the old man had troubled her dreams and entered her room would be at rest.

Having decided her course of action, she started counting off the minutes until the household was asleep. When she heard her parents coming upstairs, she pulled the covers up to her chin. When her bedroom door opened, she did her best to appear fast asleep. A moment later, her father whispered, "Out like a light," and gently closed the door. She listened to the sounds of her parents going downstairs and closing their bedroom door. The luminous face of the clock was showing 10:35 P.M. when her grandmother finally shut the door at the far end of the hall. After that, silence settled over the house, though Amanda's nerves were on edge the closer it got to 11:15 P.M. — the time she had determined to set out for the cemetery.

At exactly 11:00 P.M., she pulled on her jeans, tennies, warmest sweater, and jacket, and slipped out of the room. She moved quietly along the upstairs hall and down the stairs, avoiding the second telltale step. On the main floor, she nervously unlocked the heavy front door. She opened it just enough to slip through and then gently closed the door after her.

Outside a nearly full moon cast generous silver light over everything, and the night felt warmer than she had expected. When she was far enough from the house, she broke into a trot.

It wasn't until she was close to the darkened church that she had the uncomfortable feeling someone was watching her. But a glance all around revealed no one. Still, she slowed down and walked more cautiously around the building to the cemetery on the other side.

Though the night air was clear, an odd reddish mist

seemed to hang over the gravestones and the rangy growing things inside the iron fence. She looked at the silver watch her parents had given her for her last birthday. It showed ten minutes to midnight when she reached the lich gate and leaned forward, one hand hooked around the handle on either half of the gate.

She waited. Her grandfather had insisted she call his name exactly at midnight.

At two minutes to midnight, she unlatched the lich gate and gave it a gentle push so the two halves swung apart, giving an unobstructed view of the graveyard.

Even as she watched, the mist seemed to thicken inside the fence; a patch of it came right to the far side of the lich gate, then paused. Peering closer, the girl had the impression that people shapes were moving around deep in the mist, but she couldn't be sure.

She checked her watch again. Exactly midnight.

"James Allen Bowen," she said, using her grandfather's full name that she had only heard on the day of his funeral.

Now she was sure she saw a shape moving toward her through the mist. Her throat went desert-dry, and she could barely croak out the words "James Allen Bowen" a second time.

As the figure approached, her legs turned to water. She had to hold on to the nearest gate handle to keep from sinking to her knees in terror.

She steeled herself for the third repetition. "James

Allen Bowen," she said, her voice hardly a whisper. Quickly, she reached for the wooden halves of the lich gate to close them and complete the business.

But a hand, old and wrinkled, grasped hers and prevented her from shutting the gate. She tried to break free, but another hand locked onto her shoulder.

"Not so fast, dear Amanda," said Nana Flora. "Be patient. He'll be here by and by."

Confused and nearly frightened out of her wits, Amanda struggled in the old woman's grasp. The hold on her arm felt as strong as her grandfather's grip when he had seized her hands and made her swear to do what he told her. With a sound that was little more than a groan, she recognized the figure of her grandfather walking toward her out of the blood-red mist. He was smiling — not at Amanda, but at his widow, his wife. At the open gate, he paused for a minute, then, with an effort, stepped through to join them. He placed his hands over Nana Flora's, which were resting on Amanda's shoulders, keeping her prisoner. For a moment the two just smiled at each other.

"Back as planned," James Bowen said. "You can't keep a Bowen down."

He began to laugh, and Nana Flora laughed with him.

Impatiently, he signed for his wife to release Amanda. For a moment, she was free and ready to run, but her grandfather moved with the speed of a striking snake. He grabbed her upper arms, swung her around, and shoved her through the lich gate. Stunned, Amanda stumbled forward and fell full-length, partly on the tile flooring and partly on the brick path beyond. When she staggered to her feet, she saw a girl — the mirror image of herself — pulling one part of the gate closed, while Nana Flora drew the other part shut. The latch fell into place with a loud *click*. Then the old woman held out her hand. The girl took it, and Nana Flora led the Amanda who wasn't Amanda out of the shadows of the lich gate and back around the church toward the path home.

Inside the gate, Amanda, still shaken by what had happened, realized she was taller now. She tried to yell at the old woman and the girl, but no sound came out, though her lips moved frantically. She reached for the lich gate with a hand that was old and veined and covered with skin as thin as paper. But her fingers slipped through the wood-and-metal pickets and railing as if they weren't there. She tried time and again, but it was like trying to catch a fistful of empty air.

Around her, a wind — she didn't know if it was in the real world or the nightmare world — was rising. It began to scatter the mist within the cemetery fence, and she felt herself beginning to melt away, too. In moments, only the silver moon overhead shone on pale gravestones from which the wind was teasing the last faint ribbons of clinging mist.

Principal's Office

The principal's inner offices were functional, impersonal, and intimidating. Any student who found him- or herself in the huge space felt like a minnow in the belly of a whale. This was the desired effect. Any anger or rebellion would be swallowed up in awe.

The huge work area that Jerrod Bentley entered was carpeted in purple, with white walls and ceilings. A semicircle of five bulky white plastic chairs faced a row of four white plastic desks, each dominated by a late-model, white computer desk console.

Two women and two men, all clearly secretaries, all with frosted and lacquered hair highlighted in various colors, were having a four-way conversation at the four desks.

At Jerrod's entrance, the lacquered head (with blue highlights) nearest him swiveled around, and a frosty voice asked, "Yes?" The young woman surveyed him up and down, as if performing a medical scan.

"My name is Jerrod. Jerrod Bentley," he said, approaching the desk. "I have an appointment with the principal."

The words seemed to stick to the roof of his mouth and to his lips, unwilling to be uttered. The woman had to ask him to repeat himself. He did so, in a voice that emerged as barely more than a whisper.

"Student ID number?" she asked.

He gave her his number.

Her fingers flew across a keyboard recessed in her desk. The back of her console — like everything else in the office — was highly polished. In the white plastic rectangle, the boy could see a small reflection of himself — a pathetically tiny creature in the black slacks and short-sleeved white shirt of the school uniform.

"Fifth grade?" the woman asked.

He nodded.

"Mr. Frankle's class?"

He nodded again.

Her fingernails clattered on the keys.

"It will be just a minute, Mr. Bentley. . . . Ah, here it is now. . . ."

She dropped her eyes to the screen and read something. Then she reread it, as if wanting to be certain.

She glanced up at him, studied him briefly, and then punched a stream of information into the console.

A moment later a tiny chime signaled that she had received a second message. Once again, she read the on-screen memo twice to be certain she'd gotten everything right.

She gave him a chilly smile and said, "Won't you have a seat? There seems to be some question regarding your current status. It may take awhile to clear up."

He sat on the white chair nearest him. For all the rounded contours and the willingness of the plastiform material to adjust to his body, he found the chair the most uncomfortable he had ever sat in. It seemed to ripple around him in restless undulations that made him faintly seasick.

The secretaries' conversation died away. Suddenly, all of the slim, efficient assistants were busily at work at their desk consoles.

A raised edging served to screen each set of desk controls from anyone but the individual operator. On each desk this edging was inscribed, in tiny black letters, with the secretary's name. Under each name was a different motto. Jerrod's eyes flickered over these names and mottoes.

The desk a little to his right carried the name "Betty" and the motto *Education is a privilege, not a right.*

Next to "Betty" sat "Glen," whose console announced *There is no higher human goal than knowledge.*

At "Glen's" left sat "Duncan," and the inscription *An uneducated person lives a life without meaning.*

The woman to whom he had spoken was named "Alma"; her message was *To turn away from the getting of wisdom is to condemn oneself.*

Behind the row of desks was a single closed door. Jerrod guessed that this was the entrance to Mr. Falkland's, the principal's, office. He had only been to the outer offices before, where the school clerks and general secretary held court. His offenses (at least, at *this* school) had never been severe enough to push him beyond reprimands and warnings from the lowest-ranking assistants. Just being this close to the principal's door was making him very nervous indeed.

Alma punched a final button on her desk. She looked across at Jerrod and sighed. "I'll tell you right now, Mr. Bentley, you are in serious trouble. According to our records, you've failed all the assimilation tests, you've been on probation for three months, and yet you persist in defying your teachers, disrupting classes, and creating no end of trouble. You and your parents have been put on green, yellow, and red warnings. Still you continue to be a thorn in everyone's side."

She paused for a moment. "How many schools have you been through?" Her fingers ticked across several keys. "*Eleven!* Ten is the maximum in most cases. But your academic test scores may have been high enough to warrant this bending of the rules. Or," she added, lowering her voice to a whisper, "if your family is well-enough connected . . ."

The boy shrugged, unwilling to involve his family in what had become a frightening encounter with the powers that be. He'd had run-ins with authorities before — but this felt like much more. At other times, he had felt he could push back against the ones who were forever driving him like a calf in a cattle drive that he'd heard about in history class. *Join the herd,* he thought angrily. *Trot along with the rest of the steers. And be prepared to meet your maker at journey's end — the slaughterhouse.* This last thought dissipated his anger and left him with a cold numbness in his stomach. He clasped his hands in his lap and crossed his ankles, suddenly feeling like a very little boy.

"I'm afraid," Alma continued, "this time Central has decided, based on very careful review of the last three unsuccessful attempts to mainstream you, that there are, well, *factors* of an unspecified but very real nature that make it clear you will never be able to move on to middle school or higher."

She shrugged. "In short, on the surface, you seem to be beyond further investment in schooling. We can do nothing more for you. *But*," the woman left the word hanging unnecessarily long in the air, "they have decided to give final adjudication —"

"I don't know that word," said Jerrod weakly. Whatever fight might have been left in him had completely evaporated in the icy air-conditioned atmosphere of the principal's offices.

She smiled again, but it wasn't a friendly smile. "It means hearing and settling a case. It's like a decision a judge might make in a court. In this case, it's the principal. But *here*," Jerrod wasn't sure if she meant just in his case, or if she meant for the whole school, for always, "Mr. Falkland is judge and jury. He has special legal authority granted by the state."

Her grin widened. Now Jerrod was thinking of the "little crocodile" poem his mother used to repeat to him when he was barely more than a baby.

> *How cheerfully he seems to grin,*
> *How neatly spreads his claws,*
> *And welcomes little fishes in,*
> *With gently smiling jaws!*

The memory made him giggle — though it was more a release of nervousness than anything truly funny.

At the sound of his laugh, Alma's own smile disappeared. She said severely, "I can assure you, there's nothing to laugh about, young man."

He wanted to explain the poem, but she was no longer interested in him. She was giving her full attention to her keyboard and the console screen.

Abruptly, the panel behind the row of desks slid open. Mr. Falkland stood framed in the doorway. Though it was generously proportioned, so was the principal. His head almost touched the lintel at the top of the door, and the crown of his bushy gray hair glowed with a pearl-like sheen from the soft lighting behind the man. His shoulders left little room between him and the doorjambs on either side, yet his expensive-looking suit made him look trim in spite of his bulk. The toes of his polished shoes reflected the row lights above the secretaries' desks. Until now, Jerrod had only seen the man at a distance — addressing the two thousand students at monthly assembly or walking down a hall, talking to a group of teachers or administrators. He had never seemed so much a giant as he did now.

Jerrod, without being urged, slid off his chair and stood up — as rigid as a soldier at attention.

Mr. Falkland fixed him with a look that was neither friendly nor hostile — merely interested, the way Jerrod looked at the bugs in their glass cages in biology lab.

"Mr. . . . ah . . . *Bentley*," the man rumbled. He held out a hand. Jerrod, nodding but unable to get a word out, extended his own in return. The giant's meaty paw quickly engulfed the boy's sweaty hand and then released it. But the momentary shake had let Jerrod feel enough strength there to snap his fingers like matchsticks.

Mr. Falkland took a step backward and to the side, indicating Jerrod should follow him into the innermost office. The moment the boy was inside, the panel behind him whooshed shut.

"Please, have a seat."

Dutifully, Jerrod sat down in a shiny black plastiform chair that felt even harsher than the one in the waiting area outside. This one had arms on it; Jerrod noted that the material of the armrests felt sticky under his bare skin.

Mr. Falkland took a seat behind a huge ebony desk, which had nothing but a red folder on it. Glancing down, he began thumbing through the notes inside, almost as if he'd forgotten Jerrod were there.

Anxiously, the boy's eyes darted about, taking in the few details of the office. Framed documents and letters covered the wall on his left. Holographs of the principal by himself or with others were mounted on the facing wall. One picture showed him sitting by an old-fashioned fireplace. A woman stood beside him, resting her hand on his shoulder. A baby girl, lots of ribbons in her curly hair, sat on Mr. Falkland's lap. At his feet, two boys — twins who looked about six years old — stared into the camera. Mr. Falkland was smiling; no one else in the picture was.

There was also a picture of Mr. Falkland with a small, round, mustached man the boy recognized from newscasts as the mayor. With surprise, the boy saw that the picture next to it showed the principal alongside the president and first lady, with the White House in the background. The man must be very important, Jerrod decided, far more important than just an ordinary principal.

He felt his nervousness increasing. Directly behind the desk hung a paper banner, obviously made by a child, who had used many different colors of paint to make it look like an old scroll with hand-lettered words inside. It took him a minute to decipher what the rainbow letters were saying:

A Principal is a Prince and a Pal to Everyone!

Jerrod wondered if one of the twins — or maybe the two working together — had made it for their father.

Lastly, he glanced at a fixture with three nodes directly above his head; it was all gleaming metal and multifaceted crystal prisms. It seemed unconnected with lighting or ventilation or any functional system. Was it just there to distract the eye and mind? the boy wondered. From everything else he saw around him, it seemed unlikely. What went on here, he felt, was deadly serious.

Mr. Falkland looked across at the boy as he gently closed the folder.

"We seem to have a problem here, Mr. Bentley."

Jerrod shrugged. "What happened in Mr. Frankle's class wasn't really that big a deal," he said defensively.

"In and of itself, no," the principal said. "But as the final straw, I'm afraid it's a very big deal, indeed."

Jerrod squirmed in the uncomfortable chair as the man's eyes seemed to bore into him. A feeling of helplessness and nausea swept over the boy. His hands clutched the knobs at the ends of the chair arms, his sweat making the sticky plastiform slippery now. "I can do better," he said, managing to find his voice. He was distressed to hear how whiny he sounded.

"I have no doubt you *could*," said the man with a sigh. "The problem is that you *haven't*. We've given you chance after chance, and you've flung it back in our faces in school after school." He put his arms out on his desk, laced his fingers together into a ball, and stared with laserlike intensity at the boy.

"This was your last chance. Central even gave you one extra chance. But I don't see where anything we've done — your parents or your school or your community — has made an impact on you."

He stood up, towering over the desk, glaring at the boy. He clasped his hands behind his back and began pacing to and fro, from the holographs to the documents, then reversing his path. Each time he approached one wall, he made a show of glancing at something on it. But Jerrod was certain his mind was a million miles away, sifting facts, moving toward some kind of decision.

"I'll be better," the boy whispered.

The other ignored him. At last, the man walked to stand just behind his oversize desk chair, turned his back on Jerrod, and seemed to be studying the rainbow-colored message on the back wall. Suddenly, he spun around, clearly having made up his mind about something.

"I think this interview is at an end," he said, sounding more weary than anything else. "It's time to bring your involvement with this school — and with the community — to its necessary conclusion."

"Are . . . are you going to expel me?" Jerrod asked hopelessly.

"In a manner of speaking."

"My parents won't like that."

"I'm sure they won't."

"They'll make trouble," he said, wondering just how much trouble his parents would make. They were so worn down, they hardly spoke to each other anymore. They seemed to have lost all patience with him. His heart sinking, he realized just how badly he had pushed and argued with and frustrated everyone over the past months.

Mr. Falkland made a sweeping motion with his

fingers, as though brushing away the idea that the Bentleys — or anyone — could alter the course of what was about to happen. "The world has changed in a very few years," the man said at last. "I won't say it's for the better, but we all have to go with the program: you, me, your parents — *all of us*." His voice softened a bit. "I can't say I know you very well, Mr. Bentley. But I know all *about* you. And I know what Central requires in this case. Your parents won't interfere; they know the consequences of interfering with a Central Directive."

For the boy, for everyone, there were no two more chilling words than *Central Directive*. No one could appeal anything stamped with that seal.

"Please . . ." he said with a kind of desperation.

The principal shook his head.

"It's no use, Mr. Bentley. Even if I contacted Central, it would be a waste of time. They monitor this office as they watch everything that goes on. If there had been any willingness on their part to grant another chance, we would have heard it instantly. No override from Central means no stay of executing my decision — which is really *their* decision."

He gave a kind of wistful smile. When he spoke again, his voice was that of a teacher: impersonal, clear, every word chosen for maximum efficiency.

"Society is under the rule of **C.A.L.M.**, Mr. Bentley. You know that. Even a first grader knows what is required of her or him these days: **Conform every hour.**

Achieve every day. Labor as needed. Maximize your potential."

Mr. Falkland was shaking his head now. "You've resisted this ideal in every way you can. I don't see any hope for improvement. Not after eleven opportunities. You remain a nonconformist, a problem for yourself, but a potential threat to society." He was leaning across the desk, his fingers splayed out on the hard black surface, his massive features almost at the level of the seated boy's head. Jerrod tried to shrink back into the unyielding material of the chair, but the face only loomed closer and larger.

The principal's voice was cold but compelling. "Society moves toward the future in measured steps; everyone must pace him- or herself accordingly and *keep in step.*"

The boy had another mental vision of protesting, frightened cattle being driven to slaughter.

"But —" Jerrod began. Then he stopped. He had no idea what to say. He had run out of arguments — or even the energy to argue. Fear had taken over completely. He felt himself going limp, supported only by the back and arms of the chair.

Mr. Falkland's right hand slid open a small panel on his desk. He pushed a button with his middle finger.

The three nodes of the ceiling fixture focused on Jerrod Bentley.

Lasers burned him to ashes before he could even scream.

Electrostatic precipitators dropped the ashes and smoke particles onto the gray rug.

From underneath the chair, a thin vacuum-hose snaked out from the machinery in its base. Silently and efficiently it cleaned up the fine layer of residue.

The principal made a face that might have been regret, or merely distaste at what he saw as necessary but still wasteful. Then he punched a second button on the control panel beneath his hand. "Alma," he said, "send in the next student."

Woody

Maryanne had been sent to spend the summer with her grandmother and aunt in the little town of Arendell, North Carolina, while her parents back in Apex decided if they were going to divorce each other or give things another try. It was okay, though, as far as Maryanne was concerned; she could live with her mother or father — whichever way things turned out. At the moment, the ten-year-old was far more interested in Woody — the thing that lived, prowled, and hunted in Big Piney Woods surrounding the town.

She sat in her bedroom with her friend, Jackie, and their tagalong wannabe friend, Darleen, whom the two girls tolerated. *Just.*

"Tell me what you know about Woody," Maryanne

prompted Jackie, who had claimed the only chair in the room, next to the little book-strewn desk. Darleen, who had not been invited to share the bed with Maryanne, sat cross-legged in the middle of the braided rug.

"Well," said Jackie, "everyone knows there's *something* out in Big Piney." Through the window open to the warm summer morning, Maryanne could see the huge expanse of pine forest that stretched from the edge of town to the distant range of hills dominated by Beehive Mountain — so called because the rippled sides and rounded top reminded people of a beehive. Jackie quickly warmed to her subject. "He's at least seven feet tall, looks kinda human, but his skin is shiny black and leathery, and he has bat wings. He's got this big bird beak, and his eyes glow glittery green. When he swoops down to grab a small animal — or a little kid — he goes 'Eeee!'" Here the girl gave an earsplitting shriek that made Darleen clap her hands over her ears.

"Quiet!" Maryanne said. "Aunt Nora's reading downstairs. She'll be on my case if we bother her." Then she leaned forward and asked, "Does he really get kids, too?"

"That's what they say," Jackie replied with a shrug.

"Why do they call him Woody?" Maryanne wondered.

Jackie said, "He used to be called the Woods monster, then Woodsman, and finally just Woody."

"Like the Loch Ness monster," Maryanne said

thoughtfully. "People in Scotland who live around the lake just call her Nessie now. She's supposed to be a left-over dinosaur. Where did Woody come from?"

Before Jackie could answer, Darleen said in her heavy, flat voice, "My brother says an old medicine man put a curse here, because the first white people took the land away from his tribe. Woody *is* the curse."

"That's just silly," said Jackie. "Your brother believes everything he hears. He thought the end of the world was coming last year just because crazy old Reverend Scott said so in church one day." While Darleen's face turned red, Jackie went on, "There are really scientific ideas about Woody. He might be some kind of creature from deep down in the earth, who came up through caves. Or he could be an alien who came here in a flying saucer. I heard people talking about weird lights in the sky near Beehive Mountain. They could be UFOs. The theory I like best is that he's some kind of freaky thing that started out as a regular bear or bat or something and turned into a monster because of chemicals left over from that abandoned factory out by Big Piney. They closed it because the owners were dumping junk that was getting into the water."

"A mutation," Maryanne clarified.

"Yeah. One of those. And then there's a really boring idea that he's just some big old bird like a barn owl. But I've never heard of any barn owl grabbing kids."

"I'd like to find him and get a picture of him,"

Maryanne said. "Then we'd know what he really was."

Jackie gave a short, sharp laugh. "You won't find Woody. He'll find *you*." She slipped into a campfire-tales voice as she continued, "You'll know he's around when you hear the rustle of those leathery wings. Then you'll hear his high-pitched whistle. 'Eeee! Eeee! Eeee!'"

Maryanne wasn't sure she believed all of this, but she filed the information in her memory nevertheless. She was fascinated with the idea of a strange creature living so close by.

The more she thought about it, the more Maryanne decided this would be her summer to become famous. People had set out to photograph such legends as Big Foot or the Abominable Snowman and failed. She intended to take a photograph of Woody that would prove his existence. Of course, people had been trying for years to get such a shot. The local newspapers even offered big cash rewards for the first photograph or other piece of evidence that would verify the monster's existence.

So Maryanne set out on a "fact-finding mission." She listened carefully to all the monster stories, old and new, spent hours at the library poring over newspaper accounts, combed likely Web sites, and checked out every book that even mentioned the mystery. She got a topographical map of the area and plotted all the reported sightings of Woody. Her research led her to the conclusion that Woody's home base was somewhere on

Beehive Mountain, which lay on the far side of North Lake. The stubby landmark was reportedly honey-combed with caves. Over the years, there had been tales of spelunkers — the people who loved to explore and study caves — who had disappeared. Most people thought they'd had accidents or simply gotten lost in the largely uncharted maze of tunnels inside the mountain.

Maryanne had her own theory: Woody was respon-sible for most, if not all, of the unexplained vanish-ments. To her mind, this was tangible proof that she had guessed the location of the beast's hidey-hole. She decided the time was right to plan an expedition and check out the area.

Of course, she intended to include Jackie, even though she could be really bossy at times. But Jackie was a born athlete and belonged to the Junior Cavers, a local group that explored caves on summer weekends. She had even been in one or two of what she called "the baby caves" near the base of the Beehive. Jackie was already interested in Woody, so Maryanne didn't have to do much to convince her to come along. She sweet-ened the deal with the promise that they would find more exciting caves than "baby" ones to explore. She also promised the other girl an equal share of fame when they solved the riddle of Woody's whereabouts.

Darleen became the third member of the expedition. Maryanne had secretly nicknamed her "The D" (as in ditz, dork, or dumbbell), but Darleen had been gifted by her parents with a state-of-the-art digital camera. Maryanne knew that if she was going to get a history-making photograph, that was the way to go — much better than her own cheapo camera from her dad or any image she might capture with her cell phone. She tried to persuade Darleen to lend her the camera, but Darleen never let anyone but herself use it.

So Darleen rounded out the team.

They met early one Saturday in front of Maryanne's house. All were wearing T-shirts, jeans, and tennies. Maryanne wore an Atlanta Braves baseball cap, Jackie had a green cap with "Junior Cavers" embroidered on it, and Darleen sported a shiny pink "Hello Kitty" cap. In answer to questions from her grandmother and aunt about their plans for the day, Maryanne rattled off a prepared story about meeting friends downtown and either going to the G-rated film at the Empire or simply spending an afternoon messing around in the park. If either of the women noticed that the three girls, Maryanne and Jackie with heavy canvas backpacks, and Darleen with a petite pink "Hello Kitty" knapsack that matched her cap, were riding their bikes in the direction of Big Piney instead of town, it didn't register.

Maryanne, Jackie, and Darleen pedaled along Big Piney Road to the parking area at the edge of the forest. From there, they could see across the sea of green pines to where the Beehive shouldered its blunt way into the sky. There were a handful of cars, but no one in sight. Most likely people were hiking one of the many trails that radiated out from the parking lot or maybe just picnicking in the barbecue area a short distance away. Adjusting their backpacks, the three set off along the trail that ran straight north toward the distant mountain.

The day was warm, and they stopped often to rest and drink from the water bottles they had brought along.

"This isn't much fun," Darleen complained. "It's too hot."

"It's going to be worth it," Maryanne insisted. "You'll be famous. You'll get your picture in newspapers and magazines and blogs everywhere."

Jackie, who had less patience, just told Darleen, "Shut up! You always have to complain about everything." She moved away from the other two.

Though she agreed with Jackie, Maryanne crossed to the log where her friend had reseated herself. In a loud voice she said, "Jackie, don't be so mean. It *is* hot; I'm feeling pretty sweaty, too. Be fair."

"She is such a *creep!*" muttered Jackie.

In a whisper that only the other girl could hear, Maryanne said, "We both know she's a creep. But she's got the camera, and I *need* that."

Jackie sighed and said, "All right. But I'm going to ignore her from now on."

A few minutes later, they were on their way again, trekking for the most part in silence.

After an hour or more, they took a lunch break. As they chewed energy bars, Maryanne chattered away, trying to keep up the others' fading enthusiasm. "Maybe a film company will make a movie of how we tracked down Woody. I might even write a book and sell a bazillion copies."

Mealtime over, rested and refreshed, they repacked their knapsacks and set off on the trail again, Jackie and Darleen maintaining their bristly silence. A short time later, they reached the shore of North Lake. Directly across the lightly rippling water, the Beehive waited to give up its secrets. The trail split, running around both ends of the lake. Maryanne consulted her map and decided the easterly trail would bring them more quickly to the base of the mountain.

Another hour of trudging (and a fresh string of complaints from Darleen) brought them to the edge of this stretch of forest. Directly across a swath of thick grass loomed the base of the mountain, which had been thrust up in ages past by some tremendous underground pressure. Here Maryanne encountered her first serious problem. Jackie wanted to explore in a direction that Maryanne at first patiently, then heatedly, explained "isn't where I think we'll find Woody." But Jackie was stubborn and had a temper of her own. While Darleen fooled around, snapping pictures of trees and birds and rock formations, the other two escalated name-calling into an all-out shouting match. Abruptly Jackie stormed off in the direction she had chosen, pausing to turn and yell, "And I've got all my Junior Caver ropes and hooks and stuff, so see how you do without *them.*"

"I brought my own climbing junk," Maryanne shouted back. But Jackie had already disappeared around an outcropping of rock. "Come on," she said, grabbing Darleen's arm and hauling her in the opposite direction, ignoring the girl's protests to "Stop, you're hurting me."

Maryanne marched them for about ten minutes before releasing the other girl. While Darleen pouted and rubbed her upper arm, swearing she was going to bruise, Maryanne took out two pictures of the Beehive that she had downloaded from her aunt's computer. She compared the pictures with the actual mountain rising above them. Finally, she said, "I think where we need to go is just a little farther along that way."

"I think I'm tired of this," Darleen said disagreeably. "And I'm tired of you bossing me around."

But Maryanne just said, "Shhhh! I thought I heard, really faint, something that sounded like 'Eeee! Eeee!'"

Darleen listened and then said, "I don't hear anything."

"It sounded like Woody's whistle."

"I don't think you heard anything. You're making it up to get me to stay. I'm going home right now."

"You can't go. We need a really clear photograph. My camera isn't that good."

"That's too bad," sneered Darleen. "If you were nicer, I'd have let you borrow it." Maryanne knew *that* was a lie, but she didn't challenge the girl. Things were already falling apart. An argument wasn't going to help.

Darleen took a few more steps and then sat on a small boulder. She opened her knapsack and pulled out her cell phone. "I'm going to call my sister and tell her to pick me up at the parking area. I'm tired. I don't want to walk back and then have to ride all the way into Arendell."

She leaned over and speed-dialed a number. Then she tried again. Finally she snapped the cell phone shut. "There's no service here. I guess I'll have to call her when I get back to my bike." She glared at Maryanne. "This whole idea of yours is dumb, dumb, dumb. Woody is just a made-up story."

But Maryanne was sure she heard the distant cry of "Eeee! Eeee!" again. The first time she'd heard the sound, it was near the base of the mountain, in the general direction Jackie had headed. Now it seemed to float down from somewhere far up the Beehive.

"Listen!" she said to Darleen, making a grab for the girl, which the other neatly avoided by standing up suddenly and backing away. "Don't you hear it? That whistling way up the mountain?"

"You can't fool me," said Darleen, dusting off the

seat of her jeans. "I'm leaving."

"Maybe it's not such a good idea, going off by yourself," said Maryanne. "We should stick together. I've never heard of Woody going after two people. It's always someone alone."

Darleen paused. Then she made a face. "Now you're trying to scare me. You'll do anything to get your own way. I hate you." She held up the camera and taunted, "You want this so badly. Well, tough noogies."

Still holding the camera up for the other girl to see, she flounced off the way they had come. Maryanne watched her go in disgust. "Good riddance," she muttered. Then she took her own camera out of her pack. She wrinkled her nose. It made really awful pictures. Most of them turned out too bright or too dark. Her father had clearly bought the cheapest model he could find. Not good. She reached in farther and pulled out her own cell. To her frustration, she saw it was signaling "Battery Low — Recharge Soon." She knew well enough that meant there probably wasn't enough juice for a single clear shot.

Maryanne quickly made up her mind. If the day wasn't going to be a total bust, she'd have to catch up with Darleen and find a way to make her stay or, at least, surrender the camera. She wasn't sure how she'd do it, but she was willing to apologize, promise anything, and even eat *dirt* if the other demanded it. She *had* to get a photo. She was sure she had figured out

which of the several cave openings high above was Woody's lair.

She shrugged back into her knapsack, but had just taken a step in pursuit, when she heard — unmistakably, this time — a shrill "Eeee! Eeee!" from inside the circling trees, very near where the trail began wending its way back to North Lake. Then a second sound — a single scream — froze her in midstep. She listened, but heard nothing more than a distant whistle growing higher and fainter with each passing moment.

Now she *had* to find Darleen. Calling the other girl's name, she hurried down the narrow, pine-shaded path.

As she entered a sunny glade, she saw something glint in the afternoon light. Curious, Maryanne walked to the center of the open space and looked. A shiver went through her. It was Darleen's camera. Had the girl just dropped it? She couldn't imagine even "The D" being that careless. Picking it up, she looked around for some other trace of the girl, but saw nothing. "Darleen!" she called, hesitantly at first, then more forcefully, *"Darleen!"*

Her answer was the loud *flap! flap! flap!* of leathery wings, followed by a shrill "Eeee! Eeee! Eeee!" that nearly split her skull in two. She was still holding the camera when two immense talons bit into her shoulders. In a sickening uprush, she was jerked into the sky. The forest shrank beneath her. In a dizzying loop, her captor swooped around so that Maryanne found herself being carried directly toward a group of three cave entrances two-thirds of the way up the mountain — far from the one she had selected as Woody's nesting place. She tried to scream, but shock and terror overwhelmed her, stifling her cries.

"Eeee! Eeee! Eeee!" screeched painfully in her ears. Woody was flying unerringly toward the center cave mouth. From inside, she heard faint echoes of "Eeee! Eeee! Eeee!"

Then there came a headlong rush into the semidarkness of a cave, where she was deposited with a stunning *thump!* onto a shelf of rock. Barely able to crawl, Maryanne moved to the edge and stared down. A dozen small shrieking beaks snapped hungrily up at her. With a groan, she recognized the shreds of a "Junior Cavers" cap and "Hello Kitty" backpack amid the fluttering ebony bat wings, scaly patches of skin, and avid glittering green eyes.

The parent bird made a fluttering sound behind her. Shaking, she turned and stared into a pair of massive emerald eyes and a thick beak that jutted from an old, apelike face.

Dully she raised the camera and snapped. The flash highlighted the monster in all its terrible reality. She had wanted proof, and now she had her proof. Woody was real. Just how real was brought home when the creature took its first beakful of shirt and skin off her shoulder to drop to its waiting young.

Snow Day

The Daly house was situated on Hickham Lane, on the outskirts of the Vermont hamlet of Danby. A quarter of a mile farther down, the road ended at the Western Abenaki Native American Museum (privately funded). Beyond was the village of Wawioban, where most of the local Abenaki lived. They had no formal reservation, because the U.S. government did not officially recognize the tribe. The problem stemmed from the fact that their ancestors often hid from the Americans or fled into Canada, so they could not prove they had lived in New England continuously from the 1600s — which would be necessary for official recognition by the government. But, to Connor, good friends with an Abenaki boy, the question didn't matter. Sozap and his sister, Moli, were as full-blood as he could imagine.

Connor Daly was eleven, the same age as Sozap. His twin sisters, Jenna and Emma, were both nine, but they got along just fine with Moli, who at seven was much sharper than her years. All the children went to Ormsbee Elementary School, even though most of the Abenaki sent their children to the small school administered by the tribe.

It was a late afternoon in fall. The five friends were walking home, comparing notes on who had had the worst day. Connor and Sozap won easily, since their teacher, Mrs. Chatterton, was acknowledged hands down as the meanest teacher at Ormsbee. Her students swore she seemed to go out of her way to keep that reputation. Just a recitation of their homework assignments was enough to make the boys' sisters groan in sympathy.

"I am so over 'Crabby-ton' and her boring classes and homework and detention," said Connor. "If I didn't have to see her ugly face again, it would be too soon."

Sozap nodded. "It would be nice to sleep through the school year till summer. Hibernate like an old bear in the forest."

"Good-bye, pop quizzes; good-bye, books; good-bye, teachers' ugly looks," Connor chanted, and then made yawning and stretching motions, "Hello, sweet dreams."

"But you'd miss Thanksgiving and Christmas," said Jenna seriously.

"And New Year's and Easter," Emma added.

"Well, yeah," their brother conceded. "The best idea would be to wake up just for holidays and vacations. How cool would that be?"

"How would you do that?" asked Moli.

"I don't know — set an alarm. Who cares? You can't really do it —" Connor stopped suddenly, remembering something. "Actually, it did happen once. Sozap's cousin Orrin, who works at the museum, told me."

"When?" challenged Jenna, who was always doubtful about things — especially her brother's stories, which sometimes began with facts, but more often than not wound up someplace Jenna called "la-la land."

Connor wasn't about to let his sister derail his train of thought. "Sozap remembers. He was with me. Tell her," he said, giving his friend a poke in the ribs.

"It's just a story," Sozap muttered. "Orrin's always telling stories." Clearly he didn't want to discuss it.

Connor, however, could worry an idea like a terrier getting hold of something to chew on. "Then, I'll tell it. Before any white people moved into the area, there was already a village there: Wawioban — just like today. So what happened was, one winter the hunting had been lousy and people were weak and starving. Then they heard from a scout or something that a war party of Iroquois was coming to raid the village. Everyone was too sick or tired to run away or defend the place. But the tribe had a powerful old medicine man —"

"*Medeoulin,*" Sozap corrected. "No one calls them 'medicine men.'"

"Whatever. Anyhow, this guy could make serious magic. So he called down a monster winter storm to bury the village and drive off or kill their enemies."

"Wouldn't he have killed off his own tribe, too?" asked Jenna. "What good would that be?"

"Just listen," said Connor impatiently. "The guy had a second trick up his sleeve. He turned his people into snow men and women and children so they could sleep through the winter without freezing to death. What happened is, the raiding party was lost. No one knows what became of them. But when spring arrived, the village thawed out. The people became just people again, and they went on with their lives. But old — what was his name?" he asked Sozap.

The boy hesitated, seemingly unwilling to speak the name aloud. Then he said softly, as if he didn't want to be heard outside his circle of friends, "*Pebon.*"

"Right," said Connor. "Pebon. Anyhow, old Pebon disappeared just after the return of spring."

"What happened to him?" asked Emma.

"No one knows. It's a story," Connor said defensively.

But Moli, who had been quiet until now, made a soft, chuckling sound. "It was all that magic he used. Cousin

Orrin says you can't make big magic without paying for it big time."

"Yeah," said her brother. "I forgot that."

"Still, wouldn't it be *cool* —" Connor let the word linger, before adding, "Hey! I'm making a joke here."

The others shrugged and rolled their eyes.

"You have to admit," he continued, "it would be neat to have that kind of magic and make a snow day or snow week to close the school whenever you wanted."

"I don't think so," said Jenna. "We'd get behind in our schoolwork. And you have to make up snow days in summer."

"If it was a bad storm," Emma said thoughtfully, "it would mess people up. No one could get to work or to the store or —"

"Give it a rest!" Connor cried. "It's only an old story. You'd think someone was making you write an essay on 'Ten Reasons Why Snow Days Are Bad.'"

They had passed beyond the town and were ambling down Hickham Lane. The woods pressed close in on either side — maple, white pine, hemlock, spruce, beech, and birch trees shouldering right up to the road's edge. Connor was walking slowly now, letting the three girls drift on ahead. When there was sufficient distance between girls and boys, Connor dropped back a few paces and fell into step beside Sozap, who was bringing up the rear.

"There any truth in that old story?" Connor asked. "I mean, really?"

Sozap shrugged. "There's lots of those stories. Old people tell 'em all the time. Maybe some are true. Who knows?" He shrugged again.

"Sure would be nice to throw a few snow days at Ormsbee and Crabby-ton," Connor said.

They strolled a little ways in silence, each lost in his own thoughts. Connor, glancing out of the corner of his eye, had the clear impression that his friend was debating something in his head. He knew Sozap well enough not to push him when the other was in what he called "my thinking place."

The girls suddenly broke into a run, laughing together and holding hands, heading for the Daly house, which had just come into view. In a minute, the boys were left alone.

Sozap stood still. "It's true," he said, not looking at Connor, but gazing down the road ahead, as if afraid to look his friend in the eye.

Connor, who had been distracted by the antics of a squirrel in the branches of a nearby maple, turned and asked, "What's true?"

"The snow magic."

"You're putting me on," his friend said, grinning.

"No," Sozap insisted, turning a serious face to the other. "But if you're not interested . . ." He started walking again.

Connor grabbed his arm. "Wait! You're saying that this stuff is *real*?"

Sozap nodded and then glanced anxiously from left

to right, checking out the trees as though someone or something might be listening. "Aunt Niben — Orrin's mom — she has this medicine pouch. I've heard her talking to other grownups when they think no one is listening. Her mom gave it to her to keep when she died, and her mom's mom before her. Supposedly, it goes back to when Pebon disappeared. All sorts of stuff was found in his wigwam. The tribe burned almost everything else, but the medicine pouch was given to a wise woman of the village to keep. I dunno, maybe they were afraid that destroying it might bring down some really bad medicine."

"You've seen it?" Connor asked eagerly.

"I know where she keeps it," his friend said. "I've never touched it. I'm not supposed to know anything about it. Probably my aunt will give it to Moli, since she's the only girl-child in the family. It always goes to the girl. But that won't be for a long time."

"But you could get it," Connor began, then added hastily, "just to look at, I mean."

Sozap made a face. "You don't wanna mess with that stuff. Story is, old Pebon got it somehow — maybe stole it — from the *Meteekolenol*. They were like wizards — evil, with hearts of ice. Their magic always caused trouble."

"But Pebon saved the people."

"Yeah — and what happened to *him*?"

Connor ignored this. "Anyhow, could you get it —

just for a peek? That'd be so great!" Connor was wheedling now. Sozap looked doubtful. "Or is this just another story?"

"No, man, it's real. I've seen where Aunt Niben hides it behind a big stone on her fireplace."

"All you have to do is borrow it for a few hours," said Connor. "No one'll even know it's gone."

"I don't think that's such a good idea," Sozap protested. But Connor knew from the uncertainty in his voice that his friend was wavering. Going on the attack, Connor quickly got the Abenaki boy to agree to "borrow" the medicine pouch for a short time.

"How soon can you get it?" he asked Sozap.

Sighing, his friend said, "Saturday. Aunt Niben and Orrin always go into Danbury for shopping. They'll be gone for hours."

"Perfect!" Connor said. "We'll meet at Luther's cabin." This was a shack high up in the hills behind the Daly house. It had belonged to Old Luther, a hermit who'd died the previous year. No one knew much about the old man, but kids in the area used to tell stories of weird goings-on at night — strange lights bobbing between the trees, shadowy shapes flitting around the forest. Most people dismissed it as nonsense — the kinds of stories that were sure to be spun around an unfriendly, solitary figure, probably crazy, who was always babbling to himself or to invisible companions.

"You're just gonna look at it?" asked Sozap.

"I swear," said Connor, raising his hand like someone being sworn in at court. When it came to getting his way, the boy would do or say anything.

Sozap gave his friend a long look and then shrugged. "Saturday morning," he said. "I gotta go now. Don't let Moli stay too long with your sisters, or my folks'll get mad." He took off running down the road.

The next day, Friday, was the worst that Connor could ever remember. He left his homework at home. There was a pop quiz in math that he knew he'd blown. Mrs. Chatterton, already on his case, caught him trying to slip a note to Sozap and made him stay after school for detention.

As he sat at his desk doing extra-assignment math problems, he imagined a giant snowstorm suddenly hurtling down from the hills, driven by hundred-mile-an-hour winds. He imagined it slamming into the school, smashing through the windows, blasting through the classroom doors, and whirling away the papers on Mrs. Chatterton's desk, while she struggled vainly to reach a window to close it. Then the sheer force of the storm would punch out the classroom wall and suck his teacher into the howling, white whirlwind outside. His imagination going full steam ahead now, Connor saw the figure, still clutching a red pen and an exam paper with a big red F on it, swallowed up by the weather, with only a few fast-fading shrieks to mark her fate.

"Daydreaming won't get those math problems solved," his teacher warned, snapping him back to reality.

"Yes, ma'am," he said and bent his head over the math page in front of him. But the vision of the deadly ice storm had made him feel much better.

He got up early and did his Saturday morning chores as quickly as possible. Then, telling his parents he was going to see Sozap, he took off. A short ways down the lane, he found the nearly overgrown path that wound up and back into the hills to Luther's cabin.

When he reached the cabin, he saw that the door to the shack was partway open. Inside, leaves and pine needles and other forest litter lay thick upon the hard-packed earthen floor. An old table and two battered chairs stood near the fieldstone fireplace that took up most of one wall. A bed with mildewed covers had been pushed against another wall. Between them was a rusty wreck of a stove with a few sad pans and a dented coffeepot on top. Several nearby shelves held cans whose labels had rotted away or bottles whose contents were gray, green, blue, and gross enough to supply a witch's workshop. Several of them had exploded from the decay inside.

Connor sat at the table. He'd brought his Nintendo

DS and quickly involved himself in a game of Call of Duty while he waited for Sozap. He kept pulling his cell phone out of his pocket to check the time. When it got to be after 11:00 A.M., he began to wonder if his friend was going to show up. Maybe Sozap's relatives had changed their minds about going into Danbury.

Then he heard the door, which he'd shut as best he could, scrape open. Looking up, he saw Sozap shouldering his way in. "They were late getting goin'," the boy said. "And my old man had some extra stuff he needed me to do."

"But you brought it?" asked Connor, turning off the handheld and stuffing it in his jacket pocket.

Sozap crossed the room and dropped his worn, green backpack on a corner of the table. He dug inside and drew out a black basket the size and shape of a small soup bowl. He set this on the tabletop between them. Gently, he lifted the lid, revealing a deerskin pouch covered with designs sewn from tiny white and purple shell beads.

"What's inside the pouch?" asked Connor.

In answer, Sozap undid the leather drawstrings and shook two small white carvings into his palm. Both were eagles with outstretched wings, carved from ivory or bone, faintly yellowish.

Sozap pointed to one. "That's *Psonen*. He's an eagle-spirit that makes snow by opening his wings. The other one is *Wadzoosen*, the eagle that flaps his wings to create wind. Together, they can make a storm."

"May I hold them?" asked Connor. After a minute, the other boy gently dropped the two bird figures into Connor's hand.

"They're cold," said Connor. "They feel like they're made of ice."

"They're winter spirits," said Sozap.

"How do they work?"

"No one's told me. Maybe my aunt knows. Anyhow, now you've seen 'em, give 'em back." Sozap reached for the delicate carvings.

"Maybe just holding them is enough," said Connor, ignoring the other's request. "Maybe just telling them what you want would work."

"*Now!*" the other boy insisted, starting to get angry.

"Chill!" Connor said and added, "That's pretty funny."

"I gotta return these before my cousin and aunt come back." Clearly Sozap was not amused. He made a lunge at the other boy.

But Connor was too quick. Holding one carving in each hand, he danced around the table. In a moment of craziness, he shouted to his left hand, "*Psonen*, bring snow!" To his right, he yelled, "*Wadzoosen*, bring wind!" Then Sozap hurtled into his midriff, knocking the breath out of him, sending both boys rolling through the leaf litter, until they slammed against the old wooden bedframe, which partly collapsed under the impact.

Straddling Connor, Sozap tried to pry open his fingers; even half dazed, Connor was keeping his grip on the carvings.

"Let go before you hurt them or do something worse." Sozap sounded frantic now. His fingers dug into Connor's, the nails gouging the latter's skin.

Connor relented. "All right. Take the things." He opened his hands, and Sozap snatched the little eagles. Panting, he stood up, releasing Connor. Not looking at the other boy, Sozap returned the carvings to the deerskin bag. Then he dropped the pouch into the small basket and placed it in his backpack.

"We're not friends anymore," he said.

"I was only fooling," said Connor.

Whatever Sozap was going to say next was cut off by the howling wind that, seemingly arisen from nowhere, suddenly battered all the flimsy walls of the cabin. Startled, Connor looked out through the cabin's single grimy window, just above the collapsed bed, and saw that the sky had gone gray. The sun was giving off such a muted light, it might have been closer to evening than noon. The very air seemed to be thickening, and a bitter chill had crept into the shack, making both boys shiver. It was as though a vast, hard, gray wing had swept across the sky.

Now, from the heavens, snow began sifting down, the rising wind rapidly transforming it into a blinding storm. The pulsing flakes, charging then retreating, made Connor think of the frantically beating wings of some giant bird. The madly capering trees outside were already shrouded in white, like towering, sheeted ghosts. Connor took a branch from the pile of ages-old kindling stacked on the hearth and jammed it under the door to keep it in place. Driven snow leaked in, since the weather-beaten panel no longer fit smoothly into its frame.

"This is crazy!" said Connor. "Where did this storm come from all of a sudden?"

"From us," said Sozap dully.

"You mean the carvings?" Connor shook his head in fervent denial. "That kind of stuff doesn't work."

"Tell that to what's outside," said Sozap.

"Freak storm," muttered Connor. "We'll wait it out. You'll see, it'll blow over in a little while." He sat down at the table and pulled out his handheld. "Wanna play Call of Duty or Halo?" He made a point of ignoring the shrieking wind, the swaying tree boughs glimpsed through the blizzard, and the occasional tapping of sleet like ghostly fingertips against the glass.

Sozap shook his head, sat down in the opposite chair, and folded his arms protectively over his backpack. A moment later, he raised his hands to his ears to shut out the roar of the winds that seemed to be taking turns howling from the north and then the east, raging at the window and the door. "It isn't gonna stop," he said miserably. "You got your snow day, man. Happy?"

Connor ignored the jab, giving full attention to his Nintendo DS. "My dad always says, any storm that comes on this strong is gonna blow itself out just as quick."

The other boy sighed and, ears still covered, lowered his head onto the backpack.

Connor decided he'd better call home and let his family know that he was riding out the storm okay.

One of his sisters picked up on the third ring.

"'Lo?"

"Emma?"

"Jenna. Is this Connor?"

"Yeah. Tell Mom and Dad I'm okay, but I may have to wait until this storm blows over."

"What storm?"

"The one that began about an hour ago. It's a blizzard."

"I'm looking out the front window. There's no snow and not much wind."

"Well, it's blowing like crazy up here."

"Where *are* you?"

"Luther's cabin. There's a freaky storm trying to blow the place away."

"It must just be where you are, then."

"That doesn't make much sense," he replied, then

thought, *Nothing is making much sense at the moment.*

"Do you want to talk to Dad? I think he's in the basement."

"No — just tell him where I am and that me and Sozap are stuck here for a while."

"'Kay." Jenna hung up.

"Funny, it's not snowing down below," Connor told his friend, who had unplugged his ears and been trying to catch the conversation. "Must be a weird squall or something that will be over soon."

But just then the intensity of the storm ratcheted up outside. The walls seemed to bow in and out as though breathing in time with the buffeting winds. Then the window shattered. Connor and Sozap ducked as mixed snow and glass fragments howled into the cabin. The boys' breath emerged in streams, instantly shredded by the wind that spun around the room, determined to claim every nook and corner, shake every beam and rafter. The door began to inch open, causing the jammed branch underneath to squeal in protest.

Connor fought his way to the window. Beyond the drifts, now piled up to the window frame, swirled a white curtain of nothingness that hid even the nearest trees from view.

"I'm freezing," Sozap complained. He was wearing his school jacket with its Ormsbee Panthers logo emblazoned on the back. "Can we start a fire or something?"

Connor wished he had more than his nylon jacket.

"You got matches or a lighter?" he asked.

Sozap shook his head.

"Me neither. Let's get on the bed," said Connor. "The blankets may be funky, but we can huddle under them."

The two of them climbed onto the wrecked bed and mounded the moth-eaten covers and mildewed comforter over themselves.

"I'm calling my dad," Connor said. "They can send rangers or something."

"Just do it," his friend pleaded.

But, this time, the phone was no longer able to locate a signal. Then the screen went dark.

"Guess I kinda forgot to recharge it," said Connor sheepishly.

"You told your sister. She knows. Someone will figure it out."

In the darkness, under the piled covers, they found a little warmth. But when Connor dared to peek out, he saw the snow piling up in drifts across the floor. The air had grown so cold, it stung his eyes and nose and lips. He quickly retreated under the protective covering. The boys put their arms around each other's shoulders for a bit of extra warmth.

Then a strange numbness began to creep up Connor's hands and legs. *Is this what it's like to freeze to death?* he wondered in a panic. "I can't feel my feet or hands anymore," he said.

"Me neither," said Sozap, teeth chattering.

For a moment, Connor was too afraid to ask the question. But, finally, he said, "Are we freezing to death?"

"Maybe." Connor thought Sozap's voice sounded as lifeless as his limbs. *Don't give up on me, man,* he wanted to say. But his throat felt numb, and his lips were frozen together.

The wind-rush through the missing window got worse. It teased the edges of the blanket and then whipped it away, leaving the two boys pressed side by side against the cabin wall, no longer able to speak or move. Connor could feel nothing but bone-chilling cold. Out of the corner of his eye, he saw Sozap staring back at him, the other boy's eyebrows and lashes delicately crusted with ice. His eyes were frozen open, and Connor could see the frightened pupils darting back and forth.

More snow churned into the cabin. Soon the drifts had crawled onto the bed, forming mini-mounds around the boys' feet and legs.

Connor's own eyes were iced open, but he could still peer into the cold that was so absolute, he could almost *see* it.

There was something odd about his condition. Even though immobilized, with his body freezing down to what felt like absolute zero, he could still see and think clearly. An idea began to dawn. Part of old Pebon's wintry magic had been to freeze his people so they could survive the storm the old man summoned. They had all survived because of this second bit of magic, Connor reasoned, so wasn't there a chance that some of that magic was mixed in with the power to call up a storm? It was a wild hope, but he clung to it as the snow drifted to their waists.

He could still see that Sozap's eyes were very much alive in the ice caves of their sockets, and now Connor was sure he'd scoped it out: two magics — destruction and survival — mixed together like wind and snow to make a storm. Like two spirit-eagles doing a medicine man's bidding. He wished he could force out the words to reassure Sozap that everything was all right. *In some weird way, we're going to make it,* Connor promised himself.

The storm continued, filling the cabin with snow to chest-height on the two frozen figures. Connor wondered how far the unnatural storm extended. As the hours passed, he was surprised no one had come searching for them — but then, unless Jenna made an issue of things, no one was going to be worried for a long time if the two boys, who often disappeared together for the better part of a day, didn't show up at their respective homes.

Then, as suddenly as it had begun, the storm subsided. The gloom that had filled the cabin began to lighten. The breeze that now blew in through the window and the door was warm. Though his eyes were frozen open and his body numb, Connor saw the ice-lacing on Sozap's lashes and brows melt into tiny droplets. Soon the mini-icicles hanging from his friend's hair would start to drip away.

This whole mess may be over pretty soon, thought Connor. They'd survived the storm at its worst; maybe everything was on its way back to normal. *Maybe,* he decided, *this will turn out to be nothing but some kind of daymare.* He looked across at Sozap and saw that the despair in his eyes seemed to be giving way to something positive.

The snow inside and out was turning to slush in the rising air currents, which, compared to the cold, seemed almost tropical. Connor was sure that he could feel the feathery touch of warm breezes on his forehead and cheeks. He was sure sensation was returning to his limbs.

Everything is going to be fine, he realized. He could blink his eyes now. Feeling a smile that he would soon be able to express on his thawing lips, he glanced across at Sozap. To his astonishment, there was now a look of horror in his friend's eyes. Helpless to ask, Connor wondered what, with things going so well, could be upsetting the other boy. Then he realized that rivulets of melt were running down Sozap's face — not just from the ice-rime, *but from his skin.* Even as he watched, the boy's forehead and cheeks began to sag like the features on a wax doll that had been held too close to a flame.

Now Connor felt his own flesh softening. The numbness that held him was giving way to a sense of weakness. He felt more than snow and ice puddling on the bed beneath the two of them.

Sozap's head fell forward toward his chest. Connor felt his whole body tilting sideways into the other boy, where the two of them slowly merged as the sun shone more intensely and the warm winds flooded the room.

Connor's last thought was of Moli warning them, "Cousin Orrin says you can't make big magic without paying for it big time."

When the boys' fathers reached the cabin at day's end, they found the place pretty much the wreck it had always been, though windowless now. There didn't seem to be anything sinister, until the boys' clothes, still damp, and Sozap's backpack, soaked through, were found on the collapsed bedstead. The mystery deepened when no trace of either boy was found. The clothes and backpack contents were sifted for clues, but nothing came to light. The boys had, to all effects, vanished from the face of the earth. In fact, they became the central figures in local stories of alien abductions.

The little woven basket with the deerskin pouch inside was identified and returned to Sozap's aunt Niben. But if she, or Moli, had any suspicions about what might have happened, they kept their thoughts to themselves.

Fairy Godmother

Min Su-mi was six when she flew from Seoul to join her new American parents, Lois and Norman Gaddis. She traveled across the Pacific to San Francisco, and then on to New York City in the company of Pete and Carol Prine. The Prines worked for the Christian agency that had been caring for the girl since Su-mi's mother had brought her to St. Mary's Orphanage the year before. Deathly ill, the woman had lived only a week longer in the little infirmary attached to the orphanage. Su-mi had never really had a father; he'd abandoned the two of them when her mother grew too sick to continue supporting the family.

During the two long plane flights, the child had let

herself imagine that the Prines were going to be with her always — as her parents. Of the Gaddises, she had only a faint memory of a thin man and a heavyset woman visiting the orphanage several months before. Everything since had been done by computer or express mail. Though the couple was older than most seeking to adopt, the orphanage was quite willing to let them apply for one of their older charges.

Su-mi knew the Gaddises were very rich and owned several homes, including a big house in New York City. To the child, who had never even had a room of her own, this seemed wealth beyond dreams.

The Prines weren't rich, but they joked about it. They were always smiling or laughing out loud. Su-mi loved every minute with them. Though the people at the orphanage kept telling her, "You are such a lucky girl; the Gaddises are so *rich*," she would have felt more fortunate to be going home with Pete and Carol.

But the day came when, at the huge airport in New York, the Prines surrendered their charge to Norman and Lois Gaddis. Su-mi, clinging to Pete's hand, tried to hide in Carol's embrace.

"I know it's a difficult time, honey," said Mrs. Gaddis, "but we're your parents now." Firmly, the woman pried Su-mi free of the Prines and, gripping her left hand in her own, squeezed so hard it almost hurt the child. At a nod from his wife, Norman Gaddis took Su-mi's other hand. His fingers were warm and soft, unlike his wife's, which were cold and damp — but his grip was just as steely.

The two couples exchanged a few more words. The Prines gave the Gaddises a packet of documents.

"Say 'bye-bye,' honey," urged Mrs. Gaddis, holding up Su-mi for a last glimpse of the young missionaries. When the girl just shook her head, Lois took her limp hand and flapped it in a farewell gesture. Having no other place to hide her sorrow, Su-mi buried her face on Mrs. Gaddis's shoulder, which smelled of flowers and something the little girl could not name but would come to know as *wealth.*

She was taken to her new home in a big car — which she soon learned was called a "limousine" — driven by a man in a gray uniform with a fancy matching cap. Norman and Lois called him "Charles."

The house, when they entered through gates that opened and closed as if by magic, was three stories tall, fronted by a circular driveway with a sweep of tidy lawn and beautifully manicured trees and shrubs.

A young woman opened the front door. She wore a black skirt and a white blouse, and the Gaddises called her "Katherine."

"This," said Lois, placing a hand on each of Su-mi's shoulders, "is our little girl. Over there, her name was Su-mi. But she's our Michelle now."

Stepping into her new home, flanked by her new parents, Min Su-mi from Korea became Michelle Gaddis of America.

The interior was almost too much for the girl to take in. A long hall led to a broad staircase. Everything was painted soft gray or shades of white with, here and there, the softest hint of blue or green. Heavy curtains — which she later learned were called "damask" — framed windows that stretched from floor to ceiling.

To the girl, the halls and rooms of St. Mary's Orphanage had seemed huge. Here she felt like a mouse that had entered a giant's castle. The furniture in every room had an elegant, polished look; she couldn't imagine anybody (except Lois and Norman) sitting in one of the chairs or placing a teacup on a table in this perfect setting.

Katherine exchanged a few words with Lois and then marched down the hall, past the foot of the stairs, her crisp steps clicking hypnotically on the tile flooring.

"Come along," Lois invited. "I want to show you your room. Are you coming, Norman?" she asked her husband.

"Er — no. I want to check my e-mail."

Lois shrugged. Then, towing the girl after her, she started up the stairs.

A huge portrait dominated the landing where the stairway split, turning right and left, leading to the upstairs gallery and rooms. The painting showed a tall, thin woman reading to a child on her lap, a book open in front of them. The woman was clearly a magical being, her head crowned with an elaborate headdress that exploded with color — yellow, orange, and gold

mostly. It hinted at massed jewels and feathers and fili-
gree, yet seemed pure energy at the same time. The
woman's features and coloring — especially her
almond-shaped eyes — suggested she might have
Asian or African blood in her. Clusters of earrings
dripped from each ear. She wore a necklace of coins
or jewels — it was hard to tell which the glowing
colors suggested more. What could be seen of her
body was draped in a robe of the same shimmering
colors as her headdress. The single slender right hand,
with elongated fingers holding the book open, bore gold
rings with massive jewels of green, red, and blue.

She looked so nice at first glance — reminding the
girl of an angel or a spirit of some kind reading to a child.

"We call her 'Our Fairy Godmother,'" said Lois,
breaking the silence. She laid the fingertips of her
right hand affectionately against the gilded frame.
"She — well, the *painting* — has been in the family for
generations." Lois spoke in the hushed tones people
used in chapel, Su-mi/Michelle thought.

But, as Su-mi, now Michelle stared, she noticed
several curious things. The painted woman's long,
narrow face looked grim; her cold eyes were sharply
focused not on the book in front of her but on the very
spot where Su-mi stood. Looking more closely, the girl
realized that the shadowy drapes behind the figure
might well be enormous wings, and the thin lips were
parted just enough to reveal the hint of teeth that were
sharp, almost feral.

The image of the child was more unnerving. The girl sat a bit to one side with the strange woman's left arm locked firmly around her. While the tall figure's race was uncertain to Su-mi, the girl was unmistakably Asian, could well be a Korean child, like herself. With her thatch of black hair cut in a short bob, and her equally dark, soft eyes, she would have fit right in at St. Mary's. She was gazing straight ahead, and Su-mi had the uncanny feeling the child's eyes were staring into her own. Even more disturbing, the look on her face seemed a mix of fear and horror.

It's an awful picture, Su-mi thought. *I never want to look at it, if I don't have to.* Aloud she said simply, "It's nice."

"Come along now," said Lois. "We still haven't seen your room."

Dutifully, the girl took the woman's hand as they climbed the right set of upper stairs. She didn't turn around, but she could almost feel the eyes of the painted girl following her.

A moment later, Su-mi/Michelle stood in the center of the bedroom Lois assured her was hers. She gaped in wonder. Everything was soft pink — walls, ceiling, and fluffy rug on the floor. The bed — itself covered with a frilly pink comforter — was piled high with dolls, teddy bears, and an assortment of stuffed animals. Su-mi went right for the grinning one that had the word "Tigger" stitched in red on his yellow-and-black-striped flank.

"He is mine?" she asked.

"Of course. Everything in this room is yours."

"Then I name him *Horangi*," she said, giving the Korean name for "tiger."

"Yes, that's a good name," said Lois vaguely as the child clutched the tiger to her chest. To Su-mi/Michelle, the stuffed toy meant she had a friend who would protect her — for what kept a Korean household safe from evil spirits and misfortunes better than the spirit of a tiger?

Lois moved around the room, pointing out the walk-in closet; the bureau; the dressing table with its pink plastic hand mirror, combs, and brushes; the bookshelves jammed with an assortment of titles that meant nothing to the girl, even though she read English almost better than she could speak it.

Su-mi/Michelle nodded when that seemed the right thing to do. From time to time, she said, "That's nice" — one of the more useful phrases she had been taught before leaving for America. Her responses seemed to satisfy Lois.

The girl was already learning that things went best the happier Lois was. There had been a moment in the car when Su-mi, overwhelmed by the strangeness of everything, had begun to sob. "We'll have none of that from now on," Lois had said severely. When the girl's tears had continued, in spite of Su-mi's efforts to stifle them, the woman had ordered, "Stop that this minute!" For emphasis, she gave the child a shake. When Norman, sitting on the other side of the backseat, suggested they "let the tears run out," Lois had snapped, "What do you know about raising children?" He had simply sighed and turned to look out the window. Sensing that the woman would soon lose patience altogether — might even strike her — Su-mi had choked back her tears, though she remained miserable inside.

Now, having pointed out all the lovely things around them, her new mother said, "Play. Get acquainted with your new room. I'll send Katherine up when it's time for dinner."

As soon as Lois was gone, Su-mi began to whisper her unhappiness into the cloth ear of the tiger. After this, she felt better and lay down on the bed, still hugging Horangi, trying to imagine her new life with Lois, who insisted on having things her way; Norman, who rarely seemed to notice her; and a houseful of servants who glided around as quiet as ghosts. And there were the sad, frightened eyes of the girl in the painting — eyes that seemed to echo something of what Su-mi was feeling at the moment. Most fearful of all was the haunting, not-really-human figure of Lois's "Fairy Godmother." Su-mi promised herself she would not look at the painting when she went downstairs.

They ate dinner in the long, narrow dining room,

with an amazing light fixture — she would soon learn the word "chandelier" — hovering over the polished wooden dining set. She sat close to Lois at one end of the table. Norman sat at the other end, reading a newspaper, seemingly unaware that anyone else was in the room.

"You must be tired," said Lois, when the serving girl had cleared away the last dinner dishes — including the bowl in which Su-mi had been served two helpings of pink peppermint ice cream as part of what Lois called a "Welcome Home" celebration. That had almost made up for the bland food and the long silences that lingered over the dinner table. "I'll bet bed will seem very good."

Though she wasn't tired, Su-mi nodded and said simply, "Yes."

"Go kiss your father good night," said Lois, nudging the girl in Norman's direction. At the same time, she called out sharply, "Norman, put down your paper. Our daughter wants to say good night."

For a moment, Norman didn't look like he quite knew what his wife was talking about. Then, seeing Su-mi approach with tentative steps, he made a show of holding out his arms to her. Keeping her hands behind her back, she stood on tiptoe and gave Norman a peck on the cheek. He gave her a quick kiss on the forehead, a brief hug, and then said, "Run along to bed now."

When she was tucked in, surrounded by the dolls and stuffed animals, Su-mi lay listening as her new mother, seated on the bed, chattered away. Occasionally Lois patted the girl's hands, resting on top of the satiny pink blanket binding.

"My life — my family's life — has been like a fairy tale," said Lois. "Do you know what a fairy tale is?"

Su-mi nodded. "Carol Prine read many to us out of a book she had when she was little. It was part of English class." This was the most she'd said all evening, and it seemed to please her new mother. Su-mi was glad, since keeping Lois happy seemed to be something that she and Norman and everyone else in the house had to work at every minute. Too many times already the girl had seen anger flash into the woman's eyes — when Su-mi ran noisily down the stairs, when Norman was late to dinner, when the serving girl dripped gravy on the tablecloth.

"Once upon a time," Lois continued, starting her story like all of Carol's fairy tales, "my family was very poor. But things began to change when my great-grandfather bought the picture on the stairway. It's never been clear where it came from — or who the artist was — though the story is it came from someplace far away, like Africa or China. But old Hezekiah — didn't they have funny names back then?" Lois interjected with a smile.

Because it seemed expected of her, Michelle smiled back.

"Well, Hezekiah was only scraping by, repairing

furniture for people, or sometimes making new pieces to sell. He couldn't afford to marry or have a family. Then, somehow, he got the painting, and things changed as if by magic. It was as though he'd really found a fairy godmother — not just a painting of one. Since then, we've kept it in the family. It may sound silly, but we believe it's our lucky charm and that we'd lose everything if it ever went out of our keeping."

She gave Michelle's hand a hard, chilly squeeze. "The only thing lacking for Norman and me, living in this fairy tale like a king and queen" — here she made a chuckling sound — "was a princess for our castle. Now you've come. You're our new princess. Do you feel like a fairy tale princess?"

Again, reading the woman's satisfied expression, Michelle said, "Oh yes," with all the enthusiasm she could muster.

"Well, then, good night, Princess," said Lois, leaning down to kiss the girl's forehead. Her lips felt papery dry.

She went out, turning off the overhead light and leaving one small lamp on the bureau burning. The pink lampshade cast a soft rosy glow over the room.

As soon as the woman had closed the door quietly behind her, Michelle (who felt more like Su-mi at the moment) pushed the pale-faced American dolls to the far side of her bed and hugged Horangi to her.

Because she wasn't very sleepy — too many things had happened too fast this day — she lay awake. She thought of Carol Prine and wondered how she and Pete were doing on their journey back to St. Mary's, half a world away. Then she recalled some of the fairy tales Carol had read her. A lot of times, the princesses didn't fare too well — at least at the start. They were often captured by monsters or enchanted by witches and only survived because a hero came along to save them. Well, she decided, Horangi would be *her* hero if anything bad tried to hurt her.

Peering into his grinning face, she asked, "*Yeongeo hal jul aseyo?* Do you speak English?"

"*Anio*" — No — she imagined him answering.

"*Gomapseupnida,*" she said gratefully. "Thank you."

She sang him a half-remembered lullaby that her mother had sung to her. Shortly after this, she fell asleep only to dream of a tall figure in golden robes and bright jewels coming down a hallway toward her. But the being had a monster's head, with hot red eyes and snarling jaws full of fangs. Huge wings beat the air behind the creature. Suddenly a gigantic tiger leaped between her dream-self and the horrible beast. Horangi's roar scared the monster-headed thing back down the hall, where it disappeared into the shadows. After this, her dreams became a comfortable jumble of pleasant images, and she passed the rest of the night peacefully.

In the days that followed, Michelle was pretty

much allowed to go where she wanted in the house. Norman and Lois's bedroom was out of bounds, as was the office where Norman worked when he was home. But the other rooms were an unending source of wonder to her. She remembered a Korean fairy tale one of the cooks at St. Mary's had told her. It was about a moon-born being who came to earth to be the daughter of a simple peasant and his wife. But Su-mi, roaming the big house, felt more like an earth-born child who had gone to the wonderland of the moon.

The only thing she didn't like about the house was the painting on the hall landing. Lois called it her "Fairy Godmother," but Michelle secretly named her *Mudang*, the Sorceress, who can bring healing and good things, but who also associates with spirits of the dead. There was something distressing in the strange figure's cold, possessive stare, the frightened look of the child enfolded in her arms, and the suggestion of wings and fangs. These all hinted at a terrifying truth masked by the glowing colors, the beautiful costume and jewels, the elegance of the painting. In a way, the Sorceress reminded Michelle of Lois — all soft colors and smiles and politeness that, her adopted daughter often felt, hid things deeper and darker and dangerous in her heart.

Michelle was nearing her tenth birthday, when one afternoon she sat with her friend Julie Solberg — another adoptee in her class, who had been Kim Jin-ju when she came from Korea at age three. They were perched on one of the broad railings that flanked the stairs at the main entrance to Haddonfield Girls Academy. Though school had let out early, neither girl had felt the need to call for her respective family limo. With heavy-duty schooling and parental schedules, they found it hard enough to have any time to themselves — let alone time to share with a friend. They called each other "Su-mi" and "Jin-ju" — though not when either set of parents could hear these secret names.

"What do you want for your birthday?" asked Jin-ju/Julie.

Su-mi just shrugged, thought a minute, and then said, "Maybe to be somewhere else, by myself, for a while."

"Are you having trouble with your mom and dad?" asked Jin-ju.

Su-mi shook her head. "Not really. Lois and Norman are just . . . Lois and Norman. They never change." But she couldn't hide a note of disappointment.

"What's wrong, *really*?" asked Jin-ju, picking up the vibe.

"I don't know," Su-mi said. "But I never feel they love me. They say the right things and buy me presents all the time. But I sometimes think if I ran away, Norman would just forget about me. And Lois — well, it's like she's keeping me around for some reason of her own."

"What reason?" Jin-ju prompted, puzzled.

"I don't know," the other said, exasperated. "I guess it just feels so different from when I see you with your parents. It's clear you're the best thing that ever happened to them, and they only want wonderful things for you." Su-mi sighed. She'd felt all day as if she were coming down with a cold. She wondered if this was part of the reason for her complaining.

"Maybe Lois and Norman are afraid to love you," said Jin-ju thoughtfully. She stopped, looking embarrassed.

"Why would they be?" It was now Su-mi's turn to be puzzled.

"They lost another daughter, years before you arrived. I overheard my parents talking about it. I'm not supposed to know, but" — she shrugged guiltily — "sometimes you just *hear* things. Anyhow, she was from Korea, too. Her name was Su-yeon, but they called her Suellen."

"They've never told me. What happened?"

"She got sick or something. No one is supposed to talk about it. Maybe you kind of remind them of her, and it hurts, and they're afraid they might lose you, too." This all came out in a rush, as if Jin-ju wanted it said and done and over with.

"That's pretty weird, knowing there was another girl like me in that house."

"I shouldn't have told you," said Jin-ju. "Please

don't tell Lois and Norman. If word gets back to my parents, I'll be grounded forever."

"I won't. I promise."

Suddenly the other girl, sounding relieved, said, "Oh, there's Edward with the car." Grabbing her backpack, she added, "I really think they love you, Su-mi. Just give them time; they'll show it."

"They've already had four years," said Su-mi. But her friend didn't hear, as she was already running down the steps to the limo, where the chauffeur waited with the door open. A moment later Michelle picked up her own backpack, having caught sight of the Gaddis limousine two car lengths behind in the pickup line.

That afternoon the house seemed quieter than usual. Partly, it was because Norman was out of town on business. Lois was nowhere to be seen. But there seemed to be a heavy stillness clogging the air, hinting at the pressure before a storm. And Michelle's cold was getting worse. Her head felt so stuffed up and she was so feverish, her brain felt bogged down in glue.

Still thinking of her conversation with Julie, Michelle decided to have a nap before dinner. Eager to snuggle under the covers with Horangi, she drifted toward the foot of the stairs.

She stopped suddenly. Lois was on the landing, staring at the portrait. Michelle was sure she could hear her murmuring, although she couldn't quite make out the words. *Is Lois talking to the painting?* she wondered. The painting itself seemed to glow with an inner fire Michelle had never seen before. She tried to tell herself it was some freakish effect of the setting sun, but the heavy damask curtains had been drawn across the high windows. There really wasn't enough light to account for the strange glow. Within the gilded frame, the Sorceress's image seemed to have grown disproportionately large and bright; the child seemed to have shrunk to little more than a shadow in the curve of her arm.

Instinctively, Michelle drew aside into the open library doorway so she could watch and listen without being obvious. Now she was sure her adoptive mother was reciting a poem or a prayer, but all she could make out was the rise and fall of the sounds, the rhythm.

As she strained to hear more clearly, she caught the words, ". . . my promise. . . ." Lois suddenly broke off her murmuring, turned, and spotted Michelle, who was a moment too late retreating into the library.

"How long have you been there?" Lois demanded.

"I just got home," the girl replied, adding quickly, "I was on my way upstairs. I'm not feeling well. I think I'll take a nap."

The woman glanced quickly up at the "Fairy Godmother," then back at Michelle. The glowing colors of the painting seemed to surround Lois's head like a garish halo. "I'm sorry you're not feeling well," she said.

To feverish Michelle, she didn't sound concerned at all. Thinking only of her bed, the girl took several steps closer to the stairs.

"Who were you talking to just now?" she asked. "Or were you *praying?*"

Lois's eyes narrowed; there was a warning edge of anger in her voice when she said, "Were you listening? You know it's wrong to eavesdrop."

Michelle knew she was entering dangerous territory, but she said, "It sounded like you were making a promise up there." She waved her hand toward the landing.

For a moment the woman seemed lost for words. Then she said, "That's utter nonsense. If you're going to eavesdrop," she added nastily, "at least try to get things straight." She came rapidly down the stairs. Michelle took a step backward, but Lois grabbed her shoulder and placed her right hand against the girl's forehead. "You've got a fever." To the girl her voice sounded almost accusing. "Now, no more of this nonsensical talk," Lois said dismissively. She glanced at her watch. "Anyhow, it's teatime."

Time to back off, Michelle told herself, *and tea might be good for my nose and throat.* Aloud she asked, "Shall I ring for Katherine?"

"No, I gave her and the other servants the day off. It's just us."

No wonder the house seems so quiet, the girl thought.

"**T**ell me about school," said her mother, when they were seated in the parlor, on opposite sides of the tea table with the big silver tray between them. The tea tasted odd and so did the lemon cookies, but Michelle decided it was due to her cold. Things always tasted funny when she wasn't feeling well. The tea helped a little, but all she wanted now was to climb in bed and sleep until morning.

Trying to think of things to talk about was becoming harder. Her body felt so weary and her brain so tired, thoughts seemed to tangle up in one another. Finally she asked, "When is Norman coming home?"

"Not for several days. I told him he needed to check on the Chicago office. He didn't want to go, but I told him he had no choice. I'd already booked his tickets and the hotel." Lois poured more tea into her daughter's cup, though there was still a half-cup's worth. She hadn't yet touched her own tea or tasted the cookies, Michelle noticed.

They talked awhile longer — about classes and her friends and the upcoming winter concert when Michelle would sing with the school chorus. Lois murmured a few things, but Michelle was aware that the words only gave the illusion of conversation. There was something fiercely watchful in Lois's eyes that didn't match her empty words.

Michelle's face was growing hotter, her throat drier,

and she felt a bone-deep weariness seeping through her, deadening her arms and legs, turning her hands and feet into heavy weights. Then a dizziness swept over her that was so disorienting, she pressed her fingers to her forehead and said, "Oh!"

Lois looked intently at her. "Are you all right, darling?"

"The cold . . . I feel . . . so very tired," Michelle answered. Just getting the words out made her feel even more exhausted. She made an effort to stand up — was amazed at how rubbery her legs felt, while her head seemed to be expanding like an overinflated balloon.

"You really are ill," said her mother, rising and coming around the table. Lois laid her long, damp fingers against Michelle's forehead. "The fever is worse," she said. "Let's put you to bed. If you're not feeling better after you've rested, I'll call the doctor."

Supported by her mother, Michelle reached the foot of the stairs. She wasn't sure she could make the climb, but Lois helped her with every step. When they reached the landing, Michelle couldn't resist a look at the hated picture. The image seemed to waver in front of her blurred vision, but she was sure she could see the "Fairy Godmother's" eyes blazing with a fire that suggested hunger and — she searched her increasingly confused mind for a word and then found it — *triumph*. But there was no longer any trace of the almond-eyed child. *That's impossible,* she thought. *I've seen the picture a million times, and she's always there. Always. It's being sick. Paintings don't change.*

She wanted to tell Lois just how distorted things were becoming, but her brain seemed to have forgotten how to shape words into sentences.

"Halfway there," said her mother, and the girl's bizarre impressions flew away. The two started up the right-hand flight of steps that led to Michelle's room at the end of the short corridor.

She was completely relying on her mother to keep her upright by the time they reached the bedroom. Gratefully, she dropped onto the edge of the bed and let herself loll back onto the waiting pillows. Her mother removed her shoes and made her comfortable, carefully tucking the blankets in on either side of the girl. "Everything will be all right in a little while," Lois said, brushing back the hair from Michelle's burning forehead.

Sleep was all Michelle could think about. But before she drifted off, she said, "Bring . . . Horangi."

"I should think you're too old for him," said her mother.

"*Horangi,*" Michelle insisted.

"Very well." Impatiently, Lois shoved the grinning tiger at the girl, who folded her friend into her arms with a satisfied murmur.

Then she was asleep, wrapped in blankets of fever and something else, never hearing her mother close the bedroom door.

She came awake slowly, like a swimmer fighting her way upward through an ocean that was more warm glue than water. Her eyes felt leaden; her mouth was dry and tasted bitter. Deep, smothering dark didn't want to let go of her, but a voice far above was calling, "Wake up!" It was a familiar voice, a friend's voice — even though she wanted the voice to be quiet and go away and let her sleep. But it kept calling to her, and her dream-self followed the sound upward until the darkness began to fade to gray, hinting of light beyond.

Now she recognized the voice. It was Horangi's — just as she had imagined it when she was younger. But it wasn't filled with comfort now, it was urgent with a sense of warning. With the realization, her dream-self strove more determinedly for the light above. She imagined herself in swimming class, and her arms and legs responded, pushing her resolutely up into the gray, past the gray, into the light.

She was jolted awake — confused and fuzzy but restored to the familiar world. Her mouth and throat were dry as cotton; a pressure behind her eyes made them feel as if they might suddenly pop out of their sockets; her head pounded with the worst headache she'd ever had.

Using her arms, she propped herself up in bed. Beside her, Horangi lay grinning on the pillow. A glance at the clock on her nightstand showed her that it was 8:35 P.M. She'd been asleep for over four hours. She managed to kick off the coverlet and swivel around in the bed; the cool air felt good on her burning skin. Dropping her feet to the floor, she felt with her toes for the fuzzy pink slippers that lived under the bed's edge. She tried to stand up, felt too dizzy, sat down and waited a moment. The second time she made it to her feet, using the edge of the bed to steady herself. The house seemed utterly still, except for a soft murmuring from beyond the door. Curious, she started forward, hesitating only long enough to retrieve Horangi from the bed. She felt like a silly little girl, hugging the stuffed tiger — yet it gave her comfort, too.

Careful to make no sound, she opened her bedroom door and peered into the hallway beyond. With the door open, she could make out a voice murmuring phrases over and over, almost as if someone were praying. And now, she was sure, the voice belonged to Lois.

She rubbed her sleep- (and something else-) bleared eyes and took a step toward the top of the stairs. The hall, she noticed, was lit by a strange glow. Gold and amber and yellow, and other colors she could not name, poured up from the landing. The curtains covering the windows rippled as though strange energies were flowing through them. There were no shadows anywhere.

On impulse, she dropped to her hands and knees, crawling along the last stretch of hallway to the stairs. Unwilling to abandon Horangi, she stuffed him down the front of her uniform blouse. At last she reached the top of the stairway, gripped two balusters, and peered through the posts, down toward the landing.

Lois was kneeling in front of the picture, chanting the meaningless words over and over, her hands outstretched to the "Fairy Godmother," as the girl had seen so many hurt and frightened people praying to images of Christ or Holy Mary Mother of God back at the chapel in Korea. But their faces had been different — pleading, unsure, hopeful, and fearful. Clearly written on Lois Gaddis's face was greed and cruelty and certainty.

Even as Michelle watched, a flicker came from within the heavy gilded frame. The glowing colors of the painting grew more intense, like a light bulb when the power source receives an extra burst of energy. Michelle averted her gaze, but out of the corner of her eye, she saw something stirring within the picture. She heard the book being snapped shut. The seated figure started to rise.

On the landing, Lois had lowered her head and buried her face in her arms, but she was chanting ever more loudly and rapidly.

A huge figure, swathed in golden robes, stepped onto the landing. Risking one last look, Michelle saw a clawed foot, more like a lion's than a human's, wearing a gold sandal. It came to rest beside the muttering, prone figure of Lois. The upper part of the being was so haloed in hot light, the girl didn't dare look at it.

Panicked, she fled back to her bedroom, aware that the creature was slowly ascending the stairs. The already bright hall was seared with a radiance she imagined could be matched only by looking into the heart of the sun. She slammed the door to shut out the glare.

Su-mi ran frantically from one window to the other, seeking a way to escape the horror. But both windows gave onto the smooth back wall that dropped, sheer and without the hint of a handhold, to the terrace below.

Light streamed under the door like liquid fire. She heard the drapes in the hallway stirring as a fierce wind roared down the corridor. *Or is it the beating of wings?* she wondered.

Something — the tips of those wings? — brushed the ceiling halfway between the stairs and her room.

In the moment before the door burst open, she realized that the "Fairy Godmother" had brought Lois and her family many good things down the years. But there was always some *payment* expected. Perhaps a child born into the family, or a stolen child, or a child brought into the house with the promise of love and a bright future. With sudden, sickening clarity, she guessed that the girl in the picture — the one who had disappeared — was Su-yeon/Suellen. How many other children had been sacrificed to the monster since the painting had first entered Lois's family? Su-mi realized that there was *brightness* in the painting, but no *future*. She might follow lost Su-yeon into whatever unimaginable place the figure took her victims.

Seeing the burning shape, from whom all radiance flowed, reaching for her, Su-mi desperately pulled out Horangi and held him before her, like a shield. As she stumbled back from the approaching horror, she felt Horangi twist in her hands, then drop to the floor, growing instantly to a full-size tiger, then bigger. He flexed his claws; he roared a challenge at the approaching monstrosity, which snarled a warning back. But the creature paused, even as the tiger padded back and forth, from one side of the room to the other, defying, assessing the enemy, roaring another challenge, and all the while watching for an opening to attack. Then, in midstride, Horangi sprang at the momentarily hesitating being —

Unhappily, tiger spirits are much stronger in Korea. Horangi burst into flame. With a last cry, Su-mi watched her now-blazing defender drop to the floor. In an instant, he was reduced to the charred remains of a stuffed toy.

Smiling, so that all its cruel teeth were exposed, the monster, its wings rippling behind it, advanced on Su-mi. A moment later, the light was sucked back into the hallway, then down the stairs, and into the frame.

Lois collected herself and righted the picture, which hung slightly askew. Then she made her way slowly upstairs to the empty bedroom at the end of the hall. Here she spotted the charred remains of the stuffed tiger. Wrinkling her nose in distaste, she went to the second-floor maid's closet, pulled out a broom and dustpan, and quickly swept up the burned cloth and stuffing. She deposited the sweepings in the little pink wastebasket, then turned off the light as she left the room.

Julie, who had come to the Gaddis house with her mother, slipped away from the mourning circle of adults offering condolences to the Gaddises on the loss of Michelle. They complimented Lois, who continually dabbed at her dry eyes, on the fine mother she had been; assured a vaguely smiling Norman that he had been an outstanding father; and praised absent Michelle as a child who had been an excellent student, an asset to the family, and the best daughter such a couple could hope for.

The girl was presumed the victim of a stranger abduction, though no ransom had been demanded nor any clues found to the perpetrators. But a side door had clearly been forced and the child apparently taken while Lois was busy on the second floor in the otherwise unoccupied house. The ongoing police investigation, driven by the Gaddises' importance, would continue for a long time before being retired as a hopelessly "cold case" — one with little hope of ever being solved.

Now, needing to use the bathroom, Julie decided to find one on the second floor. Quickly she climbed the stairs, pausing to check out the portrait on the landing. What Julie was unprepared for was the second figure in the painting, the girl sitting beside the woman, leaning against her, the woman's left arm clasped tightly around her shoulder. She looked unnervingly like Michelle, who was still Su-mi in Julie's heart. Her eyes seemed to gaze into Julie's own. Though the picture was clearly old, the clothes on the girl looked curiously modern, and startlingly like the clothes Julie had seen her friend wearing the day she disappeared. With a shiver, Julie continued upstairs. When she came down a few minutes later, she took a second look at the painting. Choking back a small, fearful cry, Julie turned and fled down the stairs, never wanting to visit the house again.

Violet

The Greene family had driven from Oakland, California, to Macomber, Louisiana, in a little over a week. Since this was going to be a "working summer," Joseph's parents had made sure to do plenty of sightseeing along the way. The Greenes would spend the next eight weeks in the sleepy rural town of Macomber as part of the community-wide, interdenominational Oakland Ministries Outreach Program.

Joe's father, Jerome, drove a white panel truck, while his mother, Jessie, followed in a minivan, also white. Both vehicles displayed the OMOP logo.

Eleven-year-old Joe shared the backseat of the van with his sister, Janelle, who was six. Since Joe had never been to the area before, he was fascinated by the lush green growth pressing up to the side of the road, with glimpses of houses — shacks, really — so beaten down they looked like no one could live there. But Joe saw plenty of folks — kids playing in weedy, junk-filled yards; adults fanning themselves on shady porches. He couldn't imagine living in such places, but clearly people did.

Macomber was nothing more than a cluster of sad-looking shops, a few houses, a gas station, and, on a little rise at the north end of town, St. Cuthbert's A.M.E. Church. The steeple proudly thrust a cross into the air, but the building and the pastor's little house beside it had clearly seen better days. White paint flaked away from the gray boards underneath, and one large window of the house had cracked and been hastily repaired with what looked like duct tape. A rusty wagon and a tricycle sat on a front lawn that was more weeds than grass. It looked as if no one had tended the roses or shrubs in front of the church for ages.

The adults parked the truck and van on the rectangle of gravel to the left of the church. Joe climbed out, relieved to look around and stretch. The doors to the church were open, and a glance inside revealed the simple interior — altar, pulpit, rows of well-used pews, and a small choir loft at the back that would barely hold more than a dozen tightly packed singers. The church was empty, so the senior Greenes, with Joe and Janelle tagging along, knocked at the door of the house. A slender, thirtyish woman holding an infant opened the door. She exchanged a few words with Jerome and Jessie. Joe was close enough to hear her say she was Pastor Winnfield's wife. After a minute, she turned and called into the house, "David, the folks are here from California." Then she invited them inside. Joe was about to follow, but Janelle had spotted a swing set across the parking lot. She begged to try it, and their mother said, "All right, honey," then turned to her son, adding, "Joe, keep a close eye on your sister." The boy sighed; it felt like he was forever being pressed into babysitting service. But he put out his hand to his little sister.

Joe and Janelle walked across the parking lot to an old double swing in the shade of some oak trees festooned with Spanish moss. Joe was glad to be out of the direct sun, but the air felt warm, humid, and oppressive. He could see a long, very hot summer stretching out in front of him. The flying bugs were thick, too; he kept swiping away at them. He was glad there were several portable air conditioners in the truck, since Pastor Winnfield had told them over the phone that the place they would be staying had electricity, but no air conditioning.

For a few minutes, Janelle was happy to sit on one of the swing seats, kicking her legs and taking in their surroundings. Then she said to her brother, "Swing me." He dutifully pushed her, after first checking the swing set to be sure it wouldn't fall down the minute Janelle was in motion. But it seemed sturdy enough — just old and heavily used. He continued to push her gently, ignoring her pleas to "swing harder."

After a short while, their parents reappeared, followed by a heavyset man with prematurely graying hair and thick glasses in black frames. Their father introduced him as Pastor Winnfield, and the man shook hands with Joe while Janelle, who had grown shy, hid behind her mother.

Then he pointed down the road in the direction they'd been traveling. "Just keep going south on Ruston Road for a quarter mile. Your place for the summer is the house with yellow paint. Number 136. It's not much, but the ladies of the parish cleaned it as best they could. It's livable; I can't guarantee anything more than that."

"We'll find it," said Jerome. "And I'm sure it will be just fine."

The adults said their good-byes, and everyone piled back into the vehicles.

The yellow house was spacious enough, and everything was clean — floor recently swept, furniture dusted, sinks in the kitchen and bathroom scrubbed out. But even with the screened windows open, it was stifling inside, and a smell of cleanser hung in the air. Joe thought moving in the air conditioners should be their first priority.

Later, when the family was settled in, the Reverend Winnfield lent Joe a bike that had belonged to his older son, who was away at college. Joe liked the pastor and his wife. The pastor called their infant son Calvin, "our little *lagniappe*," which he pronounced "lan-yap." When Joe asked him to explain, the man laughed and said, "It's an old word that means 'a little something extra' or 'unexpected gift.' That's what the Lord provided us in Calvin."

The following week, the first major undertaking was to repair the roofs of the church and the parish house. Joe carried things and ran errands as needed. It was hot and tiring, but it also felt good to be doing the Lord's work in this way.

It was on these work details that Joe met Cousin Lonnie, who looked older than the hills, but was still wiry, spry, and could use a hammer or a plane with the energy of a much younger man. When they took a break to eat lunch or sip Gatorade, Lonnie would tell Joe, and other interested listeners, funny stories about "foolish Jean Sot" or "tricksy Br'er Rabbit." He knew plenty of ghost tales, too. Listening to him, Joe thought Macomber and its neighborhood must be one of the most haunted places in Louisiana.

One particularly warm and humid day, work had gone slowly, and the laborers began to knock off in the late afternoon. Joe spotted Cousin Lonnie seated on a pile of lumber, fanning himself with the old straw hat he wore every day. Joe, finishing a bottle of water, joined him. They talked about nothing very much for a few minutes, then Joe said, "You tell some great ghost stories. What's the scariest one you know?"

The old man considered awhile. "It th' story of Miss Violet's Plantation — at least, that's what folks hereabouts call it. Long time ago, it had a fancier name: *Beau Paysage*." He pronounced the French very carefully, then explained, "Meant somethin' like 'Pretty Land.' All them big ol' places had fancy names. Anyhow, th' place is still standin' 'bout a mile down Dupree Road." Here he gestured with his hat in a vaguely easterly direction. "Th' parish keep it up 'cause it's historical. Some ladies that live over to Pitreville open it and give tours on weekends. You never seen it?"

Joe shook his head. "Never even heard of it till now."

"Well, it's not a nice story. And a lot of folks 'round here don' talk 'bout it much, 'cause it made grief for some o' their families back in slave times."

He stopped and looked thoughtfully at Joe for a few moments, while he continued to fan himself. "Don' know as I should tell you. That Miss Violet, she were some nasty bit o' business, um-hmm."

"You can't stop now!" the boy pleaded. "I'm old enough to hear."

The old man sighed and seemed to study Joe's face very carefully. The boy sensed some kind of inner debate in the man. Finally Cousin Lonnie made a face, shrugged, and said slowly, "Reckon you is. But you get

nightmares, don' tell me I didn' warn you." Continuing
to fan himself with his hat, Lonnie began, "Miss Violet
were th' only daughter of a rich family back befo' th'
war."

"Do you mean the Civil War?"

"Um-hmm. Family so rich they had Beau Paysage
up here 'n' a big place down to New Orleans. Miss
Violet's ma and pa and brother all died of fever down
there. Miss Violet stayed there fo' th' mos' part, on'y
come a few times to see how this place was gettin' on.
But word got 'roun' that things were mighty strange in
that city house. Th' gal got herself mixed up with
Angeline Lestat, a voodoo woman, a one-time slave
who bought herse'f free." He dropped his voice as he
added, "They say Miss Violet done terrible things to her
slaves there. Hurt 'em, mebbe kill some. Then somethin'
happen, and she lef' the city one night, in secret, and
never gone back. She spend all her time here."

He made a face. "Things got bad here, too. She got
queer in th' head, they say. Began to act like she were a
voodoo queen herse'f. An' she treat her slaves worse 'n'
ever. She beat 'em, whip 'em, chop they toes an' feet an'
hands off, even. Some disappear, though she just say,
'He run off.' All th' time, she messin' more 'n' more with
that voodoo. But th' war were goin' bad, 'n' things was
gettin' crazy everywhere, so no one paid much attention
— jes' the slaves what fear and hate her.

"Then folks hear the Union sojers is headin' this

way. Mos' white folks took off. Miss Violet stayed. Mebbe she thought that voodoo keep her safe. But when th' boys in blue reach Pitreville, all th' slaves knew they was gonna be free. Miss Violet's slaves rose up one night. Story is, they tore her to pieces an' bury her in th' cellar, where she done mos' o' her voodooin'. They strip th' house bare. I hear they tried to burn it, but couldn' get no fire to stay lit. Then they run off. Since then, talk is, th' place is haunted by Miss Violet's ghost. Folks pass by at night an' sees red or blue lights movin' past th' windows. Sometimes they hear a woman screamin' her lungs out. Won' nobody go near after dark. Say Miss Violet won' rest easy till she catch someone alive an' do some voodoo things and mebbe she come alive herse'f. I don' know 'bout that, but you never fin' me there once th' sun sets, fo' a fact."

Joe had a ton of questions to ask his friend, but just then his dad came over, nodded to Lonnie, and told Joe, "We're heading home for dinner." Reluctantly, the boy followed his father to the van.

That evening, he told his family a much toned-down version of the story he'd heard earlier, leaving out the gorier parts. But he was eager to see the plantation for himself, and he knew his mother would be interested in this bit of local history, so he elaborated on Beau Paysage's historical importance. His mother, intrigued, suggested the family take a picnic lunch and make an outing to the place the following Sunday.

Armed with directions from Pastor Winnfield, who appeared hesitant about the visit, they set out after services at St. Cuthbert's. The pastor mentioned something about "the unsavory history" of Beau Paysage. To Joe's relief, the comment didn't register with his parents as a reason for canceling the excursion, though Joe's mother gave him a curious glance.

The plantation house stood grandly at the end of an avenue lined with oaks, its white walls and pillars gleaming, tall windows sparkling in the sunshine, and a broad, roofed veranda circling the building. On every side were carefully tended lawns and gardens.

The inside was equally impressive with rooms full of fine old furniture, though their guide, a tall, white-haired woman with a heavy accent, commented, "These are not the original furnishings. Those were lost during the Troubles" — which was how she referred to the Civil War. But when she ushered them into the main parlor, she pointed to a portrait hanging over the massive fireplace. "That is one of the few things left from the old days."

It was a life-size image of a young woman, around twenty, her jet-black hair dangling in old-fashioned ringlets that framed a face so pale, it looked ghostlike. Her eyes, as dark as her hair, seemed to burn out of the painting with a fierceness that gave her a look of disapproval, almost hatred.

"Miss Violet Ancelet," said the guide. "Her family

owned the land for three generations. When she . . . disappeared during the Troubles, the estate fell into the hands of distant cousins who largely neglected it. It was abandoned for years before the parish purchased it and the immediate grounds for our historical society."

The tour moved upstairs, where there were some nicely furnished bedrooms. But the only real point of interest for Joe was a small chapel with a handful of pews and an altar with a heavy, freestanding cross in a niche above it. "The cross is solid silver," their guide offered. "Like the painting downstairs, it's one of a handful of things that remained with the house. We suspect that the thieves who took everything else were too superstitious to take something from a sanctuary."

There were a few more things to see; then their guide escorted the visitors back down the broad staircase. She had just begun a few closing remarks, when Joe interrupted. "Don't we get to see the cellar?"

A look of distaste crossed the woman's features, but she simply said, "The cellar is not included in the tour. There are some . . . structural problems that make it hazardous. But, I can assure you, there's nothing of interest there."

She bid the visitors a good day. The Greenes went outside to get their picnic basket and join the several other families lunching on picnic tables at the back of the house.

Joe was disappointed to be denied a peek at the

basement, which was what he had *most* wanted to see. He made up his mind that someday he would get a look at the cellar.

The volunteers worked hard the following week, and by Friday, the final church repairs had been completed. Pastor Winnfield announced a Saturday night fish fry to celebrate.

But what started out as an evening of good food and fellowship, with some fine singing by the little choir, turned into a disaster. Before the night was half over, many parishioners went scurrying home, stomachs in turmoil. Clearly food poisoning was at work. The prime suspect was a mayonnaise-rich fish salad, sampled by all the Greenes except Joe, who didn't care much for fish or mayonnaise.

On Sunday morning, while the family groaned in bed or made dashes for the bathroom, Joe rode his bike to church. There were few worshipers, and the reverend, looking a bit greenish, hurried through the service and quickly disappeared. Unsurprisingly, he was not on hand to greet parishioners as they left.

Joe wasn't anxious to get back to the house, which was more like an infirmary. On impulse, he decided to ride his bike out to Beau Paysage. Maybe, if there was another guide, she would let him look into the cellar. He figured it was worth a try.

But as he neared the plantation, he noticed clouds

massing overhead into what threatened to become a major storm. He pedaled faster down the oak-shaded lane to the mansion. Just then a streak of lightning split the sky, followed by a thunderclap so loud he actually *felt* it.

Oddly, there were no cars in the parking lot, and the boy could see no lights on inside. A second blast of lightning and thunder hustled him onto the pillared porch, where he propped his bike so no one would trip over it. A sign on the double doors announced CLOSED FOR RENOVATION.

A downpour began, and a gale-strength wind drove the rain deep into the porch. Even under the veranda roof, Joe began to get soaked. He rattled the heavy brass knobs, but the doors were closed tight. He followed the veranda to his left hoping that, around the corner, he'd be out of the wind and rain enough to stay dry.

Midway along the side he spotted a dark line beneath one window sash. To his delight, he found that the window had not been properly shut. In a moment, he had raised the sash and climbed through. Inside was a small storage room, stacked with boxes and smelling faintly of mothballs. Cautiously, he opened the door and called, "Hello? Anybody there?"

No one answered. He had let himself into what he realized was the office where the guides stayed between tours. He stepped into the main hall, on the alert for signs that he was not alone. But the place seemed deserted. He decided this was the perfect time to check out the cellar. He wasn't sure which of the several doors lining the hall beyond the staircase led down, so he tried them all. The last narrow door on his left, with a NO ADMITTANCE sign, opened onto a steep flight of steps plunging down. Eagerly, he snapped the light switch just inside the door, and a string of bare bulbs flickered on above the steps. Excited — and feeling a little bit nervous — he started down into what Cousin Lonnie had indicated was Miss Violet's chamber of horrors.

At the base of the steps, he glanced around, disappointed at first. The lights were also on down here, although several bulbs had burned out so the place was shadowed and, to Joe, agreeably creepy. The floor was packed dirt, and the musty air smelled of wet earth. But, only a few steps into the gloom, he discovered hints of some very unpleasant doings. Rusty chains and manacles hung on the walls. In the center of the space was a scarred wooden post that came up to his chest. There were a number of rings embedded all over it, including a big one screwed into the rounded top. *Whipping post*, he guessed. Worst were the implements hanging on the back wall of the place — a truly disturbing selection of knives, saws, cleavers, axes, and more — all brown with what the boy hoped was only rust. . . .

He could see why the cellar was off-limits to visitors. The longer he stayed, the more unnerving the place became. He imagined the tortured ghosts of plantation

workers lingering in the shadows, still bound in some awful way to this place of suffering. He admitted to himself that what he had seen was not giving him the thrill he had hoped for — like some Halloween haunted house display. He suddenly wanted out of this evil place.

But as he started toward the stairs, something caught his eye. At first it looked like a worm, maggot-white, noodling up through the packed soil. *Gross,* he thought. But he couldn't resist peering closer. He decided it must be the uneven lighting, but it seemed to him that the worm was creeping out of the earth without actually digging free. Suddenly, it was joined by three more slender worms, and a shorter, stubbier one. With a terrified groan, he recognized them as *fingers,* deathly white, jutting up from the floor like the hand of a surfacing swimmer reaching into the air.

At a distance, another hand was rising. He saw the top of a head begin to emerge from the floor. Frozen in place, he watched as a crown of raven-black hair, pale forehead, and glittering eyes drifted up. Now, all around the basement, he saw pale shapes oozing into the light, then crawling toward the head, which had now risen up to the chin. He recalled Cousin Lonnie's words, "They tore her to pieces an' bury her in th' cellar." In shock he realized that the long-dead woman was, in some impossible way, reassembling herself.

He felt his legs about to buckle under him.

Somehow, he found the strength to make a mad dash for the steps. Behind him, he heard a woman's voice shriek, "Stay, boy! I order you!"

But Joe took the steps two by two and raced through the door at the top, slamming it behind him. Frantically, he fumbled for the lock. It took him several seconds before he realized there was none. From below, the awful voice demanded, "Stop where you are! I will not tolerate disobedience in my house!"

He ran for the front doors and grabbed both handles, but neither door would give. He tried the windows on either side; they refused to budge. In desperation, he jammed his elbow against the pane. It gave a little, but seemed more rubber than glass. Next he tried the office door he'd come in through, but it was now sealed fast. This was how things happened in the scary movies he watched with his friend Mickey when they were alone. Ghosts always had some way of making sure you couldn't get out of a haunted house.

The basement door burst open and crashed against the wall. "Boyyyyyyyyyyy!" rose a scream from inside.

Joe bolted upstairs. All the doors here were shut, too, except for the one to the chapel. With nowhere else to go, he darted in and yanked the door shut. Then he retreated until his back was against the altar.

The door to the chapel crashed inward. Framed in the doorway, looking just like her portrait, was Violet Ancelet. But now her look of anger had given way to unbridled rage. She glared at him, her mouth working furiously as she threatened, "Oh, you are going to suffer *so much* for me." She stretched out her hands toward the trembling boy and lurched forward, then paused, a look of puzzlement on her face. Her hands clutched at the empty air of the doorway as if they had encountered some kind of resistance.

Sudden hope sparked in Joe. Could the chapel, a holy place, prevent the ghastly mistress of the manor from entering? He prayed with all his might that this was the case.

With a snarl of fury, Violet grabbed fistfuls of air, as though struggling with some invisible barrier.

"This is a holy place," Joe shouted at the ghost. "You can't come in!"

"Who are you, boy, to tell an Ancelet what I may or may not do?" Furiously, she made grasping motions with her hands, then jerked her arms backward. Joe had the impression her clawed fingers were clutching chunks of some unseen material. "I will not be gainsaid," she raged. "*I will not.*"

To Joe's dismay, there came a ripping sound, like something soft and wet being torn apart. Violet thrust one hand forward. This time it came all the way into the chapel. With a triumphant cry, she grabbed the sides of what must now be a hole in the barrier. She tore and tore again, until she had forced an opening that allowed her to pass into the sanctuary.

"We have business downstairs," she said, her mouth twisted into such a snarl of rage that she barely seemed human any longer.

She started forward. Frantic, Joe looked around for something to fight back with. She was halfway to him, the rustling of her skirts filling the room, when he grabbed the silver crucifix, lowered it like a battering ram, and charged the apparition.

The top of the cross buried itself in what felt to Joe like a very real body. Then Violet screamed, "Nooooooo!" With a final shriek, she burst apart like an exploded puppet. Each bit, like a tiny comet, flared white-hot for a moment. An instant later, they winked out. Not a trace remained.

Dazed, Joe set the cross in the middle of the aisle. Then he dropped trembling into the nearest pew. He noticed, through the single round window over the altar, that the rain had stopped. Sunlight was streaming into the chapel. In a few minutes, when he stopped shaking and felt steady enough to stand, he would find a way out of the place. And, tomorrow, he'd have a heck of a story to tell Cousin Lonnie.

A Really Scary Story

Patrick held up the book so his younger brothers could see just how scary the cover was. Ian and Ethan stared at a picture of a horrible, red-eyed monster head. Whatever it was — a devil? a dragon? a giant snake? — it looked ready to pop off the front and gobble them up. When Patrick moved the trick cover back and forth, the creature's mouth opened and closed. "Gonna get you," said Patrick in a scary voice as he shoved the book at his brothers.

"Don't!" said Ian, at six the braver of the two. He made a fist as though he were going to hit the book. Then he pulled his hand back suddenly as if fearing the ugly picture might bite him.

Five-year-old Ethan, looking like he might cry, pleaded, "Stop scaring us."

Their fear only made Patrick bolder. *"Booga-booga-booga!"* he shouted and pushed the book into Ethan's face.

The little boy shrieked and ran out of the room. The others heard him making his way downstairs, calling for the babysitter. "Mrs. Gowen, Patrick's scaring us!"

"What a wuss," said Patrick. He turned to Ian. "Aren't you going to be a tattletail, too?"

"Scaring Ethy is mean," Ian said. "But just a picture can't hurt me."

"Oh no?" Patrick said with a grin. Whatever he may have been thinking of saying or doing next, he stopped when he heard Mrs. Gowen huffing up the stairs. A moment later, the babysitter appeared at his bedroom door with Ethan right behind her. In her here-we-go-again voice, she demanded, "What are you doing, scaring your brothers?"

"I'm just showing them my new book."

"Uh-huh. Well, let me see it, too."

"It's only a book."

"Show me," Mrs. Gowen insisted in her most teacherlike voice. Making a face at Ethan, Patrick handed over the book of frightening stories. The babysitter wrinkled her nose when she saw the title — *Devilish Frights and Dark Delights* — and the changeable monster face on the cover.

"This is not appropriate for the little ones, Patrick. When are you going to start using your head for something other than a hatrack?" Mrs. Gowen was always saying things like that; most of the time Patrick and his brothers didn't know what she was talking about.

Patrick shrugged. It was the best answer he could come up with.

Shaking her head, Mrs. Gowen handed the book back to Patrick. "Scare yourself silly," she said, "but leave your brothers out of it." She took Ian's hand, discovered Ethan, who had backed away to just outside the door, and took his hand, too. "I'll tell you a story that my grandmother told me when I was a little girl. A happy story."

"Are there any monsters in it?" asked Ian, who really did like scary stories — as long as they weren't *too* scary.

"There are a prince and a princess," said Mrs. Gowen.

"Oh," responded a disappointed Ian.

"I like stories about princes and things," said Ethan.

"And there is a dragon," added the babysitter.

"Dragons are good," said Ian.

"Sometimes," said Ethan.

"Wusses!" muttered Patrick.

Leading the boys away, Mrs. Gowan paused to close the door to Patrick's bedroom. "You keep your scares to yourself," she said. Then the door clicked shut behind her.

When the others were gone, Patrick looked down at the book in his hands. He jiggled it. The devil/dragon/snake's jaws gaped and clamped shut. "Who wants to hear about a stupid prince and a dumb princess?" He opened the book to the Table of Contents. He hadn't read any of the stories yet, but the titles were promising: "The Horror in the Library," "The Old Man's Revenge," "A Monstrous Surprise," and so on. He didn't recognize the authors' names, but the titles were come-on enough.

He sat on the edge of his bed, looking down at the cover. It was funny, but he couldn't remember where he'd gotten the book. It wasn't from his school library; there was no library sticker and no bar code inside the cover. And it wasn't stamped with "Avondale Public Library" in purple letters.

He tried harder to remember. Then it came back to him. Mr. Jergens, who had a house and garage overflowing with books, had given it to him earlier that day. *Why had it been so hard to remember such an easy thing?* Patrick wondered.

Now the memory came to him clearly. He'd been at Mr. Jergens's house after school with his friends Todd and DeWayne. They were bored and had decided to trash the old man's house by spray-painting what looked like gang signs on the side of the garage. They didn't know any real gang members, but they had all seen plenty of the scribbles at bus stops and on vacant buildings downtown. Mischief was all they had in mind. They didn't have any particular reason for picking on Mr. Jergens — he just seemed an easy target.

But Todd had barely gotten the first phony-gang squiggle of black paint onto the garage wall, when Mr. Jergens came hobbling down the alley, his cane raised over his head like a weapon. "Vandals! Hooligans!" he shouted. "I'll fix you for this."

The other two had beat it, but Patrick got his foot caught in a curl of garden hose and tripped. The fall onto the concrete path knocked the wind out of him, and for several moments, he was too stunned to move. Then the man grabbed him by the back of his jacket and hauled him to his feet. The guy was surprisingly strong for a geezer, Patrick realized. He looked around for his friends, but they had vanished.

"Why are you doing this?" the man yelled at him. "What do you hate? Me?"

"No, we were just messing around."

But the old man's mind had gone someplace else. "My garage is filled with books. Are you a know-nothing who hates books?"

"No, I . . . I like books, really I do," Patrick blurted out, confused by the sudden shift.

The old man's face softened into the hint of a smile.

"That's good." Then, his look hardening again, he asked suspiciously, "What kind of books?"

"Um, scary stories, mostly." Patrick wasn't sure if

this was a good answer. But it was the best he could come up with. And it was true.

"Ah!" The old man headed toward the side of the garage, dragging Patrick after him. His fingers felt like a handcuff around the boy's wrist as he pulled Patrick through a door into the gloomy garage. Shelves ran from floor to ceiling, jammed with books set every which way. Cartons of books and loose stacks littered the cement floor. An old car — which looked as if it hadn't been driven in a bazillion years — was brimming over with books. Volumes were even stacked on the hood, and more were piled on the trunk.

"You like scary stories," said the old man, his eyes searching across one shelf and then another. Finally he exclaimed, "Ah, *this* is the one I want!"

He let go of Patrick's wrist, but he was standing between the boy and the door, so there was no escape. Mr. Jergens pulled a large volume off the shelf and handed the book to Patrick. The picture on the cover shifted and reshifted as Patrick, his hands shaking from this ever-stranger encounter, took the book the old man offered him.

"You like scary stories," Mr. Jergens said. "So I give you this."

"Why would you give me a present?" the boy asked. "I mean, we weren't being very nice."

"No," the man agreed. "But you read this book. And maybe, while you are reading these stories, you will come to realize that old people can make things right one way or another. Even when dealing with bad boys who do cruel things to people who have done nothing to deserve such unkindness."

Patrick's hands were sweaty on the book cover. Something in the way the old man spoke made him shiver, though the man kept smiling. Suddenly the boy asked, "Are you going to call the police and say I stole this?"

This time the old man laughed out loud. "What a suspicious mind you have. I am giving you this as a gift. It is in your hands. It belongs to you. Take it and go along."

Patrick shook his head. "You really aren't going to make any trouble?" He could just imagine what his parents would do if they found out about his after-school activities. He'd be grounded for life. So far he'd managed to keep them from tuning in to his "pranks," as he liked to think of them.

Mr. Jergens stood aside and waved him to the door. "Go home now."

Hugging the book to his chest, Patrick hurried outside and broke into a run. He laughed with relief. He'd gotten away with no hassles — and a book of scary stories as well!

Now, in his bedroom, Patrick smiled again as he skimmed the Table of Contents. He decided to start with

"The Demon's Jaws," since a little note underneath the title said it was the story that had inspired the wonderfully creepy cover.

He began to read: *"There was once a book with a terrible curse on it. A powerful sorcerer, who had suffered at the hands of many cruel people, sent the book out into the world. To most, it would seem nothing more than a book of stories. But to anyone who chanced upon it, and who was by nature unjust and meanspirited, the book was something else again. For within the pages, unseen and unsensed by most, lurked a demon that watched and waited for a sinner's hands to turn the pages and release it."*

"Cool!" said Patrick, sprawling full-length on the bed, knowing that he was in for a night of really great scares.

But the book itself intrigued him. He studied it more closely. The pages felt thick and stiff, like old parchment. Patrick searched the title page and elsewhere for a publication date, the way the media specialist, Mrs. Braker, had taught them in library usage class. But, search as he might, he could find no clue to the book's age. It just looked and felt old. While Patrick was mainly thinking of diving into the tales themselves, a second part of him wondered just how much money he could get for the book at the Rare Book Emporium — or even on eBay, since some of his friends knew how to sell things that way, too.

An image of Mr. Jergens formed in his mind. *Stupid old fool!* the boy thought. *Too senile to realize he was giving away a treasure.* Patrick laughed aloud at the thought that his after-school prank might end up generating a bunch of cash for him.

I can hardly wait to rub Todd's and DeWayne's noses in this, he thought, recalling with a flash of anger how his friends had fled, abandoning him. *They'll expect me to do something good for all of us with the money. But I've got better friends than them to spend it on. What a great thing this book is,* he told himself. *I can read the stories, cash in on it, and get back at my so-called friends — all at the same time!*

He turned the oddly resistant pages, seeking to return to the story he wanted to start with. But the pages seemed to stick together. Out of nowhere, he had the strange idea that he was being given a last chance to put the book aside and read something else.

He gave a snort of disgust. "Let's get to the scary parts already," he said aloud. The book seemed to understand him, for the pages suddenly fanned open as if caught in a draft (though he couldn't feel any actual breeze). At the same time, a resigned sigh filled the room — so loud he wondered if someone had come in while he had been intent on the old volume. But the room was empty; the door was closed as Mrs. Gowen had left it.

He returned to the story he had just begun, "The Demon's Jaws." He read: *"The volume — no one knew how old it was — was the pride of Thomas Huntington's collection, an assemblage of books on the occult, the bizarre, the ghostly. The old man loved nothing more than a good scare* and the chance to share such frights with others. But nothing in his vast collection shocked and distressed those with whom he shared his stories as this one volume. He would never let the book go out of his keeping for fear of the horrors it might unleash, horrors far beyond those of the imagination."

Patrick was loving it.

He stopped suddenly, looking up from the thick, yellowing pages with their old-looking script and smell of long ago.

He heard the same sigh he had heard earlier — only, this time, it sounded satisfied, almost *eager*, in a totally creepy way.

Leaving the book open to his chosen story, he walked around the room, seeking the source of the strange sound. He opened the closet, checked the windows, and looked to see if his PC or his CD player had accidentally been left on. Nothing. No clue.

But the sound persisted, as though the room were inhaling and exhaling inside his head. Experimentally, he pressed his hands to his ears; the impossible sighing came through loud and clear.

He tried to interest himself in the story again, but the weirdness that suffused the room had put him off the book completely.

From downstairs, he could hear the murmuring voice of Mrs. Gowen, telling one of her "happy princess" stories, and he heard the occasional delighted laughter of his brothers at some silly thing the storyteller would slip into her narrative from time to time.

Suddenly feeling isolated and no longer looking for scares, Patrick decided to go downstairs and leave the room to its relentless sighs — whatever they were all about. He was sure it was his overactive imagination, but now he wanted to be on the first floor with the others. Of course, he wouldn't actually join the little storytelling circle, but he could sit in the kitchen, fix himself a snack, and be near them.

However, when he tried to open the door to his room, it wouldn't budge. He tried twisting the knob back and forth, but it refused to turn even the fraction of an inch. He tried rattling it; the handle remained frozen. Growing frantic, he beat on the door, but the wood felt like soft, yielding, padded cloth. He could rouse no sound from it, could make no noise to alert the ones downstairs that something weird — and growing weirder — was happening to him.

Suddenly a growl came from somewhere behind him. Stifling a sob, Patrick turned to face the bed where the book still lay open to the story.

With a *snap!* that made the boy jump, the volume closed on itself. The orange duvet on the bed began to undulate and wriggle and shift as if it were a living thing. Like some kind of worm, it coiled and lengthened, then nuzzled the old Jergens book upright. To Patrick's terrified eyes, the book cover, rocking to the motion of the worm shape, became the head of the

snake-beast, opening and closing horrendous jaws that were growing larger and wider with every bite of air they took.

Patrick spun around and beat on the door again, but his fists made no sound. He was shouting — or trying to — but his mouth and throat felt stuffed with cotton. Inside his head, the sighing-breathing grew to a roar.

He heard the book-bedclothes monstrosity slither to the floor; he turned to see it undulating toward him.

"No," he said, his voice little more than a whisper as the thing rose up cobralike to stare at him. The jaws clacked above the other sounds in his head. The monster's mouth shaped into a grin. Then the thing shot forward, jaws gaping, as Patrick gave voice to a single screech, instantly cut off with a deadly *clack!* After that, only a faint echo faded into the silence of the empty room.

Mrs. Gowen had almost reached the end of her story, when she and the boys heard a yell from upstairs. Calling, "Patrick! Are you all right?" the babysitter rushed out of the room, Ian close behind her. A moment later, little Ethan trailed along.

The door to Patrick's room stood open. The book of scary stories lay on the bed, as though the boy had just set it down a moment before. But there was no sign of him. The babysitter and the boys searched every room upstairs. Then they checked the first floor. They even searched the basement and the garage, but they found no trace.

The three returned to Patrick's bedroom. Mrs. Gowen, sounding very worried, called, "Patrick! If you're hiding! If this is a trick! Well, stop it at once! Otherwise, I'm going to have to call your parents."

There was no answer. Mrs. Gowen went downstairs to phone the boys' parents.

"Look at the book!" said Ethan, pointing. "It looks *fat.*"

"Yeah, it does," said Ian. He took a step back from the bed as if the book were dangerous — like a snarling dog or a hissing snake. He couldn't put into words why the swollen-looking book chilled him so. The horrible face seemed different, too; it wore almost a sleepy, satisfied grin.

It was Ethan who said, "It looks like Benjy Armstrong's snake when it's swallowed a mouse for its supper."

"Your parents are on the way, Patrick!" Mrs. Gowen shouted from downstairs. "You're in big trouble, young man!"

But her warning brought only a soft, satisfied sigh in return — so faint that Ian and Ethan could never be sure they had truly heard it. Yet, as if on a signal, the two boys fled Patrick's room for the safety of the babysitter's comforting presence.

Witch

Opportunity didn't exactly *knock* for Annabelle Maylie: she pulled it out of a stack of bins offering all kinds of free newspapers, most of them laden with job offers — which was just what she was looking for. She'd been searching for work for weeks, trying desperately to find something before her stepfather kicked her out of the house for dropping out of junior college in her freshman year. Of course, her mother would do nothing — just flutter her fingers and look worried and agree with whatever Hank said.

Annabelle had surfed the Internet, asked her friends for leads, had even gone around looking for work as a waitress or a salesperson. But the more she searched, the less she found, and the thinner Hank's patience grew. He wasn't sympathetic about the lack of opportunity in Bramwell, Connecticut.

And then, at the bus stop one day, she snagged a copy of *New Age Page* — a rag she normally wouldn't have given a second look. Turning to the "Employment Opportunities" section, she found the following ad:

Personal Assistant/House Help. A unique opportunity for the right young lady. Live-in position involves some cooking, light housekeeping, and a chance to learn a wealth of new skills under the training of a unique mistress of the arts of astral projection, healing, herbalism, fortunetelling, necromancy, and more. Become an expert in matters arcane and occult, inexplicable and ineluctable.

Though Annabelle didn't understand all of the words, she understood enough to know that this was — just possibly — her dream job. There were enough references to magic and sorcery and witchcraft to make this "unique opportunity" very interesting, indeed. What Annabelle desired more than anything was to break free of the mundane, everyday world and enter a realm of strangeness and magic. Not the yawn-making posturings of her boring Goth friends, whose idea of touching mysterious realms was wearing raccoon-thick mascara, blood-red lipstick, billowy black antique dresses, and lace gloves with the fingers missing. There seemed to be something encoded in the words of the ad that spoke to her. And, if she looked at it long enough, it seemed to *pop* on the page, as though the ad were written in Day-Glo ink or printed, by itself, on luminous paper.

There was no phone number or e-mail listed: just a name — Miss Hazel Starworthy — in care of a Post Office Box number in someplace called Five Points, Massachusetts. The ad instructed her to send a letter, a résumé, a strand of hair, a fingernail clipping, and a piece of cloth from a "well-worn bit of clothing." It might have seemed weird a few years ago, Annabelle realized. But she'd seen enough *CSI* programs to know that this was all connected with DNA identification. The world was changing so fast, she just assumed it was the routine next stop beyond fingerprinting. These days, it seemed everyone had to get fingerprinted for even the lowest-class job. Her friend Angela was fingerprinted just to work two days part-time in an elementary school library, for criminy's sake!

While she waited for a response to her letter, she searched the Internet for information on "Starworthy" and "Five Points, Massachusetts." There wasn't a lot of information; Five Points had been around since Colonial times and was now a burg of fewer than six hundred people.

Five Points also had — and this was an interesting

crossover — been caught up briefly in the witch-hunting madness that had centered on Salem down the road. The uproar seemed to focus on the Starworthy family — particularly two sisters, Hepzibah and Hester — who were rumored to have been witches of the most notorious kind. When the villagers turned on the Starworthys, the whole clan apparently disappeared to sit out the witch craze. When things returned to normal, they came back from wherever to reclaim their holdings in town. What skimpy information Annabelle could find suggested the family had suffered a number of losses since then and was currently reduced to a single surviving descendant: one Hazel Starworthy.

Better and better, thought Annabelle. She raced to the front door every time she heard the mail carrier. And, at last, a response did arrive: a handwritten note with the instruction to "Call me," a phone number with a Massachusetts area code, and a spidery, old-fashioned signature: Hazel Starworthy.

The girl immediately retreated to her room, closed the door, and used her cell phone to reach the woman.

After several rings, someone picked up at the other end. "Hazel Starworthy," offered a sandpapery voice.

"Oh, Miss Starworthy, I'm so glad I caught you at home. Is this a good time to talk on the phone?"

"I'm not at home. I'm visiting a friend. And I have no phone."

"But, how . . ." began Annabelle, confused.

"I was expecting your call," the other said, as if this explained everything.

Well, Annabelle thought, *this is just further proof that my guesses are right on. There's something uncanny about this woman.*

"I was wondering if —" continued Annabelle.

"You have the job, if you want it." Miss Starworthy quoted a salary that was far above what the girl had hoped for. "But I must warn you, young Miss Maylie, my home is quite rustic. I have no phone, no electricity. Cell phones refuse to work. I do have running water and a gas stove, but the amenities are very slight, indeed."

For the money offered and the possibilities far beyond the salary, Annabelle was sure she could put up with anything. They talked a bit longer, she received directions on how to reach Five Points, and they agreed she would present herself to her new employer one week from today.

"*Yesssss!*" cried Annabelle, high-fiving the empty air. Good riddance to bozo Hank and gonzo Mum and her old life. Hello to a world of opportunity. She was practically floating on air by the time she raced down the stairs to announce she'd gotten a job and would be leaving town in a week.

She took the bus to Boston and transferred as Hazel Starworthy had instructed her. The second bus left her off at the Five Points turnoff, where a fading sign announced "Five Points $1/2$ mile." A small, black, five-pointed star sat above the name; Annabelle guessed it was the town logo. Since there was nothing else to do, she shifted her backpack, hefted her suitcase, and set off down the narrow road.

When she reached Five Points, it looked pretty much deserted. A handful of vintage houses and shops clustered around the small town square. The main feature of the square seemed to be the brick church at its north end. The place looked . . . *funny* . . . not like any house of worship she'd ever seen. The tower, rising to a second story above the main building, was rounded, blunt-looking, with no trace of a cross at the top. At first, when she saw the darkened windows, she thought they were painted black. But when she climbed the nine steps to the front, she found the panes smoke-blackened, as though a fire had been contained inside.

"I wouldn't get too close, young lady," a man said. "It's dangerous."

She took a hasty step backward and turned around. An old man, with a thick mop of white hair, bushy eyebrows, and a face more lined than a Connecticut road map, was standing just back from the bottommost step.

"You mean the building's dangerous?" she asked. "A brick might fall or something?"

"Best keep your distance," the fellow said, not really answering her question.

"Looks like there was a bad fire."

"Ayup. Inside mostly. But nothing's safe about the place. It was built by the Starworthys — local folks — years ago. Abandoned a long time now."

Seizing on this, Annabelle said, "I've come to take a job with Hazel Starworthy. Do you know —" But she broke off when she saw a sour look cross his face; it was as if he'd just got a whiff of something foul.

"'Tain't none of my business, young lady — but if I was you, I'd turn my toes back the way I come and head for home." As if to emphasize this sentiment, he turned on his heel and hurried away down the street.

"Weird," Annabelle decided. She had hoped to ask him the way to Tarry Lane, where her new employer lived. She looked around for someone else who might give her directions, but all the streets feeding into the square were deserted. And the few shops looked closed for the night, though her watch assured her, in spite of the lowering dark, that it was just past four.

However, ten minutes of exploring revealed Tarry Lane, a side street that branched off Old Five Points Road, the town's main thoroughfare.

Annabelle wasn't disappointed when she reached Hazel Starworthy's cottage — gray paint, black shutters, the faint glow of flickering light. *Candles,* she guessed. *Cool.* It all added up to the perfect setting for this fantasy come true.

The old woman who opened the door looked every

bit a witch. From the tips of her black shoes, just visible under the hem of her heavy black dress, to the tip of her pointed nose, she was a classic hag. Though it was probably a trick of the evening light filtering through heavy tree branches, her skin looked greenish. Her eyes had a reddish cast, and her face — especially her nose — was warty. Annabelle's fingers itched to grasp the witchy power she felt sure would soon be hers.

"I'm Annabelle," she said simply.

"I know," said the other, in a tone that was somewhere between friendly and doubtful. She looked the girl up and down. "You seem quite young. You sounded older on the phone."

"I always do. But, believe me, I'll be everything you need — and more."

To Annabelle's surprise, the woman leaned forward and sniffed, as though *scenting* the girl's qualifications. Then she made several passes in the air with her left hand. "Ah yes. You'll do." A sudden thought seemed to strike her. "You took the bus here and walked through town. Did you talk to anyone?"

"An old man. But he was just strange and not very friendly."

"What did he look like?"

"Lots of white hair and really bushy eyebrows."

"Hmpf! Daniel Cribbens. Old fool. You cross his path again, don't pay him any mind. Anyhow, you said you were good at cooking and cleaning."

Annabelle nodded. She had padded her résumé a bit

in these regards. But she knew how to run a vacuum and load a dishwasher. Suddenly remembering there was no electricity, she realized she'd be doing all the housework by hand. Still, how hard could it be? And she had a paperback cookbook tucked in her suitcase. Though she'd never really done any cooking, she figured it would be no more difficult than following a chemical formula. She had done just fine in chem lab before she quit school.

"I'm truly eager to learn some of the . . . special things . . . you mentioned in your ad. Necromancy. Astral projection. I'm a fast learner."

"In time," said Miss Starworthy. "But right now I'm not so much looking for an apprentice as someone to help around the house."

"Fine," said Annabelle, who figured she would learn a lot just by keeping her eyes and ears open. When you worked for a witch — and she was positive that Hazel Starworthy fit the bill — you were bound to pick up the odd spell or two.

"Very well," the other said. "Come in. You can sleep in the room just off the kitchen. You'll fix and take your meals with me. We've already talked salary. You may have Sunday afternoons off."

Annabelle eagerly agreed to these terms, then followed the woman inside. The room was messy, nondescript, with books, vials, pouches, and paraphernalia of all sorts scattered everywhere. Propped in the niche beside the fireplace was a broom.

But the main feature of the cottage was an oddly colored monkey. It looked like a spider monkey the girl had seen in a nature special on TV. Only, "He's *green*," she said.

"He's from South America," her employer replied offhandedly.

Annabelle doubted *that*. She was sure the creature was the witch's familiar. Any self-respecting witch had one of those — an attendant spirit who usually took an animal form. She'd studied a lot on the subject of witches in the past week.

"His name is Ozymandias. I call him Ozzie for short."

"Hello, Ozzie," said Annabelle, extending a finger as she would to a strange cat or dog. The monkey snarled and hissed at her until she backed off.

Miss Starworthy said, "He's difficult at times and very possessive of me. For the time being, best keep your distance."

"You bet," said the girl.

While she stored her things in the chilly little back room, Annabelle tried to make conversation. "Did you get many applicants for this job?"

"Dozens. Hundreds. But most didn't pass my first reading of them, so into the fire with their letters. Only yours held some real promise. But it hinted at other things, too."

"Like what?"

"You're strong-willed. That's good in some ways;

less good in others. And you've got a lot to learn about the importance of patience. Learn to let things take their own pace here, and we'll get along just fine."

"Whatever you say," Annabelle agreed, mustering as much conviction as she could.

That night she cooked dinner by carefully following the directions in her cookbook. The meal wasn't very good, but Hazel Starworthy didn't seem to care. In fact, as the days went along, she turned out to be the easiest of employers. She didn't mind that Annabelle mended her skirts with clumsy, uneven stitches. She didn't notice that the girl never swept under the furniture or dusted any shelf higher than her head or left streaks when she washed the windows. Hazel was far too concerned with studying her craft, muttering to herself as she read from one heavy old book or another.

Annabelle asked again and again to be taught at least a *tiny* bit of magic, but Miss Starworthy only said, "All in the right time. Be patient."

But Annabelle was an increasingly impatient girl. If the witch wouldn't teach her, she decided, she would teach herself.

While pretending to do her chores, she watched as Miss Starworthy tried out various spells, mixing revolting things from colorful jars and consulting the big red and gray spell books that seemed most important to her. When Annabelle was supposed to be asleep, she spied on her employer at her work.

The familiar, Ozzie, was a bit of a problem. Though

the witch, for reasons of her own, maintained he was just a pet, the girl had caught the two of them whispering together and casting furtive glances in her direction. When Hazel was out of the house, Annabelle was aware of the green monkey's eyes following her everywhere like an in-store security camera.

Gradually, though, the girl realized he was often incapacitated, almost as if he were in a trance or coma. He seemed to sleep for hours on end. When she asked her employer about this, Hazel said, "Oh, his inner monkey is on a journey back home — sort of a memory thing. He's probably swinging through the trees in South America even as we speak."

But the stink of sulfur that surrounded the monkey in this state assured the girl that his home was in all likelihood a lot farther away, and deeper down, than South America. But she was glad to know that when she caught the stench, Ozzie was useless as a spy.

When Miss Starworthy was away on one or another of her mysterious errands, and Ozzie was surrounded by his sulfuric miasma, Annabelle would take down a red or gray spell book and try out some of the simplest spells. She made a pot of violets sing; she caused Ozzie's fur to change from green to blue to black to red and back to green while the monkey slept; she caused all the candles in the cottage to light at the snap of her fingers.

This last attempt almost burned down the house, because she accidentally caused the extra candles in a kitchen drawer to light, too. She didn't realize it until smoke began to stream from the closed drawer. Fortunately Annabelle (who hadn't learned the magic for extinguishing a flame) was able to put out the blaze with dishwater. Then she flung open the doors and windows to get rid of the smell of smoke. She worried until the witch returned. But the woman just said, "It's too chilly outside for everything to be open. Close the doors and windows at once, girl. Then bring me a cup of tea." She was far more interested in the packets and powders she had brought from town than in the lingering smell of smoke.

But it was the witch's broom that Annabelle most longed to try out. She was eager to soar and sail through the sky as her mistress did when she went to visit one of her sister witches or flew off somewhere in the dead of night.

When the girl asked about flying lessons, Hazel said, "No more talk of that! You will have to acquire skill in lesser magic before you can dream of flying."

But being told "No" only made the headstrong Annabelle even more determined to learn the secret of broom riding. She spied ever more intently on her employer. Yet she could never discover how the witch turned her broom into the magical means of carrying someone far and away through the air.

Then, one night, while the witch was skrying — gazing into a mirror she had rubbed with magic oil to let her see distant places — she suddenly gasped and cried,

"My sister in Far Hathaway is very sick! I must go to her at once. Fetch my cloak! Bring me my red bag of potions! *Hurry, girl!*"

As Annabelle did these things, the witch grabbed her broom. When she had the cloak around her shoulders and the red bag firmly in hand, she hastened out onto the porch. She was not aware that Annabelle hadn't quite closed the door and was, in fact, watching and listening with all her might. For the first time the girl heard Hazel Starworthy's words of power.

The witch's hands made three sets of figure eights in the air over the broom as it lay flat on the porch. Then she whispered, "*Alikki* — up!" The broom floated to waist height. Miss Starworthy seated herself on the broom — bristles to the front — and said, "*Alikki* — high and away!"

The broom and its passenger shot up and away into the night sky.

"Yes, yes, *yes!*" cried Annabelle, dancing around the cottage. "I know the secret. Soon I'll fly myself!"

Hazel Starworthy returned late the next morning.

"How is your sister?" asked Annabelle, trying to sound very concerned.

"She's mending," said her employer, unaware that the girl could hardly keep her eyes off the broom, now back in its chimney nook.

But Annabelle had to wait another two days before she could try out what she had learned. On a sunny afternoon, Hazel said, "I am going into the woods to gather herbs and mushrooms. I should be back in three hours. Have supper ready then — something hot."

"Yes, ma'am," said Annabelle.

The choking smell of sulfur around Ozzie convinced her that the moment had come, and as soon as Miss Starworthy was gone, the girl snatched up the broom and ran into the yard. Her hands shook with excitement as she wove figure eights in the air over the broom in the grass.

"*Alikki* — up!" she commanded.

The broom shuddered and seemed almost unwilling to obey, but then it floated up and hovered in front of her.

Annabelle seated herself as she had seen Hazel Starworthy do so often. Then she ordered, "*Alikki* — high and away!"

The broom shot into the air so quickly that the apron she was wearing blew back into her face, momentarily blinding her. By the time she had the apron under control and could look around, she realized she was high above the forest. The trees below looked like twigs covered with moss, Miss Starworthy's cottage was smaller than a doll's house, and the road to town wound like a brown ribbon through the twig-and-moss forestscape.

The broom soared and dipped; it flew in circles and figure eights, following sky paths as though it had a mind of its own. For a time this was exciting, but Annabelle began to grow bored.

"I should go someplace, then get back before Miss Starworthy returns and finds out what I've been up to." (She laughed at her own accidental joke.)

"*Alikki* — to town," she said.

The broom dipped and then doubled back on its course, making yet another tiresome figure eight in the air. The girl tried command after command — always starting with the word *Alikki* — but the broomstick paid no attention. Slowly she began to realize there might be another word — or maybe several other words — of power that would make the broom obey. As a last try, she ordered, "*Alikki* — down!" then "*Alikki* — to home!"

The broom spiraled up.

Annabelle began to get truly worried. The broom continued to do what it wanted, go where it wanted. She had no say in the matter.

As the day faded toward evening, she grew cold. She wrapped her apron around herself like a shawl. She was hungry and thirsty and tired. To keep up her hope, she promised herself, "Miss Starworthy will set things right when she returns. Though she will probably be very angry with me."

Up and down, round and about, went the broom and its passenger.

When Hazel Starworthy returned to her cottage a bit later, she was puzzled to find the place empty — no

Annabelle and, what annoyed her more, no supper. Looking around, she quickly realized the broom was gone. Remembering the girl's eager eyes when she had asked about flying lessons, the woman guessed what had happened.

"Foolish girl," she muttered.

She went out on the porch and, shading her eyes against the late afternoon sun, peered at the sky. But she saw no trace of her missing broom or the disobedient girl. "Ah, well," the witch said, returning inside, "I'll have to spell a new broom. That's a bother. But the child couldn't cook or clean or mend very well. Hopefully, the next girl I hire will do better."

As for Annabelle . . .

Sometimes people looking skyward, especially in the late afternoon, saw high above what looked like a stick carrying a bundle of rags and twigs. Pilots in the area occasionally reported strange encounters of a witchy kind, which got even less credibility than tales of encounters with UFOs. Most of what was Annabelle dried up and blew away over the years, like the broom's bristles. But there is still enough left to glimpse forever riding the winds if a person happens to look up into the sky or out an airplane window at just the right moment.

Red Rain

The camping trip had been a disaster from the get-go. The ten boys and two scoutmasters had pitched their tents in central Oregon's Gold Ridge State Park. The nearest town was Bend, where on Friday afternoon they had stopped at a grocery store for last-minute supplies: water, Sprite, energy bars, and extra hot dogs.

Dean, the group whiner, had started in complaining about how long the ride was taking, that he might be getting carsick because of all the turns in the road, and on and on.

Marc, sitting in the front passenger seat of the van, saw Mr. Reeves's plump hands tighten their grip on the steering wheel. He sensed that the assistant scoutmaster was getting fed up with Dean's endless bellyaching.

Marc wondered how long it would be before the man lost his temper completely. Deciding to take matters into his own hands, Marc turned to face Dean, who was in the middle seat of the van. "Will you shut up?" said Marc. "I'm tired of listening to you."

For a moment Dean was too surprised to respond. Jacob, sitting beside Dean, suddenly became very interested in the thick trees that formed a green wall beside the highway. In the backseat, a grinning Darrell nudged Manuel, and the two of them made a poor job of concealing their laughter.

"What's so funny?" Dean demanded, turning away from Marc, who continued to watch him as if challenging the boy to utter one more word of complaint.

"I was telling Manuel a joke, wasn't I, man?" said Darrell, starting to laugh again. He turned and nudged his friend.

"Oh yeah! It was funny," Manuel said. "See, it's making me laugh all over again."

"If it's so funny, tell it to the rest of us," said Dean.

"If you didn't catch it," said Darrell, "too bad. It's never as funny the second time." He tugged at the little gold peg in his left ear and winked across at Marc.

With a sigh, Mr. Reeves said, "Do you think we could have five minutes of silence? Be like Jacob. Enjoy the scenery. This is one of the prettiest parts of Oregon."

"*I'm* not doing anything," Dean pouted. "Besides, Marc started it."

"Look!" Jacob cried suddenly, jabbing his forefinger against the window. "A deer — no, two of them. And a fawn."

The other boys strained to catch a glimpse of the animals — all except Dean. "Big deal," he said. "You can see loads of them in the petting zoo near Portland. You can buy ice-cream cones filled with food pellets, and they'll eat right out of your hand."

Mr. Reeves, Jacob's father, sighed again. Marc could tell the man was dreading the weekend ahead. In front of Mr. Reeves's black van, Mr. Bragonier, the scoutmaster, led the way in a later-model, silver-gray van carrying the other five scouts. For the umpteenth time, Marc wished the scoutmaster's van had been saddled with "Dean the Downer." But the boy had been determined to be a part of Mr. Reeves's group, and since his father was rich enough to make generous donations to the scouting organization, what Dean wanted (within reason), Dean pretty much got.

"Mr. Bragonier's slowing down," Marc pointed out.

"I see," said Mr. Reeves, doing the same. The left turn signal on the van ahead began blinking. The van slowed, then swung onto a narrow gravel side road, advanced a short ways, and waited for the second vehicle to follow. Mr. Reeves put his own signal on, checked the road for oncoming cars, and, seeing it was clear, turned left onto the other road.

"Does this mean we're getting close?" asked Dean.

"I hope so." .

"Not far now," Mr. Reeves assured everyone. Marc had the impression he was just as anxious as the others to get out of the van and away from Dean's nasally complaining.

Fifteen minutes later, they had reached a graveled parking area. A number of cars, a pickup with a camper mounted on back, and two motorcycles were parked higgledy-piggledy. The van drivers managed to find space a little ways apart from the others where they could park side by side. A brown wooden sign with bright yellow letters marked the trailhead — the path that led to the campsites beyond.

"No more free rides," joked Mr. Reeves. "From here on out every man packs his own gear."

The boys scrambled out of the van, stretching arms and legs and greeting their buddies from the other vehicle.

Jacob took a deep breath. "The air is wonderful!" he said. "I can smell juniper and sage and —"

"Who cares?" said Dean. "How far do we have to walk to set up camp?"

"Not too far. A half-hour climb should get us there," said Mr. Reeves. "Pull your stuff out of the back, men, and let's haul it. I want to get the tents up before the sun goes down."

They started up in a ragged line, with Mr. Bragonier leading his half of the troop, and Mr. Reeves and his scouts following.

Dean, who was in the rear, kept up a steady string of complaints. His backpack was too heavy. The trail was too steep. He kept slipping on the leaves and pine needles that carpeted the path. The other boys closed ranks and refused to pay attention to him. But he was seriously souring everyone's late-afternoon hike through the woods.

Marc and Jacob kept pace with Mr. Reeves. As they climbed, they took turns pointing out interesting rock formations or unusually shaped trees. A little behind them, Darrell and Manuel kept cracking each other up with jokes that (Marc was sure) were the kind no adult was supposed to overhear. They only broke off from time to time to yell back at Dean. "Hurry up, dude! We won't get nowhere till midnight, if you don't move your sorry rear!"

Dean muttered something — plenty of somethings — back, but too softly for the other boys to understand or take offense.

It was after 4:00 P.M. when they finally reached site #41, a grassy expanse that sloped gently down to the banks of broad, clear Lake Duchene. In the soft evening light Marc could see dimples in the water and hear faint splashes. "Rainbow trout," said Jacob, the troop's naturalist. "They're after mayflies and caddisflies. There should be good fishing here."

Gratefully, the boys dropped their gear and broke out a round of Sprites. But they'd barely had time to catch their breath before the scoutmasters were urging them to set up the pup tents and get ready for the night. Although the distant Cascade mountaintops were still aglow, the shadows under the trees were fast pooling together, ready to flood the forest with darkness.

"I can't get any cell reception," said Dean, who was wandering around the clearing.

"It's almost impossible here," Mr. Bragonier explained. "Don't even try."

"But I *have* to call my father," the boy protested, as if that would force sky or woodland to provide him a signal. Finally, after twice circling the area where the other scouts were hard at work, he shoved the useless phone into the pocket of his khaki uniform trousers. "Stupid place," he snarled to no one in particular. "Who picked out this dumb campsite, anyway?"

The scoutmasters exchanged eye-rolling glances and went on setting up their own, larger tent. The boys continued the policy of ignoring Dean, who was letting his tent-mate — Jack from the other van — secure the stakes, raise the tent poles, fasten the snaps that held the two canvas half pieces together, and bind the structure with ropes. Under the scoutmasters' direction, the boys had arranged the tents in a semicircle facing the lake. The adults' shelter was in the center, with two smaller tents on one side and three on the other. Darrell and Manuel made sure theirs was the third on that side — farthest away from the scoutmasters.

There was already a stone-lined firepit midway between the water and the tents. Using charcoal, Mr. Reeves started a fire and began heating vegetable soup and roasting potatoes on a grill he had brought with them. The boys were sent to find and sharpen sticks so they could roast their own hot dogs. Mr. Bragonier set out a packet of buns for the scouts to toast on the grill. From time to time, coyotes sounded a hunting call, heralding the arrival of sunset and the coming of darkness. The sound sent a collective shiver through the boys.

Dean's first hot dog fell off the roasting stick into the ashes.

"Smooth move, Ex-Lax," Darrell called from across the fire. The rest of the boys laughed as if this were the funniest thing they'd ever heard. Even the scoutmasters smiled a little.

Then Mr. Bragonier, supplying a replacement frank, said, "If that's the worst that happens this trip, don't worry. But watch what you're doing this time."

"I *was*. It just *slipped*. It wasn't my fault."

Nothing ever is, thought Marc. But he avoided saying it out loud.

After dinner, which the boys insisted was the greatest meal they'd ever eaten, they sat around the campfire and told ghost stories, most of them so old the boys had heard them lots of times. But the rising wind in the trees, the occasional call of a night bird, and the thousand and one other sounds of the woods after dark made even the most tired story seem fresh and immediate and frightening.

Marc's was the best, hands down. Before he launched into it, he told his listeners, "This story is absolutely true. When my cousin was studying in Japan, he heard about an elementary school nearby that kids couldn't go to, because it was haunted by the Split-Faced Woman. She was this woman who thought she was very ugly, so she went to a plastic surgeon. She begged him, 'Make me beautiful.' But she didn't have much money, and he wasn't very good. He did something terrible to her face so that her mouth opened from ear to ear in a horrible smile."

"That's gross," Darrell said.

"I think it's cool," said Manuel, giving his friend a push. That almost led to a shoving match, until Mr. Reeves said, "Knock it off and let Marc finish."

When they had settled down, Marc went on, "When she saw what had happened, she went crazy. She killed the doctor and his nurse, and ran away with her face covered by a red surgical mask. The police chased her into the basement of this school, and they shot her or something; anyhow, she died. But ever after, they say, her ghost hangs around, always wearing the red mask. If she meets anyone alone, she will shyly ask, 'Am I beautiful?' If the person says yes, she yanks off her mask and says, 'Even like this?' And if you yell 'No' or try to run away, she follows you, and grabs you, and you die of fright. And they always know she did it, because when a person is scared to death by her, their mouth twists up into a kind of horrible smile that runs from ear to ear."

Abruptly, Dean stood up. "I don't like scary stories, so I'm going to my tent. My father says you have to be really weird to *like* scaring yourself."

He left the other boys shaking their heads.

"Good riddance," said Marc.

He was a first-rate storyteller. The boys had sat spellbound. But no one volunteered to follow up with another ghost story.

The scoutmasters stretched and yawned, then announced it was time to "hit the hay." The boys were free to fish or explore or do what they wanted in the morning; in the afternoon they would go on a nature hike.

The boys visited the porta-potties some distance away from the main camp, then retreated to their tents, where they quickly snuggled into their sleeping bags.

But the camp wasn't really very quiet. Darrell and Manuel kept up a steady stream of chatter and laughter — not loud enough to understand, but loud enough that everyone else in the camp could hear them. The scoutmasters told them several times to be quiet, but after a few moments of silence, they'd be talking and chuckling again.

Unable to sleep, Marc listened to the night sounds and the loud snoring from the adults' tent. He regretted telling the story of the Split-Faced Woman, because he found himself endlessly thinking about her and half imagining some red-masked ghost thrusting its face past the flaps into the tent. He envied Jacob who was sleeping soundly a few feet away.

At last, he started to drift off — only to be awakened by Dean. The boy was standing outside the scout-masters' tent, announcing loudly, "My air mattress popped. What am I going to do? I can't *sleep.*"

Marc had the distinct impression that if Dean couldn't sleep, *no one* was getting any sleep.

The adults' tent was next to his own. Marc could clearly hear the two men rousing themselves. Wide awake, he crawled to the end of the tent and looked out. Mr. Reeves, who had thrown his jacket over his T-shirt and jeans, was trying to calm Dean down.

Dean wasn't buying. "I have to go home *now!* I don't want to be here anymore!"

Mr. Reeves explained in a voice that alerted Marc the man was forcing himself to be reasonable, "It's — what? — after midnight. We can't break camp and try to find our way out in the dark."

"Yes, we can. Or just you or Mr. Bragonier can take me. I don't care about the others."

Now both scoutmasters were trying to reason with Dean, but the boy had worked himself into a tizzy. "I have to go *now!*" he screeched. It was the same sort of tantrum Marc's two-year-old brother, Tad, would throw when he didn't get his way. Marc could barely stand seeing a baby act like that; watching Dean carry on was seriously pathetic, he decided.

If Dean had intended to involve the whole camp in his meltdown, he'd succeeded. Faces peered from every tent. Even Jacob, who could sleep through almost anything, had crawled over to join Marc.

Dean was now thrashing from side to side and pounding on Mr. Reeves's arm as the man tried to grab the boy's shoulders to bring him to his senses. Suddenly, tall, thin Mr. Bragonier — who *never* raised his voice — bellowed, "Get a grip, guy!" His roar was so uncharacteristic, everyone just stared at him gape-mouthed. Even Mr. Reeves seemed stunned. He was gripping Dean's shoulders, but now it looked as if he were holding a boy-sized doll. Dean had gone limp, his eyes wide and his mouth frozen in an O of surprise.

"That's better," said the scoutmaster. "Now, you come into our tent where we can sort things out." Then, casting his eyes around the half-circle of tents, Mr. Bragonier said loudly, "The rest of you settle down. If I hear one more sound out of anyone tonight, I'm canceling the next two days. *Got me?*"

Everyone got it. Heads were yanked back into tents; flaps dropped into place. After a few rounds of (very soft) whispering, a genuine silence fell over the camp, except for murmurs from the adult tent. But Marc didn't sleep; nor did Jacob. Marc had the feeling that no one in the camp was sleeping — just honoring the "pipe down" order.

A little later, Marc overheard the scoutmaster and Dean going to the boy's tent. A few minutes later, a single pair of footsteps returned to the main tent. Marc folded his hands behind his head and stared up at the seam where the two halves of their shelter had been snapped together. He'd given up the idea of sleep. He lay listening to the woods until the first light of dawn seeped past the loose flaps beyond the foot of his sleeping bag. *Definitely, our adventure is off to a bad start,* he decided.

Everybody looked and sounded dragged out in the morning. Breakfast was a haphazard affair of lumpy oatmeal, greasy sausages, burnt toast, and Gatorade. The scoutmasters sat apart from the boys, talking softly over steaming cups of coffee. Both of them looked as unrested as Marc felt.

Dean sat by himself, picking at his food. Word had gotten around that Mr. Bragonier had given Dean his own air mattress until repairs could be made on the boy's. Marc couldn't imagine trying to sleep on the bumpy, stone-littered ground without an air mattress. *No wonder the guy looks half-dead,* he thought.

Every now and then, the men glanced toward the

west. Though the morning was sunny and warming up fast, dark clouds massed in the distance. Marc hoped it wasn't a thunderstorm brewing. He had no desire to be caught in rain, thunder, and, worse, lightning, in the wilderness. *Might be a good idea to bag this whole trip,* he thought. He was aware of the soft patter of dew dripping off the branches of the trees around them. He hoped it wasn't a preview of a rainstorm to come.

He had brought his fishing pole, so he went down to the lake to try his luck. A couple of others joined him. The water was pure blue a little ways out, but crystal clear near the shore. They could see the iridescent flicker of trout threading their lazy way through the water plants or snapping at low-flying insects. But though Marc cast and recast his line, none of the rainbows seemed attracted to the handcrafted flies he had spent months making as one of his merit badge projects. Most of the other boys had lost interest and were sitting on boulders, dangling their feet in the cool water and looking bored. Dean wandered by, complained of "too many mosquitoes," and left. *Nothing about the trip feels right anymore,* Marc told himself. He glanced again to the west. The clouds were measurably heavier and darker, though the sunshine in the immediate area of the camp kept assuring a pleasant day.

Half an hour later, the scoutmasters called everyone to the center of the camp. "There's just a chance we might have some rain later," said Mr. Bragonier, "so we're going to get an early start on the hike. We'll fix sandwiches, take plenty of water, and bring along some energy bars. We'll have lunch on the trail and make up for it with a good dinner when we get back."

Everyone looked a little livelier at the chance to get moving and *do* something. Even Dean seemed enthusiastic. He made a point of showing off the fancy compass and new hiking boots his father had let him pick out for the trip.

In short order, they set out single file along the hiking trail the scoutmasters had selected. It was a moderate uphill trek that promised a great view of Stairstep Falls. Mr. Bragonier set the pace and served as trail guide, while Mr. Reeves, who worked for the Portland Wildlife Conservancy, acted as naturalist. Jacob helped in pointing out things the others shouldn't miss.

Marc walked a little ways behind Jacob and his father, not wanting to miss anything they had to share. All the boys seemed to be having a good time as they followed the trail that wound upward through the fragrant, sun-warmed woods. Occasionally a break in the trees allowed a glimpse of lush, green forest that stretched for miles, revealing half-hidden canyons, towering rock outcroppings, and the occasional fragment of a lake or stream shining in the sunlight.

They paused for lunch on a broad ledge overlooking Stairstep Falls, admiring the play of water over stone as they chewed their sandwiches and sipped from their canteens. Marc noticed that Dean, as usual, was sitting by himself. He had his new boots off and was rubbing his heels. Then he pulled his socks off and peered more closely at each foot.

"Something the matter?" asked Mr. Bragonier, who happened to be passing.

"My feet hurt. I've got blisters."

The scoutmaster looked down and whistled. "Those are the size of silver dollars," he said. "Your boots must be too tight. Didn't you make sure to get them roomy enough? Didn't you break them in like we told you?"

The boy shrugged.

"We'll have to do something," the man said. He got the first-aid kit and applied a generous amount of antiseptic ointment to the blisters. After putting a pad of gauze over each of the boy's heels, the scoutmaster helped him carefully draw on his socks. But when he tried to help Dean pull the boots back on, the boy yelped in pain. "They're too tight," he complained. "You're hurting me."

The boots came off again. "I don't suppose you brought your tennies along just in case?" Mr. Bragonier asked, his voice suggesting he already knew the answer.

The boy shook his head.

"Well, I don't know what we're going to do here."

"I'll walk in my socks."

"Socks won't do much good on these rocks. And you

need the boots to protect you from insect bites or poison ivy or even a snake."

At this last, Dean shuddered. "What am I going to do?"

"Put your feet up; they're probably a little swollen. You may be able to manage the boots by the time we're ready to move out."

At that moment, there came a deep, dull rumble from the west, followed a moment later by a distinct clap of thunder. As one, the entire company swiveled their heads toward the source. It was easy enough to locate. While they had been eating lunch and watching the falls, the mass of thunderheads had advanced halfway toward them across the parkland. Frequent sizzles of white-purple lightning mixed with the churning clouds.

Mr. Reeves looked anxious, but he said lightly, "Time to call retreat, I think."

"Clean up your stuff as fast as you can," Mr. Bragonier told them. Marc and the others could clearly hear the concern in his voice. They gathered up the remains of their lunch and hurriedly stuffed things into backpacks and fanny packs.

Several more bursts of thunder helped speed things along.

"What am *I* supposed to do?" Dean wailed.

"Let's try the boots again," said the scoutmaster. He and Mr. Reeves managed to get the boots on, though

Dean winced and yelled and once even tried to kick Mr. Reeves. But when he tried to stand up, his legs almost buckled under him. "It's *killing* me!" he cried.

The clouds were swirling closer.

"Everybody back to camp *now!*" Mr. Bragonier commanded. To Mr. Reeves he said, "We'll have to carry him chair-style." The two men interlocked their hands and formed a "seat" between them. Dean sat like a prince on the improvised throne. The men, adjusting their grip and balance to his weight, started for the path downhill. Without being asked, Marc and Jacob took charge of the men's backpacks, leaving the scoutmasters free to deal with Dean.

From time to time, the men had to shout a warning to the scouts to slow down. Things seemed much steeper on the descent than they had on the way up, Marc realized. The two men in front of him were panting from navigating the downhill slope and supporting the burden they shared.

By the time they had left the rock ledges near the falls and entered the canopy of trees, the threatening clouds were a solid mass overhead. Most of the scouts were on a steep part of the trail when a flash of lightning seared the sky from horizon to horizon. Marc saw every leaf and branch of every tree suddenly lit up as if touched by the beam from a laser wand. A minute later came a KABOOM!

Like a sonic boom, Marc had time to realize. Then the

ground rose and fell underfoot as if the earth had been turned to liquid.

Everyone, at all points along the trail, was tossed up and dropped down like so many rag dolls. Marc hit the ground on his right shoulder, felt pain shoot through like a red-hot wire, and prayed he hadn't broken something. The scoutmasters slammed into each other, and then were tossed apart. A shrieking Dean spilled onto the path and began rolling down to where the forward guard of the troop lay sprawled on the trail, or in the bushes and weeds beside it. Dean bumped to a stop against Manuel, who lay stunned, staring up at the nearly pitch-black sky, eyes still dazzled by the light-burst. Marc, clambering to his feet, thought, *Earthquake!*

Then rain poured down. *Red rain.* It cascaded off the trees overhead like . . . *blood,* thought Marc. A drop fell on his hands; it burned. The scoutmasters, still dazed, struggled to get up. Farther down the trail, scouts began to scream as burning red raindrops touched them.

Marc helped Mr. Bragonier to his feet. "There's something wrong with this rain," he said. "It burns."

"Some kind of acid rain, maybe," said Mr. Reeves, who had made it to his knees. "Get the boys under the trees."

"What about lightning?" shouted the other scoutmaster over the roar of the rising wind and the *spatter-hiss* of the thickening downpour. Now Darrell

was screaming, and Marc could see that his arm was puffy, red and swollen like boiled lobster, where a spill of red rain had soaked it.

"We'll have to take our chances," Mr. Reeves shouted back. "Lightning is a maybe; this red stuff is deadly."

Now a second downpour of leaves and needles spilled from the trees overhead. Shriveled gray, burnt leaves from the upper reaches of the trees pattered down on all sides. When they hit the ground, they turned to ashes. The wet grayness stuck to the boys scrambling to reach better shelter near the tree trunks. It smeared their hands and legs and faces, but it didn't burn like the rain did.

"Get out of the rain!" the scoutmasters cried in tandem. "Get off the path. Get under the trees."

Most of the boys had gotten the message, urged on by burns and blisters from the corrosive rain.

But Dean, his arms folded over his head, the pain from his new boots forgotten, was charging down the path toward camp, screaming as each drop of the red wetness burned him. He slipped, fell on his rear, and slid down the rain-slicked, ash-covered slope.

"I've got to stop him!" cried Mr. Bragonier. Mr. Reeves tried to hold him back, but the scoutmaster pulled free and hurried after the screeching, terrified boy.

Another bolt of lightning split the sky. A tree beside

the path exploded. The scoutmaster went down in a shower of charred bark and branches.

Then, as suddenly as it had begun, the storm ended. Red rain ceased falling. The shower of shrunken, dead leaves stopped. The clouds overhead began to scatter to the four corners of the world.

Emerging from the shelter of the trees, the dazed boys looked at each other and shook their heads, as if to free themselves from this nightmare that had affected all of them.

Marc was the first to reach Mr. Bragonier and begin brushing the leaves and splinters off him. The scoutmaster didn't look right. One side of his face and most of his neck was badly swollen. He seemed barely conscious as Mr. Reeves leaned over him and tried to shake him into awareness.

Marc glanced around. Everyone was here — shocked and blistered, but present and accounted for, except Dean.

It took him a minute to focus. He'd last seen Dean charging down the trail, screaming. As the others clustered around the injured scoutmaster, Marc took it upon himself to look for Dean.

He didn't have far to go. The downhill path curved sharply around a massive oak, then leveled off. He found the missing scout facedown in a puddle of blood-red rainwater.

Trying not to touch the water, Marc grabbed the back

of Dean's khaki shirt and pulled him out of the puddle. The effort overbalanced Marc, and he tumbled backward, hauling Dean with him. They landed on their backs in a mush of gray ash and dead leaves.

To Marc's relief, the wetness only felt cold and unpleasant. The red rain seemed to have lost its potency within minutes of touching the earth. Pushing himself to his hands and knees, Marc bent over Dean. The other boy's eyes were closed. Marc turned his face to the side. Trickles of red water ran from the corners of the boy's mouth, his nostrils, and his ears. Marc tried to remember the rules for helping a drowning victim, but he was having a problem connecting one thought with another.

Then Dean's eyes popped open. He coughed up a lungful of now-harmless red water. Then he coughed again. He got to his knees, staring at Marc.

"Why are you here?" he asked. "You don't like me."

Deciding that the other boy was only a little more confused than he was, Marc said, "Don't say that. I like you fine. Everyone does. Everyone will be glad you're all right."

Dean said nothing, just struggled to his feet, letting Marc help him, though Marc felt just as wobbly.

Now they could hear the others, carefully coming down the slick path around the huge oak. The rest of the troop looked beat-up but holding it together. Then Mr. Reeves appeared. He and Jacob were supporting Mr.

Bragonier, who lurched along upright, but whose head lolled on his chest. To Marc, his face and neck and arms looked as if they belonged to someone who had just been pulled out of a fire.

"We've got to get Roger to a doctor," said Mr. Reeves. Then his eyes fell on Dean. "And he's . . . ?"

"Doing okay," said Marc. He put a supportive arm around the other boy and was surprised to feel that Dean's shoulders were icy cold. *Shock*, he decided, remembering something from the scout handbook. *He needs a doctor, too.* He asked the other, "How are your feet holding up?"

"Fine, I guess." Dean looked as if he didn't know what Marc was talking about. He wriggled free of Marc's arm and began to walk a little ahead, as if wanting to distance himself. His first few steps seemed uncertain, but then he was striding along behind the rest of the troop.

With the rain over and the sky clearing, the scouts made their slow way back toward camp. *It's weird,* thought Marc. *The rain really burned Mr. Bragonier, but it didn't seem to hurt Dean, even though he swallowed some of it.* Over his shoulder he asked Mr. Reeves, "What was that rain all about?"

"Got me. I heard about something like this happening in India years ago. It could have been reddish dust from who knows where that got washed down by the rain. Over there someone suggested it might have been spores from lichens growing in the forest." He shrugged. "I think there was even one scientist who suggested the redness came from microscopic bits of a meteor that exploded when it hit the earth's atmosphere and got mixed with a rain cloud."

"That might explain the loud boom and the flash just before the rain began," said Marc. "And the earthquake."

"That's pretty far-fetched," the man said. "It's more realistic to think dust or plant spores or some kind of pollution."

Marc looked at the groaning scoutmaster supported by Mr. Reeves and Jacob. "Acid rain would explain what happened to him," he said, pointing at Mr. Bragonier. "It could."

Marc was about to raise the other question of why Dean didn't seem harmed, just vague to the point of not feeling the blisters on his feet. But just then Jacob asked, "Marc, could you spell me for a minute? This guy's a lot of dead weight."

"Sure," said Marc, happy to give his friend a break. The scoutmaster seemed really out of it, and his frequent stumbles meant a sudden extra burden on the others until he found his footing. In a short time, Marc's shoulders and calves were aching. He wondered how Mr. Reeves was managing without relief.

They struggled on for two hours, taking occasional rest breaks, with Marc and Jacob spelling each other.

Mr. Bragonier seemed to be coming around a little. He was walking more steadily and seemed better able to support himself, though he rambled a lot when he tried to talk.

Then, thankfully, Darrell came hurrying up the trail to tell them, "Manuel's spotted the camp. We're almost there."

Mr. Reeves nodded, clearly too winded to say anything.

Once back, they let Mr. Bragonier rest in a folding chair with a blanket around him, while the others broke camp. Marc couldn't wait to be on the road back home.

At one point, Darrell came over to him and held out the back of his hand. Where there had been a rain blister, Marc now saw a circle of what looked like tiny red snake scales, crimson at the center, shading to pink at the edges.

"Gross," said Marc.

"It's happening to some of the other guys who got burned. But not everyone. Hey, Manuel!" Darrell shouted. "Come here. Show Marc your wrist."

Manuel did so. There had been a burn line where red drippage off a tree branch had etched a "bracelet" onto Manuel's wrist; now the burn was almost completely healed, except for a pale smudge that seemed to be fading even as the boys watched.

Mr. Reeves paused in breaking down his tent to join them. "Never have seen anything like this. It's almost as if it's reacting differently to different body chemistry." He made a face and said, "Looks like we're all going to have to be checked out by doctors when we get home." He went back to finish stowing his and Mr. Bragonier's gear.

"Man," said Darrell, "this really sucks." He rubbed the spot on his hand and then looked closely. "Hey, this thing's growing!" He shoved his hand at Marc then Manuel. "Doesn't it look like it's getting bigger?" The other boys nodded. The red patch that had been about the size of a penny was now bigger than a quarter. "I gotta get to a doctor."

Marc took the other boy's shoulder and squeezed reassuringly. "I'm sure it's no big deal. The doctor will give you some meds, and you'll be fine. Finish packing up. Everyone else is almost ready to go."

As Darrell and Manuel drifted off, Marc glanced around the camp. The others were working in their assigned two-man teams to dismantle the tents and repack their gear — except for Mr. Reeves, who was trying to keep an eye on Mr. Bragonier. The man was still seated on the folding camp chair, swathed neck to ankles in a plaid, thermal blanket. He seemed to be staring wide-eyed at nothing in particular. *The sooner he gets to a doctor, the better,* Marc thought.

Then he noticed that Jack, Dean's tent-mate, was struggling alone to break down their shared tent. Since Marc and Jacob had completed their work in record time, and Jacob was helping his father, Marc wandered over to assist Jack.

"Where's Dean?" he asked as he helped pull up stakes and roll the canvas halves of the pup tent.

Jack gestured with his thumb in the direction of the porta-potties, separated from the camp by a screen of trees. "Guess he had to use the can," he said. "I'm never gonna team with him again. He leaves all the work for me and just talks about how stupid everything and everyone else is."

Marc stowed Dean's stuff in the missing boy's backpack while Mr. Reeves made a quick check to be sure everything was shipshape. Then they were ready to move out. The assistant scoutmaster did a quick nosecount. "Where's Dean?"

"Latrine," said Marc.

"Would you get him? Unless he's fallen in, I want him here *pronto*. While you do that, I'm going to rouse Roger as best I can." He took a step in the direction of the scoutmaster while the rest of the boys milled around, anxious to be away from the place. Several of them, Marc noticed, were comparing rain marks.

He followed the short path that led to a row of three pale green porta-potties standing in a small clearing. The doors to two of them hung partway open. The third was closed, clearly locked from inside.

"Dean?" Marc called. There was no answer. He advanced to just outside the potty, calling the other boy's name, and then tapping gently on the door. "You in there? It's Marc. You okay?"

He heard something between a groan and a growl.

"You being sick? Want me to get Mr. Reeves?"

Now the sound from inside seemed like some strange blend of snarl and hiss. It reminded Marc of an angry raccoon he'd accidentally disturbed prowling around the garbage cans on another campout. But this sounded much scarier.

He tapped one last time on the door. "I'll be back with help."

From inside came a deep rumbling, almost like very distant thunder, with scrabbling against the door and walls that sounded almost like claws. Marc felt his body go cold, while his stomach did a flip-flop. The sounds grew more frantic; the door seemed to bulge outward. He couldn't take his eyes off it. At the same moment, he heard screams from somewhere nearby. An instant later, he realized they were coming from the campsite. He tore his eyes away from the potty that was now rocking back and forth, door and walls bulging and shaking as though something very big were very angry at being stuck inside.

The screams and shouts from the camp had grown fainter. Maybe the other boys were running away. Just then a deafening roar burst from the potty, and Marc ran for it. A moment later the door of the latrine went hurtling end over end, narrowly missing him before coming to rest in a tangle of bushes beneath a pine.

Whatever was inside was out now. Marc glanced over his shoulder and saw something tall and red and scaly lurch away from the wreckage. Two eyes, of different sizes, located in a swollen red mass of a head, now fixed on the runner. The mouth broke into a horrible grin that would have stretched from ear to ear — if the thing had *had* ears. Then the mouth-slit twisted and rippled as if trying to shape words it was never meant to speak. *"Yuh dunsh ike muh. Eh dunsh ike yuh."*

Marc put on a burst of speed. He hurtled down the path, nearly stumbling over his feet, until he reached the campsite. It was a shambles, packs and supplies scattered everywhere. There was no sign of anyone.

No, he realized. *Wrong.* Something red and on all fours crouched over a plump khaki-brown shape. Shreds of plaid cloth lay scattered all around. As he raced through the clearing, Marc was dimly aware of an elongated grinning face, covered with surprisingly delicate red scales, that snarled at him and then hissed a greeting to the thing that shambled into the abandoned camp in pursuit of Marc.

He ran as he had never run before. He assumed the rest of the scouts had fled down the path toward the cars and other campers. He wondered how soon he'd overtake them. And he wondered what he'd find when he did. *What about Darrell and the others marked by the red rain?* he wondered. *Were they just changing more slowly? And how many other camps have been drenched?*

Tree branches snapped somewhere behind him.

Something snarled. A second something roared a response.

Then he had no more time for wondering. There was only the steady pumping of his legs and heart and lungs as the world narrowed to a single thought: *Keep running.*

Marc ran.

Cabin 13

Noah was tired and cranky by the time his dad finally pulled the family van onto the dirt-and-gravel parking area of the Mountain View Motel, somewhere off the highway between Denver and Fort Collins in Colorado. The family was on its way to visit Noah's aunt and uncle in Casper, Wyoming. His dad had wanted to push on for another hour or two to cut the next day's driving time, but Honey, Noah's mom, argued that the kids were exhausted and needed to eat and get some sleep in "real" beds — not bouncing around the seats of the van. To keep the peace, Noah's dad had grudgingly agreed, and Noah felt relieved. It was no fun being trapped in a van with seven-year-old

215

Leah and five-year-old Steffi, who were even crankier than he was.

The L-shaped motel featured a row of old-fashioned, but tidy-looking units, painted white with red trim on the doors and window frames. Individual roofs overhung porches with a white metal chair or two on each. The office and owners' residence stood at the end, a white, single-story building at a right angle to the rental units. Behind the office were a few scattered outbuildings and several cars and trucks in various states of repair.

Eleven-year-old Noah and his younger sisters crowded into the tiny registration office behind their parents. Noah glanced at some tired-looking brochures in a rack. They featured places of local interest — none of them exciting. Meanwhile, his dad and mom talked with the woman behind the desk.

"There's two double beds," she was saying. Noah noticed that her fingers all displayed big, glittery rings. And her hair was the weirdest shade of orange he had ever seen. Beneath the ugly, curly mop of hair, her eyes — pinkish-red behind thick, round glasses — reminded the boy of the eyes of a vulture that had been feasting on road kill when the family van disturbed it. The heavy bird had liftoff problems and had barely gotten out of the way. Noah had stared into its eyes as it slid past the passenger side of the van. In some similar fashion, the motel woman creeped him out.

"There's pretty good eats across the road at Cogburn's Lounge and Grill," she said. "Steak is good; lamb chops is fair-to-middlin'; salmon's passable." She lowered her voice. "Don't risk the meat loaf."

"Thanks for the warning," Noah's mom said. "Knowing this crowd, it'll probably be four burgers and a salad for me."

"They make good margaritas, too," the woman offered.

"We'll skip those, I think," Dad said with a laugh.

The motel owner shrugged and handed them two keys to Number 5. "Cogburn's opens for breakfast at 7 A.M. And don't you worry; I'll send my husband, C.J., over with the rollaway bed as fast as I can find him."

"Thanks again," said Noah's dad. On the way out, Mom paused to snag some of the pamphlets from the rack. No matter where they went, or how long they stayed, Honey always tried to learn a little about the area. Since she taught American history in the middle school back in Texas, Noah decided it made sense. But, casting a glance at the woman, who was moving her lips as she read something off their registration form, he knew he'd be only too glad to leave the Mountain View Motel far behind.

The room was one of the shabbier ones they'd stayed in on any family trip. It held the two double beds with icky green chenille spreads, a desk, a bunged-up bureau with six drawers, a closet that was only a niche without a door, and a bathroom with stingy tubes of shampoo and conditioner and two skimpy bars of face and bath soap.

"It's good we brought our own overnight kits," said Honey. She pulled back the covers to check the sheets and pillows. "More patching than sheets," she decided, "but no problems." Problems, Noah knew, meant bugs or stains or other unacceptable things. His mom was a stickler about cleanliness. He knew her fussing drove his father crazy, but Dad put up with it "to keep the peace."

They'd just about unpacked enough for one night, when a knock came at the cabin door. Honey peered through the spy hole, then called, "Jim, the rollaway's here." As she pulled the door open, Noah and his sisters looked up from the video game they were playing on the TV. Even a funky place like the Mountain View had a few video games available, though they were oddball ones the kids had never heard of before. Still, any game was better than none.

The two younger children immediately returned to the game on the video monitor. But Noah couldn't take his eyes off the man, who had to be the other half of the motel-owning couple, the husband the woman called "C.J." He was skeleton-thin and old as the hills — or older, by Noah's figuring. His pale skin seemed to be drawn so tightly over his lanky framework that every bone showed in his hands and neck and skull-like face.

He wore a black cowboy hat; when he removed it briefly and nodded to Honey, Noah saw that his head was completely bald, save for a few wisps of white hair. Around his neck was a bolo tie — thin, braided black leather clasped with a solid silver steer's head, with horns that looked almost two full inches apart. The man's thin lips barely covered a mouthful of surprisingly perfect teeth. His eyes were sunk so deep in their sockets, they seemed to be staring from the depths of deep, matching caves. Noah had the uncomfortable feeling that, of everyone in the room, the ancient had singled him out. His look struck the boy as every bit as hungry as that of his orange-haired, pinch-faced wife.

Jim Caxton rushed to help the old man maneuver the rollaway bed up the two steps into the cabin. When the furniture had been rearranged to allow for unfolding the extra bed, and it had been put in position under the green-curtained window, C.J. said, "You need anythin', just call the office. Me or the old woman will fix you up as best we can. Oh, they'll be folks you don't know in the office tomorrow. Our son and daughter-in-law are takin' over. Me and the missus have to drive down to Colorado Springs first thing. Family business."

As C.J. left the room, he gave Noah one last lingering look. Noah shuddered. The guy creeped him out just as much as the woman had. He was getting only bad vibes from the place, even though no one else seemed to notice anything strange. He was glad to hear the old couple would be gone before the Caxton family hit the road in the morning. Just knowing the motel owners with their strange, greedy eyes were anywhere nearby was an unpleasant thought. Wyoming couldn't arrive soon enough, Noah decided.

Starving and ready to eat, the kids waited outside for their parents. Noah watched Leah and Steffi race each other up and down the row of cabins. When they finally paused in their running, Leah reported to Noah, "I counted two times. There are fourteen little houses —"

"Cabins," Noah corrected automatically.

"Okay, *cabins.* Anyhow, there are only fourteen of them. There's no Cabin 13. It goes up to 12, and then skips to 14 and 15. Did someone mess up when they put the numbers on the doors?"

"I don't think so," said Noah, who liked to read and knew all kinds of curious facts. "A lot of people think the number 13 is unlucky, so they don't put it on anything. The motel owners probably thought no one would want to stay in Cabin 13."

"That's stupid," Leah announced. "It's just a number."

The discussion went no further, since their parents had emerged from their own unit to take them to dinner across the road.

The burgers at Cogburn's were undercooked, and the fries lay limp and greasy on their plates. Even Steffi, who loved fries and was forever stealing from others, hardly touched any. Honey's salad looked soggy, with a few anemic veggies sprinkled over sad-looking lettuce leaves, the whole mess buried under globs of ranch dressing that seemed more like dollops of Elmer's glue. She left most of it on her plate, ignoring her own rule to "eat all your vegetables."

"I think we'll skip breakfast here and see what we can find farther down the road," said Jim, pushing aside his half-eaten burger — still way too red even after sending it back to the kitchen for extra cooking. The waitress — "Inez" her badge said — had dutifully carried it back and forth, but made it abundantly clear that customer satisfaction was way down on her list of priorities. Noah, who paid attention to details, noticed his father put the absolute minimum tip on their Visa slip when the check came. Then the kids were hurried back across the deserted road to the Mountain View. Leah wanted to point out where Cabin 13 was missing, but no one cared.

Inside their unit, Noah and the girls begged to play a last round of video games, but their parents nixed this. "Time for bed, period," said their dad. "We've got to get an early start tomorrow."

For Noah, the thought of putting distance between here and anywhere else made it worth the sacrifice, though he *had* been enjoying a game called Haunted Houseful, with blast-'em pop-up ghosts, werewolves, skeletons, and vampires — although the last two somehow reminded him of C.J. and his orange-haired wife. *Weird,* Noah told himself as he settled under the covers of the rollaway that was his for the night.

The boy had hoped he could just bag all his uneasiness about the place and sleep till dawn, when they'd continue their trip north. But, after an hour, he found himself wide awake. He was roasting. He kicked the covers off the bed. But the room seemed stifling, even though he could hear the air conditioner purring in the far wall.

Oddly, on the other side of the room, his mom and dad slept deeply; he could hear his father's louder snoring as a counterpoint to his mom's softer tones. His sisters, sharing the double bed in-between, also slept soundly, with only a sigh or a murmur to indicate dreams.

Even with the covers kicked aside, it was just too warm for Noah to sleep. He sat up on the side of the bed, grateful that the ancient bedsprings didn't give off more than a few soft squeaks and squeals.

He glanced at the luminous dial of the radio alarm on the nightstand between the double beds. It read 12:57 A.M.

Moving quietly, he slid a pair of jeans out of his

suitcase, which lay unzipped on top of the waist-high bureau. Quickly he tugged them on over his pajama bottoms, then slipped his bare feet into his tennies and laced them up. His pajama top was as good as a shirt — who was going to see him? Gently he pulled open the front door of the cabin and snuck out into the night, leaving the door unlatched. His parents would be upset if they knew what he was doing, but he planned to have himself back in bed long before their alarm went off.

The air outside felt blessedly cool. It was still, except for the *chirr* of crickets in the grassy emptiness around the motel or the occasional faint horn blast from a truck out on the highway. The porch lights were on in front of three units besides their own. Cabins 1 and 2, closest to the office, had pickups parked in front. In the other direction, a single light was burning near the end of the row.

Noah decided to stroll along the line of cabins to the vacant lot that marked the far end of the property. He savored the breeze that was blowing from the direction of Cogburn's. A few dim lights inside the restaurant separated it from the sweep of darkness that marked the road. In the distance pinpoints of moving light indicated cars on the highway that curved back toward Denver.

Ambling along, his tennies making faint scrunching sounds on the gravel, the boy was aware of just how desolate — and *spooky* — the spot was. Absently, he ran the fingertips of his left hand along the picket fencing that separated the cabins from the parking lot.

He was just passing the far cabin with the glowing porch light, when he paused, noting the number 13 in big white raised numerals on the door. *How is that possible?* Noah wondered. He remembered Leah telling him that the number 13 was missing. Well, his sister had been wrong — big surprise! He'd have fun teasing her in the morning about how she couldn't even count to 13 properly.

"Bit late, ain't it, boy?" a whispery voice asked from the shadowed corner of porch. Shading his eyes against the light's glare, Noah saw a stick-thin figure settled into the cushions of a chair. The orangey hair revealed it was the woman motel owner seated to the left of the front door. Her bony fingers clutched the chair arms as if she were getting ready to spring at him. The rings on every finger of her hands sparkled and glittered above her swollen, knobby knuckles.

Noah hesitated to answer. Even at eleven, his mother's warning never to speak to strangers still sounded loud and clear in his head. But, then, he reasoned, the motel owner had met the family earlier, so she was probably no longer classified as a stranger.

He replied, "Yes, ma'am," adding unnecessarily, "I couldn't sleep." Feeling an explanation was expected, he said, "It was too warm in the room."

"Weren't the air conditioner runnin'?"

"Yeah — but somehow, it didn't seem enough."

"Well, a little night air might could be a good thing, then," she said, leaning forward. The light caught her moist eyes, making them glitter like her rings.

"I guess," said Noah, wanting to be away from those hungry, bird-bright eyes. "I suppose I better get back."

"You've hardly had a chance t' cool down," she said. "Come on up and set a spell. There's another chair." She waved her hand at the matching chair to the right of the door.

"Um, I'd better not." He took a step backward.

"Well, who've we got chere?" asked a paper-dry voice behind him. Noah felt a hand with vise-strong fingers clamp on his right shoulder. Turning to confront his captor, Noah found himself staring into the skull-face of the other motel owner, the man called C.J. "Oh, sure. Number 5," the old man said, nodding.

Noah tried to twist free of the gripping hand. He had the impression that the man's fragile-appearing body concealed a great reservoir of strength.

"Ease up, C.J.," the woman cautioned. "You're gonna hurt 'im."

"Oh." The fingers relaxed, but the hand continued to rest lightly on Noah's shoulder.

"Boy couldn't sleep. Found it cooler out here. Invited him up to talk a spell, but he's shy. You know kids," she said with a shrug. All the time she kept watching Noah as if he were the most interesting thing in the world.

"No need t' be shy with Lucia or me," the man insisted. "G'wan, set. Take a load off. Enjoy the coolin' air."

"I — I need to get back before someone misses me," Noah protested weakly.

"At 1:00 A.M.? I doubt that, boy. Go on; do like Lucia suggests." A bony finger with a thick, sharp nail jabbed him between the shoulder blades.

Feeling foolish and threatened at the same time, Noah pushed his way through the little gate, aware of the old man following close as his shadow.

Trying one last time to get away, Noah said suddenly, "Didn't I hear you say you're leaving tomorrow — I mean, *today*? Don't you need to pack or something?"

Lucia waved a dismissive hand. "Nothin' much t' worry 'bout. The youngsters'll be here by dawn. Me 'n' C.J. don't sleep much. Old folks don't," she added in a confidential tone. "Now, sit you down."

Reluctantly, the boy sat facing her. C.J. paused on the top step, watching Noah every bit as intently as his wife.

"C.J.!" the woman spoke sharply. "Stop standin' 'round. Go see what kind of ade's in the pitcher in the fridge."

When the old man had gone inside, Lucia leaned across and patted the boy's knee. He could barely hide the repulsion that made his whole body want to shudder at her unwelcome touch. He felt relieved when she settled back into her chair cushions.

"Nice frosty glass o' lemonade or limeade will finish coolin' you down. You'll sleep like a baby — though you don't seem like much more'n a baby t' these old eyes." She leaned across again to touch his leg. This time, her fingertips lingered a bit too long on his knee. He felt their faint pressure, as though she were testing the firmness of the flesh below the denim. Then she pulled back again, content to sit wordlessly, just watching him.

Increasingly uncomfortable, the boy cast around for something to say. Abruptly he blurted out, "My sister Leah didn't think there *was* a Cabin 13. She kept telling my folks and me that the numbers jumped from 12 to 14."

"Might's well *not* be here," Lucia said with a sniff of disgust. "Folks shy away from anythin' with that number 13: hotel floors, motel units, seats on a airplane — y'name it. *Superstition*" — she sounded out every syllable of the word for emphasis — "pure 'n' simple."

"That's what I said."

"Foolishness. Me 'n' C.J. use it as our special place — 'part from our reg'lar space back o' the office." She turned her head and shouted, "C.J.! You died in there? How long's it take you t' poke your nose in a fridge?"

A moment later, the old man returned to the porch, carrying a blue pitcher and a single glass that looked to Noah as if it had once held jelly. "Lemonade," he told them, nodding at the pitcher. "I turned the air conditioner all the way up. It's coolin' down the inside even better than out chere."

"Then I vote we go inside and let the boy have his lemonade there," announced Lucia, heaving herself out of the chair with the slowness and distress brought on by accumulated years. She held the cabin door open for Noah, indicating with a sidewise motion of her head that he should enter.

Noah got up, but he made no effort to follow. "I think I'd better get back to our cabin," he said with all the forcefulness he could muster.

"Nonsense," said C.J. "'Sides, it'd be rude t' turn down what's been offered in a friendly way." He added a second jab to Noah's shoulder for emphasis.

"Some o' my fresh-squeezed lemonade in a cool room," said Lucia, "you'll be ready for bed in no time t'all."

To avoid another poke, Noah walked past the old woman into the main room of Cabin 13. A moment later, the two oldsters followed him in. He heard C.J. close the door softly behind them.

There were no beds in the cabin. It looked more like a dining room inside with a big round oak table dominating the space. Four spindly, high-backed chairs surrounded it. Curiously, there was no other furniture in the room except a big wooden sideboard. Pictures of couples covered the walls. Sometimes the people were dressed in old-fashioned clothes; other times they looked quite modern. Some of the photos were old and brown; some were black-and-white; some were in color. What was curious was that the couples in all the photos looked a lot like C.J. and Lucia, though in some they were young, in some they looked middle-aged — but there were none of the old couple who ran the motel. The backgrounds varied from forests and mountains and deserts to landmarks that Noah recognized as the Empire State Building, the Eiffel Tower, and the Taj Mahal.

"Family?" he asked.

"Sure is," said C.J. with a grin.

"Our nearest 'n' dearest," said Lucia, smiling back at the old man. Then she told Noah to sit. When he was settled in one of the uncomfortable chairs, she plunked the single glass in front of him and filled it to the brim with lemonade. "Drink," she ordered.

He felt like a prisoner seated between two standing guards. "Aren't you having anything to drink?" he asked.

"Later," Lucia said offhandedly. "Time enough later."

Having no other choice, Noah brought the glass to his lips and sipped. It was way too sweet, but he forced himself to swallow. And it *was* cold. After a second sip, he put down the glass. "I think I've had enough," he said.

"Drink up," said C.J. His attempt at good humor

seemed to have vanished. "Don't want Lucia t' think you don't like her special homemade lemonade." His eyes bored into the boy's.

Noah dutifully drank. He was vaguely aware that the oldsters had inched closer, and each had a hand on one of his shoulders. A moment later, he was glad their hands were there to steady him, for he felt light as a feather — as if he would float up to the ceiling if it weren't for the restraining hands. The shine of Lucia's rings and the sheen of C.J.'s silver-steer bolo blazed, filling the air around him.

And then he felt as if he were shrinking, his skin evaporating into the cool air, drawn in two different directions like mist being pulled into an air vent. Even his bones — and he could feel every one of them, icy-cold and aching — were growing thinner, smaller, brittle as twigs and straws.

Noah felt a sudden shock of surprise, followed by confusion, then emptiness — all of which dissolved in an instant. His consciousness, his being, faded into a puff of air and a single mournful sigh echoed by two contented sighs. Then there was nothing but a whisper like twigs and straw spilled on a wooden floor.

Honey, awakened when the 6:30 A.M. alarm went off, discovered that Noah was missing. When she saw that a pair of his jeans and tennies were gone, she assumed he had gotten up early and was waiting for them outside. But a hasty search of the parking lot turned up nothing.

The construction workers in Cabins 1 and 2 were just piling into their pickups. Honey's hasty questioning revealed they had no idea of what might have happened to her son. As they roared off toward the highway, she began banging on the office door, ignoring the Closed sign.

After a few minutes, a strange (yet vaguely familiar) young woman, her fingers covered with showy rings, her hair bright red, unlatched the door. She started to protest that it was "Awful early t' rent a room." But when Honey frantically explained that her son was missing, she went to fetch her husband so they could join in the search.

As the three hurried to be sure Noah hadn't somehow turned up back at Cabin 5, the young woman, whose name was LuAnn, explained that she and her husband, Charlie, had arrived only a short while before. Her mother-in-law and father-in-law were heading to Colorado Springs on business. Honey noticed, then quickly forgot, that Charlie had the exact same bolo necktie his father wore.

While Leah and Steffi watched fearfully from the porch of their unit, the adults combed the parking lot and the surrounding fields. Jim even went over to check out Cogburn's restaurant. But there was no trace of the boy. Even when the local sheriff arrived, and an AMBER

Alert had been issued for "possible stranger abduction," no clue to Noah's whereabouts showed up. A full search of every unit of the Mountain View Motel likewise proved fruitless.

At one point, Steffi found a little pile of what seemed to be polished white sticks and a part of a curved white shell. But when she pointed this out to Leah, her older sister said, "Ewww, *gross*. That's a bunch of bones and probably a piece of a skull from a field mouse or some other animal. Don't touch it. You might get rabies."

They backed away quickly and never mentioned what they'd found in the space between Cabins 12 and 14. They didn't like to think about it, and the adults had bigger problems to concern them.

Smoke Hands

Natalie was sitting across the tile tabletop from David in San Francisco's SFX-Café. They were only two blocks from their school — they were both in the sixth grade at Bateman Middle — sharing their regular morning lattes as they went over homework assignments and exchanged the latest tidbits about their classmates. The ritual made them feel sophisticated. There were some seventh graders at a nearby table, but no one spoke to anyone from another class.

Natalie, going over an algebra problem, was startled, as was David, when the little boy at the next table suddenly smacked his hands against the window glass just behind Natalie's head. "Mom," he said, "it's him again."

"Who, honey?" his mother murmured, clearly more interested in the *Chronicle* spread out in front of her.

"I *told* you," the boy said, sounding exasperated. "The man with the smoke hands."

Without looking up from her newspaper, the woman said, "His hands are dark?"

"No! They're made of *smoke*."

Sighing, his mother glanced through the window. Natalie, curious, looked too. David — momentary interest gone — was bent over his iPhone, texting someone. The girl saw nothing — just a street person in ratty jeans jacket and funky slacks with a pattern of black-and-white checks, disappearing down the hill in the direction of the school.

Clearly the child's mother hadn't seen anything unusual, either. Now she said, "You have an active imagination, Jake. You make up really wild stories." With an even bigger sigh than before, she gathered up her coffee cup and saucer, Jake's half-finished glass of orange juice, and her newspaper. She deposited the dirty dishes in black plastic tubs on a side table and put the paper back on the recycled newspaper rack. "We've got to get you to day care, bub." She lifted down the boy, who was still standing on his chair, peering out the window.

"You don't think I saw him," said the boy stubbornly as she took his hand and started for the door. "But I *did*. And his hands really are smoke."

"Look at the nice doggy," said his mother to distract him. Then they were gone.

"We'd better get going," Natalie said to David. "I don't want to be late for homeroom." She watched mother and son strolling up the hill away from them. "Kids are funny."

"Hmmmm," her friend responded, not looking up from texting.

"Some of them have so much imagination, they believe they're really seeing things that can't be." She paused a moment, then added, "I guess that's true of all kids. When I was little, I was sure I saw a weird figure, like a dwarf — Mister Peek-a-boo. He used to watch me. I'd see him hiding behind trees or peeking over a fence or looking in a corner of my window when I was in bed."

She was surprised how clear and disturbing the memory was, even after so many years. She no longer cared if David was listening or not. She went on, "I'd only see an eye or his smoke-blue fingers — they're my most vivid memory — clutching a tree trunk or resting on my window sill. My mother was a fresh-air fiend; she'd leave my window open every night. But I'd close it right away. I couldn't sleep otherwise, imagining Mister Peek-a-boo's fingers creeping into my room, touching my stuff. Ugh! Still creeps me out to think about it."

"Wow!" said David, who'd caught the last part.

"Stalked by a dwarf. That sounds like a great idea for a horror flick."

Natalie ignored his teasing, unable to let go of the memory-thread she was following. "His fingers were long and thin — wispy and pale-blue — like smoke." Her voice trailed away.

"You're right; that's creepy," said David, shutting off his iPhone. "What else do you remember?"

She shook her head, as much to get rid of the memories as to end any further discussion. "We're going to be late," she said.

"Holy — !" shouted David, looking at the clock over the counter. "Why didn't you say something sooner?"

"I did," Natalie said. "You didn't tune in. Next time, I'll text you." She gave her latte a final slurp and followed David, who was double-time marching toward Bateman Middle School.

That afternoon David, his arm around Natalie's shoulders, walked her a block and a half to the Muni station to wait until the streetcar came to take her home. Sometimes they'd let a car or two go by, having a lot to talk about, or just enjoying each other's company. But, today, Natalie felt only a desire to be left alone. David must have sensed that she wasn't listening, because he broke off streaming a long, pointless story about something that had happened in gym that day. "Everything okay, Nats?" he asked.

"Yeah," she answered, knowing she didn't sound a bit convincing. In fact, her mind was endlessly replaying two things that had happened — or she *thought* had happened — to her earlier.

The first had been when she reached her locker and spun the combination repeatedly, but couldn't pull the door open. It was almost as if it were being held from *inside*. In frustration, she had suddenly wrenched the handle, which no longer resisting, sent her flying backward, dropping her onto her tailbone, scattering the books in her arms and letting the contents of the locker cascade around her feet. For just a moment, trying to get up and regain some dignity while gathering her spilled belongings, she had the impression that a flat, gray shape with pale eyes was pressed against the back of her locker. Then, as the second bell rang, the image vanished, leaving only the space into which she hurriedly crammed unneeded books and supplies. Fortunately, her homeroom teacher accepted the "stuck lock" and didn't hassle Natalie. She soon convinced herself that she had only imagined glimpsing the hated nightmare figure.

The second incident was more unnerving. After last class, she had stopped in the girls' bathroom. The place was empty when she entered. But while she was still in the stall, rebuckling her jeans, she thought she heard someone whisper her name. The voice was so soft, it had to come from someone standing just on the other side of the stall door. Hardly daring to breathe, she bent over and checked the space under the door, but saw no trace of feet.

Suddenly the stall door began to rattle violently, as though someone were trying to pull it off its hinges. She had the crazy thought that whatever had taunted her from *inside* the locker that morning was now *outside* the door, trying to frighten her.

"Go away!" she screamed. The rattling stopped, only to be replaced with a soft *skritch-scratch,* as if the claws of a very large cat were scraping against the wood. Then the mocking whisper came again, so faint she had to strain to hear it. *You've been thinking about me, and your thoughts are a very strong magnet.* This was followed by a quiet, unpleasant laugh.

"Oh!" cried Natalie, then clapped her hand to her mouth.

No good hiding, I'm coming to seek. Now the clawing was replaced with soft pattings, as though a pair of hands, small and delicate as a child's, were feeling their way up the stall door. Fearfully, the girl fixed her eyes on the top of the grimy and graffiti-covered green panel.

Peek-a-boo, I'm coming for you.

More pats higher up. The soft, seeking sounds were almost at the top.

Then four long smoke-blue fingers curled over the rim, followed by a second set.

Peek-a-boo, I've found —

But the bald, domed head had gotten no higher than a pair of pale, blue-gray eyes, when several laughing, shrieking girls burst into the bathroom. The fingers and half-head vanished in twirls and a puff of smoke.

Natalie was aware of a voice disappearing into the distance (*Or just into the depths of my mind?* she wondered) with the single frustrated cry, *Soon!*

Cautiously, she left the stall. Three girls from her class were talking loudly and laughing by the windows beyond the row of sinks. They glanced up at Natalie, smiled briefly, and returned to their interrupted conversation.

Natalie leaned on the nearest sink and splashed water on her face. Then she searched the bathroom for any sign of her tormentor. But she found no trace. She hurried to find David, although she didn't intend to tell him what had happened. She was already trying to convince herself that she had imagined this second incident as well. But it wasn't as easy to dismiss as the locker event.

The moment she saw David, she knew she needed to be alone more than anything else. She needed to think things through, since no one would believe a childhood terror had become real and was turning her life into a nightmare once again.

"**J** Church is coming," David said. She looked along the track and saw the streetcar just pulling away from the next stop up the hill. It would reach them in a matter of moments.

"Want to talk about anything?" David prompted.

She was surprised and even touched by David's unexpected sensitivity to her mood. Any other time, she would have welcomed a sign that they were connecting on a level that couldn't be interrupted by a text message. But today wasn't the day, she realized. She was feeling on overload. So all she said was, "I just need to get home. Lots of homework tonight."

He seemed to buy the explanation. "Fine," was all he said.

The streetcar pulled up with a squeal of brakes. The doors clattered open, and a few people clambered off.

"See you tomorrow," Natalie said. She scrambled up the steps, flashed her Fast Pass, and claimed a seat beside a window near the front of the car. A moment later a Latina settled in the aisle seat, pulled a cell phone out of her purse, and began rattling away in Spanish. This was just what Natalie wanted — to be left to herself and her own thoughts.

"The man with the smoke hands," the little boy had said that morning. *That's what started all these thoughts,* Natalie realized. After the business with her locker, she'd barely been able to keep focused on her classes; she'd been overwhelmed with memories of her childhood terror, Mister Peek-a-boo. She had thought he was safely dead and buried in the recesses of her mind. She wanted him

gone — not like her vanished sister, Kirsten, who seemed to be laid to rest in the family's memories, yet remained a restless spirit who refused to lie quiet. None of the family could forget her; each kept hoping she'd be returned to them one day against all odds.

As the streetcar rolled along the tracks, pausing at almost every stop to let off or take on passengers, Natalie surrendered to remembrances she had been pushing aside.

She'd first seen Mister Peek-a-boo when she was four years old. She had woken up suddenly, having fled some dream for the night-light comfort of her bedroom. But she quickly discovered that a small piece of her dream had followed her into wakefulness.

Peek-a-boo, said a soft voice from somewhere in the dimly lit room, where the only illumination came from her Ariel the Mermaid night-light. *I see you.*

Still only half awake, the girl had asked, "Who's there?"

I see you. Can't you see me?

"Where are you?" she demanded. "Stop being mean."

Why, I'm right here, the voice replied. To little Natalie, it now seemed to come from the shelves across her room where stuffed animals and dolls watched her through the night. More curious than anything else, she shifted to a sitting position, her bare feet dangling off the side of her bed.

Peering more closely at the toys, she quickly spotted what seemed to be a small, gray figure, about the size of a ventriloquist's dummy she had seen on some Saturday morning television show. He was perched on the edge of the higher shelf with his arms around a stuffed penguin and a Princess Jasmine doll.

Peek-a-boo, he began, *I see —*

"You! I see you, Mister Peek-a-boo!" Natalie finished, clapping her hands delightedly.

Yes, I believe you do, said the little man. *We're going to be good friends, you and me. We'll be seeing a lot of each other. My visit tonight must be a short one, but I'll come back. Oh yes, indeed!*

Abruptly he faded away. The dolls flanking him tipped sideways into the spot where he'd been a moment before.

She called, "Mister Peek-a-boo," several times, but he didn't answer.

He did, however, make good his promise to see her often after that.

He began popping up unexpectedly every day, darting behind trees and bushes, hanging over fences, or staring in her bedroom window, even though her room was on the second floor. There was not a moment of the day or night when he wasn't watching her, studying her, waiting for . . . *something.*

Neither of her parents could see this creature with his staring gray eyes, bluish gray skin, and twisted

fingers of blue smoke. When she tried repeatedly to convince her mother of Mister Peek-a-boo's presence, the woman only said, "Stop making up these stories; it's not healthy." And her nine-years-older sister Kirsten just told her to "Shut up!" when she mentioned Mister Peek-a-boo. Though Kirsten insisted she didn't believe in the little man, she seemed scared whenever Natalie mentioned him. Once or twice Natalie caught the other girl turning to look at a certain spot moments before Natalie saw Mister Peek-a-boo looking at her — at them both. But the younger girl could never get her sister to admit she saw anything.

Natalie didn't want to disobey her mother or frighten Kirsten. But Mister Peek-a-boo was real. She couldn't wish him away. But — and this is where Natalie in the here and now was most troubled — she *had,* in some way she couldn't understand, wished him into existence. She was sure of it. She had been so alone — her parents both working, her sister living in a world of friends and goings-on that shut her out, no friends her own age, and often no one to talk to but the babysitter, Mrs. Ortega, who mostly watched TV and napped.

Miserable in her loneliness, Natalie had longed for a special someone who would be her friend and hers alone. And then one day she had seen someone no one else could see. In the end, she had grown totally frustrated by the little man's teasing, his invisibility to everyone (except, maybe, Kirsten), and being told over and over by adults that she had to stop talking about him. He was making her sadder and angrier every day. Finally, she decided to banish him, as kings in fairy tales banished those who angered them.

The next time he appeared in her bedroom, sitting on her dresser, leaning against the mirror (which never showed his reflection), she said, "I want you to go away."

No you don't, he had said, but she was sure she heard a hint of anger and worry in his voice.

"Yes I do. Go away now." Then, pointing a finger at him, she said in her most kingly voice, *"I banish you."*

And he had gone from her room. But a moment later she heard a pattering like rain falling softly on the window. And there he was, hovering just beyond the glass. She had rid the house of him, but no more. So he continued to tease her — though from now on his teasing grew more nasty and frightening. She wanted to be completely free of him, but that seemed hopeless.

The streetcar suddenly jounced over a bumpy stretch of tracks, pulling Natalie back into the present. Listening to her seatmate chatter on, she wrestled with the idea that she had somehow caused a nightmarish figure to be born into the everyday world. At the same time a more adult inner voice assured her, *Such things don't happen.*

Her own neighborhood was coming into view now. They rolled past the familiar cluster of shops — pizzeria, bakery, and the corner grocery store–deli — that were still the area's heart. She'd loved to go shopping with her mother on Saturdays, or accompany her father to pick up a pizza for dinner, before everything ended with Kirsten's disappearance.

In the days just before Kirsten vanished, Mister Peek-a-boo had been everywhere. Natalie had grown so afraid of him, she would try to hide or run away when she saw his pale shape flicker from tree to tree in the park a block from their house, or when she saw him peep through the purple bougainvillea blossoms twining a neighbors' porch, or press his soft, wispy blue fingers against the windows of any room she entered.

She had heard him say, *I'm coming to get you.*

And she — only four — began to understand that he wouldn't leave her until something terrible happened.

No one would listen to her. Her parents forbade her to talk about Mister Peek-a-boo. Her sister avoided her when they were not forced together at meals or watching TV as a family, something their parents often insisted upon. But even with a reality show or comedy blaring from the TV set, a turn of Natalie's head would, like as not, reveal a pale face and fingers of smoke lightly touching a nearby window. And if she woke Mrs. Ortega up from a nap or interrupted a soap on

Telemundo to make her look, the woman would just shush her and say, "Be a big girl. Put such foolishness away."

But all the time, Mister Peek-a-boo's voice was becoming louder and more insistent. *I'm lonely*, he complained. *Your loneliness brought me here, and only you can stop what you started.*

Natalie leaned her face against the streetcar window, then pulled back suddenly as long smoky fingers began to stroke the other side of the glass.

"Oh!" she cried. *Kirsten!*

The woman next to her broke off her phone conversation and asked, "Are you all right, *niña?*"

But Natalie couldn't answer. She just nodded, pushed past the woman, and left the car, impatiently brushing away the tears that wouldn't stop coming.

"**A**re you feeling all right?" asked her mother later that evening. "You've hardly touched your dinner."

Natalie made an effort to bring herself mentally back to the dinner table. She focused on the plate in front of her, noting meat loaf, mashed potatoes, string beans, a sourdough roll — using this inventory exercise to pull her more firmly back into reality.

"Everything okay at school?" her father asked, a forkful of meat loaf halfway between his plate and his mouth.

"Fine, everything's fine," the girl insisted, trying not

to sound impatient. "I'm just a little tired. I think I'll go to bed right after dinner."

Her parents nodded, indicating this was a satisfactory answer. Her mother looked like she was going to ask again when Natalie refused dessert — peach cobbler à la mode, a favorite of hers — but then she just sighed and said, "I hope you're not coming down with something."

Natalie cut her off. "Really, I'm just tired." She kissed them each and wished them good night. Then she raced upstairs to her room.

First she called David, hoping to see him, but he told her he'd been grounded for staying out too late the night before. His parents were always punishing him for something, he complained. Most of the time it was for stuff they'd imagined he'd done or for stuff that was so silly, most normal grownups wouldn't give it a thought. Natalie had the opposite problem. Since Kirsten's vanishing, her folks often seemed so distant, it was like they were on another planet. They were so wrapped up in guilt and grief that Natalie sometimes felt she could set fire to the house, and they'd hardly even notice.

She wanted to talk to David and tell him more about the man with the smoke hands. But, over the phone, he was far more interested in ragging about his parents, who were always comparing him to his "perfect" older brother, Luis, a straight-A student who was graduating from high school with honors. The frosting on *that* cake, he assured her, was that Luis had won a college scholarship, so there wasn't a prayer that his younger brother, with barely passing marks, would ever measure up.

After a few minutes of this, Natalie gave up hope of a heart-to-heart and rang off. She tried her friend Mary-Louise, but only got her voicemail. She didn't bother to leave a message. She simply bagged her hope of really talking to someone and set to work finishing her homework assignments.

She could hear the TV going downstairs, but she had no desire to join her parents where, she knew, they'd be sitting side by side on the couch, each lost in his or her own thoughts. Sometimes Natalie wondered why they just didn't get a divorce. But, then, it seemed pointless. They were already light-years apart from each other — and from her.

Homework done, she flopped down on her bed and picked up the latest in a series of "romantic vampire" books she was following. Usually she got happily lost for an hour in the pages. But, tonight, the story didn't interest her — well, actually, it creeped her out a little. The beautiful and handsome young vampires, who experienced adventure and love and never let a little thing like death stand in their way, kept teasing her mind back to a shadowy figure with long fingers of curling vapor and ash-colored eyes that were only smoke swirls in otherwise empty sockets.

Tossing the book onto her nightstand, she lay back on the bed, trying to clear her mind and relax. But thoughts and memories kept flooding in. . . .

It was on a night very much like this that Mister Peek-a-boo had come to her window for the last time. "Go away!" little Natalie had ordered him. "Go away now!"

Naughty Natalie, the frighteningly familiar voice had whispered in her ear. *Why are you so mean? You asked me to be your friend, and now you don't want to play.* His mouth, a slit in his pale oval cloud-puff of a face, turned from a faint grin to an exaggerated frown.

"Go away! I hate you!" she had screamed. "I'm telling!"

Her parents had gone out to dinner, so she ran to get Kirsten, hoping that her older sister's presence would chase the nightmare figure away. But by the time she'd managed to convince her sister to come upstairs, Mister Peek-a-boo was gone.

Kirsten went to the window, angry at being dragged away from her favorite cable TV show — one that was off-limits when their parents were around. "You know, you've got to stop this junk. You're driving Mom and Dad crazy with your stories. And now you are really bugging me! Look," she said, pointing at the darkened window glass. "There's nothing there." She unfastened the latch and threw open the window. "You know, for a while, you almost had me believing in your little gray man, but I'm over that. You'd better get over it, too!"

"Don't," begged Natalie weakly.

But Kirsten was out to prove her point. She leaned into the warm night air. "Hey, Smokey-doo, if you're really there, let's see you. *Get in here now!*"

When nothing billowed or swam through the clear night toward Kirsten, she turned to her sister. "You and your stories!" she said disgustedly.

"Close the win —" was as far as Natalie got.

Mister Peek-a-boo, visible as a swirl of blue smoke, abruptly hovered in the air outside. Then his impossibly long, snaky, gray arms were reaching through the open window toward Kirsten. Natalie, terrified, felt her muscles lock so she couldn't move; even the muscles in her throat froze, preventing her from choking out the smallest warning. The room filled with the smell of wet smoke, like that from a freshly doused campfire. Kirsten, stunned by her sister's stranger-than-usual behavior, took a step toward Natalie. Then the unearthly arms — now thick and solid as ropes — wrapped themselves around the older girl's waist. She began to scream. Natalie screamed, too.

I want a friend. The fierce voice thundered in her head. *Either will do. Which will it be? Come with me, and I'll let your sister go.*

"No!" said Natalie, surprised to find she still had a little power over him. He couldn't make her go away; she had to say "Yes."

Instead, she said, "You let Kirsten alone!"

But her small power couldn't protect the other girl.

This is your last chance, whispered the little gray man. *Promise to come with me, or I take her away. Forever.*

Natalie, pressing her hands to her ears, fled the room. She hurtled down the stairs, taking them two at a time, yanked open the front door, and, shrieking like a banshee, raced toward the nearest neighbor's house.

By the time the police arrived in answer to the neighbor's 911 call, Kirsten was gone. There was no clue as to what had happened. One of the officers commented on the smell of smoke in the room. A few smudges on the window provided nothing in the way of fingerprints or DNA to aid the investigation. Kirsten's disappearance was quickly ruled a kidnapping, by a person or persons unknown.

No one listened to Natalie babble about a nightmare figure. It was supposed that the shock of witnessing a stranger invading the house and fighting with her sister had somehow gotten jumbled up with her fantasy of Mister Peek-a-boo. According to more than one therapist she saw in the aftermath, fact and fantasy had woven together, "as it will in the mind of a young and highly impressionable child."

But though she learned to give lip service to this explanation — came, in fact, to half believe it herself at times — deep down, Natalie knew that Mister Peek-a-boo had stolen her sister to be his "friend." And what was even worse was the knowledge that she had run away and let her sister take her place in the nightmare world she had brought to life.

And now he's back, Natalie thought miserably. *It couldn't be coincidence that the little boy was sitting right next to me when he told his story.*

He's up to his old tricks: The watching. The teasing. The waiting. And when he's done playing with my mind, he'll try to take me wherever he took Kirsten.

For a long time, she lay quietly. Her personal nightmare made her think of some of the scary DVDs she and David watched all the time. The young woman in *Halloween* had to face down the death-masked, ghostly killer from out of her past. The teenaged heroine in *Nightmare on Elm Street* had to find a way to vanquish the monstrous, knife-fingered Freddie who kept breaking out of her dreams into the real world. Even *Buffy the Vampire Slayer* reruns seemed to have something important to suggest to her.

The more she thought about it, the more she realized that the message in all of these stories was the same: *You have to face your fear in order to overcome it.* Anxiety and discouragement began to give way to something more positive in her. She wasn't a four-year-old anymore. If things were going to be different this time around, they'd be different because *she* had changed the rules. And maybe — just maybe — she could also make up for having abandoned her sister all those years before.

Gradually, she decided what she must do.

Natalie went to the window, opened it, and called

softly into the night, "I know you're back. Well, I'm here, and I'm waiting. Where are you?"

Almost instantly, a patch of air swirled with fog. She breathed in the too-familiar wet smoke smell. Ash gray eyes and a grinning mouth took shape inside the now smoky blue swirl. Arms that ended in smoke fingers drifted toward her.

Natalie slammed the window shut. The smoky palms flattened against the glass, leaving faint smudges like wet soot.

That's not fair, the thin, reedy voice complained, the words forming inside her head.

"You took my sister," Natalie said, keeping her voice calm and stern — even adultlike. "*That* wasn't fair."

I need a friend. I'm that part of you that has always needed a friend.

"You have Kirsten."

She's not you. The faint voice sounded both sad and angry.

Natalie took a deep breath. Then she said, "Give back my sister. Let me take her place."

Yes! We should never have been separated from the start. Eagerly, the voice said, *Open the window, and it's done.*

"You promise?"

I am many things, but never a liar. Mister Peek-a-boo sounded hurt that she could even think such a thing. And, because she knew him as well as she knew herself, Natalie believed him.

The moment was here. Natalie felt her hands

shaking as she reached for the window. Slowly she unlocked it and raised it all the way up.

Smoke poured into the room, filling every corner with haze and smell, enveloping her. But it didn't make her afraid, because, as she breathed in the taste and scent, she also breathed in a sense of desperate loneliness. Hers? Mister Peek-a-boo's? The both of theirs?

"I'll go with you, for now. But I won't stay. I'll find my way back."

Kirsten never could. Why should you?

"Because I'm not her."

His arms wrapped around her, steel-strong, though made of smoke. *You'll see; you can't get away.*

He was laughing, but Natalie was already promising herself, *I will find my way back,* as they whirled away into someplace beyond night or day or anything familiar.

When Kirsten woke from a sleep deeper than any normal sleep, she barely recognized where she was. For a time she lay huddled on the floor, letting the breeze blowing through the open window gradually lure her to full consciousness.

Finally feeling strong enough, she opened the bedroom door, made her way unsteadily down the hall, using the walls for support, then wobbled downstairs to rouse her frightened and ecstatic parents from where they were dozing in front of the TV set.

No one — detective, preacher, scientist, or mystic — was able to solve the riddle of Natalie's disappearance and Kirsten's return, older, but wearing the same clothes she had worn when she disappeared years before. That she had no memory of what had happened in the time between her kidnapping and her miraculous reappearance only added to the layers of confusion surrounding the event. Of course, her parents' joy at her return was overshadowed by the loss of her sister. But Kirsten's unexpected homecoming gave them hope that Natalie, too, would be restored one day. And that merest glimmer of hope made their second loss somewhat easier to bear.

Moonrise

Far off in the distance, something howled. Anxiously, Peter Navarre twitched aside the curtains at the dining room window. He peered beyond the shatterproof glass and the thick, black vertical bars that gave every room the feeling of a fortress or (more to Peter's thinking in his present state of mind) a maximum security prison. Though the bars looked impressive enough, the creatures whose marauding they had been designed to withstand were beings of almost incalculable strength.

The boy let his gaze sweep back and forth like a surveillance camera. He was relieved to see no sign of movement close to the house, where the winter-blasted remains of his mother's flower and herb gardens cowered beneath a coverlet of burlap and mulch. Nor did anything stir in the fields beyond, where, in the limited warmer days of Michigan's Upper Peninsula, his father raised corn, hay, and a few cold-resistant root crops like turnips, rutabagas, and potatoes. A flurry had passed through the area a few hours before, and a light dusting of snow still lingered. It seemed to glow in the last rays of the late-afternoon sun.

To one side he could see the barn where the dairy cows were safely housed behind steel-reinforced walls and doors almost as heavy as those on a bank vault. The doors boasted time-controlled locks that would not be released until the morning sun was fully risen. All the armoring made the building effectively soundproof. Even from a few feet away, you couldn't hear the cattle inside lowing, once the place was sealed.

Finally, Peter turned his attention to the tree line beyond the farthest fields. This was the direction from which, he was sure, the howling had come. But, again, he satisfied himself that nothing was amiss in the lengthening shadows below the birch, pine, and other trees of the forest that surrounded the farm.

The boy knew how far and clearly sound could carry in the chill winter desolation. Whatever had been howling might, in fact, still be way off in the wilderness beyond the Navarre Farm acreage.

With a sigh, he let the curtain drop back into place and turned to face the room. It was decorated for his thirteenth birthday. His parents had strung up signs that read HAPPY BIRTHDAY, BEST WISHES, and CONGRATULATIONS in big, shiny metallic red and gold letters. There was a crisp red tablecloth and a place set for three with the bone china that his mother had inherited from her mother, Grand-mère Leclerq. The old woman and Grand-père Leclerq had been the first of the family to move from Canada into this remote section of Michigan, not so very far from the border. Peter had few memories of the two elders; they had died before he was quite four. Whenever he asked his mother about this, she never gave any specifics, just said, "It was their time."

Looking at the party preparations, Peter realized that his parents were far more excited by the prospect of his thirteenth birthday than he was. To him, birthdays had become merely a way of marking the end of another year of loneliness, isolation, and steadily growing frustration. His mother insisted on homeschooling him, so he was not allowed to attend classes in the town of Coeur de Bois. He rarely went into town, and then only when accompanying one or both of his parents on a shopping run or some other business. The few children he saw on those occasions seemed always to be watching him and whoever was with him with suspicious, even hostile, looks. The men who worked on the farm arrived at sunrise and left each day well before dark.

Peter dreamed of going away to school, perhaps as

far as Marquette, the county seat, which had a good university. Better yet, he dreamed of going someplace far, far away where it would be warmer, and there would be so many people he couldn't help but make friends. Florida and California loomed large in his imagination, and he devoured every television show or magazine article that so much as mentioned these places. But when he raised the subject, he was met with the same blank, uncomprehending look from each parent, and the same response, "None of us go away from here. The farm is our life. It will be your life, too."

Not if I can help it, he promised himself. He had no real plan, only a growing determination not to be trapped in his parents' world. Of course, he understood all the reasons for their stubborn refusal, but he couldn't accept that what bound them would bind him. *I am different; I am strong. I will get to the world beyond Coeur de Bois, and I will never look back. Never.* This he vowed as he snapped out the light, consigning the festive wall signs and table to darkness.

As he crossed the hall to the living room, the cell phone in his hip pocket began to play the opening bars of the *Star Trek* theme. He grabbed it, flipped it open, recognized the caller's number, and said, "'Lo, Dad. What's up?"

After a burst of static, his father's voice crackled into his ear, "Son, we had an accident —"

Peter's stomach knotted with fear. "How bad?"

"I was taking the back way to bypass a wreck on

Miller's Road. A semi jackknifed, and a lot of passenger cars got caught in a chain reaction. But we haven't done much better. We must've hit a patch of black ice out here — slid across the road. Fortunately, there were no oncoming cars, though it's hardly surprising, since the road isn't used very much. . . ."

His father was rambling. Peter wondered if this was a sign of shock.

"How are you? How's Mom?" he asked hurriedly, trying to get the other to focus.

"We're just shaken up. No bones broken or anything, but we'll probably have some bruises and aches for a few days."

Peter let out a sigh of relief. "Where's the car?"

"Off the road, nose down in a ditch, with ice water up to the windshield. Not a chance we'll get it free without a tow."

"Did you call Billy's Garage? Should I?"

"Wouldn't do any good. I spotted Billy's truck earlier helping to clean up the mess on Miller's Road. Fred Northgate's two trucks from Danville are there, too. I doubt there's anyone countywide not helping with the smash-up."

"Should I call the police?"

"They've got more important things to do."

"Well, what *should* I do?" He couldn't keep the frustration out of his voice.

"You just sit tight. Marie and I are going to hike it. We're not that far."

"The moon will be up soon," Peter protested.

"We'll cut through the woods. We'll move fast."

"The woods aren't *safe*." He was going to tell about the howling he'd heard earlier, but his father's voice suddenly broke up into a series of static sputters and crackling. Then Peter's cell phone went dead. He instantly tried calling back, but neither this nor his next three attempts got through. Reception in the area was notoriously iffy. Sliding the phone back into his pocket, he thought about taking the truck but quickly dismissed the idea. He was just learning to drive; in all likelihood, given the hazardous road conditions, he'd wind up in a ditch himself — or worse. Besides, he'd have to stick to the secondary road, and his folks were probably already striking out across the woodland. Of course, they knew the territory as well as anyone, but that wasn't the point. The full moon was the issue. When it rose, all bets were off about what could happen to the two adults.

He shuddered to think of his parents caught in the open. He'd overheard them saying that several strangers had been spotted recently in the area. Something, that had formerly been a *someone*, was on the prowl, he was certain, on the lookout for an unwary partridge or rabbit or deer or human.

Werewolves were real; they were a fact of life, he knew.

He was always amazed when he heard visitors or newcomers to the area make fun of the locals — especially the old-timers — who spoke in hushed tones about the creatures that were not entirely of this world, but still very much a part of it. The strangers would assure everyone within earshot, *There's no such thing as a werewolf or windigo or Big Foot haunting the woods*. Well, Peter couldn't say one way or the other about Big Foot or the windigo. But the northern forests were vast — and the world an even vaster place. Who knew what secrets it might conceal? But werewolves had been a reality both in Canada and Michigan for centuries, though their origins remained obscure.

Peter had heard all the old stories. . . .

How, long ago, in Detroit there had been a man who loved a young woman. He pleaded with her to be his bride, but she told him she was to become a bride of Christ, a nun. Frantic at the thought of losing her to the convent, he went to a local witch, where he traded his soul for the power to become a werewolf, or *loup-garou*. In this terrifying form, he hoped to force his beloved to abandon her promise to the Church and wed him. One moonlit evening he followed her to the convent garden where she had gone to meditate and pray. When she saw the snarling, slavering wolf stalking her, she sought help by clinging to the statue of the Virgin Mary. The wolf leaped at her, but an unearthly light from the statue swept over him so he was turned into stone in midleap, then crashed to the ground, where he shattered into dust.

Another less fortunate woman was seized by a werewolf on the night of her wedding and dragged into the forest. Her bridegroom, driven mad by her loss, spent the rest of his life tracking the creature through the woods, brandishing a silver knife that his neighbor had given him, with the assurance that this alone could slay the beast. At last he cornered the creature on the shore of Lake Superior. There, forced back by the threat of the silver blade, the creature leaped into the water and disappeared. The avenger afterward claimed that it had jumped down the throat of a huge catfish. Though most doubted this part of the story, Peter knew that many older locals still refused to eat catfish.

Countless tales from all over paraded through Peter's mind. With a shake of his head, he forced himself back to the here and now. When one last try to reach his dad by cell phone failed, he suddenly felt cut off, not only from his parents, but from the whole world.

He moved through the house, now looking out this window, now that. Finally he settled in the living room. He switched off the lamps, which were kept on most of the day, since the winter gloom began to thicken indoors shortly after noon. And the smallish rooms, each with its burden of heavily barred windows, were hardly cheery even on the sunniest summer day.

When the lights were off, he pulled the heavy floor-to-ceiling drapes a few inches apart — just enough to let him keep watch on the curve of road that led from the graveled parking area in front of the house back toward the encircling forest that quickly swallowed up all trace of the roadway. Kneeling on the sofa, with his chin propped on the back, he prayed for a glimpse of his folks.

Just as intently, he watched the patch of sky where a pale radiance was edging toward an almost white-hot brilliance, heralding the full moon. Soon it would be climbing into the heavens from just below the horizon.

Very soon now . . .

He stared back at the road, willing his parents to appear.

But it was the moon that appeared, disentangling itself from the interlocking tree branches that now seemed drenched in liquid silver. It floated balloonlike into the night sky, its brightness radiating in waves that banished the lesser light of the stars and laid claim to the greater portion of the heavens.

A small "Oh!" escaped from the boy, overwhelmed by the sight. In all his years of watching the rising of crescent, quarter, half, gibbous, and full moons, he'd never seen anything like this. The brightness seemed to stab through his eyes, deep into his brain and his very being. The light set the skin of his face and neck and arms that jutted from his T-shirt tingling as though he were standing under one of the power poles that marched across the eastern pastureland into the forest, their looping wires bringing energy from a distant plant.

Everything seemed to be changing somehow. Even

the blotchy shadows that made up the face of the moon were reconfiguring themselves. What seemed at first glance a man's face rapidly changed into a wolf's muzzle. There were the jaws; there the nostrils (did they flare and shrink?); there the black crater eyes, hiding fathomless hot silver pools in their twin centers. Their gaze bored into him, following the path of the moon's rays.

He grabbed for the drapes, one hand on each side, ready to pull them together and shut out every trace of moonlight. Suddenly he saw two shadows hurrying down the road toward the house. Even as he watched, they changed in the moonlight — torsos sinking closer to the ground, elongating, all four legs foreshortening. What might, a moment before, have appeared human, was now lupine, wolfish.

When he saw the beasts, he knew his parents were not coming home to him that night.

He was on his own to face whatever the full moon would hurl his way. Refusing to give in to despair, he pushed his terror to the back of his mind and ordered, *Get a grip. Focus. One step at a time.* He hurried to the front hallway and double-checked the lock on the heavy oak door with its steel backing. Then he hastily checked the other doors and windows to be sure they were secure. All were sealed tight.

He had just started upstairs when two massive *thumps!* slammed into the front door, one right after the other. The panels withstood the attack, but he heard howls of frustration moving back and forth as the beasts padded the length of the porch, seeking a way in. Patting, scratching, and then storms of fury ensued as the creatures looked for a weak spot in the house's defenses. Peter raced up to the second floor to make sure the windows were equally secure there.

Now he heard heavier crashing below. He had the impression that the beasts were doubling and redoubling their attacks at the front door. Each loud slam sent a shiver through him. He took comfort in the fact that all the windows on the upper floor had their blackout curtains drawn. Shutting out every trace of moonlight helped him feel safe, in spite of the howls and unrelenting assaults on the door below.

Standing in the brightly lit hallway, he reminded himself, *I'm Peter. I'm me. I'm going to make it through the night. I'm going to follow my dreams to Florida or California. And I will never, ever come back to this nightmare!*

But the nightmare insisted on following *him*.

With a *crash!* the front door burst inward. It had never been tested against an attack of such ferocity. *Live and learn*, thought Peter, dismayed at the terrified giggle that bubbled out of his throat.

He retreated to his bedroom, where his folks had insisted he remain every full-moon night. Each time, they ordered him not to unlock the door until true morning light filled the spaces between the bars on his window. He knew his father had taken special pains to make this room a safe place. *Well, now we'll see just how safe it is,* he told himself, backing away from the door to sit on the bed.

Peter could hear scraping, growls, and the clatter of claws on wooden floors downstairs. *Oh yes,* thought Peter, *werewolves exist.* Tonight they were in the house with him.

He continued to stare at the locked bedroom door as the sounds from downstairs grew even more fearsome. Amid the howling he heard almost human cries and groans. But those quickly ceased — replaced by the animal noises that would not stop even when he pressed his hands to his ears.

His nerves like red-hot wires, he began pacing the floor — only pausing to peek out one of the two windows, each shielded by heavy blackout curtains. Beyond the snow-covered fields, beyond the circling woods, the lights of Coeur de Bois glittered like stars caught in the webs of shadowy tree branches. Peter felt just as caught — trapped in his room in a house surrounded by woods where creatures with fierce yellow eyes hunted their prey.

Again he thought of all the times he had pleaded with his mother and father to move — or at least send him away to school — anything to put miles between himself and this nightmarish place where the moon ruled. Every month, his mind grew peaceful again when the moon began to shrink, but his misery grew as the moon swelled once more toward fullness.

"Leave here? What nonsense!" his parents always said. "This farm is our life. It's always been in our family. You must stop filling your head with dreams of running away to who knows where because of your fears about werewolves. Your future is here, on the farm, with us. Accept what you can't change."

Even his approaching thirteenth birthday — which his parents were so excited about — could not make him feel better about himself or his life.

"Thirteen," his mother had said, smiling at him as she frosted the humongous birthday cake on which a gold "13" — composed of two big candles — glowed under the kitchen light. "Soon you'll really be an adult. When the time comes, make a wish, then blow out your candles. But don't tell what you wished for, or it won't come true." She had said the same thing every year for as far back as he could remember.

He hadn't said anything aloud, but his wish was clear in his mind, not just because it was his birthday, but because he had held the same wish in his heart from the time he was a toddler: *I wish I were far away from here. I wish I didn't have to stay another day on this farm, in these woods. I wish we could all just . . . go away and lead different lives.* Of course, he kept this wish to himself. His parents would be shocked to realize the depths of his dislike for — and, yes, *fear* of — his present life.

"Welcome to 'lucky thirteen.' You're almost there."

His father had patted Peter on the shoulder as he and Peter's mom climbed into the shiny black Bronco for their last, soon-to-be-disastrous trip into town.

Unlucky thirteen, Peter thought. *Bad to worse. Worse to worser,* as some character on a TV sitcom had said.

And now the full moon that threatened to illuminate the most awful moment of his life had arrived. The werewolves were downstairs. It was only a matter of time before they came for him. Carefully he adjusted the blackout curtains across both windows so that not a seam of silver light shone through. *Maybe that will be enough,* he thought.

Something heavy crashed to the floor downstairs. A moment later he heard the sound of shattering glass. Peter could imagine the mess being created below. There would be a lot of cleaning up to do tomorrow.

Why am I thinking of something so stupid? Peter asked himself. *The only thing that matters is getting through the night to morning. If I can, if I do, I'm going to run, run, run until I run so far, I won't even remember this horrible night!*

There was sudden quiet downstairs. He opened his door a crack and put his ear to the tiny opening. He listened, but heard nothing. He imagined yellow-eyed monstrosities listening back in the dark. Then he heard the stealthy *pad-pad-pad* of paws climbing the stairs.

In a moment of panic, he called, "Mom! Dad!" although he knew his parents were lost to him.

From the darkened stairway at the end of the hall, he

heard a snarl that was answered by a softer growl — almost a purr. The boy put his eye to the crack.

Suddenly there came the *click-clack* of claws on the hardwood floor of the hall. Two shapes bounded on all fours toward him as two sets of blazing yellow eyes hurtled for his door.

He slammed it and turned the key in the lock. A moment later something big hit the door with a dreadful *whump!* Peter spun his head from side to side, looking for something to help defend his bedroom. His old-fashioned, six-drawer bureau caught his eye. With a strength born of panic, he shoved it in front of the door.

A second and a third *whump!* shivered the wooden panels.

The boy looked desperately around for some escape. In the full-length mirror on the closet door, he saw himself freaking out like a mouse he'd seen dropped into a snake's cage on a nature show on TV. The mouse sensed he was about to become dinner and wasn't taking it calmly. And Peter wasn't about to take his own situation calmly.

But what could he do? The barred windows offered no hope. The closet's thin sliding door offered less hope against the creatures hurling themselves furiously at his bedroom door.

A crack appeared in the plaster where one of the hinges of the heavy oak-and-metal door was fastened to the wall. The massive bodies kept up the barrage as both hinges, though solidly reinforced, inched away. Their last hold gave; the door crashed inward, pushing the bureau several inches into the room. A hairy snout wriggled through the narrow opening, followed by a leering, wolfish head with blazing yellow eyes and fangs only slightly duller yellow. In an instant, the beast had shouldered its way into the bedroom. Behind it, a second creature, eyes ablaze and jaws gaping like the first, appeared.

Retreating, Peter kept his eyes on the two creatures as they crisscrossed back and forth in front of him, gradually drawing nearer.

The boy closed his eyes. *I don't want this. I want to be miles away and living another life.*

Abruptly, the werewolves sat back on their haunches. The bigger cocked its head slightly to the right; the smaller turned its head a bit to the left. Both looked as if they were studying him.

Lucky thirteen, Peter thought bitterly. *You're an adult. Accept what you can't change.*

"All right," the boy whispered. "You win." He walked to the window and, in angry frustration, yanked so hard on the blackout curtain that he pulled both curtain and rod down. Moonlight flooded the room. He hurled the now-useless curtain and support into the farthest corner.

In the mirror on the other side of the room, he saw himself changing as his watching parents had changed already. They growled eagerly now — anxious to be off on the night's hunt as a family, as a true *pack*. For years they had protected him from rogue predators, from *themselves*, with the house and inner safe room barred against threats to the boy, who, until he reached thirteen, would not come fully into his "inheritance" (as his parents called it). And though the moonlight was working its mysterious effect on his now-adult body, he still thought of it as a curse.

His parents watched with doglike patience and an innate sympathy for suffering, even though their awareness was no longer remotely human.

They didn't, *couldn't*, heed — or care about — the tears that gathered in the corners of Peter's now-yellow eyes and began to stream down his muzzle.

The Maple-Vail Book Manufacturing Group   York, PA, USA
September 2009   1st printing